Bombay Islam

The Religious Economy of the West Indian Ocean, 1840–1915

As a thriving port city, nineteenth-century Bombay attracted migrants from across India and beyond. Nile Green's *Bombay Islam* traces the ties between industrialization, imperialism and the production of religion to show how Muslim migration from the oceanic and continental hinterlands of Bombay fuelled demand for a wide range of religious suppliers, as Christian missionaries competed with Muslim religious entrepreneurs for a stake in the new market. Enabled by a colonial policy of non-intervention in religious affairs, and powered by steam travel and vernacular printing, Bombay's Islamic productions were exported as far as South Africa and Iran. Connecting histories of religion, labour and globalization, the book examines the role of ordinary people – mill hands and merchants – in shaping the demand that drove the religious market. By drawing on hagiographies, travelogues, doctrinal works and poems in Persian, Urdu and Arabic, *Bombay Islam* unravels a vernacular modernity that saw people from across the Indian Ocean drawn into Bombay's industrial economy of enchantment.

Nile Green is Professor of South Asian and Islamic History at the University of California, Los Angeles. He is the author of many books, including *Indian Sufism since the Seventeenth Century: Saints, Books and Empires in the Muslim Deccan* (2006); *Islam and the Army in Colonial India: Sepoy Religion in the Service of Empire* (2009); *Sufism: A Global History* (2012); and *Global Muslims in the Age of Steam and Print*, co-edited with James Gelvin (2013).

Bombay Islam

The Religious Economy of the West Indian Ocean, 1840–1915

NILE GREEN

University of California, Los Angeles

CAMBRIDGE
UNIVERSITY PRESS

CAMBRIDGE
UNIVERSITY PRESS

32 Avenue of the Americas, New York NY 10013-2473, USA

Cambridge University Press is part of the University of Cambridge.

It furthers the University's mission by disseminating knowledge in the pursuit of education, learning and research at the highest international levels of excellence.

www.cambridge.org
Information on this title: www.cambridge.org/9781107627796

First published 2011
First paperback edition 2013

A catalogue record for this publication is available from the British Library

Library of Congress Cataloguing in Publication data
Green, Nile.
Bombay Islam: the religious economy of the west Indian Ocean,
1840–1915 / Nile Green.
p. cm.
Includes bibliographical references and index.
ISBN 978-0-521-76924-2 (hardback)
1. Internal migrants – India – Bombay – History. 2. Muslims – India – Bombay –
History. 3. Iranians – India – Bombay – History. 4. Bombay (India) –
Commerce – History. 5. Economics – Religious aspects – Islam.
I. Title.
HB2100.B66G74 2011
330.954792031–dc22 2010027650

ISBN 978-0-521-76924-2 Hardback
ISBN 978-1-107-62779-6 Paperback

For Nushin

Bombay is not a good place for ghosts. There is too much activity, too many people, and too great an amount of gas and electric light.

James Douglas, *Bombay and Western India* (1893)

Samandar dariyā sē bāwā jān dānā awliyā.
Baba took from the seas and oceans and gave life to the friends of God.

Murjān Sīdī Nangasī, Afro-Indian prayer song (*c.* 1890)

Contents

Illustrations

Acknowledgements

Bombay Islam did not begin in Bombay, but like the religious 'firms' whose activities it traces, it set out from Tehran and Hyderabad on the far fringes of what in the nineteenth century became Bombay's wide religious marketplace. There, tracing histories of Muslim organizations which I originally understood in terms of the regional and national, I pursued the peregrinations of men such as Safi 'Alī Shāh and Habīb 'Alī Shāh, whose own trails would ultimately lead me to Bombay. And so, over the course of more than a decade, what began as a search for neglected regional side-lights on the Muslim nineteenth century became an inter-regional survey converging on a city which, were it not for the persistency of my sources in drawing me towards it, I would never have recognized as the religious centre it became from the mid-1800s. When the penny farthing dropped and the focus of the project turned to Bombay itself, I was pushed to other directions in turn, from the dockyard shrines of Bombay proper to their reproduction across the ocean in the distant port of Durban. Linked as it was to these outlying markets by vernacular print and the steamship, Bombay offers the urban historian as large a canvas as might be managed. While tracing case studies in Iran and South Africa of Bombay's links to a larger maritime market of faith, I hope to have at least drawn an outline on enough of that canvas to give a sense of the steam-driven pulse of 'Victorian' Bombay and the responses to those rhythms at every node of its capillaries. That said, the book is deliberately restricted to the Muslim experience of Bombay. Partly this is justified because so little has been written about Bombay's Muslims; partly because for all its neglect by historians of Islam, Bombay was a crucial oceanic hub for Muslims navigating the age of empire and industry. But if Islam is the major theme,

I have kept in mind the experiences of the city's non-Muslim groups at every step, and would venture so far as to suggest that parallel cases could be made for Bombay's variegated Hindus, Zoroastrians, Christians and Jews. Bombay's religious market was ultimately open to all traffic.

Like any new initiate to multi-sited research, I incurred many debts along the way, and I would like now to repay these, if only in the meagre coinage of acknowledgement. In Bombay, I am thankful for the cooperation of the staff of the Asiatic Society of Bombay; Bombay University Library; the Maharashtra State Archives; and the Library of the Shia Imami Ismaili Tariqah and Religious Education Board (in particular Husain S. Jasani, Yasmina and Khairunnisa, none of whose views are reflected in what follows). Personal thanks to Mohammed Hanif Gaya and Mrs Shahnaz Habibi; Minhaj Ali of Bismillah Shah dargah; Abdullah Wahedna of Baba 'Abd al-Rahman dargah; and Papu the Urdu bookseller in Bhindi Bazaar. In Hyderabad, I am indebted to the staff of Osmania University Library and the Salar Jung Library (in particular Dr A. Nagemder Reddy and Dr Syeda Asfia Kauser). Thanks and *adab* to the custodians of the many shrines and family book collections to which I was given access, especially Faisal Yar Khan Habibi Siddiqi and Mohammed Ali Chishti Husayni. In Tehran, I am most grateful to the lineal heirs of Safi 'Ali Shah (who for reasons of security I will not name) for introducing me to the writings of Safi 'Ali and opening to me the library of their *khanaqah* and the various locations of his career around the city of Tehran. Though she is not associated with this brotherhood, I am especially grateful to Fatima Nejadveisi for the lasting pleasures of books and friendship. In Durban, I am most grateful to Naeem Khan Chishti for supplying various texts and opening many doors to me in KwaZulu-Natal. In addition, I was helped by many other members of KwaZulu-Natal's Muslim community, especially Shah Mohammed Saied Soofie (Sajjada Nasheen of Soofie Saheb and Badsha Peer), Shah Abdul Aziz Soofie, Moulana Mohammed Farouk Soofie, Moulana Goolam Mohammed Soofie, Hazrat Goolam Mohayudeen Kazi, Hafiz Mohammed Fuzail Soofie, Fiona Khan, Imtiaz Khan, Mohammed Salih Jhaveri and Saajid Arbee. On the institutional front, I am much obliged to the Durban Cultural and Documentation Centre (in particular Nasreen Salig and Yatin Singh); the Durban Local History Museums (in particular Neela Dullabh) and the Documentation Centre at the University of KwaZulu-Natal, Westville Campus (in particular Mr K. Chetty). In Munich, I am indebted to Dr Winfried Riesterer for help in accessing the rare books collection of the Bayerische Staatsbibliothek.

The research and eventual writing of *Bombay Islam* were pursued during my tenure at Oxford University, the University of Manchester and the University of California, Los Angeles. At Oxford, I am grateful for the support of Frances Lannon, Principal of Lady Margaret Hall, and the trustees and committee of the Milburn Research Fellowship. At Manchester, I learned more than I can easily summarize from my colleagues Jacqueline Suthren Hirst and John Zavos, and received sound counsel and good company from Atreyee Sen, Soumhya Venkatesan, Anindita Ghosh, Andreas Christmann, Youssef Choueiri, Tilman Frasch and Lady Catherine Croft. I am especially thankful to Rylands Professor George Brooke and the School of Arts, Histories and Cultures for support in funding my research in South Africa. At UCLA, I have been fortunate to be exposed to a veritable *cuadrilla* of accomplished scholars and unfamiliar ideas. Among the many who between casual observation and extended conversation have helped me sharpen my arguments, I am most appreciative of Edward Alpers, Andrew Apter, Amy Catlin-Jairazbhoy, Caroline Ford, James Gelvin, Lynn Hunt, Margaret Jacob, Nikki Keddie, Ghislaine Lydon, David Myers, Gabriel Piterberg, Teo Ruiz and Sarah Stein. Special thanks to Sanjay Subrahmanyam for setting an unfailing standard of inspiration and support. Thanks also to Alex Lowe and Carlos Hernandez for patient help with my many scan requests. In the Los Angeles area more generally, thanks to Arash Khazeni, Karen Leonard and John Wills for invitations and discussions. In the wider realms of academia, I am grateful to the following colleagues for various interventions and suggestions (and luncheons): Thomas Metcalf, Polly O'Hanlon, David Washbrook, Michel Boivin, Clare Anderson, Daniel Sheffield, Teena Purohit, Elizabeth Lambourn, Jim Masselos, Scott Reese, Omar Khalidi, Scott Kugle, Mitch Numark, Sean O'Fahey and Torsten Tschacher. Much gratitude to Terenjit Sevea, Syed Farid Alatas and the National University of Singapore for enabling my visits to Singapore and Malaysia and all the comparative insights that came with them. An especial word of recognition is due to Kai Kresse and Edward Simpson for initially encouraging me to frame my work in an Indian Ocean setting and to Francis Robinson for unfailing encouragement and intellectual generosity. Several graduate students also helped at various stages: Banu Demir worked with care on my revisions to the manuscript, Daniel Haines helped track down additional material in Bombay and Nir Shafir made astute suggestions as a reader. Final thanks to Marigold Acland at Cambridge University Press for agreeing to take on another book on working men's miracles, and to Mary Starkey for the careful editing of my words.

I am grateful to Sage/Society, the British Institute of Persian Studies and Cambridge University Press for permission to reprint revised sections in Chapters 2, 4 and 7 from the following articles: 'Moral Competition and the Thrill of the Spectacular: Recounting Catastrophe in Colonial Bombay', *South Asia Research* 28, 3 (2008); 'A Persian Sufi in British India: The Travels of Mirza Hasan Safi'Ali Shah (1251/1835–1316/1899)', *Iran: Journal of Persian Studies* 42 (2004); and 'Islam for the Indentured Indian: A Muslim Missionary in Colonial South Africa', *Bulletin of the School of Oriental and African Studies* 71, 3 (2008).

Given the fact that in 1997 the official Indian name of Bombay was changed to Mumbai, a final word is required on my choice of toponym. In this, my decision was determined by the sources I have used for what is in essence a historical study: for the writers of Arabic, Persian, Urdu and English on whose works I have drawn for the period surveyed in *Bombay Islam*, the name was always Bomba'i/Bombay. The partial eclipse by Marathi of the old name and of the oceanic and imperial languages that used it marks the dilemmas of a different age.

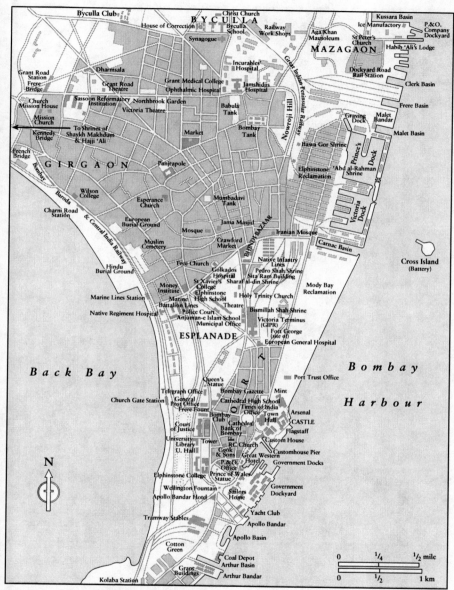

MAP 1. Map of Bombay, India

The map contains the following labels:

Byculla Club
Christ Church
BYCULLA
House of Correction
Kussara Basin
Ice Manufactory
P. & O. Company Dockyard
Byculla School
Railway Work Shops
Aga Khan Mausoleum
St Peter's Church
Synagogue
MAZAGAON
Habib 'Ali's Lodge
Grant Road Station
Frere Bridge
Dharmsala
Incurables' Hospital
Dockyard Road Rail Station
Grant Road Theatre
Grant Medical College
Jamshidjis Hospital
Clerk Basin
Church Mission House
Sassoon Reformatory Institution
Ophthalmic Hospital
Northbrook Garden
Babula Tank
Graving Dock
Frere Basin
Mission Church
Victoria Theatre
Malet Bandar
Malet Basin
To Shrines of Shaykh Makhdum & Hajji 'Ali
Market
Bombay Tank
Bawa Gor Shrine
Kennedy Bridge
French Bridge
Panjrapole
'Abd al-Rahman Shrine
GIRGAON
Elphinstone Reclamation
Prince's Dock
Baroda
Wilson College
Esperance Church
Mumbadavi Tank
Victoria Dock
Charni Road Station
European Burial Ground
Jama Masjid
& Central India Railway
Mosque
Iranian Mosque
Muslim Cemetery
Crawford Market
Carnac Basin
Hindu Burial Ground
Free Church
Native Infantry Lines
Cross Island (Battery)
Golkados Hospital
Pedro Shah Shrine
Sita Ram Building
Mody Bay Reclamation
Marine Lines Station
Money Institute
St Xavier's College
Sharaf al-din Shrine
Native Regiment Hospital
Marine High School
Elphinstone
Holy Trinity Church
Battalion Lines
Theatre
Police Court
Bismillah Shah Shrine
Anjuman-e Islam School
Municipal Office
Victoria Terminus (GIPR)
ESPLANADE
Fort George (site of)
European General Hospital
Back Bay
Queen's Statue
Port Trust Office
Bombay Harbour
Telegraph Office
Bombay Gazette
Mint
Church Gate Station
General Post Office
Cathedral High School
Times of India Office
Town Hall
Arsenal
Frere Fountain
Bombay Club
CASTLE
Flagstaff
Court of Justice
Cathedral
Bank of Bombay
Custom House
University
Library
Tower
Cook & Sons
RC Church
Customhouse Pier
U. Hall
P. & O. Office
Great Western Hotel
Government Docks
Elphinstone College
Prince of Wales Statue
Wellington Fountain
Sailors' Home
Government Dockyard
Apollo Bandar Hotel
Tramway Stables
Yacht Club
Apollo Bandar
FORT
Cotton Green
Apollo Basin
Kolaba Station
Coal Depot
Arthur Basin
Grant Buildings
Arthur Bandar
N

0   ¼   ½ mile
0   ½   1 km

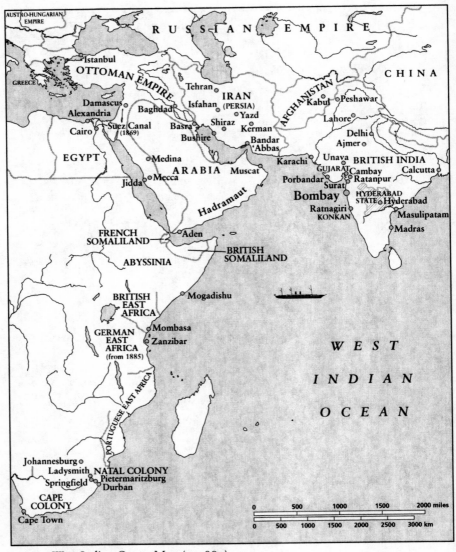

AUSTRO-HUNGARIAN
EMPIRE

RUSSIAN EMPIRE

Istanbul

OTTOMAN EMPIRE

CHINA

GREECE

Tehran

Damascus
Alexandria
Cairo
Suez Canal
(1869)

Baghdad

Isfahan
Basra
Shiraz
Bushire

IRAN
(PERSIA)
Yazd
Kerman

Bandar
Abbas

AFGHANISTAN

Kabul
Peshawar

Lahore

Delhi
Ajmer

BRITISH INDIA

EGYPT

Medina
Jidda

Mecca

ARABIA

Muscat

Karachi
Unava

Calcutta

GUJARAT
Cambay
Porbandar Ratanpur
Surat
Bombay HYDERABAD
STATE Hyderabad
Ratnagiri
KONKAN

Masulipatam

Madras

Hadramaut

FRENCH
SOMALILAND

Aden

BRITISH
SOMALILAND

ABYSSINIA

BRITISH
EAST
AFRICA

Mogadishu

GERMAN
EAST
AFRICA
(from 1885)

Mombasa
Zanzibar

WEST

INDIAN

OCEAN

PORTUGUESE EAST AFRICA

Johannesburg
Ladysmith NATAL COLONY
Springfield Pietermaritzburg
Durban
CAPE
COLONY
Cape Town

0		500		1000		1500		2000 miles
0	500	1000	1500	2000	2500	3000 km		

MAP 2. West Indian Ocean Map (c. 1880)

xvi

Introduction

A RUMOUR OF MIRACLES

At 10.15 on the night of 31 May 1903, the D-block of the recently completed Sita Ram Building in Bombay 'suddenly came down with a crash'.[1] Most of the multi-storey building was unoccupied, but on the ground floor was a saloon bar which over the past months had done a brisk and boozy trade with the port's many British sailors. It was mainly the customers of the bar who made up the dead and injured when the building collapsed. Because the Windsor Bar stood right across the road from the shrine of a Muslim saint, rumours spread quickly that the disaster occurred through an insult to the holy man by the Hindu bar-owner and his bibulous Christian patrons. But for all his defence of the anti-alcoholic norms of *shari'a*, the saint in question was himself something of an oddity. His name was Pedro, and according to urban legend he was a Portuguese sailor who had converted to Islam two centuries earlier. This Pēdrō Shāh was no more commonplace a saint than his feat of levelling a tower block was an act of everyday grace. From his shrine's location in the heart of Bombay's bazaar district, his spectacular miracle was symptomatic of the larger pressures of cosmopolitan modernity that helped create a marketplace of religions in the city surrounding him.

The implications of Pēdrō Shāh's story – that the moral life of the metropolis was regulated by supernatural policemen, that capitalist cosmopolitanism could be undone at the whim of a dead Muslim – have profound implications for the ways in which the trajectories of religion in the nineteenth-century Indian Ocean should be understood, and it is the goal of *Bombay Islam* to unravel these implications. The fact that rumours of

1

righteous supernatural indignation causing Sita Ram Building to collapse spread so quickly tells us something important about the moral landscapes and vernacular imagination of a city which at the turn of the twentieth century stood at the vanguard of industrialization in both India and the Indian Ocean. For Pēdrō Shāh's cult was not the superstitious detritus of an earlier age, but part of a larger supply of religious productions being generated by the experiences of modern urban life. If such supernatural interventions as that seen in the punishment of the Windsor Bar drinkers are not part of the familiar story of the industrial city, then, like the internationalized Yoga of Swami Vivekananda in Chicago and the scientific table-tappers of Victorian London, they comprised the ruptures and reprises of culture that accompanied the ascent of the no less invisible powers of capital.[2]

At the same time that, in London and Manchester, Marx and Engels were attempting to identify the vast but hidden forces that governed the industrializing process, the labourers and merchants of Bombay were developing their own readings of those powers. Just as the two overseas Germans made their models from the building-blocks of their continental intellectual heritage, so did the Muslims who gathered in Bombay from all around the Indian Ocean resort to their own cultural resources to make sense of their brave new world of cotton mills and dockyards. With its saints and miracles, its theologies and pamphlets, its festivals and schools, Bombay Islam was no less a response to industrial change than the leftist ideologies and working-men's clubs that form the familiar stock-in-trade of the labour historian. If the Methodist, Spiritualist and other alternative Christianities of the proletarian Atlantic are now well known, this book tries to draw from their shadow a parallel oceanic Islam of the industrial era.[3]

While the collapse of Sita Ram Building was an unusually dramatic intervention of enchanted agency in the humdrum life of the city, it was unusual in scale and not kind. For in Bombay and its continental and maritime hinterlands, the new social conditions of modernity were highly receptive to an Islam of holy men and their strange powers. The survival – indeed, the increasing production – of such 'old' religious forms in the industrial epicentre of the Indian Ocean demands a reconsidering of industrial modernity and the ways in which Muslims responded to and experienced it. If the story here is one of Bombay, then it is one of a Muslim city which has long stood in the shadows of other Bombays, whether British, Maharashtrian or Parsi.[4] It is also a story of the oceanic reach of Bombay Islam that through railways to Hyderabad and Gujarat and steamships to Iran and South Africa found markets far beyond the city's own platforms and quays.[5] As the rumours of a Portuguese Muslim imply, the picture painted by *Bombay Islam* also differs from familiar depictions of other globalizing Asian or African cities of the nineteenth century, where the social and intellectual forms of modernity have been read through secular or national trajectories.[6] Seated similarly in the second carriage is the colonial, for *Bombay Islam* is constructed in the main from indigenous materials that, in reaching beyond the colonial archive, question the scale of imperial influence on the urban lower classes. In focusing on the Indian products of Bombay's 'economy of enchantment', the following chapters place Muslim writings in the trans-regional languages of Persian, Urdu and Arabic at centre stage to explore an industrial and cosmopolitan environment that was at the same time enchanted with imaginaries and energies that industrialization did as much to empower as suppress.

With shipping routes connected together from every direction, such was the city's status as travel hub of the west Indian Ocean that even Muslims making the *hajj* from Africa, Central Asia or Iran found themselves on layover there.[7] Muslim Bombay was to maritime itineraries in the second half of the nineteenth century what Dubai would become to aeroplane journeys in the second half of the twentieth. All underwritten by commerce, these steamship and sailboat networks ferried in African deckhands and Iranian merchants to add to this character as Islam's industrial *carrefour*. Drawing Muslims from far and wide, in the mid-nineteenth century Bombay emerged as the cosmopolis of the Indian Ocean, a global city in which Muslims were forced to deal with the competitive pressures that also shaped its Atlantic counterpart, New York.[8] Bombay's industrialization was signalled to these Muslims in many different ways. Its mechanical advances offered urban visions of a progressive future; its iron printing-presses produced books in Persian and Arabic, English and Urdu, Malay and Swahili; its steam-fed factories created a jostling of new Muslim proletarians; its sheer size allowed Muslims to alternatively discover the collective unity of the *umma* or to learn instead that they were above all 'Indian'. By the mid-nineteenth century, not only was Bombay *urbs prima in Indis* (as its proud citizens were fond of calling it), but also a primary city of Islam.[9] While in the same period Istanbul, Alexandria and Beirut experienced comparable patterns of demographic and cosmopolitan expansion, in scale and speed none could compete with Bombay's industrialized pace of growth, and the oceanic rather than Mediterranean remit of its pluralism. From Africa, India and the Middle East, Bombay attracted Muslim industrial workers; from the small towns of the Konkan came others in their tens of thousands, along with shiploads of Iranian pilgrims whose journeys to Mecca now involved a stopover of weeks or even months in Bombay. For the Muslim aristocracy of landlocked Hyderabad, Bombay served as a window to the world; for Iranian political and religious exiles as a place of refuge. For a new breed of Muslim missionaries the city's demoralized workforce offered fertile ground for proselytization, while the wealth of its Muslim merchants lent these missionaries the routes and resources to expand beyond Bombay. The city brought together far more linguistically and ethnically diverse Muslim groups than the smaller *dār al-Islām* of the ports of the Mediterranean.

In the earliest major source on Bombay Islam, the Persian *Jān-e Bombā'i* (Bombay soul), written in 1816, the port was already presented as the crossroads of the world. In addition to the English, Portuguese, Greeks, Dutch, Zoroastrians, Jews, Chinese and the many 'sects' (*farqa*) of Hindus described as residents of the city, *Jān-e Bombā'i* spoke of a bewildering range of Muslim groups who also lived there: Arabs and Turks, Iranis and Turanis, Sindis and Hindis, Kabulis and Qandaharis, Punjabis and Lahoris, Kashmiris and Multanis, Madrasis and Malabaris, Gujaratis and Dakanis, Baghdadis and Basrawis, Muscatis and Konkanis.[10] These Muslims did not collapse themselves into an indistinguishable and uniform religious community, and the author of *Jān-e Bombā'i* tells us that each group deliberately made themselves appear different through their forms of dress: 'Every one of them has invented an attractive and different style of tying their turbans (*dastār*) and of curling the locks of their hair in individual ways.'[11] Drawing Muslims from Iran and Iraq, Central Asia and Arabia, as well as every corner of the Indian subcontinent, with its wide pull of visitors Bombay came to serve as the mercantile shadow of Mecca that would in time produce its own Islams in boisterous counterpoint. Bombay's structures of migration were moreover unique in channelling the mass movement of an industrial Muslim workforce and not the smaller flows of technocrats, ideologues and merchants attracted from mid-century to the likes of Istanbul and Alexandria. The gravity of capital thus ensured that the full medley of Muslims from Bombay's vast maritime marketplace was represented on its streets and wharfs. As one of the city's residents described the dazzling assortment of Muslims visible there in 1912:

> There, mark you, are many Bombay Mahomedans of the lower class with their long white shirts, white trousers and skull-caps of silk or brocade ... Arabs from Syria and the valley of the Euphrates; half-Arab, half-Persian traders from the Gulf, in Arab or old Persian costumes and

FIGURE I. Many kinds of Muslim: Samples of Bombay Muslim headdress

black turbans with a red border. Here again comes a Persian of the old school with arched embroidered turban of white silk, white 'aba' or undercoat reaching to the ankles, open grey 'shaya', and soft yellow leather shoe; and he is followed by Persians of the modern school in small stiff black hats, dark coats drawn in at the waist, and English trousers and boots. After them come tall Afghans, their hair well-oiled, in the baggiest of trousers; Makranis dressed like Afghans but distinguished by their sharper nose and more closely-set eyes; Sindis in many buttoned waistcoats; Negroes from Africa clad in striped waist cloths, creeping slowly through the streets and pausing in wonder at every new sight; Negroes in the Bombay Mahomedan dress and red fez ... Malays in English jackets and loose turbans; Bukharans in tall sheep skin caps and woollen gabardines, begging their way from Mecca to their Central Asian homes, singing hymns in honour of the Prophet, or showing plans of the Ka'aba or of the shrine of the saint of saints, Maulana Abdul Kadir Gilani, at Baghdad.[12]

The attractions of the city to these Muslims is self-evident: between 1840 and 1915 Bombay became the third-largest city in the British Empire, the largest port in Asia and, after overtaking Calcutta, the industrial centre of all India and the economic centre of the west Indian Ocean.[13] From the beginning of its great expansion around 1840, Bombay drew Muslims as diverse as the merchants and political exiles of Iran and the rural poor of the surrounding country in the Konkan and Gujarat. From mid-century

onwards, its growth came to rely on migrant labour from its continental hinterland, creating not only a Muslim labour force but huge market
demand for religious productions. In 1850 Bombay was already home
to around 100,000 Muslims.[14] By 1872 the number had grown to some
137,000, around one-fifth of the city's overall population, and by 1901
over 155,000 Muslims lived there.[15] This position in turn afforded the
city's producers and consumers of Muslim religious forms an impact on
religious consumption across this vast region. Yet Bombay was not an
indiscriminate Muslim melting pot in which difference was dissolved
into a single Muslim community demanding a single formation of their
faith. In its cosmopolitan environment, different Muslims protected their
customary community boundaries; and in the period with which we are
dealing, the idea of an Indian Muslim 'nation' or a collective Pan-Islam
was still a minority discourse of the privileged and few. Bombay's distinct
mohalla quarters housed separate *jamā'at*s or communities of Mughal,
Irani, Habashi, Konkani, Pathan, Hadhrami, Mēmon, Bohra and Khōja
Muslims, who married among their own and kept their working and
religious lives in similarly communitarian distinction. The city's mosques
were typically affiliated to these community groups: Bombay's oldest, the
Jami' Masjid (founded 1217/1802), was ruled by an exclusive board of
Konkani old families, while the Zakariyya Mosque (founded 1238/1823)
served only the Mēmon community.[16] In the eighteenth century the many
Iranian Shi'ites who gathered in Bombay founded their own mosque
in turn, shipping ceramic tiles from their homeland as a visual symbol
of their separation. Other Muslim communities had their own distinct
places of worship. In such circumstances, Pan-Islamic visions of a single
umma under Allah were insubstantial indeed, and visions that, in circumstances of increasing religious production, comprised only one of many
Islams on offer.

The period between 1840 and 1915 was therefore not only the heyday of Bombay's commercial and industrial dominance over its oceanic
and continental hinterlands; it was also a period in which the fracturing
effects of a new kind of pluralizing and competitive religious marketplace
emerged. For as different Muslim individuals and groups migrated to
Bombay, they realized (often for the first time) how different they were
from other Muslims. The responses to this predicament with which this
book is concerned are not the solutions of the Muslim Nationalists or the
Pan-Islamists, even though in the persons of Muhammad 'Alī Jinnāh and
Jamāl al-dīn 'al-Afghānī' the cosmopolitan pressures of Bombay have a
claim to the origins of both ideologies.[17] Instead, the main subject of this

book is the process by which distinctive and often mutually competitive Islams were produced or refined in Bombay, and in some cases exported from there to the far regions of the west Indian Ocean. While Bombay's economy of Islams did not disappear in 1915, as the year before the Bombay lawyer Muhammad 'Alī Jinnāh became president of the Muslim League, that year forms a symbolic end point for our survey. From that period, the new imperatives of nationalism and the search for a unified Indian Muslim 'community' symbolized by Jinnāh pulled Bombay's Muslims in other directions, whether seen in their participation in the nationalism of the Muslim League or the internationalism of the Khilāfat movement. The point at which these larger and self-consciously national or transnational visions of community sought to draw together and 'monopolize' Bombay's plural marketplace of Islams marks the beginning of a different age in the history of the city and the ocean's Muslims. And so, with Jinnāh's rise to political prominence, the symbolic date of 1915 marks a point of closure for this survey. Unlike the leaders of the Pan-Islamist Khilāfat movement and the Islamic nationalist Muslim League, the organizations scrutinized in the following chapters had no interest in toppling the colonial government or creating a new Muslim state, and confined their activities to what, in its ideological and legal contours, colonial modernity had rendered as the private and thereby unregulated sphere of 'religion'.[18] By promoting religious productions that did not contradict the colonial formulation of religion as the private business of individual conscience and community custom, the individuals and groups discussed in the following chapters drew their success from being located in this sphere of 'religion' rendered distinct from 'politics'. Unlike the political activities of the Jinnāhs and the al-Afghānīs, the 'Wahhabis' and the Pirs of Pagaro, which became so thoroughly registered in the imagination and archive of empire as to offer historians the double attraction of being automatically 'important' and abundantly documented in colonial records, the Muslims discussed in *Bombay Islam* left no such imprint in the colonial register and, comprising hagiographies and etiquette manuals, poems and travelogues, prayer-books and contracts, the documentation they left is their own. In this sense, their place in nineteenth-century history is raw: their motivations and status have not been preordained by the colonial information order and its long echoes in academia.[19]

If the production of such unproblematically non-political forms of 'religion' passed under the radar of the colonial state, their neglect belies the efficiency of their producers' response to the displacement and anomie of a new Muslim working class and the moralities and anxieties of an

ascendant Muslim middle class. For, as the earliest steamships in the Indian
Ocean entered Bombay's waters in 1825, the first train in Asia departed
the city in 1853, and its streets were illuminated by gas lamps a decade
later, this oceanic urban herald of industrialization produced forms of
enchantment that were no less modern than the ectoplasmic enthusiasms
of metropolitan London.[20] What the following pages offer is therefore
not an account of the kind of Islamic modernity – global and derac-
inated, rational and individualist, disenchanted and 'Protestant' – that
has long been the familiar face of the Muslim nineteenth century.[21] For
the swifter and cheaper travel of the nineteenth century that enabled this
plurality of Islams had only one of its trajectories in the direction of Pan-
Islamism, and the Reformist Islam of a small class of intellectuals was in
turn only one response to the new social conditions.[22] While Bombay did
help produce such Pan-Islamist and Reformist Islams, the greater number of religious productions to emerge there were made of the same stuff
as the towerblock-busting Pēdrō Shāh.[23] Looming large over a market
that stretched between Durban, Tehran and Hyderabad, Bombay produced and exported a bewildering supply of Muslim cults and services
whose chief attractions were the promise of miracles, intercession and
patronage.[24] As late as 1911 an Arab Christian observer could still note
of Bombay's Muslims that, 'to the practice of white magic, soothsaying, and the procuring of luck-charms and amulets, they have, like other
Moslems, no objection', adding, in a pointer to the economic dimensions
of such services, that 'their advisors in soothsaying and witchcraft are
poor Saiyids'.[25] In the industrial heart of the west Indian Ocean, such
enchanted practices and the 'entrepreneurs' and 'firms' that produced
them found a ready market of consumers: among not only the Indian and
African workers in the cotton mills and dockyards, but through networks
of commerce and labour as far as the towns of Iran and the sugar fields
of Natal. For as the following chapters detail, Bombay's Islams were not
limited to Bombay itself and, produced by the largest player in a maritime
marketplace, spread from the northern to the southern reaches of an oceanic economy of religious exchange.

BOMBAY'S RELIGIOUS ECONOMY

As an interpretative model which analyses the holistic interactions of the
'producers' and 'consumers' of religion in a given environment, religious
economy (or the economy of religion) offers a way to track the relations
of the large numbers and varied types of religiosity that typify complex

modern societies.[26] To use such a model of religious economy is not to make judgements on the ontological or epistemological value of religion, nor is it to reduce religion to solely material or financial forces. In this respect, it is important to bear in mind that the model of religious economy is a product of sociological rather than economic thought. The general principle of such analysis is that the complexities of religious activities and interactions are *like* commercial activities and interactions in their capacity to be rendered intelligible through the interpretive model of economy. Further, religious economies are *like* commercial economies in that they constitute a market of potential 'customers' or 'consumers', a set of 'firms' competing to serve that market, and the religious 'products' and 'services' produced or otherwise made available by those firms.[27] As a product of sociological thought, religious economy is concerned with the social life of religion, and as such addresses such fundamental questions as why one type of religiosity flourishes in a certain environment and not another, and how different types (or rival versions of the same type) of religiosity compete with one another. Religion is in this sense conceived as a social and collective enterprise, the result of interactions between different persons. One of the most important aspects of religious economy is therefore the way in which it brings together both the production and consumption dimensions of the social life of religion: the careers of thinkers, prophets or miracle-workers are held to be inseparable from the responses (or lack thereof) of those around them. The model of religious economy also has the advantage of being equally capable of explaining very different trajectories of religious development. In being fundamentally data driven and capable of envisaging a multiplicity of outcomes from the interaction of the participants within its purview, unlike certain forms of classical (particularly Weberian) sociology it avoids teleological explanations of religious development. For these reasons, the model has rich potential for making sense of the social history of religion, particularly in periods and places characterized by religious variety.

Theoretical models are meant to explain complex data and render it comprehensible. Since the model of religious economy was originally developed to explain highly pluralistic religious environments, it is particularly useful in making sense of the vast plethora of Muslim religious organizations or 'firms' that have emerged since the nineteenth century. The latter has usually been seen as a period in which a new Muslim conscience of 'reform' emerged and became increasingly hegemonic as the century progressed.[28] As research has excavated the range of voices and positions in these nineteenth-century debates, it has become increasingly difficult to discern clear defining positions between them. The implicit heuristic model typically used to map this fracture between 'tradition' and 'reform' is one of a dialogue in which two polemical parties can be distinguished.[29] But as research on the range of parties involved has unearthed a cacophony of voices between which no clear dividing line can be discerned, the model of a dichotomous dialogue seems less and less helpful. It is here that the model of religious economy proves its usefulness. For as the cumulative research of recent decades has demonstrated, what we see in the nineteenth century is not the emergence of a smaller number of dominant religious 'movements' among India's Muslims and of agreement between a small number of theological 'parties', but on the contrary a bewildering array of new religious 'entrepreneurs' and 'firms' whose positions on different subjects overlapped as much as they contradicted one another. The model of dialogue, or two-way debate, simply does not fit the evidence, and has the additional disadvantage of reflecting the self-proclaimed Reformists' own rhetoric by collapsing their opponents into the static and monolithic category of 'tradition'. While standardizing, nationalizing and even globalizing organizations did emerge by the 1900s, so did increasing numbers of sectarian, dissenting and localizing organizations.

In focusing on the city's many Muslim productions – indeed, its many Islams – *Bombay Islam* is concerned with the way in which this larger and newly competitive religious economy both created and exacerbated fractures *within* what are too easily assumed to be either pre-existing religious communities of 'Muslims' or newly unified ones of Muslim Nationalism or Pan-Islamism that emerged in the nineteenth century. While the following chapters do occasionally touch on the more familiar topic of inter-religious competition (as with Bombay's famous Hindu–Muslim riots) they are more concerned with challenging the notion that modernity created more standardized – 'uniform', 'global' or 'national' – forms of Islam.[30] Far from creating such a standardized or homogenous Islam, in the period from 1840 to 1915 at least, in the most industrialized city in the west Indian Ocean, industrialization and capitalist modernity encouraged the creation of an ever-increasing diversity of religious producers and consumers, with the latter made more demanding through their exposure to a growing marketplace of religious products and services. Bombay Islam was not one kind of religious production, but many.

What is seen overall in the nineteenth century is therefore a massive increase in Muslim religious production. In part, as in the case of Bombay, this came through the availability of new technologies of communication and reproduction (steam travel, printing) and the creation of new and old forms of social organization (missions, associations, brotherhoods). What emerged from this increasing production of religious sites, texts, persons, practices and organizations is not the clarity of the dialogue but the cacophony of the marketplace. In contrast to Weberian sociology or modernization theory, the principles of religious economy maintain that whether scriptural or charismatic, individualist or collectivist, none of these different Islams was intrinsically any more 'modern' than its competitors. Unlike in the formulations of classical sociology and its heirs in contemporary globalization theory, the model of religious economy helps explain the persistence of forms of religiosity that appear to contradict the familiar trajectories of socio-historical development. For in the most industrialized, technological and cosmopolitan city of the west Indian Ocean, the most successful religious productions were not 'modern', disenchanted, 'Protestant' Islams, but cults that were enchanted, hierarchical and ritualistic. They were neither uniform in characteristics nor cosmopolitan in outlook, but highly differentiated and parochially communitarian. They were neither reformed nor modernist, but customary and traditionalist. While conventional theory fails to explain their success – indeed, expansion – the model of religious economy at least offers the elegance of simplicity: they succeeded because they satisfied the demands of a wide range of consumers.

Since religious economies emerge from the interactions of the religious 'producers' and 'consumers' in any place and period, the model of religious economy could also be applied to maritime and continental India before the nineteenth century. Different religious economies – monopolistic or liberal, active or stagnant, closed or connected – emerge in different periods and places. What this book argues was specific to the period and place it surveys was the emergence in Bombay from around 1840 of a new kind of pluralistic, competitive and 'liberal' religious economy. This new nexus of production, interaction and consumption – or, more simply, this marketplace – emerged through the collusion of several distinct but overlapping factors. The primary enabling factor in the emergence of Bombay's new religious marketplace was the colonial deregulation of religious interactions. In theory at least, the colonial government operated according to the liberal principle of non-interference in religious affairs. Having its origins in the mercantilist attitudes of the East India Company, the principle was gradually formalized in legislation that culminated in Act XX of 1863, which formally banned the colonial government from direct support or control over religious institutions. In terms of social (that is, market) administration, this official policy of non-interference shaped a religious economy in which the state promised and largely appeared not to intervene to favour one competitor in the marketplace over another. This was a significant factor, for as the sociologist Rodney Stark has noted, 'to the degree that a religious economy is unregulated, it will tend to be very pluralistic'.[31] If the subtle religious pressure or indirect interference of the colonial administration has been well charted by various scholars, this was not the same as overt control; and when it did intervene in the market in Bombay the goverment was as likely to do so on behalf of indigenous religious parties as British ones. While the colonial government was therefore not always true to its liberal principles, except in exceptional circumstances (when, as in Chapter 5, colonial law could be called on to assist Muslim no less than Christian groups), the state was not a significant visible player in the economy.

This was particularly true of Bombay compared to the role of the colonial state in such cities as Delhi or Lucknow, where pre-colonial histories of Muslim settlement and rule had created *waqf* endowments and other forms of financial support. The lack of a substantial pre-colonial history of Bombay left little such legacy for the state to interfere with by way of religious buildings or endowments. By the same token, this laissez-faire policy did enable the entry into the Indian marketplace of sophisticated and wealthy foreign 'firms' by way of Christian missionary societies possessing new forms of religious technology in terms of organizational infrastructure and vernacular printing equipment. As the missionary firms expanded in Bombay from the 1820s onwards, their conception of 'religions' as having relational exchange values in which the characteristics, ethics and even utilitarian value of different 'religions' could be compared and chosen between by the rational religious consumer acted as both an ideological and organizational catalyst that furthered the degree of competition in the religious economy.

In this way, the foreign missionaries triggered responses from indigenous religious firms, whether old priestly families or new reforming associations, who borrowed the Christians' techniques and methods, particularly with regard to vernacular printing. The outcome of this dual pattern of governmental deregulation and the arrival of missionary firms was not only the increasing pluralism of a religious market from which none were excluded, but also the competitiveness brought by missionary polemic and counter-missionary apology. Initiated by the vexed collusion of liberal colonial rules on religious toleration and missionary conceptions of the exchangeability of religious affiliation, Bombay's religious

FIGURE 2. Muslims from far and wide: Bombay cafeteria scenes, *c.* 1890

marketplace became an increasingly plural and competitive arena as the nineteenth century progressed. Given the dominant role of India – and particularly the commercial and administrative elites of Bombay in an Indian Ocean that has been conceived as a sub-imperial 'Indian Empire' in its own right – this blend of imperial deregulation and evangelical opportunism reached beyond the shores of India herself.[32] Whether in British domains in East and South Africa, or in independent regions such as Zanzibar and Iran, through the increasing interactions of the nineteenth century and the role of Bombay within them, to a greater or lesser degree the Bombay religious economy was replicated and its productions exported overseas. By way of example, at the northern and southern ends of this oceanic marketplace later chapters take as case studies Bombay's religious traffic with Iran and South Africa. While it is not the aim of this book to portray Bombay as the sole agent in the creation of a religious economy that transformed every corner of the west Indian Ocean, it hopes to present Bombay as the largest urban player in a religious economy that was inter-continental in its extent.

After the 'liberal' colonial conditions and the arrival of missionary 'catalysts', the other major factor in the creation of Bombay's religious economy was the concentration there of a diverse body of religious producers and consumers.[33] The Muslim demographic of this religious economy reflected the sheer volume of Muslim migration to the city from a catchment area that stretched from Gujarat and Hyderabad to Mombasa, Mecca and Shiraz. For the emergence of the city as the economic centre of the west Indian Ocean created a complex pattern of demographic change, concentrating Muslim capitalists in a new industrialized setting at the same time that it attracted a vast rural workforce to its mills and dockyards and created a new middle class of professionals and compradors. It was not only occupation and wealth that divided Bombay's Muslims, but language, ethnicity and place of origin. As one Bombay Muslim explained to readers of *The Times of India* in 1908, 'the most essential fact to be learnt about the Mahomedan community of Bombay is that there is no such community. There are various communities in this city which profess this religion.'[34] After the 'deregulation' of the economy and the 'kickstart' entry of the missionary firms, the third major element in the creation of this plural and competitive religious economy was therefore the presence of a large and diverse market of Muslim religious consumers, whose tastes lent shape to the city's religious productions emerging from the supply side. Moving into Bombay in large numbers, and distanced from the religious products of their homelands, the decisions made by these religious consumers and the responses of the producers who supplied them were the crowning factor in the creation of a thriving religious economy.

With so many Muslims brought together in this way (many of them from socially and religiously homogeneous village environments), Bombay's cosmopolitanism afforded new possibilities of *comparison* between the many different beliefs and practices on display there. The step between the social visibility of religious variety and individual acts of inspection and comparison can be seen in action in as early a source as the 1816 Persian *Jān-e Bombā'ī*, which included in its panoptical survey of Bombay keen descriptions of the religious practices of each of the city's religious groups, before comparing and commenting on their respective degrees of enlightenment and civilization.[35] Such acts of comparison were even more powerful between members of what were nominally the same but in practical terms quite different religious groups. Illusions of Muslim social or theological unity quickly dissolved when different Muslim communities came together in Bombay. Whether between 'co-religionists' or members of more transparently different religious communities, these acts of everyday comparison were an important factor in the creation of a more plural and competitive religious economy. For to compare is to relativize, to make subjective judgements of value and ultimately to make choices. The sum total of such individual acts of comparison fed the motors of competition that led in turn to further religious production.

These issues of comparison, choice and competition point towards the changes being wrought in nineteenth-century Bombay that separate its religious economy from those of earlier periods. For while modernity should not be simplistically equated with individualism, a variety of factors did emerge in the period covered in this book that placed religion increasingly into the hands of individuals as both wage-earning consumers and 'entrepreneurial' new producers.[36] In this, there were many factors at work. Partly this individualization emerged through the petty surpluses of cash that new wage-earners could spend on religious products and services; partly through Christian missionary promotion of an ideology of religious choice and individual conversion. Partly it emerged through the spread of printing and private access to religious texts and ideas; partly through the arrival in Bombay of religious entrepreneurs supplying new products and services. The aggregate of these new social forces encouraged an individualization of patterns of religious 'consumption' in the metropolis that was guided by thousands of private acts of comparison and choice. The majority of changes in patterns of religious consumption that Muslims made were between different Islamic productions rather than changes

('conversions') between the larger 'brand groups' of Islam, Christianity
and Hinduism, even though each of these 'brands' was itself characterized
by increasing and pluralizing production in Bombay.[37] The relatively small
number of 'conversions' that vexed the Christian missionaries therefore
belied the larger pattern of comparison and change that occurred within
such larger 'brand groups' as Islam. For as more and more Islamic products and services became available in Bombay, Muslims 'consumed' them
as rational agents, comparing different religious products or services on
the basis of their explicability or usefulness to their own lives.[38]

If this diverse Muslim population speaks to the demand and consumption side of the economy, then what were the religious 'products' and
'services' that were generated in Bombay, and who were their 'producers'
and 'suppliers'? In outline, products and services could take the form of
pilgrimages and rituals, printed books and preachers' doctrines, moral
consolations and bodily cures, as well as the persons and cults of the
intercessionary holy men whose charisma was no less the production of
the new economy. For in a context of diverse patterns of religious consumption, religious producers increasingly differentiated their persons no
less than their products and services as offering rival paths to salvation
in the hereafter – or, no less often, in the here and now. As the following chapters show, their miraculous productions and charismatic marketing techniques appealed to the demands of the industrial labourers
and expatriate merchants brought to Bombay by the lure of capital. The
production and distribution of these new religious products and services
also relied on the industrial technologies of steam travel and vernacular printing, technologies which offered new avenues of propaganda and
advertisement for holy men and their impresarios. If for heuristic purposes the main religious productions discussed in *Bombay Islam* can be
grouped together beneath the larger market 'trends' towards Reformist
and Customary Islam described below, at ground level these 'firms' comprised a fourfold spectrum of organizational formats.

Seen over the following chapters are four basic types of religious firm
operating from Bombay. Despite the rhetoric that the more self-consciously Modernist of these firms supplied, the vast majority of firms operated on the family business model, in which control over their symbolic
and capital resources was shared primarily along the horizontal stratum
of brothers and male cousins, and transferred along the vertical stratum
of fathers and sons. For the sake of brevity, the four major types of firm
can be labelled the *anjuman*, *jamā'at*, brotherhood and shrine. The *anjuman* or 'association' was the newest organizational type of firm, typically

governed by a board of directors and supported by subscriptions or other modes of formalized charity. The *jamā'at* or 'community' comprised a customary form of an endogamous religious group over which one or more different leaders might struggle for hereditary or, more rarely, elective leadership. Most often associated with the Sufi orders, the brotherhood (or *tarīqa*, literally 'way') was a customary form of voluntary association characterized by the authoritarian and charismatic rule of a living holy man who (depending on his success) expanded the reach of his firm through the distribution of 'deputies' (*khulafā*) to attend to his different constituencies of followers. Finally, shrine firms were centred on the mausolea of saintly holy men (often, but by no means always, Sufis) and, depending on the degree of success that a particular descendant of the saint had over other descendants, were controlled by one or more descendants of the saint in question. Since shrines represented the most concretely localized type of firm, they were often also linked to brotherhoods as a means of expanding the geographical reach of the shrine towards wider consumer bases. However, in densely populated urban environments, shrines had the advantage over other types of firm of having a highly visible and recognizable physical presence which, when combined with long-standing beliefs that such Muslim saints distributed their charisma equally to all, allowed them to potentially attract larger and more religiously diverse sets of consumers than any other firm.

Despite the kin-based popularity of the family business model, the organizational format and strategies of outreach that these firms applied varied considerably, and these were important factors in their relative success. While *anjuman* firms comprised new kinds of modern associations with formal agendas, philanthropic programmes, membership dues and newsletters, the organization of shrine firms ranged from individual entrepreneurs who established 'franchise' shrines connected to parent shrines elsewhere to larger pilgrimage centres and communities of charisma organized on the model of the hereditary family business. While the services of individual wandering *faqīr* mendicants did contribute to the religious economy, more effective were those holy men associated with the organizational framework of the brotherhood, whose customs of hierarchy and discipleship are seen in following chapters providing an effective framework for expansion between Bombay, Durban and Tehran. Through using new technologies and techniques to reach the vast Muslim marketplace in the city and its hinterlands, it was ultimately such customary religious firms of individuals and families operating through charismatic shrines and brotherhoods that emerged as the most successful and characteristic firms of Bombay's Muslim religious economy.

The success of these customary firms points to the fact that market conditions do not necessarily favour innovation. Even if in his essay on 'The Harms in the Observance of Customs', the great Indian Reformist Sayyid Ahmad Khān declared around 1875 that 'the observance of customs is everywhere an obstacle to progress', when faced with the entrepreneurial deployment of familiar religious customs, the sheer novelty of the Reformists' Islam was an impediment to success.[39] In a competitive marketplace, the familiarity and security of custom therefore served to recommend certain religious productions as 'tried and tested', playing into the hands of the customary intercessors and holy men rather than the Reformists, even if many of these customary individuals and firms were entrepreneurial *arrivistes* in their own right. So there was nothing contradictory in the fact that so many of Bombay's religious consumers preferred the familiarly enchanted Customary forms of their forefathers to the disenchanted productions of the Reformists. It is on this basis that Bombay's religious economy can be characterized as an 'economy of enchantment'.

Finally, it is important to note that whatever the confines of the present study, the processes it maps did not apply uniquely to Bombay's Muslims. While the colonial administration applied its laissez-faire policy to all regions of India under its control, its enabling role in the creation of a plural and competitive religious market in Bombay was all the greater for the vast influx to the city of different religious groups from around the Indian Ocean no less than India itself. The unprecedented level of interaction afforded by the cosmopolitanism of what was by the early 1900s a million-strong industrial city affected every group that came there, Hindu and Zoroastrian no less than Christian, Jewish and Muslim. Through such organizations as the Manav Dharma Sabha, founded in 1844 by Durgaram Mehtaji Dave (1809–76), the Ārya Samāj, founded in 1875 by Dayanand Saraswati (1824–83) and the many lesser-known organizations that spread out to the Hindu diaspora in Africa no less than Gujarat and Maharashtra, Bombay was as important to the new Hindu religious economy as it was to the Muslim.[40] As Jews from various regions in India, Iran and the eastern provinces of the Ottoman Empire seeking refuge or commerce converged in Bombay, the city also came to play an important role in the reconstruction of Jewish religiosity in the city's wider oceanic arena.[41] As shown in Chapter 4, the city was also the source of an unprecedented level of Zoroastrian religious productivity, which was in turn exported to Iran.[42] Bombay's Muslim religious economy, then, was part of a larger multi-religious economy from which it borrowed in various ways.

LABELS FOR AN ECONOMY OF ISLAMS

Where the collective weight of scholarship suggests that the nineteenth century belonged to the Muslim Reformists, *Bombay Islam* places these players into the same marketplace alongside the customary purveyors of enchantment who were no less attuned to the industrial age. In place of the term 'Sufism', the following chapters use the category of 'Customary Islam' to refer to the patterns of Muslim religiosity that, while evolving in the centuries before the emergence of the more competitive religious economy of the nineteenth century, still held sufficient – and indeed expanded – appeal in the new conditions so as to be successfully reproduced for new sets of consumers. Yet in Bombay's competitive religious economy, such reproducers of custom could not pass on their Islam unchanged. The model of custom put to use here echoes E. P. Thompson's understanding of the customary idioms of English labour groups, for whom custom was less a static entity than a 'pool of diverse resources' whose various usages placed custom in a creative tension of perpetuity and change.[43] In industrializing India likewise, change was an integral part of even the reproduction of custom, in some cases by ensuring larger public approval through self-consciously 'Islamic' behaviour when visiting shrines or emphasizing the harmony between custom and *sharīʿa*.[44] In the rapidly changing urban environment of Bombay, there was therefore never any simplistic perpetuation of custom, and the strategies and mechanisms of its reproduction by Customary Islamic firms are examined in the case studies of the following chapters.

Against a historiographical drama in which Reform has long held centre stage, *Bombay Islam* argues that in industrializing oceanic India, Reformist Islam was only a marginal player in the period under scrutiny. As a result, in Bombay and its wider marketplace relatively few Customary Islamic firms felt the need to expressly respond to the 'threat' of Reform, and for these generally later organizations the label 'Counter Reform' is adopted. The picture was different in continental North India, arguably because, stuck with a diminishing economy of agricultural landholdings and a rural or provincial service class clientele, Customary Islamic trends there lacked the oceanic economy of industry and commerce that in Bombay sustained the market for Customary Islam so well.[45] It was therefore in the north that from the 1880s the most important Counter Reform organization began to emerge by way of the 'Barelwi' *madrasa* network established by Sayyid Ahmad Riza Khan of Bareilly (d. 1340/1921).[46] A classic example of the logic of Counter Reform, his Ahl-e Sunnat organization has been described as 'reformist in the self-consciousness of its practice, and in its insistence on following the sunna of the Prophet at all times'.[47] While through such organizations Counter Reform became an important element in India's overall religious economy by 1900, and some of Bombay's Muslim reproducers of custom similarly voiced its apologetic and self-modificatory logic, for the most part what flourished in Bombay was an economy of enchantment in which Customary Islam felt little competition from the city's limited number of Reformists.

While the labels Customary, Reformist and Counter Reformist Islam are helpful, they should not be reified as constituting coherent 'movements', and are used here as heuristic labels to designate widespread but often quite disparate and internally competing 'trends' within the market. Such was the competitive logic of the new economy that, despite the similarities they pose to the observer, Reformist firms frequently opposed one another, as did Customary Islamic firms. What can be observed therefore remained first and foremost a marketplace of many distinct competing organizations and individuals, albeit a market in which certain larger trends towards Reform and Customary Islam can be observed from the outside.

THE ECONOMY OF RELIGION AND THE HISTORY OF LABOUR

Compared to the more richly culturalist historiography of labour that has developed over the past half-century with regard to Britain and the United States, for the nineteenth century at least the literature on Indian labour history presents a far less detailed picture of the interface between labour and culture. Although excuses can be made about the relative paucity of sources for India rather than the Anglosphere, the fact is that India's industrialization in the nineteenth century led to the production of an unprecedented array of printed materials in almost every vernacular language of the subcontinent. While many of these emerged from the bailiwick of the middle class, there were also large numbers of chap-books produced for those lower down the social scale. This was particularly the case in large Indian urban environments, where the mid-1800s saw the emergence of thriving print markets geared towards the tastes of the urban masses.[48] If Bombay offers a similar abundance of such printed and otherwise written materials, then written documentation is not the only source material that the city offers onto the religio-cultural imagination of its workforce. For while texts were one kind of religious production that emerged from Bombay's religious economy, from festivals and musical gatherings to healing practices and new forms of sociability, there were also many other kinds of religious production that emerged in the city in response to the demand of the urban masses. It is here too that the model of religious economy proves its value, for in showing how religious products are the result of the interaction between consumer groups and the suppliers competing for their support, the model presents a variety of evidence for the cultural life of the city's labouring groups by way of religious productions created in response to the demand of the lower-class consumer.

Given the fact that the greater proportion of Bombay's Muslims consisted of the new industrial workforce that the city pioneered, the study of the religious consumption of a new Muslim working class contributes to long-standing debates in labour history, in particular on the place of 'custom' in labour culture. For the religious idioms that appealed to the Muslim labour groups that emerged in Bombay during the nineteenth century were writ through with customary hierarchies that governed the metaphysical no less than the social and political imagination.[49] The patterns of the inheritance and reproduction of Indian labour culture were quite different from those imagined by Marx and the early E. P. Thompson: this was not the egalitarian inheritance of the 'liberty tree' that Thompson saw behind the English workers' movements of the nineteenth century.[50] In spite of this distinction, the religious productions consumed by Bombay's Muslim labourers did hold in common with English labour culture an emphasis on custom, which the later Thompson saw as the labourers' 'rhetoric of legitimation for almost any usage, practice or demanded right'.[51] From a comparative perspective, it is this shared idiom of the customary rather than its distinct egalitarian or inegalitarian expressions that appears as the more general characteristic of labour culture.

Yet the customary idioms that appealed to Muslim labour groups were not the sole resource of the labourer, and were often most effectively mobilized by wealthy religious entrepreneurs and merchant groups. Such was the hierarchical character of the symbolic resources of custom (*dastūr*, *'ādāt, rasm*) that the production of a metaphysically elevated 'leader' (and not a 'representative' *primus inter pares*) was a necessary element of customary productions, whether they originated among labour or merchant groups. One of the key contentions of this book is that the religious productions, and thereby the larger history, of such groups cannot be easily separated. For as the following pages show, in an economy of religious enchantment relying on the client–patron ties of the devotee and saint, the religious economy of both labour and merchant groups was typically interactive – and at times mutually dependent. The empowerment lent to such inegalitarian customs by the capitalist enterprises of Bombay helps explain the survival among workers in colonial Calcutta of the 'precapitalist, inegalitarian culture marked by strong primordial loyalties of community, language, religion, caste and kinship' that was problematized by Dipesh Chakrabarty.[52] For such customs did not simply 'survive': in the religious economy of an industrializing environment they were reproduced more efficiently than ever. By pointing towards the continuing, if protean, importance of custom among the Muslim workers of Bombay, *Bombay Islam* therefore hopes to move beyond the search for emblematically 'modern' forms of labour organization that until recently typified the study of Indian labour.[53] Seen in this light, the body of vernacular materials drawn together in this book provides the kind of index and archive of nineteenth-century working-class life that has so far eluded historians of Indian labour.[54]

By inspecting the Muslim corner of one of the most productive religious economies to emerge in the nineteenth century, *Bombay Islam* suggests that the conditions of industrial modernity did not necessarily lead to fewer 'Reformist', 'uniform' or 'globalized' religious forms any more than they favoured processes of rationalization and disenchantment.[55] Looking at a specific religious economy that centred on Bombay demonstrates how industrialization created a range of social conditions for its different participants that in turn shaped a diverse and often contradictory set of religious demands. While an English-educated comprador class demanded a 'Protestant' Islam of scripture and sobriety, the workers in their warehouses sought a religion of carnival holidays and practical little miracles.[56] The increasing social complexity of a cosmopolitan and class-differentiated capitalist city thus found expression in increasing religious production and diversification rather than standardization. But among the many religious productions that emerged from Bombay's oceanic shipyard of modernity between 1840 and 1915, the most successful trend to emerge was that of Customary Islam. Despite having roots in the pre-industrial past, the reproductions of custom created by Bombay's Customary Islamic 'firms' spread widely due to their resonance with the working conditions of industrial capitalism and its broken social landscape of individuals uprooted from their ancestral backgrounds. For many Muslims, a world with no helper other than a distant Allah was a lonely world indeed. With their shrines and lodges near the cotton mills of Bombay and the plantations of Natal, the charismatic shaykhs who form the focus of *Bombay Islam* were infinitely closer to their clients than a faceless and absent God. Led by spiritual aristocrats, patronized by wealthy merchants and consumed by labourers, the religious productions traced in the following chapters were not simply 'popular Islam', and expressed themselves in a plethora of modern printed genres, from newspapers and travelogues to biographies and guidebooks. Powered by the new social and technological forces of labour migration and steam travel, they were not merely 'local Islam' either. Like the maritime cults of Muslim Tamil migrants in colonial Singapore, the stories of European vampires that followed African labourers into the mines of the Copper Belt, and the movement of fortune-telling promoters of the 'refugee god' Wong Tai Sin to Hong Kong harbour, these were forms of religion that were inseparable from the mass labour migrations that transformed Asian and African societies in the nineteenth century.[57]

I

Missionaries and Reformists in the Market of Islams

CHRISTIANIZING CATALYSTS: THE IMPACT
OF THE MISSIONARY SOCIETIES

Before turning towards the new Reformist firms that emerged among Bombay's Muslims in the mid-nineteenth century, we must first trace the activities of the ideological and organizational catalysts in the city's transformation into a competitive and pluralizing religious economy. These were the Christian missionary organizations whose great assault on the religions of Bombay formed the background to the emergence of the first Parsi, Hindu and Muslim Reformist groups in the city. While the Christian missions did not influence every group among the city's Muslims alike – Bombay's Iranian Muslims, for example, remained largely unaffected – their importance cannot be overlooked for the earlier part of the century, when the missions were the first substantial importers of unfamiliarly new religious productions to the city's growing populace. In triggering a set of defensive responses from Reformist organizations from across the spectrum of Indian religions, the missionaries played a key role in triggering the increasing pluralization and increasing production that would typify the religious economy of Bombay Islam. As an imperial port city, Bombay was intrinsically connected to developments in the imperial centre, even as its parallel existence as an Indian Ocean port ultimately held the potential to wash colonial influences beneath stronger tides of more regional cultural provenance. In religious terms, the most important example of these interconnections between Britain and its empire was the development of the missionary society. While the importance of the missionary societies for religious developments in the

North Indian 'bridgehead' of Calcutta is well known, this chapter argues that the arrival of the Christian missionary societies in Bombay from the early 1800s was similarly crucial to the development of dozens of new religious entrepreneurs and organizations among each of the city's groups. In turn, these indigenous Reformist organizations expanded from Bombay into the city's wide continental and oceanic hinterlands, to Gujarat and Maharashtra, Iran and South Africa.[2] As the nineteenth century progressed, there emerged in response to the decision to allow Christian missionary organizations to operate in British India in 1813 an unprecedented level of competition between the various Muslim, Hindu, Sikh, Jewish and Parsi Reformist organizations.

As catalysts in the creation of the competitive religious marketplace with whose Muslim participants we are concerned, the missionary societies provided two crucial elements in the 'liberalization' of the region's religious economy. The first was ideological: the revolutionary idea that religious identity and the social affiliations that came with it were freely changeable through an act of individual choice based on private conscience. The second was organizational: the 'missionary' forms of social and communicational technology that propagated Christianity and castigated its competitors. The point here is not to argue that the missionaries were the sole agents in 'freeing' their marketplace to new levels of competition. Competition and comparison between socio-religious norms were an inevitable result of the influx of so many different peoples to Bombay, and the greater agency here was in some senses the basic cosmopolitan lure of capitalism. If they were not sole agents, the missionary societies were important for the novel way in which their very model of conversion rendered religious identity changeable through individual choice, lending 'religion' as such an immediate and simple exchange value. Empowered by the industrial apparatus which in the period of the dawn of Indian-language publishing disseminated hundreds of thousands of printed tracts and scripture portions, the missionary societies were ultimately more important for their ideology of free religious exchange than for their actual success in converting Indians to Christianity. Transforming industrial printing into a polemical publicity machine, they provoked alternately self-critical and defensive responses from Bombay's various Indian communities. In turn, these methods and the ideology they expressed found their echo among the new religious organizations that developed among each of Bombay's communities.

Based on critique, comparison and free exchange, this new ideology of religious exchange or 'conversion' was further amplified through new organizational forms of religious outreach by way of schooling, public preaching and organized charity. It was through this growing number of individual, family and associational organizations that the Bombay religious marketplace became not only more diverse but also more competitive. As the formative background to the spread of the 'enchanted' Muslim religious productions explored in later chapters, this chapter traces the emergence of the Christian missionary firms in Bombay, and the first Indian – and among them Islamic – responses to them. In this respect, it is important to note here the 'Protestant' character of not only the Christian missions but also of their immediate Reformist responses from indigenous groups. For, as we will see, a disenchanted and egalitarian religiosity based on scripture, reason and salvation ultimately held less appeal to the mass of proletarian consumers than more familiar customary religious products based on miracles, rituals and the intercession of charismatic saviours.

For Bombay, the most important of the British missions were the Scottish Missionary Society (SMS, founded in 1796) and the Church Missionary Society (CMS, founded in 1799), whose foundation marked a turning-point in the relationship between Britain's society at home and that of its empire in Asia. Of comparable importance, particularly early in the century, was the American Board of Commissioners for Foreign Missions (ABCFM, founded in 1812). The Evangelical movement that these organizations exemplified was a response to the new cosmopolitan pressures brought by the increasing circulation of personnel and knowledge between Britain and India.[3] Under leadership of the missionaries Gordon Hall, Samuel Nott and Samuel Newell, the ABCFM arrived in Bombay within months of the lifting of the East India Company's ban on Christian missions in 1813.[4] Working on the frontline of the Evangelical revival, these men were fully committed to the eradication of 'heathenism' in any shape in which they found it.[5] As heirs to the Enlightenment they were also pioneers of English education, which would become a filter for their ideas among the merchant middle classes of Bombay, and so to the modernist wing of Muslim Reformism. By 1816 the ABCFM was teaching three thousand pupils in Bombay, and in 1824 opened a pioneering school for Indian girls. While its pedagogical interests were mainly among the city's Hindus, as pioneers of the city's printing infrastructure the ABCFM's impact was ultimately far wider. Having begun printing in Marathi as early as 1816, the ABCFM gradually expanded its output of polemical tracts and scripture portions into the Gujarati, Urdu and Arabic languages familiar to the city's Muslims.[6] The game was afoot.

While the ABCFM was the earliest of the pluralizing catalysts of competition, the Reverend John Wilson (1804–75), the most influential missionary to work among Bombay's Muslims, served as a pioneer of the
journal publishing that created the public sphere of information on religious products and services that a competitive liberal market required.
He established the *Oriental Christian Spectator* magazine in 1831. Sent
to Bombay as the representative of the SMS in 1829, Wilson spent the
next forty-seven years preaching and printing in refutation of native religions.[7] As with all of the city's missionaries, his impact was felt among
every community present in Bombay, triggering cumulatively pluralizing
responses from Hindus and Parsis as much as Muslims. Within a year of
his arrival he was preaching in Marathi, but more importantly for our
purposes, over the following years Wilson improved his linguistic arsenal
by learning Persian, Urdu and Gujarati, as well as the scriptural languages
of Arabic and Sanskrit.[8] As early as 1830 he began what would become a
long series of public disputations with Indian religious leaders, beginning
with Narayan Rao, who in an early instance of local competitive productivity wrote a response to Wilson's tract *An Exposure of Hinduism.*[9] A
teacher of English at the Raja of Satara's school, Narayan Rao reflects the
class and occupational profile of the city's Modernist Muslims discussed
below, many of whom were similarly linked to Anglicizing educational
institutions. Wilson's investigations of Zoroastrian texts and critiques
of contemporary Zoroastrian practices also prepared the way for the
exchanges with local Parsis that laid the ground for the production of the
Reformist Zoroastrianism discussed in Chapter 4.[10]

The responses to such attacks did not manifest themselves merely in
the sphere of ideas, but also in their modes of production and in terms
of the greater impact on the marketplace; the medium was ultimately
more important than the message. For in 1828, in response to attacks on
Zoroastrianism, the Bombay Parsi Mullā Firōz bin Mullā Kāvus became
possibly the first Indian to acquire one of the new lithographic presses and
to turn it towards publishing in both Gujarati and Persian. The text in
question was *Risāla-ye istishhādāt* (Book of certificates), which sought to
defend Zoroastrianism against various polemical charges by publishing the
certificates or rulings of various Muslim as well as Parsi scholars.[11] Printed
in Persian from one side and in Gujarati from the other side of the book,
Risāla-ye istishhādāt was a remarkably early and significant step in the
adaptation of the new industrial technology of lithography for publishing
in Asian scripts.[12] As the transfer of a colonial and missionary technology
for local religious production, Mullā Firōz's *Risāla-ye istishhādāt* shows

just how tangible the catalytic effects of missionary activity were. For as Chapter 3 traces in more detail, over subsequent decades the spread of lithography among Bombay's other religious firms widely distributed one of the religious economy's most important means of production.

The effects of Wilson's attacks were not only felt in the Zoroastrian corner of the emerging marketplace. Not content to criticize only Hindu and Parsi practices, Wilson went on to print a whole series of tracts in the languages of Bombay's Muslims attacking the 'licentiousness and imposture' of Muhammad.[13] The first of these 'Refutations of Muhammadanism' appeared in 1833 in Urdu (as *Musulmānī dīn ka radiyya*) and Persian (as *Rad-e dīn-e musulmānī*).[14] In 22 short chapters of 120 pages of neat lithography printed at a time when the new technology and its imported Bavarian stones were still very new to the city, Wilson's scripture-based 'refutation' dealt first with the purity and truth (*pākī aur sachā'ī*) of the Torah and Gospels.[15] The text then went on to attack the crooked morality of the Prophet Muhammad over several chapters and then, by exegetical method, demonstrate the 'contradictory phrases of the Quran' (*qur'ān kē ikhtilāf aqwāl*) and the false reports the scripture made on Alexander the Great (Sikandar Rūmī) so as to deny that the Quran was a 'heavenly book' (*āsmānī kitāb*) like the Bible.[16] In what was still a very early period in printing in the Muslim languages in India – the first indigenous Muslim text only being printed in around 1820 in Lucknow – Wilson's tracts were widely distributed, and had an impact whose gravity drew on the power of the new technologies of religious production and distribution that missionaries had at their disposal through their mechanized presses and colporteurs.[17] Bombay's Muslim scholars were triggered into defending Islam in both the discursive terms and informational medium set by their polemical interlocutor. One of these defenders in Bombay was was Hājji Muhammad Hāshim, a learned *mawlwī* originally from Shiraz or Isfahan, who responded to Wilson by publishing a long tract in Persian and Gujarati in defence of the Quran.[18] Reaching a still wider public marketplace, their ongoing dispute was carried into the pages of the city's emergent Indian-language newspapers.[19]

This brief outline of Wilson's career tells us several things. First, that the better-known pattern of Evangelical printed polemics and public *munāzara* debates that spread from Calcutta to such North Indian cities as Delhi, Lucknow and Agra in the 1820s and 1830s were also characteristic of Bombay.[20] Indeed, Wilson's 1833 Persian and Urdu publications pre-dated by six years the Indian printing of the famous *Mizān al-haqq* (Balance of truth) by which Karl Gottlieb Pfander (1803–68) triggered Muslim responses in the north.[21] Second, that as with the emergence of

Islamic Reformism in North India, its appearance in Bombay must be understood as at least in part a product of competition with scriptural-izing Protestant Christians.[22]

The American and Scottish missions were by no means the sole Protestant ideologues in Bombay. In 1820 the CMS began operating there under Reverend Richard Kenney. Another educational pioneer, Kenney had within six years opened ten schools catering to some three hundred pupils; he had also translated and printed the Psalms and Liturgy into Marathi.[23] After Kenney returned to England in 1826, the CMS mission in Bombay was taken over by William Mitchell and S. Stewart, who founded more schools and began the CMS outreach to the city's Muslims.[24] From mid-century the CMS thus continued what Wilson had initiated among the Muslims of Bombay. Beginning in 1859 with Reverend J. G. Deimler, who led the mission until his retirement in 1895, its targeted outreach to Bombay's Muslims continued to operate until 1907 under Reverend Henry Smith, who had begun his career as a preacher among the working men of Birmingham.[25] From their base in Bombay, the CMS also made its first excursions into East Africa, as Bombay's Muslim religious firms would later. Deimler and Smith were not alone in this work, and the social reach of the CMS mission was expanded through the help of Indian preach-ers and the establishment of a women's *zanāna* mission under the leader-ship of Deimler's wife.[26] In the combined high and low point of Deimler's career he converted a Bombay Muslim called Mirzā Sulaymān ʿAlī Ghōr, who claimed to be a grandson of the last Mughal emperor, before being unmasked as a fraud after Deimler announced his success.[27] Worse was to come, and local opposition to the CMS's attempts to capture public space was given violent vent when Daʾūd Mukham, another of Deimler's Muslim converts and a native catechist, was stabbed and seriously wounded in a Bombay street.[28] While the sociological impact of the mission is clear enough from such violent protests, in terms of the development of a new kind of religious economy it was the more efficient new modes of religious production and distribution represented by such foreign firms as the CMS that were to have the longer-lasting effects. Deimler's description of these activities illustrates the multiple levels on which the religious productions of the Christian missionaries infiltrated Muslim society in Bombay. The CMS mission's modes of distribution included:

> receiving Native visitors and inquirers; attendance at meetings of vari-ous societies; examination of Urdu tracts presented for publication; the superintendence of a [book distributing] colporteur to the Mussulmans; occasional duty in the Society's English Church; instruction of inquirers

and converts; the superintendence of the Society's catechist; a weekly
service in Urdu; visiting shops, houses, the Native hospital, the poor
house, the Sipahis' [Indian soldiers'] lines, the gardens, the bunders
[dockyards], the Native hotels, street preaching, translational work.[29]

Along with their new modes of proselytizing distribution, which Muslim
isha'at (outreach) or *tabligh* (preaching) firms would later copy, what
was most distinctly modern about the missionary societies was their turn
towards the urban labour communities that had emerged with industrialization. Pioneered by the homeland missions in cities such as Manchester
and London, and the subsidiary missions to specific groups of 'demoralized' workers such as perennially licentious Navvies, in the second
half of the nineteenth century Christian missionaries also began working among colonial labour groups. As in Britain's cities, from around
the 1870s the rapid development of labourers' quarters or chawls in
Calcutta and Bombay had not taken account of the need for religions or
other social institutions, and it was into this gap – concretely architectural as much as abstractedly spiritual – that the mission houses inserted
themselves. While historians have drawn attention to the emergence of
trade unions and political parties in Bombay, such hallmark criteria of
'modernity' have overshadowed the missionary dimension to industrialization that was present among the mills of Bombay as much as those
of Manchester.[30] What was new about this religious modernity in terms
of social relations was its positioning of the middle-class missionary as
the moral tutor of the working class. In India in particular, we must
not underestimate the radicalism of the idea that a man of gentle birth
should plunge himself on a daily basis into the company of the lowliest
in society; not merely the country folk (who in both India and Britain
acted with the deference of those who knew their place), but the unruly
labourers of the city. In India as in Britain, this radical idea lit the fuse
for the explosion of indigenous missionary firms – Christian, Muslim,
Hindu – that so characterized the second half of the nineteenth century.
In a sense, the activities of Mr and Mrs Deimler represented the 'family
business' model of religious production that is seen in later chapters as
characterizing several of the new Muslim cults that emerged in Bombay.
But while there was a familial element in the day-to-day running of the
Christian missions, they are better conceived as the religious counterparts to transnational corporations such as the East India Company, if
forced to operate without the protection of a monopoly. Supported by
capital raised overseas and equipped with social and mechanical technologies developed in the cities of industrializing Britain and to a lesser

extent United States, the Christian missionary firms represented new and characteristically modern ways of both producing and organizing religion. If, as is seen in later chapters, the missions were by no means the only religious import into an entrepôt located in an ocean with longer associations with Islam than Christianity, the missions still introduced innovations and resources that it took local groups some years to master and muster. But this they surely did; and as we will now see, the results were to bring new Muslim firms into a marketplace which would in turn become more plural and fragmented.

REFORMIST RESPONSES: NEW RELIGIOUS PRODUCTIONS

Combining with the widespread collapse of Muslim political power in India in the previous half century, the extensive polemics in which the Christian missionary societies engaged from 1813 fed an existing Muslim crisis of conscience, on the back of which a range of new piety organizations were able to spread their messages. The emphasis on *islāh* (mending, reforming) and *tajdīd* (renewing) that characterized the pietism of these firms was accompanied by a stern critique of prevailing custom (*dastūr, 'ādāt, 'urf*), particularly that associated with shrines and holy men, the old 'firms' against which the new Reformist firms would ultimately have to compete to establish themselves in the Muslim corner of the marketplace. It was around these issues that in the second half of the nineteenth century there came about a parting of the ways between Custom and Reform. In Customary Islamic terms, the dead saints and their living representatives were the keystone of the bridge between God and his creatures. In a context of mass illiteracy and manuscript rather than print production, the use of scripture as an intermediary between man and God was of very limited value. More important – more accessible, reliable and downright reassuring – was the tangible, talkative and emotive presence of God's mercy made manifest in the persons of his living representatives. But as the old social order of religious notables broke down and the spread of printing made book-religion practical on a new scale, there emerged a trend towards the disenchantment of the social world of holy men and miracles. At the behest of a growing number of Reformist organizations, books replaced bodies as both the bridge between man and God and as the prime locus of religious authority.

One of the most important characteristics of the new Muslim organizations that from the mid-nineteenth century promoted this ideology of Reform was their adaptation of the new social technology of the mission to the local conditions of religious marketplaces which they ultimately knew better than the foreign mission firms. Recent scholarship has argued that one of the key facets of Bombay's modernity is to be located in its role in the spread of associational culture.[31] In its religious expressions at least, this new culture cannot be separated from the organizational example of the Christian missionary associations. The organized voluntary associations that emerged in Bombay from around 1850 have been seen as Indian parallels to the explosion of clubs and societies that, in the wake of Jürgen Habermas, have been seen as crucial to the emergence of a modern public sphere.[32] Nineteenth-century Bombay was indeed characterized by the spread of voluntary associations, beginning around 1840 through the efforts of its small Anglophone Indian elite, particularly the section of society that Christine Dobbin described as Bombay's Indian 'intelligentsia'.[33] By this time the Christian missionaries had been operating in Bombay for several decades, founding their earliest schools there in 1813, and with the CMS having almost five hundred students on its school registers in Bombay by 1840.[34] Bombay's wealthier Indian merchants were spurred to react to the critiques and innovations of the Christians, and from the 1840s began founding rival associations that with all the logic of market competition absorbed much of their Protestant competitors' critique of Indian religious customs. As with the 'Bengal Renaissance' that had emerged from this same infrastructure of transnational Christian religious firms in Calcutta a few decades earlier, the Indian response in Bombay was predominantly by way of religious firms aimed at the reform of customary religious practices.[35] This was a development that first emerged among the city's Parsis and Hindus, and took several decades before it reached the Muslims of Bombay.

The wealthy comprador elite at the heart of Bombay's Parsi community were among the earliest and most effective responses to the Christian catalysts of the marketplace.[36] Their intentions were paradigmatic of the larger Reformist project that also emerged among Hindus and Muslims: 'the restoration of the Zoroastrian religion to its pristine purity'.[37] Largely drawn from former students at Bombay's Elphinstone College, in 1851 the Parsi Reformists founded the Rahnuma'i Mazdayasnan Sabha (Religious Reform Association) under the leadership of Naoroji Furdoonji.[38] Already exposed to the Christian missionary polemics that catalysed the new era of religious competition, the Rahnuma'i Mazdayasnan Sabha had three principal aims: to present Zoroastrianism as a form of pure monotheism; to place the text of the Gathas as the sole religious authority; and to eradicate all forms of customary ritual without sanction in the Gathas so as to create a religion based on 'original pure belief'.[39]

Teachings such as Khorshedji Rustamji Cama's Parsi Reformism also evolved in contact with Protestant scholarship and European notions of 'true religion' more generally. On his return to Bombay from Europe, Cama began teaching the Gathas in the 'Protestant' mode that he had learned by studying with European scholars in 1859. Aiming to slough off centuries of custom, Cama sought to educate a new kind of Parsi priest who would lead the community through mastering scripture, modelling himself on the 'original' virtues it expressed.[40] Naturally enough, the critics of the new priests labelled them 'Parsi Protestants', and the influence on them of Christian Protestants was quite clear through the acts of visible comparison that the Bombay marketplace offered.[41] However, it would be a mistake to see the changes among the Parsis as affecting only themselves. For as some of the wealthiest men in the city, the ideas and institutions promoted by the Parsi merchant elite had widespread effect. While in Chapters 4 and 5 we see their Reformist doctrines reaching as far as the towns and villages of central Iran, their most notable early impact on wider religious competition in Bombay occurred when an article on the Prophet Muhammad appeared in a Parsi Gujarati newspaper accompanied by a 'hideous picture' of the Prophet, leading to the bloody Parsi–Muslim riots of September 1852.[42] As with the Christian missions, the productions of the new Parsi associations were similarly powered by the new technology of vernacular and, in this case, also illustrated printing. Here was the negative social equity of Parsi life in the oceanic cosmopolis.[43]

In the wake of the Christian missions, a range of Hindu Reformist associations also contributed to Bombay's new forms of religious production. Among these other early non-Muslim Reformist societies were the Paramahamsa Mandali (Society for the Supreme Being, founded in 1847), the Prarthana Samāj (Society of Liberal Religionists, founded in 1867) and eventually the more famous Āryā Samāj (Noble Society, founded in 1875), which went on to become the most important of the new Hindu missionary societies.[44] Just as Parsi Reformism would reach out across Bombay's oceanic arena to Iran, so would the city's Hindu Reformists quickly establish franchise operations in the city's continental hinterland in Gujarat and Maharashtra and, by the century's end, through the 'Hindu' diaspora in its oceanic hinterlands in East and South Africa as well.[45] In line with the theology of the Christian missionary firms by which they were influenced, the indigenous Reform associations were

characteristically 'Protestant' in expression, promoting such causes as
religious rationalism and modern education while suppressing the 'superstitious' mediation of customary rituals and holy men not legitimized
in the scriptures. In a classic expression of the scripturalist character of
Reformism, the Āryā Samāj set itself the 'object of effecting social and
religious reform on the authority of the Vedas'.[46] Led by the comprador
elite among Bombay's merchants, the distinctive mechanisms that these
Reformist 'association' firms were able to develop through their mobile
representatives, school-building and journal-printing was intimately connected to the transformation of the city's economy as a whole. While they
were never simply reducible to one another, the religious and the material
economies of Bombay were always connected.

It is therefore important to position the religious pluralization of
Bombay Islam within this broader pattern of Reformist productivity that
affected every religious group in the region, from Hindus and Zoroastrians
to neo-Buddhists and Jews. In response to the wider transformation of
Indian society concomitant with the creation of a competitive religious
marketplace, the new religious products designated under the heading
of Reform were trans-religious in their remit.[47] In order to salvage local
religious products from the attacks of the new Christian firms, the indigenous Reformist associations sought to discard the pernicious influence of
'superstition' to leave what they presented as a pristine form of their own
religious brand. In the urban marketplace, one of their key attractions
was their amenable stripping away of custom to render them more adaptable to the aspirant lifestyles of an emerging middle class. One important
aspect of this was the attack on the pan-religious forms of customary
community organization that are usually designated as 'caste', customary structures which were no less common to Bombay's Muslims than its
Hindus.[48] Other middle-class attractions included the Reformists' promotion of such causes as female education, scientific and English medium
instruction and the easing of taboos on social interactions, each with
their implications for bourgeois mercantile and civil careers in the modernizing colonial cosmopolis.

PRODUCING REFORMIST ISLAMS

Bombay's Muslims were similarly active, if slower, in founding such
Reformist associations, the emergence of which must be seen as part of
the same competitive marketplace, triggered by the Christian missions,
in which their Hindu and Parsi counterparts operated. With their access

to English-medium education and their closer interactions with British Christians, it was Bombay's Muslim comprador and bureaucratic middle class that first moved towards the production of the self-consciously 'modernist' Islam that was one pattern of the wider trend of Reform. In large part, Bombay's Muslim Reformists were also responding to the Christian missionaries, but, within the increasingly pluralistic religious economy of the 1870s, they were also responding to the new religious productions of the Parsi and Hindu middle class. The most important of these new Muslim firms was Bombay's Anjuman-e Islām (Islamic Association), its very associational structure a pointer towards the influence of the missionary and educational societies from which it took inspiration.[49] Established in 1876, the founder and leading figure in the Anjuman was Badr al-dīn Tayyibjī (1260–1324/1844–1906), a Bohra Muslim and high court judge.[50]

Tayyibjī was reared in a family deeply exposed to British ideas, and his own father had written a book in Gujarati-inflected Urdu, *Gulbun-e hidāyat* (Rosebud of guidance), defending Islam against the criticisms of Christian missionaries.[51] At the age of fifteen, Tayyibjī junior was sent to study law at London's Highbury College and subsequently at the Middle Temple, before returning to Bombay to begin his career at the bar.[52] While his father's response to the missionary critique was primarily intellectual and textual, Tayyibjī's, a generation later, was practical and institutional, in effect creating a means of religious productivity to mirror the schools and missionary presses of the Christians. From the late 1860s Tayyibjī began to involve himself with a range of social issues affecting Bombay's Muslims, a pattern of activism that culminated in his founding of the Anjuman-e Islām. Tayyibjī himself served as its secretary for around sixteen years, though other members of the civil service and merchant elite of Gujarati Khōja and Bohra Muslims were also active in the organization, including his brother Qamr al-dīn Tayyibjī, who served as the Anjuman's president (*sadr*) from 1876 to 1889.

Working towards the same ends as Tayyibjī was another Muslim figure from the city's Konkani Muslim community. This was Ghulām Muhammad Munshī, who earned his living through official appointments teaching Hindustani Urdu to British civil servants. In 1869 he published two Urdu pamphlets in Bombay, in which he urged his co-religionists to seek modern forms of education; he eventually rose to the position of vice-president of the Anjuman-e Islām.[53] In 1880, after petitioning wealthy Muslims and the colonial administration in Bombay, he finally succeeded in opening the first Anglo-Hindustani (here, English-Urdu) school in

the city.[54] In the words of a report on his motivations in the newspaper
Native Opinion, his efforts drew on the middle-class Muslim dilemma
that 'the greater [the] efforts of the Government to civilize the people,
the deeper do the Mahomedans seem to sink, socially and morally'.[55]
In some ways, the joint Urdu–English medium schools that Ghulām
Muhammad founded were less a gesture towards vernacularization than
an attempt to promote a common language among the city's linguistically divided Muslims. In this, Ghulām Muhammad and the Anjuman
echoed the proto-nationalist efforts of such North Indian Modernists as
Sir Sayyid Ahmad Khān, who was a personal friend and correspondent
of Badr al-dīn Tayyibjī. But, as we will see in the Urdu-spreading efforts
of the customary firms examined in later chapters, Modernist firms such
as the Anjuman-e Islām held no monopoly over the growing production
of Urdu, which had cosmopolitan and enchanted dimensions no less than
its better-known nationalist and Reformist trajectories.

Like many other Reformist associations, the Anjuman-e Islām was
chiefly concerned with the provision of what it regarded as a modern
education. Part of its success with the colonial administration on this
front came through its official policy of separating social issues from
political ones.[56] According to the statement of aims (*maqāsid*) composed
for its first Annual Report for 1876, the Anjuman aimed in general for
the 'progress of the Muslim community' (*apnī qawm kī taraqqī*), and saw
the means of achieving this as being through the spread of the 'new civil-
ity' (*tahzīb-e nō*) by way of education in 'science and the arts' (*'ilm aur
honār*).[57] As a charitable association on the model of Bombay's earlier
Parsi *anjuman*s, the Anjuman-e Islām did gradually move into a range
of activities, from managing its own new charitable endowments (such
as the Sir Sayyid Memorial Fund) and more traditional Muslim *waqf*
endowments to trying to raise the marriageable age for Muslim girls and
attempting to ensure that irresponsible poor *hajj* pilgrims bought return
tickets before embarking on steamships to Mecca.[58]

In order to assess the impact of the Anjuman's and wider colonial
educational initiatives among Bombay's Muslims, it is helpful to turn
to the statistics on Muslim education that emerged from an official
Director of Public Instruction survey in 1880–1.[59] The survey revealed
that in terms of higher education, among 175 students at Bombay's
Elphinstone College (founded in 1856), only 5 were Muslims, while
St Xavier's College (founded in 1869) reported a single Muslim among
the 71 students enrolled there.[60] The Government Law School and
Grant Medical College counted 6 Muslims between them from a total of

434 students.[61] The figures for high school education were scarcely better, with a total of 36 Muslims among the 1,470 pupils at the Elphinstone and St Xavier's high schools. Given that Muslims made up around 20 per cent of Bombay's population, these participation figures of between approximately 1.5 and 2.5 per cent were strikingly low. Neither did the figures point to any unusual dip around 1880, for among more than 1,500 students who had passed the Bombay university matriculation examination between 1859 and 1881, fewer than 50 were Muslims.[62]

This is not to say that no system of education existed among Bombay's Muslims, but rather that they were not participating in the modernizing education system established by the colonial state, the missionaries and the Reformists. In terms of primary education, in 1880 there were 104 traditional *maktab* schools operating in Bombay's various *mohalla* quarters, in which the pupils were taught Quran reading, Urdu, sometimes Persian or Gujarati, and basic arithmetic.[63] Similarly, in terms of higher studies, there were six Arabic-medium *madrasas* funded by *waqf* endowments and teaching the *dars-e nizāmi* (Nizami syllabus) that had emerged in early eighteenth-century Lucknow, rather than the curriculum associated with the Deoband *madrasa* network.[64] Most of these institutions had emerged in the period from around 1840, so forming indigenous Muslim responses to the spread of the city's Christian missionary schools in the same decades. For the period until 1880 at least, this shows the relative importance in Bombay of the private customary *maktab* and *madrasa* as opposed to the missionary or government schools, a pattern that has echoes in the larger growth of *madrasas* throughout British India.[65] Unlike the sponsors of the self-consciously Islamic curriculum of the *maktabs* and *madrasas*, the founders of the Anjuman-e Islām sought a new Modernist curriculum, and after the 1880 report immediately set about raising funds for an at least partially English-medium school that would teach young Muslims the forms of knowledge that the Anjuman's fathers considered essential for the modern age. In 1880 the Anjuman's first school was opened, in a building belonging to the Zayn al-'Ābidin *imāmbārā* or mourning hall, its teaching supported by grants of 300 and 500 rupees per month from the Anjuman members and the Bombay Municipality respectively.[66] Its syllabus sought a 'liberal Islamic education' by combining Quran reading, Urdu and Persian alongside English, mathematics, history and geography, each subject defined by specially designed textbooks.[67] Reflecting the self-conscious Islamic Modernism envisaged in educational terms at the Mohammedan Anglo-Oriental College founded at Aligarh by Sir Sayyid Ahmad Khān in 1875,

FIGURE 3. Discipline and reform: The Anjuman-e Islām High School (completed 1893)

the Anjuman school thus taught the classical Islamic languages of Arabic and Persian alongside English and modern science.[68] Like Aligarh in the north, the Anjuman school in Bombay would produce several generations of students imbued with a newly rationalistic faith in which the customary Islam of shrines and holy men held no attraction. A new Islam was in manufacture.

A year after the school opened in its *imāmbārā* lodgings, in an echo of the new institutional apparatus that the Anjuman espoused, a new 'committee' (*komīti*) was set up to raise funds for a proper building for the school. The methods of funding employed to establish this most famous of Bombay's Muslim schools reveals the economic strategies that the Anjuman used to spread its ideas. First, with the close contacts its leaders had with the city's administration, the Anjuman prevailed on the Bombay government to commit an annual grant of 6,000 rupees for the project, before building on this pledge to persuade the Municipal Corporation to promise a further annual grant of 5,000 rupees.[69] Second, well-known non-Muslim philanthropists such as the Parsi lawyer and municipal commissioner Sir Pherozeshah Mehta (1845–1915) were offered key positions in the committee.[70] Third, the associational structure of the Anjuman itself was put to work by raising the tremendous sum of 110,000 rupees from its members for the actual construction of the school and an additional 50,000 rupees by way of an endowment.[71] As one 'progressive' pledge led to another in the philanthropic competition of fundraising, the Bombay government agreed to grant a free site for the school, along with an additional 38,000 rupees towards final construction costs. Opened in February 1893, the new Anjuman-e Islām High School on Hornby Road voiced an impressive visual statement of the place of this new Islam in the urban landscape. As D. A. Pinder's 1904 *Illustrated Guide to Bombay* described it,

> The building is in the Saracenic style, the modern requirements for the construction of a school, and the harmonising of it with the several public buildings surrounding it being borne in mind. The school has three turrets, surmounted with domes of Porebunder stone, two of them being erected at the southern, and one at the northern facade of the structure. The tower is 125 feet high, and is capped with a dome having a circumference of 16 feet. The facade of the building, as also the tympanums and drums of the domes, the lower frieze and the arched wings of the several windows, are ornamented with coloured tiles. The general facing is of dressed blue stone, the several columns and the arches being made of Porebunder and yellow Coorla stones, relieved in places by red Hemnugger stone. The capitals of the front columns bear carvings of various pretty designs. Over the windows are placed stones carved in various geometrical designs. On the ground floor are four large and two small class-rooms, there being also apparatus, library and masters' rooms. On the first floor there are four class-rooms and a large hall measuring 63 feet long and 37 feet wide, with a gallery above it. The second floor has four class-rooms, which are very lofty and airy. There is no lack of ventilation in the school, which has spacious verandahs on either side of it.[72]

With the attractive school buildings now tangible enough to appeal to the parental private investors willing to commit money to their own family's future, the fund was finally able to subsist on subscriptions and fees from the families of its pupils. In this joint enterprise of bringing together government grants with associational fundraising and private subscription, the Anjuman-e Islām school was the most successful project of the new organizational and financial methods that Bombay's Reformists drew on. Yet the fact of the matter was that the Anjuman High School could only educate a tiny proportion of the city's Muslims, and those few were drawn from the ranks of the upper middle class at that. Under the care of thirteen teachers, in its first year the school enrolled some 429 students, 40 per cent of whom were Gujarati Bohras, with Konkani and Deccani Muslims making up around 15 per cent each.[73] Amid a Muslim population in the city that was approaching 200,000 by this time, the few hundred boys being educated at the school at any given time were a drop in a much larger ocean. Despite the liberal opinions of the Tayyibjī family itself, the Anjuman did not, aside from small primary schools, involve

itself with girls' education in any significant way until after 1915.[74]
As Benjamin Fortna has argued with regard to the modernizing Ottoman
schools of the same period, the impact of the Anjuman school was therefore ultimately very limited beyond a small social stratum.[75] While the
Anjuman-e Islām and its school were significant in the production of a
Modernist Islam among the city's small middle class, their school lessons had to compete with a much larger economy of enchantment that
appealed to the wider sections of Bombay's working-class Muslim population. While its embrace of English education was unusual among
Bombay's Muslims, the Anjuman-e Islām conceived of its activities
through the same language of moral (*akhlāqī*) improvement shared with
a range of religious firms that viewed the moral degradation of industrial
urban life with disdain.[76]

For all its conspicuous modernity, this middle-class and modernist
profile of Reform was only part of a broader set of reactions by Bombay's
Muslims to the problems created by modern urban life. The same years
that saw the creation of the new associational culture exemplified by
the Anjuman-e Islām also saw the growth of a Traditionalist pattern
of Reformism, seen most vividly in the foundation of new *madrasa*s in
Bombay that had an older history than the high schools associated with
the Anjuman. The Konkani merchant Muhammad Ibrāhīm Muqba had
founded *madrasa*s in the Bombay districts of Kalura, Thora, Mazagaon,
Mahim and Nagpada in the first half of the century, and this proliferation of new *madrasa* schools continued in Bombay into the 1900s.[77]
As with the comprador Parsi Reformists and the Traditionalist *ulamā*
Reformists of Deoband in North India, Muhammad Ibrāhīm Muqba's
project emerged in contact with both colonial ideas of proper education
and the missionary critique of Muslim superstition. He had served on
the first board of directors of the Bombay Native Education Society, and
in 1839 was a signatory to a letter to the Chief Secretary of the Bombay
government complaining about the 'outrageous attacks of missionaries
on Indian religions'.[78] Later Konkanis founded other types of *madrasa* in
Bombay, such as Mawlidī Abū Ahmad Dīn, who established his Ghaws
al-'Ulūm *madrasa* in the suburb of Kamatipura.[79] While these were not
self-consciously 'modern' or 'Anglo' institutions promoting English and
technical education like the *anjuman* schools, the proliferation of these
Traditionalist Reform networks of *madrasa*s was very much a part of
modernity as a process.[80] In several such ways, Christian organizations
such as the CMS therefore acted as catalysts for the Muslims' own educational and missionary ventures. As Prashant Kidambi has noted, in

terms of their methods and organization many of Bombay's new religious societies 'clearly derived their inspiration from the activities of Christian missionary societies'.[81] As the Christian missionaries were themselves aware, part of the reason for their failure lay in the Muslims' effective response to what had been the Christians' innovations.[82] An example was the foundation of schools itself: one CMS missionary specifically cited the Anjuman-e Islām's grand High School opposite the Victoria Terminus train station as such a stumbling-block to Christian success.[83] But the new shrines, *madrasa*s and *khanaqah*s examined in later chapters show that Customary Islamic firms were no less responsive. For all the Gothic architectural splendour of its mission to defeat superstition with scripture and science, the Anjuman was ultimately a small player in the larger urban landscape of dockyards and shrines, and amid the more enchanted Islam that they produced between them.

Typified by Badr al-dīn Tayyibjī and Ghulām Muhammad Munshī, it was the mercantile and bureaucratic middle class who initiated the production of Muslim Reform in Bombay by creating the new associational organizations, schools, publishing ventures and fundraising initiatives that lent their ideas means of production and distribution that were ultimately borrowed from the Hindu and Parsi Reformists and the Christian missionary associations before them. Other middle-class Muslim philanthropists sponsored the foundation of modern schools for their own *jamā'at* (communities), as when the Gujarati Mēmon businessman Sēth Cummū Ja'far Sulaymān founded a school for Mēmon girls in Bombay in 1880, so (in the pluralizing logic of the marketplace) diluting the drive of the Anjuman towards standard schools for all groups of Muslims.[84] Upper- and middle-class Konkani Muslims established their own schools in this way too, further splintering religious productivity by way of their own curricula, producing adult Muslims imbued with variant models of Islam. Schools aside, other Reformist Muslim associations such as the Konkani Club and the Anjuman-e Arbāb-e Safā (Society of the Lords of Purity), were also founded. On the ideological if not always practical level, Bombay's relative proximity to the great Muslim princely state of Hyderabad also saw the spread of ideas of Modernist Reform from there. In many respects the Reformism that Hyderabad exported to Bombay was a southern version of that developing in North India, which had reached Hyderabad through the employment of North Indian Muslims (many of them Aligarh graduates) in the Nizam's civil service. The most significant example of this was Mawlwī Chirāgh 'Alī (1844–95), another Modernist civil servant who, after failing to find gainful employment in the colonial administration in his native North India, moved to Hyderabad in 1877 and on the recommendation of Sir Sayyid Ahmad Khān rose through a number of positions before reaching the office of finance secretary. Although he wrote widely for the new Urdu journals of the period, including Sir Sayyid's Modernist *Tahzīb al-akhlāq* (Moral reform), it was Chirāgh 'Alī's English work, *The Proposed Political, Legal, and Social Reforms in the Ottoman Empire and Other Mohammadan States*, that offered the clearest synthesis of his ideas.[85] Published in Bombay in 1883 in reply to an article by Reverend Malcolm MacColl in the *Contemporary Review* of August 1881 entitled 'Are Reforms Possible under Mussulman Rule?', Chirāgh 'Alī's *Reforms* offered the classic statement on Islamic Modernism:

> I have endeavoured to show in this book that Mohammadanism as taught by Mohammad, the Arabian Prophet, possesses sufficient elasticity to enable it to adapt itself to the social and political revolutions going on around it. The Mohammadan Common Law, or Sheriat, if it can be called a Common Law, as it does not contain any Statute Law, is by no means unchangeable or unalterable. The only law of Mohammad or Islam is the Koran, and only the Koran.[86]

Arguing for a purifying recreation of Islam based on the rejection of custom by means of a renewal of religious law through the exercise of *ijtihād* (legal reasoning), Chirāgh 'Alī helped create the intellectual framework for producing new Islams for the modern age. For in essence, the doctrine of individual *ijtihād* opened the intellectual means of religious production beyond the old *'ulamā* scholars to any Muslim equipped with reason and a knowledge of scripture. Religious justifications and doctrines in general could in this way be generated by a far wider range of producers, beyond the traditional biopoly of scholars and saints, and so setting in motion the manufacture of a series of new doctrines, organizations and – ultimately – new forms of Islam. As with Bombay's homegrown Modernists whom he influenced, Chirāgh 'Alī was thus able to create 'Islamic' justifications for such classic liberal causes as women's education and monogamy rather than polygamy (causes which in turn point to the catalytic role of Christian missionary critiques in the emergence of such Reformism). What the formation of a Reformist Islam represented was not so much a picture of Weberian 'religious change' in which new disenchanted versions of Islam came to replace customary forms, but rather a picture of new religious productivity in which new religious firms began to compete with, and in turn trigger changes among, pre-existing firms operating in the same marketplace.

In other strategies of Reformist entry to the marketplace, Hyderabadi Reformists visited Bombay to spread their ideas in person rather than print, using the city's new civic institutions to give public speeches. This method was exemplified in the Urdu lecture on the classic Reformist theme of the decline of India's Muslims made by the Hyderabadi civil servant Nawwāb Muhsin al-Mulk in 1891. Muhsin al-Mulk was another close associate of Sayyid Ahmad Khān and subsequent joint secretary of the new Muslim political party, the All India Muslim League, founded in 1906 as the nationalizing heir to the associational organizations of the previous generation.[87] As with other Reformist groups' modes of distribution, the lecture was translated into English in Bombay, and printed for distribution there.[88] In classic Reformist mode, Muhsin al-Mulk identified the principal reason for Muslim decline as the misapprehension of the Quran's true teachings.[89] As with Ja'far Sulaymān and Ghulām Muhammad Munshī's attempts to promote an education that was at once 'modern' and 'Islamic', here was an attempt to cure the varied social maladies faced by Bombay's Muslims through rejecting the 'superstitious' customs that the city's Muslim workforce brought with them from their former rural and small town homes. As expressions of a new kind of middle-class religiosity in India, the scripturalist and anti-syncretistic opinions of Bombay's Reformist Muslims thus bore much in common with those of other middle-class groups, Hindu no less than Muslim, in northern Indian cities at the same time.[90] Like Muhsin al-Mulk's speech, agendas found new written outlets in vernacular print. In the last decades of the century the Konkani Club, for example, published a magazine, *Risāla-e Kawkab-e Konkan* (Konkan star), which included regular articles on social and religious reform, particularly the writings of its philanthropist founder, Muhammad Hasan Muqba.[91]

By seeing the various versions of Reform as new productions operating in an increasingly dynamic religious economy, we are able to make sense of the fact that, rather than any 'replacement' model of change taking place, what actually occurred was a pluralization of types of Islam available, each of which was perpetuated and sustained through its particular appeal to different sections of the population. In the increasing plural religious market that emerged in complex urban environments such as Bombay, the Modernism of men such as Mohsin al-Mulk, Muhammad Muqba and Chirāgh 'Alī appealed to a middle-class set of patrons and consumers who sponsored schools and sent their children to them, while nonetheless remaining only one Islam among a wider set of religious productions that appealed to other sectors of society. The model of religious economy therefore helps us understand the fact that while Modernism interacted with customary forms of Islam through competition and the product adjustments we usually term as 'influence', in the long run what we see is coexistence rather than replacement. In other words, a modernity characterized by an increasing pluralization, rather than a progressive standardization, of religious forms.

If the Christian missions failed to convert significant numbers of Bombay's Muslims, this is not to say that the Christian missionary societies failed to make an impact on the city's religious economy. As we have seen, Christian missionaries pioneered a number of innovations in the technology of religious production and distribution, placing preachers into new social spaces and among new social groups in a way that was largely without precedent. For schools and education formed only one way in which Bombay's religious economy became more productive through the responses of indigenous Reformists to the critiques and techniques of the Christian missionaries. The new ideology of the exchange-ability of religious identity and affiliation – the conceptual cornerstone of the mission – also found expression in the creation of Muslim missions as well as schools, so affecting innovations in the distribution of new religious productions that reached beyond the relatively small audience of the class room. With the assurance of their bourgeois certainties, in India the Christian missionaries initiated a programme of outreach that brought their message to such new settings as the factory and such older but closed settings as the female domestic quarters. In both cases, what Christian missionaries pioneered, the Muslims continued with greater success. It would be a mistake to see the Christian effort as solely a white man's endeavour, and much of the work of cultural transfer – of passing on the missionary model and its methods no less than its message – was done by the 'native catechists'. In many cases it was these Indian converts who were chosen for the infiltrative excursions to the workplace and home. It was these intermediary men and women who were the most effective exponents of the Christian message and, more importantly, of the social technology of its dissemination: the mission.

In Bombay such native catechists included the converted Hyderabadi Muslim Reverend Jānī 'Alī, who after his conversion in 1855 spent almost two decades preaching in Bombay and Calcutta.[92] While not of Muslim background himself, another such native preacher in Bombay and its surrounding towns was Samuel Rahator (1866–1936). From the 1880s much of his work in Bombay was conducted among its factory workforce of rural migrants.[93] Among the hyperbole of his biography, we get a vivid sense of the broad reach of the native preacher in Bombay's cosmopolitan milieu:

> No man ever had a more varied audience. Pathans, Sikhs, Arabs, Jains, Jews, Parsees, Hindus of all castes and no caste, Moslems of every order, wanderers from every corner of Asia, brigands and budmashes [villains] rubbed shoulders as they listened to this eloquent Indian declaring the Gospel of God's seeking and saving love.[94]

In response to such conversions as that of Jānī 'Alī, Bombay's Muslim religious leaders made greater efforts to maintain their own market share, and rejoiced at the news of anyone converting to Islam from Christianity. When the American consul at Manila, Muhammad Alexander Russel Webb, gave a public lecture at Bombay's Framji Cowasji Institute in 1892 on the reasons for his conversion to Islam, an audience of over five hundred of the city's Muslim notables turned out to greet him. Making maximum capital of the conversion, his speech was converted into Urdu and printed by 'Abd Allāh Nūr, the leader of one of Bombay's new Muslim missionary organizations, the Majlis-e Daw'at-e Islām (Council for the propagation of Islam).[95] Similar publications greeted the news of the conversion of the Englishman William Abdullah Quilliam (1856–1932) in the connected port city of Liverpool. Printed in Bombay in 1891 for the North Indian Anjuman-e Ishā'at al-Islām (Society for the propagation of Islam), the *Moslem Guide* stated that it was written because 'the far off town of Liverpool, in England, has responded to the voice of the Arabian prophet, and it is hoped that others will soon see the truth of a faith and doctrine that claims to be catholic and universal'.[96] Consisting of basic instructions on the faith and practice of a Reformist Islam stripped down to 'reasonable precepts which immediately recommend themselves to philosophic minds', in connecting Bombay to Liverpool the *Moslem Guide* is testament to the range of missionary agendas in which Bombay's Muslim firms also became involved. Conversion – the voluntary and individual act of private, rational conscience – had now become an important feature of Muslim public life: here was the market's operation as public competition.

It is in this emergence of a cosmopolitan and competitive religious economy in Bombay that we must see the most crucial religious development of the nineteenth century. For it was this newly 'liberal' and pluralizing market that lay behind the emergence of the new ways of organizing, comparing and ultimately producing religion that characterize the period. The implication of this is that we should not consider some organizations of the period as inherently more 'modern' than others, whatever their own rhetoric and self-representations. Like the Customary Islamic firms discussed in later chapters, each of the Reformist associations that developed in Bombay was in this way a response to the same development: the creation of a liberal religious marketplace and the incentives garnered by its competitiveness towards the evolution of new technologies of production and distribution. What we have seen over the previous pages is that despite their own presentations as providing 'rational' and 'modern' forms of religiosity, in terms of gathering followers the direct impact of both Christian missionaries and Muslim Reformists was ultimately limited in Bombay. Even as late as 1911, missionary intelligence could offer the following assessment from its informants in Bombay: 'Reform has not found a strong echo in the hearts of Bombay Moslems. The reformer who comes from North India or elsewhere does not find a good reaping in Bombay, where each head of a Moslem community only exercises influence over his own community and is never recognized by members of another division.'[97] Instead, the Reformists' impact came in triggering an increasing level of religious production by a range of new firms. The Christians were likewise more successful in catalysing the foundation of Muslim Reformist firms than in converting Muslims to Christianity. And with its limited appeal beyond a comprador elite and bureaucratic middle class for whom European style, manners and scientific educations had some degree of applicability in their lives, the Modernist trend that most characterized Bombay's Muslim Reformists had its greatest effect in the similarly indirect terms of increasing competitive production among other Muslims. As we will see in Chapters 6 and 7, despite the limited direct success of the Reformists, by the end of the nineteenth century these other forms of production included the more explicitly Counter Reformist Customary firms that sought to defend Customary Islam from the critiques of Christian missionaries and Muslim Reformists alike.

The larger effect of the missionaries and Muslim Reformists was not only to help create a more competitive religious economy, but also to encourage new methods of religious production and distribution. This competitive productiveness was enabled by the 'free market' conditions created by the legal freedom of religion that was a central tenet of the colonial state's claims to progressive modernity. Life in Bombay thus confronted the believer with an unprecedented number of religious possibilities, possibilities which the polemical public culture of critical missionaries and apologetic Reformists encouraged the believer to compare. Of course, this was by no means a perfect free market, and the personal histories of Indian converts to Christianity, shunned by their friends and families on conversion, speak eloquently of the social constraints on free consumer choice. At its most effective, the religious marketplace did not therefore operate most effectively through 'conversion' in its traditional sense of the outright rejection of one religion for another, but rather in the range of possibility, comparison and competition it created between producers of alternative versions of the 'same' religion.

Like other agents in the marketplace, religious consumers are often conservative in their 'brand' and 'product' loyalty, such that shifts of allegiance in market behaviour tend to be marginal rather than drastic. Faced with multiple Islams as well as multiple religions per se, what Bombay's marketplace offered its Muslims was not solely the unattractive option of rejecting their ancestral faith entirely. It also presented the possibility of choosing between a range of Islams. The intervention of the Reformists did therefore not bring about a unification of Bombay Islam, but in a cosmopolitan context of so many different Muslims only added further to the increasing pluralization of Islams in the marketplace. We have seen how Bombay's Reformist organizations produced rationalized forms of Islam based on stripped-down versions of scriptural religion freed of the constraints of customs re-read as 'superstition'. Yet the Muslim middle class to whom Bombay's Modernist Reformers appealed was only a small minority of a much larger Muslim labouring population attracted to the city by the demand for cheap labour, and this larger demographic felt little attraction towards the Islam of the Reformists. Instead, the labouring classes preferred the rituals and enchantments associated with a more firmly established class of religious producers and suppliers: the saints and holy men associated with the familiar 'brands' of well-known Sufi orders. The Christian missions were themselves quite aware of the relative importance of the different Muslim players in the religious marketplace. Using their Muslim converts to gather this market data, we see this recognition of the relatively greater importance of the customary Muslim forms associated with Sufi holy men in such texts as the autobiographical *Wāqi'āt 'Imādiyya* of the Punjabi Muslim 'Imād al-dīn, published by the CMS in 1874.[98] For in the conversion narrative of his journey towards Christianity, 'Imād al-dīn did not reject the Reformists, but rather the Sufis; and it was they whom missionary organizations such as the CMS rightly recognized as the more important obstacles to their success in the religious marketplace. 'Imād al-dīn graphically described the practices associated with the Customary Islam that competed so successfully with Christian missionaries and Muslim Reformists alike:

> As soon as I was entangled in this subtle science I began to practice speaking little, eating little, living apart from men, afflicting my body, and keeping awake at nights. I used to spend whole nights in reading the Koran. I put in practice the [litanies of] Qasīda-e Ghawsiyya, the Chihil Qāf, and the Hisb al-Bahār, and constantly performed the Murāghaba-e Mujāhida, and the special repetitions of the Koran, and all the various special penances and devotions that were enjoined. I used to shut my eyes and sit in retirement, seeking by thinking on the name of God to write it on my heart. I constantly sat on the graves of holy men, in hopes that, by contemplation, I might receive some revelation from the tombs. I went and sat in the assemblies of the elders, and hoped to receive grace by gazing with great faith on the faces of Soofies. I used to go even to the dreamy and intoxicated fanatics, in the hope of thus obtaining union with God. And I did all this, besides performing my prayers five times a day, and also the prayer in the night, and that in the very early morning and at dawn; and always was I repeating the salutation of Mohammed, and the confession of faith. In short, whatever afflictions or pain it is in the power of man to endure, I submitted to them all, and suffered them to the last degree; but nothing became manifest to me after all, except that it was all deceit.[99]

Even if 'Imād al-dīn was ultimately disillusioned with this enchanted Islam, as we see in the following chapters, to the larger demographic of Bombay's working-class Muslims these old customary ways still held great appeal. In the midst of industrialization, the conditions of workers' lives led not to a large demand for self-consciously modern schools that exchanged 'superstition' for science, but instead to a demand for the foundation of shrines that provided the kinds of customary services that the urban poor found more useful and pleasurable. Among the vast majority of Bombay's Muslims who could not enter the new schools and for whom scripture portions and controversial tracts offered little intelligible solace for their hardships, those firms that could supply the tangible rewards of miracles and the easy enjoyment of carnivals were far more likely to receive their support.

2

Cosmopolitan Cults and the Economy of Miracles

SHRINES FOR A MIGRANT WORKFORCE

The self-conscious modernism that was symbolized by the hybrid Anglo-Oriental architecture of the Anjuman-e Islām School ultimately played a limited role Bombay's religious economy. For the members of the labouring classes who made up the majority of the city's Muslims the appeal of a scientific and scriptural Islam was limited, and their own patterns of religious consumption were as distinct as they were widespread. For many of these labourers from rural and small town backgrounds, the growing number of shrines that emerged in Bombay as the nineteenth century progressed offered the chance to reconnect with the secure roots of custom and so enter a more reassuring cityscape enchanted with the powers holy men made available at their gravesides. This chapter traces the role played in the increasing religious productivity of Bombay by migration from the city's continental hinterlands in Gujarat and the Konkan, whence most of its Muslim labour force originated.[1] On the trail of these demographic shifts, 'franchises' of older inland pilgrimage centres in Gujarat and the Konkan were established in Bombay, some of which were especially associated with particular ethnic groups such as Afro-Indian Sīdīs, others with specific activities that typified the city's new way of life, such as the specialist 'traveller shrines' beside the sea and railways. As Rodney Stark has observed, 'To the degree to which a religious economy is pluralistic, firms will specialize.'[2] In this way, Bombay saw both the production of new shrine firms appealing to unfamiliar urban experiences and the reproduction of older ones catering for established but relocated clienteles from the provinces.[3] What we see in both the range of shrine buildings and the distinct narrative and ritual ways in which they marketed their miraculous services is not the more standardized or disenchanted form of Islam more usually associated with modernization, but instead a pattern of increasing diversity and product differentiation in which customary and enchanted religious forms performed especially well.

In 1914 one Bombay resident proudly asked his fellow citizens, 'Is it not literally true that in modern Bombay we witness a truly cosmopolitan population in which every nationality is represented … ?'[4] Yet rather than conceiving of the Muslim shrines that were founded in response to the demands of migrant labourers as 'tolerant' spaces of urban harmony, the following pages explain how shrines also expressed the tension between the cosmopolitanism pressures and possibilities caused by mass migration and their relationship in turn with the pluralizing tendencies of the religious marketplace. Most famously seen in the Hindu–Muslim riots that repeatedly rocked Bombay in the 1890s and 1900s, these tensions found more discreet expression in stories associated with the city's saints and shrines and the tensions surrounding its Muslim carnivals. By tracing these more subtle expressions of cosmopolitan urban pressures, the chapter draws attention to the conflicts surrounding the Muharram carnival and the rumours associated with shrine cults created in Bombay through the immigration of Muslims from many different regions. Here the chapter explores paradoxes that have been neglected in the recent celebratory literature on cosmopolitanism. Looking at the rumours that surrounded urban carnivals and 'cosmopolitan' migrant cults, it draws attention to the at times chauvinistic and communitarian narratives that surrounded certain shrines at the same time that other Muslim shrines in Bombay attracted followers from every religious background. In doing so, the chapter explores the social fault lines of a city whose religious pluralism was founded on the competitive logic of the marketplace. If Bombay was above all an urban market of labour and goods, of morals and life-ways, then in rumours of vengeful miracles no less than communal riots we see the fractured promises of the cosmopolitan that were themselves the religious productions of a competitive economy of interaction.

What we explore in this chapter are the implications of this cosmopolitanism in a religious economy in which different migrant groups participated. For Bombay's diverse 'communities' of Muslims were made up of Indian groups as different as Mēmons from Gujarat and Pathans from the far north, or African and Arab lascars who manned the many ships that crossed the ocean. The collision of the customary forms of Islam these migrants brought with them to Bombay led to still greater diversification through certain 'entrepreneurial' migrants' production of new religious sites and shrine firms. Comparative and competitive, the logic of the marketplace favoured increasing 'product distinction', and while certain 'standards' emerged among its many productions (particularly with regard to legalistic observance and public propriety) the overall picture was of increasing diversity. While later chapters focus on case studies of brotherhood firms, in this chapter the focus is on the tangible impact of the religious economy on the physical topography of the city. These concrete expressions of the religious economy took the form of the shrines that created an enchanted cityscape whose alleyways teemed with the rumours of miracles.

Examining the city's shrines and popular festivals brings with it certain openings as well as closures. It opens to us the religious world of the lowest classes of the city in a way that even their preachers and moralists, examined in later chapters cannot. But at the same time, it closes the possibilities of direct access permitted by the writings of men such as Habib 'Ali and his literate class of deputy preachers to whom Chapter 6 will turn. This is not to say that we are left with no sources, but rather that the sources are different: they consist of rumours and stories of holy men who often lived centuries ago but whose cults were imported to Bombay with the migration of their followers from Gujarat, the Deccan and the Konkan. Wherever possible, evidence is drawn from written sources, typically the cheap print hagiographies long associated with India's Muslim shrines. But in other cases, with shrine firms that never found written expression, we must rely on oral traditions in which the legends of the saints are preserved.[5] In drawing on these sources, the chapter aims not only to further demonstrate the range of Islams available in the Bombay marketplace, but also to explore the inherent tensions in its product diversity, tensions that not only separated Muslims from one another but also from the Hindus who made up the far greater proportion of the city's inhabitants. As Luise White has noted with regard to rumours of vampires in colonial Africa, 'stories and rumors are produced in the cultural conflicts of local life; they mark ways to talk about the conflicts and contradictions that gave them meaning and power'.[6] Here in Bombay, we will see the dual effects of the rumours of miracles whose narrative forms attracted the support of a religiously diverse clientele while at the same time cementing older fractures between Muslims and their 'idol-worshipping' Hindu others. Yet the fact remains that the shrines that emerged beside Bombay's markets, mills and dockyards were the production of a distinctly modern religious economy of proletarian consumers who earned precarious but nonetheless cash wages that by way of petty patronage, gift-giving and the consumption of goods sold at the shrine carnivals was invested into a religious economy of enchantment.[7]

FROM MILLS TO *MAZĀRS*

By the 1840s Bombay's ruling classes had embarked on a programme of civic improvement that lent the face of Bombay a physiognomy more fitting with its ascent in the world of commerce.[8] While colonial architectural ventures in Lucknow and Cairo saw 'oriental' cities being rebuilt as architectonic symbols of European modernity, the burghers of Bombay were able to create a public architecture for a city that had little by way of an older history to compromise.[9] The city's new dockyards in Mazagaon were among the great architectural projects of the age. As nineteenth-century travellers remarked, in monolithic basalt or carefully whitewashed plaster, Bombay's seaward public face could scarcely offer travellers a greater contrast to the mud-brick walls and date-palm dwellings of the older ocean ports of Bushire and Muscat.[10] As time went on, new forms of social technology were adopted from the civic improvement schemes of Birmingham and Manchester to police the city's morals in the name of public order and hygiene.[11] Bombay was not only a modern city in a material sense, but also by writ of its administrative fabric. And yet amidst these transformations there also emerged an Islamic architecture of enchantment – of shrines (*dargāh*s) and pilgrimage places (*mazār*s) – whose development was the religious collateral brought by the recruitment of a Muslim labour force.[12]

Despite the recent emergence of urban history in India, the importance of this geography of shrines to the new colonial cities of the nineteenth century has been largely neglected.[13] Yet these sites were no less an aspect of the workings of the modern city than the train stations and writers' buildings that have traditionally defined the era. Even if the customary powers of Bombay's saints were located in humbler architectural settings than the great palaces of steam power, for thousands of urban dwellers such *mazār* shrines were no less important a factor in the smooth operation of urban life. This expansion of the city's sacred spaces was coeval with the demographic expansion of Bombay, a process which was intimately entwined with its industrialization. As Dipesh Chakrabarty and Arjan de Haan have argued with regard to Calcutta, the influx of rural labourers to that city's jute mills was accompanied by an influx of religious practices and social bonds.[14] The same forces were at work in Bombay, and in the Muslim case this meant affiliation to an Islam based around Mausoleum shrines, and holy men and the miraculous services they gave access to. Here was a certain historical irony. For while on the one hand the emergence of an educated Anglophone intermediary class in the great colonial cities such as Bombay and Calcutta laid the ground for religious firms promoting self-conscious modernization, the transition of these cities from bureaucratic into industrial centres caused an influx of rural labourers for whom ideas of disenchanted rational religion had little appeal or even meaning. The evolution of the city's saintly shrines thus forms the neglected counterpart to the modern associations and trade unions with which Indian urban historians are more familiar. Like the suppression of the foundational role of the opium trade in the city's development in favour of a 'progressive' picture of industrialization and the cotton trade, the growth of Bombay was not only coeval with train stations and factories but also with sites of the anti-scientific power associated with relics, rituals and holy men.[15]

THE WORKERS' CARNIVAL OF MUHARRAM

All around the Indian Ocean, shrine foundation had been part of the migration process long before the nineteenth century, and the onset of industrial labour migration brought continuity with this older pattern.[16] Although the expansion of Bombay's religious topography also occurred in terms of the mosques and *madrasas* discussed in Chapter 1, it was the city's saintly shrines and processional routes that formed the most important medium of its urban enchantment. The role of processional routes in symbolically claiming urban territory is well known to anthropologists, and even nineteenth-century European observers noted how Bombay's Muharram processions formed a potent reversal of colonial public order.[17] Although in principle a period of mourning for the Prophet's martyred grandson, with its colourful floats bearing the stylized *tābūt*s (coffins of Husayn) and the frenzied drumming and dancing that accompanied them, Muharram was effectively the city's great Muslim carnival. This picture of the cityscape was widely reproduced on chromo-lithographic postcards of thoroughfares crammed with marchers. As one local observer described the scene,

> From morn till eve the streets are filled with bands of boys, and sometimes girls, blowing raucous blasts on hollow bamboos, which are adorned with a tin 'panja' – the sacred open hand ... Youths, preceded

by drummers and clarionet-players, wander through the streets laying all the shopkeepers under contribution for subscriptions ... while a continuous stream of people afflicted by the evil-eye flows into the courtyard of the Bara Imam Chilla near the Nal Bazaar to receive absolution from the peacock-feather brush and sword there preserved. Meanwhile in almost every street where a 'tabut' is being prepared, elegiac discourses ('waaz') are nightly delivered by a maulvi ... while but a little distance away boys painted to resemble tigers leap to the rhythm of a drum, and the Arab mummer with the split bamboo shatters the nerves of the passer-by by suddenly cracking it behind his back.[18]

Far from being a narrowly Shi'ite event, the festive – and often licentious – atmosphere of Muharram attracted celebrants of many religious backgrounds, particularly young working-class men. Like other reproductions of custom for the religious marketplace, the carnival held great appeal for a certain clientele at the same time that the competitive character of the religious economy compelled other Muslims to condemn it. Although this carnivalesque form of Muharram had pre-colonial antecedents elsewhere in India (particularly in the Hyderabad Deccan, from where it was probably imported) its re-creation in Bombay involved a transformation of the festivity in distinctly modern 'disciplinary' ways.[19] First, the proletarianization of a previously rural workforce rendered Muharram a working-class carnival that had as much in common with the processions

FIGURE 4. Custom in print: Postcard of Muharram carnival in Bombay, *c.* 1880

of industrializing cities such as Barcelona and New York as with the old
agrarian fairs of the Indian interior where it had originated. The social
make-up of its supporters now comprised the anonymous workers of the
metropolis rather than the familiar neighbours of village society, and its
spatial setting now lay between factories and coal depots rather than amid
the huts and havelis of former times. Second, the routing of Muharram
processions through the cheek-by-jowl neighbourhoods housing Hindu
no less than Muslim workers made the carnival a focus for the growing
phenomenon of the communal riot, pointing to the fractious potential
of the religious economy's productions.[20] Over time, the combination of
these factors led to two further and disciplinary developments by way of
the legal regulation of processions by the city police and their moral regulation by the city's Muslim Reformists.

As in other regions of the British Empire to which carnival similarly
spread through the movement of Indian labour, the old custom of carrying the blessing-laden symbolic coffin of the dead Husayn through the
streets of the living was regarded with suspicion by policemen, missionaries and Muslim Reformists alike, each of whom attempted to control its
riotous reversal of public order.[21] The decorated and artfully constructed
tābūts were set up in dozens of streets throughout the city, from which
points they were carried in procession throughout the surrounding areas.
In such ways, customary processions were vehicles of an entanglement of
competing and discordant interests. Vilified by these varied critics, for its
participants Muharram brought the blessing of Husayn's re-created coffin to the streets where they lived and worked. But crucially, like the death
anniversaries of saints which were celebrated in the forms of 'wedding'
or *'urs* described below, the Muharram festival was similarly conceived
of as a festival of life no less than death, an affirmation symbolized in the
vows of many participants to act as the *dulhā* (bridegroom) during the
festival. Linking festive action and its enchantment of urban space to the
bodies of the participants themselves, these *dulhā*s would often enter a
state of ecstasy, the blessings of which would be in turn transmitted to
their friends and fellow proletarian participants:

> Then on a sudden the friends rise and bind on to the Dula's chest a pole
> surmounted with a holy hand, place in his hand a brush of peacock's
> feathers and lead him thus bound and ornamented out into the high-
> way. Almost on the threshold of his passage a stout Punjabi Musulman
> comes forward to consult him. 'Naya jhar hai' (this is a new tree), mean-
> ing thereby that the man is a new spirit-house and has never before been
> possessed. A little further on, the procession, which has now swelled to a

considerable size, is stopped by a Mahomedan from Ahmednagar, who seeks relief. He places his hand on the Dula's shoulder and asks for a sign ... So the Dula fares gradually forward, now stopped by a Kunbi with a sick child, now by some Musulman mill-hands, until he reaches the Bismillah shrine, where he falls forward on his face with frothing mouth and convulsed body. The friends help the spirit which racks him to depart by blowing into his ear some verses of the Koran.[22]

The peacock-feather *morchchal* fan, the double-headed *zū'l-fiqār* sword, the five-fingered *panja* hand, the brightly painted *tābūt* of Husayn's mausoleum: every element of the hardware of sanctity charged urban space with an energy more benevolent than that which powered its gas lamps and steam engines. Through procession and possession, the Muslim lower classes of Bombay used the minimal resources of their own bodies and ritual implements of bamboo and tin commodities to channel the infinite power of the sacred into their hands and channel it to their friends and co-workers. If Muharram afforded this opportunity only once per year, then for the rest of the time there were the shrines that contained the no less empowered bodies of the saintly dead. Here the new shrine firms and their entrepreneurs entered the economy.

OCEANIC PATTERNS OF SHRINE PRODUCTION

One of the most important aspects of the expansion of Bombay's religious economy was the development of a series of saintly shrines, both within the city itself and in its hinterland. The products of movement to Bombay of both saintly families (on the supply side) and a larger urban workforce accustomed to a shrine-centred Islam (on the demand side), the shrines were products of the religious economy itself. In turn, they became important centres for religious production in their own right by way of rituals and festivals, medicines and talismans, healing and miraculous services and the hagiographies that 'advertised' these products. This enchantment of the city's topography was a process that was helped through the development of sacred spaces in the very urban fabric of Bombay, *mazār*s consisting of holy graves and domed mausolea that served to render permanent the blessing power of the saintly body. Each of the shrines to the holy dead tapped into the financial economy of the city in a range of different ways, whether through the donations of pilgrims, the fees paid for particular services or the selling of what were by this period mass-produced pilgrimage souvenirs, such as blessed roses and *'atr* perfumes, talismans and textile shawls, chap-books and chromolithographic postcards. In this sense the shrines served as outlets for a range of religious products and services. By 1915 the city had come to possess a large number of such Muslim shrines.[23] Since the villages that Bombay's nineteenth-century expansion swallowed already possessed a number of minor Muslim pilgrimage sites, some of these graves were older than the metropolis itself. Anchored into the earth and pre-dating the movement of most of the Konkani, Gujarati and Hyderabadi Muslims into Bombay, these graves served as topographic evidence for historical and aetiological charters that staked the Muslim presence in the city in the firm foundation of the past. The influx of large numbers of Muslim workers lent a special significance to these older sites as purported evidence of Bombay's 'Islamic' rather than 'Hindu' roots.

The initial foundation (if not flourishing) of most of Bombay's shrines dated to the last decades of the eighteenth or the opening decades of the nineteenth century. An account of the Muslim shrines of the city as they existed in around 1820 is found in the Persian *Jān-e Bombā'ī* (Bombay soul). As the earliest Persian text on Bombay Islam – indeed, on British Bombay's religiosity *in toto* – the evidence of *Jān-e Bombā'ī* is crucial in allowing us to date the main period of shrine expansion in the city. For while *Jān-e Bombā'ī* describes a series of Muslim pilgrimage places as already being active in the city in around 1820, with the exception of that of Makhdūm 'Alī Parō, which was described as possessing a dome (*gumbad*), the specific terms that the text used to describe the city's pilgrimage places refer to them as graves (*marqad, maqbara*), simple 'places of visitation' (*mazār*) or retreat huts (*chilla*) rather than using the language of the fully developed shrine (*dargāh, qubba*).[24] Several of the saints discussed below – such as Shaykh Misrī, Bismillāh Shāh and Pēdrō Shāh – were already referred to in *Jān-e Bombā'ī*, pointing to the familiar importance of temporal precedence in the success of any given shrine firm, positioning the saints as urban founder figures from the era of the city's prehistory.[25] While the concrete architectural presence of Bombay's shrines seems to have been largely limited to enclosed graves rather than the more elaborate mausolea that were built over them as the nineteenth century progressed, *Jān-e Bombā'ī* does suggest that the ritual life of their pilgrimage cults was already in production. The text refers to several saintly wedding or *'urs* festivals, expressions of Customary Islam that as we see below would become vastly popular with the city's proletarians as its population expanded. It was as purveyors of such pleasurable and festive forms of custom that these often rudimentary sites were patronized and expanded as the city's Muslim population grew through the migration of labour to its factories and dockyards. The old, small religious shrine firms described in *Jān-e Bombā'ī* as already present in the city around 1820 were thus to find a new body of consumers for their services. Yet the process was by no means automatic, and each of these firms required effective and sometimes entrepreneurial management in order to capture the interest of the growing population. *Jān-e Bombā'ī* is in this respect no less important for the number of Muslim pilgrimage sites it described in 1820 that were subsequently never able to gather the following and investment to transform themselves into proper mausolea, and in some cases disappeared from the city's historical memory altogether. Like the grandest of the saints, Makhdūm 'Alī, being buried first in the city was certainly a cultic advantage; but in a competitive marketplace in which many religious entrepreneurs were active, such temporal precedence was only one factor in a saint's posthumous success.

As their biographies maintained, many of Bombay's local saints were in fact foreign bodies, the enchanted remains of men born in distant parts of the city's oceanic and continental hinterlands.[26] The stories of sea journeys in previous centuries that were related for each of Bombay's saints help explain their appeal in forming aetiological myths that provided the comfort of vicarious roots and past parallels for the Muslim migrants who listened to them in latter-day Bombay. In the north-east of Bombay Island was the shrine of Shaykh Misrī, who, as his name suggested, was believed to have come to Bombay from Egypt around the fifteenth century, though as with many of the city's other shrines, by the nineteenth century that of Shaykh Misrī was maintained by a more local Konkani family firm. Other shrines grew from the old graves of the city's cemeteries, such as the three neighbouring shrines of Sayyid Qādir Shāh, Sharaf al-dīn Shāh and Bahā' al-dīn Isfāhānī (d. 1134/1722) in the Dhobi Talao quarter. Rumour held them to have been itinerant soldiers from Arabia and Iran – a cross-pollination, then, between the economy of soldiering that brought Arab soldiers through Bombay into Hyderabad well into the twentieth century and the posthumous economy of pilgrimage.[27] Since neither of these holy soldiers was mentioned among the list of pilgrimage sites in *Jān-e Bombā'ī*, it appears that their shrine firms only developed in the period after its composition. From pious soldiers (as rumour had it) buried beside many others in the large cemetery around them, their graves were transformed by some unknown entrepreneurs into fonts of benediction and, as sufficient capital was gathered, the two graves were surrounded by walls, topped with domes and softened with silks. As a *munāqib* praise-poem on the wall of Bahā' al-dīn's shrine described it:

Muqaddas āstān bābā kā bāb-e fath wa nusrat hai
Woh jin kā rawzā pur-nūr ahl-e dil kī jinnat hai
§
Baba's holy threshold is the gate to triumph and victory;
An illuminated garden that is the paradise of the heart-followers.

If this was a shrine built to pious soldierly migrants from the Middle East, shrines were also established for migrants from other regions of Bombay's oceanic hinterlands. Several shrines emerged in Bombay dedicated to Afro-Indian 'Sīdis' (from *sayyidī*, 'my lord'). Dedicated to holy men from Africa, these shrines embodied in concrete form two levels of migration. At one level Bombay's Sīdī shrines drew on an older era of African slave migration into Gujarat that saw the establishment of saint cults fusing African possession rituals with Muslim shrine traditions and the respectable idioms of the Sufis.[28] At another level they drew on the more recent nineteenth-century migration of Gujarati Muslims into Bombay itself, which, as seen with regard to the Bohra migrants in Chapter 5, led to the recreation of Gujarati forms of Customary Islam in a new urban setting. It is notable that none of these Sīdī shrines were mentioned in *Jān-e Bombā'ī*. This fact could point to either their being ignored through their low-status association with black Muslims of African origin rather than the Arab origins that had greater prestige or to their establishment after the composition of *Jān-e Bombā'ī* through the immigration of clients by way of the African Muslims who worked the engine rooms and coal barges of Bombay's steamships and of the Gujarati Muslims to whom saintly Africans were already familiar. Further evidence seems to point to the latter option, with migration from both Africa and Gujarat having fed demand for shrines to saintly patrons already familiar to Muslims from those regions. For Bombay's Afro-Indian Sīdī shrines were not the burial places of the saints as such, but satellite or 'franchise' shrines of the mausolea proper in Gujarat which were established in Bombay by migrant impresarios of these more distant shrine firms. In this way there developed in Bombay the shrine of Sīdī Bāwā Gōr in a gully in the heart of the Dongri quarter as a local franchise of the famous shrine of the Afro-Indian saint of the same name at Ratanpur in Gujarat. Like the other saints described above, Bāwā Gōr in some legends was also held to have been an itinerant soldier from East Africa.[29] During the nineteenth century the Dongri quarter in which his satellite shrine developed was chiefly settled by Gujarati Muslims and Iranians, and takes its name from the Gujarati term for the hillock on which the settlement developed. While it

FIGURE 5. African magic in the market: Franchise shrine of Bāwā Gōr of Ratanpur, Bhindi Bazaar, Bombay

is unclear precisely when Bombay's Sīdī Bāwā shrine emerged, its current custodians date it as late as the 1880s.[30] Due to the fact that it developed in a corner plot of the Khōja cemetery that emerged with the movement of Gujarati Khōjas to the city from the 1830s, it was presumably coterminous with the Gujarati Muslim influx to the city after this time.[31]

As in the case of the Afro-Indian Sīdī shrine of Pīr Bābā Habashī discussed below, it seems likely that the Sīdī Bāwā shrine in Dongri was established by a religious entrepreneur who originated in Gujarat, perhaps near to the original shrine at Ratanpur itself. Since the shrine firm is run by a Sīdī family to this day, this entrepreneur was presumably one of the low status Afro-Indian Sidis themselves, who in the corner of a graveyard would have required minimal initial capital to set up his franchise operation before donations and fees for the saint's intercession eventually funded the construction of the small domed building. Judging by period descriptions, it appears that the shrine and its rituals appealed to a specific section of the market, namely the East Africans and Afro-Indians who as coalers and boiler-room assistants played a central part in Bombay's steamship industry, so pointing to African no less than Gujarati migration as a factor in the establishment of the city's Sīdī shrine firms. Writing in the early 1900s, the Indian Police officer S. M. Edwardes described the dancing ceremonies that typified the gatherings at Sīdī shrines in Bombay 'in which both sexes participate and, which commencing about 10–30 p.m., usually last until 3 or 4 o'clock the following morning'.[32] Edwardes's account carries echoes of the *ratīb* performances associated with black 'Zanzibari' Muslims throughout the west Indian Ocean, not least through the element of showmanship and paid performance he described. At the same time, it points to the economy of oceanic commerce that carried the shrines' African participants, and their rituals, in and out of Bombay:

> One of them, as he passes, shouts out that he sails by the P. and O. *Dindigul* the next day and intends to make a night of it; another is wearing the South African medal and says he earned it as fireman-serang on a troopship from these shores; while a third, in deference to the English guest, gives vent at intervals to a resonant 'Hip, hip, Hurrah,' which almost drowns the unmelodious efforts of the 'maestro' with the kerosine-tin.[33]

The services of Bombay's Sīdī shrines were not solely confined to the provision of music as entertainment. At the practical level, with which the economy of enchantment so frequently concerned its transactions, certain musical performances at the Sīdī shrines were famous for their ability to cure black magic and possession, while 'the "Damali" and "Chinughi" [dances] are said when properly performed to give men the power of divination'.[34] In this, the specialist rituals of the Bāwā Gōr franchise entered an important corner of the religious marketplace, particularly that occupied by the lowest class of workers and women.[35] Unable to take part in many of the male-dominated gatherings organized by living shaykhs, and unaffected by the women's education organizations of modernizing Reformists which affected mainly the Muslim bourgeoisie, the women of market districts such as Dongri bought into the small and economically marginal firms that developed around saints who specialized in possession, trance and music, their Thursday night gatherings becoming important spaces for the public gathering of lower-class Muslim women. The same pattern is seen again below in such dockyard districts as Mazagaon.

Showing how entrepreneurship and effective spatial positioning was at least as important as a saint's pre-colonial temporal origins, the somewhat later shrine of Bābā 'Abd al-Rahmān (d. 1336/1918) developed a short distance away in one of the main streets of the Dongri bazaar. This too had a predominantly lower-class clientele. 'Abd al-Rahmān was a Tamil

Muslim from the town of Salem in north-central Tamil Nadu who came to Bombay to serve as the *imām* of the mosque on Bapu Khodi Street. Reflecting the stories of many other 'holy fools' (*majzūbs*), one day 'Abd al-Rahmān suddenly tore off his clothes outside the mosque and turned to living rough in the streets.[36] Thereafter he became a regular sight, collecting scraps of food from the vegetable market in Dongri. One day he picked up the stinking corpse of a dead rat and began to hug it like a baby in front of the appalled crowds of shoppers, before putting it into his basket and taking it home with him. By morning the dead rat had turned into gold, allowing him to break off limbs to give to the poor.[37] The local poor and sick crop up frequently in the rumours of 'Abd al-Rahmān's miracles that still circulate through Dongri bazaar. One example concerns the case of a female devotee who regularly gave 'Abd al-Rahmān tea until one day he left four pieces of charcoal in the cup, which on his departure turned into gold. Another example concerns a man who suffered repeatedly from fainting fits, and asked the holy fool for help; when the man fell down one day, the deranged 'Abd al-Rahmān poured acid into his mouth and effected an unexpected cure. In stories such as these we get a sense of the figures referred to in the Persian memoirs of the Iranian traveller Safī 'Alī Shāh, who wrote of meeting miracle-working beggars in the streets of Bombay in the 1860s.[38] When 'Abd al-Rahmān died, the spot on which he used to sit in the market was purchased by local shopkeepers and a dome was raised above it. A location for the provision of 'Abd al-Rahmān's services was formalized by way of a shrine with its own front men that was set up between two shops in the Dongri bazaar. Like the proverbial corner shop it resembled, the shrine was open all hours. Through rendering permanent and round-the-clock access to 'Abd al-Rahmān's charisma, the shrine ensured that his miraculous cures were now guaranteed to continue after his death. The key to the saint's assistance was the sprinkling of inexpensive flowers bought from the shrine's shop and the uttering of the simple graveside cry: *yā Dādā Rahmān, sab mushkil āsān!* (O grandpa Rahman, all my problems gone!). At the same time that Bombay's Christian missionaries and Muslim Reformists were busy decrying such 'superstitions', the shopkeepers and poorer residents of Dongri were investing in a shrine around the remains of a mad street-dweller.

MIGRATION MEMORIALIZED

As with the graves of the Sīdīs and Arabian soldiers, many of Bombay's shrine firms promoted stories of migration woven into their clients' historical memory – and in some cases into their material fabric. The most vivid example was the shrine of Sayyid Bismillāh Shāh Bābā, which was built into the very structure of the great Victoria Terminus train station and which we have seen as the destination of the possessed Muharram 'bridegroom' in the procession described earlier. Designed by the government architect Frederick William Stevens (1847–1900) and completed in 1887, 'VT' was built in a monumental gothic style that befitted the Victorian headquarters of the Great Indian Peninsular Railway. As one architectural historian has described it, the station is 'a riot of polychromatic stone, decorative ironwork, marble and tile'.³⁹ Since the pilgrimage site was mentioned in the Persian *Jān-e Bombā'ī* in around 1820, it clearly pre-dated the construction of the Victoria Terminus, though in the text it was merely mentioned as a small 'footprint site' (*qadam-zad*) rather than a proper burial site or mausoleum.⁴⁰ Not only did this minor pilgrimage site to a spot where a saint had supposedly walked survive when the railway station was built, it also managed to acquire a fine stone mausoleum which was architecturally contiguous with the Victoria Terminus, so embedding itself into the grandest of all Bombay's celebrations of steam power. Like several other shrines established in Bombay through Gujarati migration to the city that are discussed below, that of Bismillāh Shāh was also a satellite franchise cult related to an older shrine, that of Sayyid Kamāl Shāh (d. 1146/1734) at Baroda in Gujarat. It is little coincidence that Baroda was one of the first cities that Bombay was connected to by rail as part of the Baroda and Central India Railway founded in 1856; and as the trains brought the migrants, the migrants brought their customary cults. As with many other migrant shrines, the unknown grave of Bismillāh Shāh was 'rediscovered' in miraculous circumstances. Oral tradition describes how during the years in which Victoria Terminus was being constructed, whenever rail tracks were laid in this particular corner of station property they mysteriously disappeared – or else were snapped in half overnight. Only after many inquiries did the British surveyors and their local workmen learn that a Muslim holy man lay buried there, and in recompense the rail company funded the construction of the small domed mausoleum that covers Bismillāh Shāh's grave.⁴¹ Drawing on the global commodities of the nearby markets, no fewer than fourteen hanging lamps were purchased to illuminate the tomb chamber, all of them manufactured in the Val Saint Lambert Cristalleries, founded in 1825 in distant industrializing Belgium. Whatever the factual circumstances of its construction, judging by its position and construction material the shrine was clearly coeval with the VT railway station itself. And once

FIGURE 6. The saints at sea: Shrine of Hājjī ʿAlī, located off the coast at Worli, Bombay

established it was resorted to by travellers who wished to assure them-selves of a safe journey, and the donations of its regular throng of visitors assured the shrine's managers of a steady income.

Other shrines bore such connections with movement and migration through their locations on the shoreside. An example is the most famous of all of Bombay's Muslim shrines, that of Hājjī ʿAlī, whose connection to oceanic travel was made manifest by its liminal position between land and sea. Perched on a rocky outcrop at the end of a rough and low cause-way reaching far into the ocean from the esplanade at Worli, the shrine rose out of the waves to face some of the wealthiest merchant residences in Bombay. Hājjī ʿAlī himself was rumoured to have been a wealthy local merchant who after setting sail for Mecca centuries ago was drowned at sea, only for his body to be washed back to shore in Bombay, directed home by the power of his piety. As a result, the shrine that grew around his eventual place of half-at-sea burial became associated with the pro-tection of travellers, who would come to his shrine before boarding ship. Since Hājjī ʿAlī's shrine is not mentioned in the list of saintly shrines in the Persian account of the city, *Jān-e Bombāʾi*, written in 1231/1816, it

seems probable that it developed no earlier than the mid-nineteenth century, the age of the great expansion of maritime travel that came with the
steamship.⁴² In this way, the development of a shrine for a supposedly
'medieval' saint probably reflects the same 'invention' or 'discovery' of
tradition that has accompanied the foundation of Muslim communities
elsewhere.⁴³

In the case of the city's other main maritime protector, we have evidence that the shrine was much older than the nineteenth century, in
turn suggesting that in some cases Bombay's saintly shrines did reflect
the earlier trans-oceanic migrations that so long characterized the human
geography of holy sites along India's western littoral.⁴⁴ The shrine in
question was that of the Arab scholarly migrant Shaykh Makhdūm ʿAlī
Parō (d. 835/1432), which dated originally from the period of the sultans
of Gujarat but grew in importance as Bombay expanded towards its location at Mahim in the northern suburbs of Bombay. In developing ties to
the shrines of their own community saints that did not disappear as the
modern age dawned, the Muslim maritime communities of western India
reflected these wider patterns. A sense of the importance of the coastal
shrines of western India on the cusp of the colonial era may be gained
from the *Qissa-ye ghamgīn* of Munshī ʿAbbās ʿAlī, completed in 1779.
Written in the form of an Urdu *masnawī* poem, this 'doleful tale' (*qissa-e
ghamgīn*) recounted the history of the last *nawwāb* of Broach and his
personal and political travails as British power crept along the coast of
Gujarat to absorb Broach into the Bombay Presidency in 1803. From
Parsi traders to Afghan soldiers and Hadrami *sayyids*, the personalities
who appear in the text echo the cosmopolitan society of the region's ports,
though the text is of especial interest for its description of the *nawwāb*'s
pilgrimages to the shrines of the many Muslim saints of Broach, holy men
whose ancestral names reflected the ethnic diversity of the port.⁴⁵ The
nawwāb's pilgrimage to the shrine of Shaykh Makhdūm ʿAlī at Mahim
on the edge of Bombay is also described in the *Qissah-ye ghamgīn*, pre-
senting him as reciting the opening verse of the Quran before Shaykh
Makhdūm's tomb as he passed between his own sphere of influence in
Broach and that of the British in Bombay.⁴⁶ The *nawwāb*'s pilgrimage
marked a turning-point in the region's religious economy in which, despite
the longer-term role of the merchant classes, the patronage of a princely
and aristocratic elite would be replaced by that of a cash-earning urban
proletariat. This turning-point is captured in *Jān-e Bombāʾī*, in which the
shrine of Shaykh Makhdūm was described as the only one of Bombay's
Muslim pilgrimage sites possessing a dome (*gumbad*).⁴⁷ The reference

points to the pre-eminence of the shrine's status prior to Bombay's expansion in the decades after the text was composed around 1820. In the new industrial cities especially, over the following half-century the patronage of Sufi shrines by independent Muslim rulers faded with not only the rise of British power but of new classes of indigenous patrons. In being able to maintain their connections with both maritime merchant communities and a new clientele of urban workers, the shrines of Bombay such as that of Shaykh Makhdūm were more fortunate than many similar institutions inland. As the old ports of Gujarat fell into the shadow cast by Bombay, the saintly tombs of the new entrepôt of Bombay grew correspondingly in prestige and, as we see later in the chapter, the nineteenth century saw either new or previously negligible shrines in Bombay flourishing with the donations of the city's growing Muslim populace.

Although Shaykh Makhdūm lived in the medieval period, and his shrine first developed through the patronage of a pre-colonial economy of notables of whom the *nawwāb* of Broach was one of the last, the growth of Bombay increased the importance of his multi-member shrine firm through its links to both the expanding Muslim travel on the Indian Ocean and to the expanding proletarian population of the city itself, so providing the shrine with a vastly increased clientele who were attracted by the proven antiquity of its blessing powers. In 1875 this reinvigoration of the cult led to the writing of a new Arabic hagiography entitled *Zamīr al-insān* (Most scrupulous of men).[48] Written in neat and elegant *naskh* and completed on 17 Muharram 1292 (23 February 1875), in a reflection of both the continued prestige of Arab bloodlines on the Indian side of the ocean and the importance of the death anniversary to the shrine's annual *'urs* celebration, *Zamīr al-insān* began by recounting the history of Shaykh Makhdūm's death and family lineage, fitting him into the Arab ancestries treasured by the Konkani Muslims who managed his shrine and made up a large part of the labour-class Muslims of his clientele.[49] In reflection of the importance of this data, the author showed off a series of citations of living scholars and books from which he had drawn to verify the saint's lineage (*nisba*).[50] The text then provides several narrative 'service charters' of Shaykh Makhdūm's special powers through accounts of the seaborne rescues in which he specialized from his shoreside shrine.[51] Scrawled in Persian in the margins of the Arabic manuscript, a subsequent reader used the customary *abjad* system of numerological reckoning to calculate a verse containing the saint's death date: the result was *jinnāt al-firdaws*. The term for a 'heavenly garden' traditionally used as a metaphor for the shrines of the saints, the marginal scribble is a pointer to the city as it appeared in the imagination of its Muslims. Not a brooding seaside huddle of satanic mills, but as in the 'illuminated garden' of the saintly soldiers' shrine in the Dhobi Talao quarter, Bombay was imagined in terms of the horticultural and holy, as a city of the tranquil gardens of the saints.

As its fame grew, the shrine firm of Shaykh Makhdūm's stake in the miraculous economy expanded, and the reach of its blessing power eventually extended to services on land as well as at sea. In the Bombay-printed Urdu hagiographical compendium *Awliyā Allāh kē zinda karishmāt* (Living miracles of God's friends) the public were advised that Shaykh Makhdūm's powers reached through gullys no less than waves to all of the city's residents.[52] If anyone were sick at home, the cheap print pamphlet advised, a relative should immediately rush to Shaykh Makhdūm's shrine, repeat a prescribed formula ('O Shaykh Makhdūm, I sit here in your court, and pledge to feed so-and-so many people if you will pray for the illness of such-and-such to leave and for them to recover at once.').[53] Advertised and distributed by means of cheap vernacular printing, the procedure for this curing service depended on an economic transaction in which the saint's intercession came through the promise to feed (as the text then recommended) either ten, twenty, forty or a hundred poor people, a pledge whose financial arrangement would be managed by the shrine custodians. These cures were also often made by living holy men who served as custodians or worked as healers in the courtyards of these shrines, with a description from 1912 detailing the ritual of curing a sick child of evil through a technique of 'pass[ing] the end of a twisted handkerchief seven times over the sick child's body, murmuring at the same time certain mystic formulae which he, as it were, blows over the child from head to foot'.[54] The price for this expelling of the evil eye (*nazar*) was set at 'eight annas to a rupee'.[55] This model of transaction between pilgrim and saint, pleader and intercessor, was an essential element of the economy of enchantment, and drew on an older customary logic of reciprocal exchange that was expanded by means of printed advertisement to a larger urban marketplace.[56] One colonial British resident of Bombay explained the logic of such transaction in relation to the lack of appeal of the Protestant Christian emphasis on faith alone: 'A shrewd native cannot understand a man's having belief and yet making no visible sacrifice for it. Chintamon, who willingly expends two-thirds of all he possesses on his father's funeral obsequies; Badrudin, who sacrifices two years of his life for a journey to Mecca; or Nouroji, who says twenty prayers and makes one hundred genuflexions each day, cannot understand [the logic of *sola fide*].'⁵⁷ The economy of enchantment thus relied on a system of both symbolic and material transactions in which pilgrims offered prayers, penances and cash in exchange for the intercession of the holy dead, whose living stakeholders in turn offered a more or less specialized range of services, in the case of Shaykh Makhdūm ranging as widely as the cure of sick bodies to the rescue of whole ships (and their cargoes) at sea.

As Bombay expanded, the shrine of the Arab migrant Shaykh Makhdūm became chiefly associated with Bombay's Konkani Muslims, who ascribed their own origins to similarly venerable Arab migrants.⁵⁸ This development is suggestive of the shrine firms' role in supporting the fragile identities of the city's migrant workforce, among whom the Konkani Muslims loomed so large. Faced with a pluralistic and competitive new environment, the shrine firms offered such small-town labour migrants a historical tradition that was near at hand and accessible by the uncomplicated act of pilgrimage and petty donation that required minimal commitments of workers' limited time and resources. Hardwired into the social no less than topographic fabric of the city, shrines became proof of the longevity of certain communities' residence on Bombay's soil: they were concrete testament for contested claims to being Bombay's first settlers. Amplified in the nineteenth century through new hagiographies such as *Zamīr al-insān*, the shrine of Makhdūm ʿAlī served as a concrete historical statement that Bombay was irrevocably Muslim territory that no degree of colonial government or Parsi wealth could alter. To borrow a phrase from Egypt, the powers of the saints were those of a 'hidden government' which worked more efficiently than that of the city's more visible British rulers.⁵⁹ In such ways, the shrines served as safe-houses and indeed, through pilgrimage and printing, as reproduction centres of custom and historical identity in a way that the smaller social reach of the Reformists' Anglo-Mohammedan schools could not match.

All of Bombay's Muslim shrines hosted annual celebrations for the ʿurs, which comprised the 'wedding' or death anniversary of the saint buried there. These celebrations were typically accompanied by fairgrounds and markets, as well as the kinds of religious ritual that later chapters describe such individual promoters of Customary Islam as the migrant Hyderabadi shaykh Habīb ʿAlī Shāh producing. As in the case of the Muharram carnival, the saintly festivals were similarly contested events which different Muslim religious firms sought to control, not least because of their popularity with the city's working class. By 1909 the *Bombay Gazetteer* listed ten such festivals that were large enough to be worthy of official notice.⁶⁰ Most of the shrines to which they were linked dated from the first half of the nineteenth century, and of these that of Makhdūm 'Alī hosted the largest and most popular *'urs* festival. As a counter to the European-style bars and music halls that were attracting a growing Indian clientele in a city typified by increasing levels of consumption, the shrines of the Muslim saints offered a more licit and self-consciously indigenous form of entertainment.[61] Compared to other forms of producing pleasure, the *'urs* festivals offered both the familiarity and respectability of custom; and this in turn assured them large audiences. This is not to say that the shrine festivals were static and old-fashioned events; on the contrary, the emotional safety net of custom offered their organizers a free range for entrepreneurial flair in the provision of half-penny amusements for the labourers' customary holidays. The *'urs* tapped into the same demand for entertainment that funded the expansion of music halls in Bombay and, in the years after 1915, cinemas as well. In their common forms of love-song (*ghazals*) and parades of dancers there lay an important link between the economy of music production in the shrines and the subsequent film studios of Bombay, both of which directed themselves to the period's new audiences of mass urban consumers. At Bombay's saintly 'weddings' the visitor would encounter 'stalls and booths of every description', kite-flyers and minstrels, 'merry go rounds and pleasure boats': these were the Indian sisters of the fairground attractions of industrial working-class Britain.[62] The attraction of entertainments that people of all religious backgrounds could enjoy underlay the festivals' popular appeal to Hindus no less than Muslims. Even as the saint was seen to truly belong to the Konkani Muslims, for the flourishing of the shrine there was an economic logic in allowing Hindu as well as Muslim participants. For in a city in which Hindus outnumbered Muslim by roughly five to one, such festive inclusiveness maximized the pilgrim traffic and its revenues to the shrine firm. The same could be said of the many Muslim shrines in the small towns and countryside in Bombay's continental hinterland where religious inclusiveness held similar incentives. If in its mixing of many peoples this was a kind of cosmopolitanism, then it was one built at least in part on the broad market appeal of entertainment and the basic business demands of any shrine for revenues to support its buildings, workers and services.

PILGRIMAGE IN A COSMOPOLITAN RELIGIOUS ECONOMY

What can be observed at such shrine festivals was therefore the religious expression of new patterns of consumption created by the availability

of a vastly expanding urban labour force with a small surplus of cash.
Popular with both Muslims and non-Muslims through the appeal of
its entertainment forms, the great *'urs* ('wedding' festival) at the shrine
of Shaykh Makhdūm attracted thousands of pilgrims each year. By the
end of the nineteenth century, on an average year between 70,000 and
200,000 visitors attended Shaykh Makhdūm's week-long 'wedding' festival, enjoying not only the stalls and the mechanical fairground but also
the musical concerts which for many pilgrims formed the highlight of its
attractions. While most visitors came from the city itself, smaller numbers
of pilgrims travelled from outside Bombay, including from Hyderabad
and the Konkan coastline.[63] Yet these were not only places of pleasure
but of moral competition as well, for Shaykh Makhdūm's wedding festival also acted as a magnet for both Christian and Muslim critics of the
easy appeal of Customary Islam. Among the Christian contingent was the
CMS missionary Henry Smith, whose mission to the city's Muslims was
discussed in Chapter 1. Smith left the following description of his proselytizing visit of 1902, which gives a good sense of the festivals' place in
the wider industrializing economy of Bombay:

> Mahim is a small fishing village to the north-west of Bombay Island.
> In it is situated the tomb of a Muslim saint, or 'pir', called 'Makhdum
> Shāh' in whose honour a fair is held annually. On such an occasion a
> very gay sight is witnessed. Booths are erected on either side of the long
> village street, where the vendors of every imaginable species of ware ply
> a busy trade, and the proprietors of various 'shows' and the promoters
> of the worship of many Hindu gods, with the help of stentorian lungs
> and deafening 'music' do their best to attract visitors. Here you may see
> articles of native make, by the side of Sheffield knives, Wolverhampton
> locks, and Birmingham toys and brassware as well as German goods.
> The clothing of everybody is of the brightest possible hue, and the com-
> binations of colour and material would surely baffle the skill of the
> cleverest plate artist.[64]

In such ways, the economy of enchantment in which the shrines and their
miracle stories played so great a role was encouraged by the incorporation
of the city's shrine festivals into Bombay's larger commercial economy
by serving as marts for all manner of petty consumer goods. Alongside
the manufactures of the English Midlands which the former Birmingham
schoolboy Henry Smith was proud to point out, his visit to Shaykh
Makhdūm's *'urs* shows how the shrines were forced to openly compete in
the religious marketplace we have seen emerging in Bombay: even on his
own 'wedding day' Shaykh Makhdūm was challenged by his Christian
rivals for the affiliation of his urban clientele. Smith had arrived at the

fair with six other missionaries, and together they spent the three days of the festival preaching and selling cheap-print copies of the Gospel in Gujarati. In Bombay's competitive religious economy, the missionaries' presence at the festival was regarded with suspicion, particularly since one of the preachers was himself a Muslim convert. After being jibed as a disgrace to his community and having his beard roughly tugged in shame, the native preacher was chased away, along with Smith's other companions, under a shower of stones, leaving several of the party with bruises as they escaped to the safety of one of the train carriages that ferried pilgrims to the festival. It was not only Christian missionaries who saw the saintly festivals as an opportunity to capture the religious loyalties of the workers and, as we will see in Chapter 6, Muslim preachers also gave their attention to the *'urs* festivals. As centres of community identification, miraculous services and popular festive consumption, the city's shrines served not only to channel the saved energy of the saints into the new urban environment, but also as key locations for the competition for a stake in the market of Bombay Islam.

Other festivals, such as that at the originally eighteenth-century shrine of Dīwān Shāh (d. 1076/1665) at Bhiwandi, lay outside the city. Linked by rail, they served as semi-rural retreats for Bombay's labour force that were easily accessible on single-day holidays, so placing such shrines into a close relationship with the city's religious economy. Situated to the north of Bombay beside the early Bombay–Thane rail line, Bhiwandi itself was populated by Konkani Muslims and Hindu Marathas. Its commercial no less than religious economy was transformed by its position in Bombay's hinterland, and industrialization began there in the early twentieth century when the North Indian Muslim migrant Hājjī 'Abd al-Samad signalled a change in its economy with his slogan *sōnā bēchō aur lōha kharīdō* ('sell gold and buy iron'). Within a few years of such investments, in a transfer from Bombay, electric-powered textile mills were being founded in Bhiwandi.[65] Other hinterland shrine towns were similarly drawn into Bombay's orbit. Directly inland to the east of Bombay was the shrine of Hajj Malang Shāh Bābā at Kalyan. Like Bhiwandi, for much of the nineteenth century Kalyan was a supplier of migrant Konkani labour to Bombay, and we will encounter the town again in Chapter 7 as the home of the Customary Islamic 'exporter' to Natal, Ghulām Muhammad, who, on leaving Kalyan in 1892 to travel to Bombay in order to make the *hajj*, came into contact with the Bombay shaykh who would send him to South Africa. For other migrants from Kalyan to Bombay, the forty-odd mile journey back to Kalyan was short enough for many of them to

travel back annually for the *'urs* festival of Hājj Malang Shāh Bābā. As
an important early railway junction for the mainland routes branching
in and out of Bombay, Kalyan made for a particularly easy pilgrimage
from the city. As the hagiographical *Awliyā Allāh kē zinda karishmāt*
practically spelt out the matter, 'the town is only an hour by train from
Bombay'.[66] Located on top of an attractive hill and surrounded by ruins
of a possibly Mauryan-era fort, the shrine's attraction as a workers' day-
trip from the confines of the chawls and factories of their everyday existence can easily be imagined. Despite its many attractions, the shrine of
Hājj Malang illustrates the pressures that were put to bear on Bombay's
pluralistic cosmopolitanism, pressures which though multiplied by the
intense competition of life in the capitalist metropolis drew at least in
part on pre-industrial fractures between the region's different communities. Like that of Shaykh Makhdūm, the shrine of Hājj Malang attracted
a broad clientele of followers. In the words of one cheap-print text, people came there 'without regard to religion and caste (*mazhab aur millat*)'
such that the saint's followers include 'Hindus, Muslims, Parsis and others'; all the peoples, then, feeding Bombay's religious economy on which
the shrine drew as the wealth of the city and its relations with Kalyan
expanded.[67] There is reason to question whether the social differences
between these pilgrims did ever melt away in a Turnerian experience of
'communitas'. To begin with, the shrine's cultic identity was read in different ways: for Muslims it was the grave of Hājj Malang Shāh Bābā,
for Hindus the *samadhi* of the Nath Yogi Machindranāth.[68] Served by
their respective community specialists, who were employed at the site and
were paid to perform rituals and prayers on their behalf, the different pilgrims bought into the miraculous economy of the shrine firm in different
ways. While there was conceivably a certain camaraderie generated by
the shared train journey and lengthy climb up the hill, in a period before
the bonding ideology of nationalism there are reasons to doubt whether
the pilgrims returned to Bombay filled even briefly with Turner's spirit of
brotherly love.

The fractures in the cosmopolitan potential of the shrine's broad market appeal are most clearly seen in the aetiological legends that surrounded
Hājj Malang, legends that reflect those of many other saints in the regions
from which Bombay's Muslim labour groups migrated. In the most
famous of these narratives it was said that before Hājj Malang arrived
in Kalyan and brought the light of Islam there, the town was draped in
the darkness of 'infidelity and oppression' (*kufr wa zulmat*).[69] For before
his arrival, Kalyan was prey to a *dēvi* (goddess) whose *jādū* (magic) was

so powerful that a light poured from her head that was visible for miles around.[70] Along with her many offspring, the goddess oppressed all the people of the area like the infamous pharaoh, and compelled everyone to worship her. Then along came Hājj Malang, with his two Muslim companions. Approaching the hill where the goddess had her fort, the saintly migrants were greeted with a hail of rocks. Confronting the goddess with their spiritual power (*rūhānī tāqat*), Hājj Malang and his companions engaged in nothing less than a 'war' (*jang*) in which the two Muslim companions died as *shahīd*s (martyrs). Seeing the death of his friends, Hājj Malang began to chant the Great Name of Allah (*'ism-e a'zam*) and, on this, the goddess and her followers were all finally turned to stone. By way of proof, the author of the Urdu pamphlet, 'Abd al-Majīd Qāzī, assured his readers that pilgrims can still visit the ruins of the goddess's castle and see there the stone forms of her petrified offspring.

In a competitive pilgrim economy, aetiological legend could also be turned to the advertising of tourist attractions, pointing to the way in which cheap-print hagiographies served as an indigenous form of vernacular tourist guides for brief proletarian excursions. But in such stories as this, the most famous legend associated with the shrine of Hājj Malang, we also see a kind of narrative anti-cosmopolitanism that was one outcome of the comparative possibilities of a pluralistic religious marketplace. There was nothing here of the attempts seen in Chapter 4 by the likes of the Iranian traveller Hājjī Pīrzāda to place Hindu goddess worship on some kind of equal comparative footing with Islam. Instead, the story of the defeated *devī* offered only a caricatured version of Hindu practices in the form of 'infidelity and oppression' (*kufr wa zulmat*). Of course, there is also an important sense in which the story was not about Hindu practices, but was a symbolic charter of the saint's power to destroy any source of oppression in his followers' lives. As such, the *devī* symbolized the oppressors of the shrine's Hindu no less than Muslim clients. But the disturbing elements in the story cannot be explained so easily, for they formed part of a wider repertoire of saintly narratives which centred on feats of competition between Hindu and Muslim holy men and the latter's sites of triumphant pilgrimage.[71] In the narrative charter, Hājj Malang's 'war' was such market competition writ large.

Another example of such competition through stories relates to the shrine of Shams al-dīn Shamnā Mīrān at Miraj, another railway junction and pilgrimage town connected to the Bombay economy. As with many of Bombay's other saints, Shamnā Mīrān was said to have been born outside India, and was associated with stories of a long sea journey made with the aim of spreading Islam. In his case too, we hear how before his arrival the town of Miraj was draped in ignorance and darkness.[72] As with Hājj Malang's war with the goddess, pilgrims to Shamnā Mīrān's shrine heard how before the saint reached Miraj, the town was in the thrall of a magician from Bengal called Ganganā Dhōbī. Along with his magician wife (*jādūgarnī*), Dhōbī was forcing the townspeople to worship a *mūrtī* (statue) that demanded sacrifices of human blood.[73] On hearing this, Shamnā Mīrān summoned the soldiers of his 'army' (*fawj*) and invaded the town, putting an end to its oppression and freeing Dhōbī's wife from the *bhūt* demon with which she was possessed by forcing it to enter a bottle. Like others among the Deccan's many medieval warrior saints, Shamnā Mīrān was said to have been eventually killed in battle, in 896/1491.[74] As in the case of Hājj Malang, there are two levels at which the story operated in the context of the marketplace and its rivalries. At one level it offered a narrative advertisement of the shrine's speciality service by way of the curing of possessed women, a service offered by many of the region's Muslim shrines with lower-class clienteles. On another level the legend made the association between wickedness and the worship of statues, using *mūrtī*, the correct Hindu term for a statue rather than the generic Islamic term *butt* (idol). Here it was not only pointing to the fractured pluralism of the religious economy but positioning the statue-free shrine as superior to neighbouring Hindu temples with which it competed for a broad-based clientele, particularly of lower-class women with psychological problems conceptualized as demonic possession.

Similar stories of competition surrounded the shrine of Pīr Changī Bābā at Porbandar in Gujarat, from where many families migrated to both Bombay and Durban. Here the saint was connected to an aetiological myth of Porbandar's very foundation when the raja of a nearby town wished to build a port on the coast and, constantly failing, enlisted a powerful *yogi* to help him.[75] A master of astrology and a rider of tigers, the *yogi* was given many cash grants (*in'ām*) by the raja in request for his help, but none was forthcoming. Pitying the raja, Pīr Changī then challenged the *yogi* to a competition in which he froze the *yogi*'s tiger and then banished them both from the kingdom, which then was able to flourish anew. In another legend, Pīr Changī challenged a *yogi* to make a group of palm trees walk, and once again won the wager.[76] As with the legends of Shamnā Mīrān, the stories are on one level cultic advertisements for the shrine firm's provision of a superior miraculous service: Pīr Changī was able to offer his royal client stronger supernatural resources than the *yogi*.

But at the same time, they were also narratives of competition rather than coexistence. In the context of the newly competitive marketplace that emerged in nineteenth-century Bombay, such legends can therefore also be set against the attempts from the 1890s by the Bombay-founded Ārya Samāj to 'revert' the Muslims associated with such shrines in Gujarat 'back' to their ancestral Hinduism.[77] The older legends of Customary Islam thus took on new urgency in a more competitive era.

Associated with the shrines to which many of Bombay's Muslims were connected by either birthplace or pilgrimage, such legends were part of the cultural knowledge and social attitudes that migrants carried to the city in their quest for work. As such, these legends of increasingly competitive enchanted interactions made up part of the raw material of Bombay Islam. In some cases, labour migration patterns reconstructed these older cults as part of the built environment of the industrializing city. An example is seen in the cult of the Gujarati warrior saint Sayyid Mīrān 'Alī Dātār (d. 898/1492). The original shrine in the town of Unava was a popular pilgrimage centre in central Gujarat, from where we have already seen Bombay drawing many of its migrant workers. In the early years of the twentieth century, the shrine's Bombay franchise was opened by a migrant Muslim *sayyid* from the Gujarati port of Cambay, to the south of Unava.[78] Although not the saint's burial place, the Bombay shrine was constructed as a complete replica mausoleum, in the centre of which stood a cenotaph for the dead saint as the ritual focus of the pilgrims' dedications. Located around thirty metres from the sea, Mīrān 'Alī Dātār's Bombay outpost stood in Goghari Street, surrounded by the dockyards and warehouses of the Mazagaon quarter and the squalid houses of the dockyard workers. It was a mere short walk away from the house in Dockyard Road where the Hyderabadi holy man Habīb 'Alī Shāh is seen in Chapter 6 preaching in the late 1800s. While operating close to the house of this living holy man, the entrepreneur from Cambay who established the Mīrān 'Alī Dātār franchise was offering a very different religious product from that of his Hyderabadi rival, and one of which the latter would certainly have disapproved. For both the Unava shrine and its branch in Bombay were effectively purveyors of female possession. Although theoretically specializing in the exorcism of possession by spirits and the removal of the spells of black magic, the services that the cult provided required repeated visits, ritual performances and the offering of cash or purchased animal sacrifices that fed into this specialist niche of the shrine economy. The Indian police official S. M.

Edwardes described how the shrine firm's founder provided the painful course of one such cure in the early 1900s, which involved a possessed local Muslim woman called Afiza:

> The Syed [from Cambay] came into the house and gave Afiza a potion composed of incense-ashes and water from the Miran [Dātār] shrine. But the evil spirit was terribly violent; and it required regular treatment of this nature for fully twenty days ere it could be dislodged. Evening after evening Afiza was taken into the presence of [the] Syed, who summoned forth the spirit with a drink of the sacrosanct water; and at home [her husband] Abdulla and his mother who had been supplied with water and ashes by the Syed, were wont likewise to summon the spirit at any hour which they felt would cause it inconvenience. Thus the struggle between the powers of light and darkness for the soul of Afiza continued, until at length the evil spirit deemed it wise to depart; and on the twenty-first day, when it was racking Afiza for the last time, it demanded as the final price of its departure the liver of a black-goat. So Abdulla hearkened to the spirit's will and buried the pledge of his wife's recovery in a new earthen pot just at the spot where the four roads meet near his house. And Afiza was at peace.[79]

While offering a very different kind of Islam to that supplied by the more decorous Hyderabadi shaykh up the road, the *sayyid* who brought Mīrān 'Alī Dātār's cult from Gujarat clearly had a good sense for his corner of the market. Setting up his branch of the Unava shrine in the poor back alleys of the dockworkers' quarter, as Edwardes noted of him, 'the Syed of Goghari Street has earned well-merited fame among the poorer Musulman inhabitants of that quarter'.[80] And the shrine flourished.

Within the same building as the Mīrān 'Alī Dātār shrine in Bombay there also stood a separate cenotaph dedicated to another Gujarati saint, Pīr Bābā Habashī. Another franchise outpost of a main shrine, this time located in the coastal town of Ankleshwar in Gujarat, the firm of Pīr Bābā Habashī was associated with the Afro-Indian Sīdī community whose shrines specialized in the cure of possession through music and who we have already seen establishing a franchise shrine in the Dongri quarter.[81] It is little surprise to find the shrine firm of Pīr Bābā Habashī transferred the heart of the dockyards, for, as Edwardes observed, the main employment of Bombay's Sīdīs was to 'supply the steamship companies with stokers, firemen and engine-room assistants, and the dockyards and workshops with fitters and mechanics'.[82] The main dockyard location for Bombay's mobile community of African and Indo-African ship workers was certainly the logical place to establish a branch of a shrine with which they were not only familiar but at which they were, as low-status black Muslims, welcome in a way they were not at many of the city's mosques and other religious spaces. Managed by its entrepreneurial founder from Gujarat, the shrine of the two imported saints served as a venue for Thursday evening performances of *naqqāra* kettle drums at which black Muslims and lower-class women sought procedures that as the contemporaries of Freud's psychoanalysis it is tempting to label the 'dancing cure'. While officially specializing in expelling malevolent spirits, in practice the firm equally provided the more plainly pleasurable services of enduring states of trance. For workers who spent much of their time in the confined spaces of the boiler room, the drumming nights lent them the brief freedom of ecstasy as they danced around the courtyard with women who likewise abandoned themselves to the music with (as the loaded vernacular expression has it) 'open hair'.[83]

Such were the attractions of a firm introduced to the lower classes of Bombay's dock district by an entrepreneurial *sayyid* from Cambay; it is not difficult to understand the shrine's success. But as with the other saints discussed above, the miracle stories brought to Bombay with Mīrān 'Alī Dātār carried similarly anti-cosmopolitan tropes. Like that of Shamnā Mīrān, the biography of Mīrān 'Alī Dātār centred on legends of conquering cities to destroy cruel statues, such as the idol for which the king of Mandu captured hundreds of prisoners to sacrifice to every day.[84] Inland from the dockyards at the shrine of Shāh Dawla Dātār (d. 1228/1813?), in the Khōja graveyard in the Dongri quarter, similar stories transposed this older narrative geography of the spread of Islam to Bombay itself. Spreading like rumours through the alleys and tenements that surrounded the graveyard, stories recounted how Shāh Dawla had arrived in Bombay from Medina at a time when Dongri was plagued with *rakhsha* demons and *jādūgar* magicians.[85] From his example the local people learned not to worship these figures, and saw that Islam offered the correct path. In some accounts Shāh Dawla was said to have been the brother of Hājj Malang of Kalyan, who we have already seen bringing the light of Islam to one of the neighbouring towns of Bombay and turning its demons to stone.[86] What is seen in these folk histories is the way in which the aetiological charters of the older narratives of custom were carried into Bombay as means of locating the Muslim presence solidly into the topographic, and historical, fabric of the city. Reproduced in new urban contexts, these were old solutions to new migrations and the anxieties of belonging that they brought with them.

Such Muslim legends were by no means the era's unique narratives of chauvinism: this was after all a period that saw the emergence of fiercely anti-Muslim attitudes among many Bombay Hindus and the fierce bigotry of Christians. In their less appealing moments, the tales carried into Bombay of the heroic Muslim warrior saints of Gujarat and the Deccan echoed the rise of the warrior Sivaji as the Muslim-slaying hero of Maratha nationalism.[87] Moreover, the picture we have seen was not one in which Muslims became unified *en bloc* in the face of their Hindu 'others', not a simplistic binary communalism, but instead a process by which the very fragmentation and multiplication of Islam exacerbated internal fractions among Muslims themselves. The shrine firms were producers of rival and mutually contested Islams. Many of the shrines and cults examined in this chapter were communitarian in nature, but their appeal remained confined to mobile regional and linguistic communities, to Konkanis and Gujaratis, rather than to the larger imagined communities of subsequent religious nationalism, to Muslims as a whole.[88] This perspective reflects what has been described in Singapore in the same period, where diverse migration patterns led to an 'ethnicization of ritual' among the city's various Muslim groups, with the emergent religious geography of Singapore replicating the splintered small-town homelands of its different Muslim inhabitants.[89]

MORALS, COMMUNITIES AND MIRACLES IN THE MARKETPLACE

The previous pages have shown that, like other public spaces in pluralistic settings, the shrines of Bombay's Muslim saints could alternatively encourage or discourage cosmopolitan sentiments. While the saintly wedding celebrations of Makhdūm 'Alī attracted Bombayites of all religious backgrounds, other shrines acted as vehicles for sectarian narratives of Muslim superiority. Many of these were older stories that had originated long before the rise of Bombay, to be later carried there as the cultural baggage of its workforce. Yet such legends were not only the lagging weight of tradition, but, like the vampire tales colonial Africans attached to European doctors and firemen, were new cultural products made intelligible by the familiar dressing of custom.[90] As in the case of the enchanted economy of book production discussed in Chapter 3, Bombay produced no less than it consumed rumours of miracles. Not only the stock-in-trade of shrine firms appealing to the illiterate denizens of the dockyards, these supernatural stories also belonged to the sphere of written and printed religious production. While the previous pages focused on stories of the saints triumphing over pre-modern landscapes

FIGURE 7. The market of morals: Bhindi Bazaar, location of Sita Ram Building (1900)

of castles and hilltops, the remainder of this chapter turns to expressions of the saints' power over the capitalist cityscape of Bombay itself. The saint on whom we will focus bore the unusual name of Pēdrō Shāh: we have already heard rumours of his miracles with the collapse of Sita Ram Building in Bhindi Bazaar in 1903. In the writings that followed the building's collapse, Pēdrō Shāh became the focus of a moral contest pitting the social habits of English seamen against the mercantile interests of a Hindu businessman and the partisan mores of a dead Muslim saint. For as Bombay grew, so did the degree of moral competition between its various inhabitants, particularly when in public their spaces began to infringe on one another. A decade before the Sita Ram Building catastrophe, these tensions had erupted in the Hindu–Muslim riots of 1893.[91] If discussion of such competition and conflict has previously been interpreted only with regard to the city's religious processions and riots, the enchanted topography of saintly shrines also served as centres of narrative production for rumours that vented resentments. Bombay's shrines were, after all, entangled in densely urban environments in which, as in other cosmopolitan port cities of the nineteenth century, different communities struggled for control over moral no less than physical space.[92] In the case of Pēdrō Shāh's shrine, the atmosphere of competition was all the more charged through its location amid the shops and stalls at the heart of the market quarter of Bhindi Bazaar.

Given that Pēdrō Shāh (d. 1215/1799 or 1245/1829) was popularly believed to have been a Portuguese sailor who converted to Islam, he was an ironic choice as a defender of Muslim manners. But when a popular saloon bar was founded in Bombay's newly built Sita Ram Building in 1903, whatever Pēdrō Shāh's earlier credentials, he became a Muslim saint in the right place at the right time, since his shrine was located directly opposite the Windsor Bar in question. The curious series of events and rumours that developed in connection with the shrine shed revealing light on the cosmopolitan pressures that were an inevitable product of Bombay's religious marketplace. Of particular interest is the manner in which the collapse of the building was reported in a Muslim publication: published in 1903 under the combined English–Urdu title *A Sketch of the Life of His Holiness Saint Syed Pedro Shah, and His Miraculous Deeds – Pēdrō Shāh Sāhib kī karāmāt* (Pēdrō Shāh's miracles), the cheap-print pamphlet is one of the most revealing documents to have survived on Muslim life in colonial Bombay.[93] With its curious blend of journalism and hagiography, of English and Urdu, in its hybrid form the *Sketch* sought to widely advertize the miraculous powers of the shrine firm, showing the way in which the use of English was by no means exclusive to Muslim Reformists. Yet this did not prevent the *Sketch*'s author from using his hybrid genre to voice distinctly anti-cosmopolitan sentiments. While previous sections focused on cults associated with Bombay's lower-class Muslims, the text is particularly revealing for the attitudes it displays that a middle-class Muslim held towards the different communities living cheek-by-jowl around him in the city's main market district.

A local Muslim bookseller called 'Abd al-Karīm Munshi, the author was not content to provide only an account of Pēdrō Shāh's destructive wrath. In a reflection of the use of saintly legends to create a Muslim history for Bombay seen earlier, 'Abd al-Karīm also aimed to correct what he saw as grievous errors in both popular and governmental accounts of Pēdrō Shāh's life and so use his book to present a distinctly 'Islamic' history for the city at large. Bearing history on the back of hagiography, the *Sketch* began with a summary of the early settlement of Bombay, focusing on the etymology of its Portuguese (*Bonba'i*), Muslim (*Bomba'i*) and Hindu (*Mumba'i*) names as well as the rise of British power under the Company and Empire. In a similarly etymological method the *munshi*'s linguistic training turned to the service of the saint instead of empire as the text addressed the problematic name of 'Pēdrō'.[94] It was here that the author took his first contentious turn, arguing in Urdu against the widespread oral tradition of Pēdrō Shāh as a Portuguese convert by putting forward a biographical counter-narrative that portrayed him instead as an Arab merchant from the Makran who belonged to the Qādirī lineage of Sufis, came to Bombay on a trade mission and died there in 1215/1799.[95] The saint's unusual (and clearly Christian) name of Pēdrō (that is, the Hispanic Pedro) was explained by 'Abd al-Karīm as a mere nickname given to him by the Portuguese of Bombay out of respect for his piety, which was such that they compared him to their own St Peter.[96] Finally, the author claimed that true name of the saint called Pēdrō Shāh was Sayyid 'Abdullāh Shāh Qādirī. Like the city itself, and the towns of its hinterland, the saint of Bhindi bazaar was no less in need of an unambiguously Islamic ancestry.

In an English appendix printed on the back cover of the Urdu text, the author reprinted a letter he had sent to the *Advocate of India* newspaper, explicitly challenging the version of Pēdrō Shāh's life given in the 1901 *Census Reports* that had described him as 'a Portuguese convert, who on conversion to Islam obtained the honour of sacrosanctity'.[97] Since the account in the *Census Reports* (which also appeared in various editions of the *Bombay Gazetteer* and other nineteenth-century publications) presumably drew on the oral traditions of local informants, we should be cautious in automatically conferring authority on the more 'Islamic' picture painted in the *Sketch*, not least considering the banality of the 'original' name of 'Abdullāh Shāh Qādirī offered in its place. Given that the margins of the history of pre-colonial European encounters with Islam are replete with such conversions – particularly among the sailors and merchants who had most to gain by such acts of re-affiliation – there is nothing inherently unlikely about the story of a Portuguese convert.[98] It seems conceivable that 'Pēdrō Shāh' was the product of an older religious economy in the Indian Ocean, an earlier chapter in the region's history in which Arab merchants dominated trade and conversion to Islam made easy entry to the market; we cannot know. But it is not in any case the 'facts' that are at stake here. As Luise White has written in connection with colonial vampire stories, 'gossip is a reliable source because it traces the boundaries created by talking about someone'.[99] What is more important, then, is the play of familiar tropes in 'Abd al-Karīm's counter-history, for the ascription of an Arab (and particularly a *sayyid*) ancestry to Muslim saints was a long-standing part of the hagiographical and saint-making process in India, in which an Arab bloodline became virtually a prerequisite for any saint worth his salt. The continued emphasis on such prestigious bloodlines was one of the key characteristics in the reproduction of the inegalitarian social structure of Customary Islam well into the twentieth century.

The similar insistence on Arab bloodlines for Bombay's other saints such as Hājjī 'Alī (despite alternative claims of his Afghan lineage) show the same Arabocentrism at work in a market comprising Muslims of many ethnic backgrounds, claims that reflected the predilections of the 'Arab-descended' elite among Bombay's Konkani Muslims. This emphasis on an Arab bloodline and merchant occupation surely appealed to the city's Konkani Muslims, who treasured the genealogies of merchant Arab descent that set them apart from many of the city's other Muslims. Konkanis were certainly well represented in the Muslim institutions of Bombay: they controlled such important shrine firms as that of Shaykh Makhdūm 'Alī and, a short walk away from Pēdrō Shāh's shrine, Bombay's main Jami' Mosque. They were also well represented among the literate producers of Urdu and Arabic texts in the city, and so there is good reason to suspect the author 'Abd al-Karīm, the Munshī or 'secretary', was himself a Konkani Muslim. Such genealogical revisions of historical identity were also engaged in by other groups in Bombay's larger marketplace, as in the attempt by Hindu Pattana Prabhus to claim the status of high-caste *ksatriya*s, a struggle which like 'Abd al-Karim Munshī's also involved the contradicting of descriptions of their history by colonial scholar-administrators such as Captain Molesworth.[100] Perhaps what is most striking about Munshī 'Abd al-Karīm's *Sketch* is finally what it left out: aside from blood and trade, there were no details of Pēdrō Shāh's life at all. It was a question of to which Muslim group the saint, shrine and his miraculous capital belonged.

Perhaps this was because the rumours that did survive of his life presented a less attractive picture to the middle-class Munshī. The stories preserved by the present custodians of his shrine seem to confirm this in painting a very different image from that of 'Abd al-Karīm's noble merchant. Problematic as the comparison of sources may be, in the oral history of the shrine's hereditary servants Pēdrō Shāh was a coolie, one of the thousands of day labourers who literally carried the city's commerce on their backs. A saint of the streets like the rat-hugging 'Abd al-Rahmān of half a mile distant, Pēdrō Shāh was no less holy for his subaltern status. To the *ahl-e nazar*, the 'people of insight', Pēdrō Shāh was known to be one of God's hidden friends. Not intolerant of non-Muslims, it was only to a Parsi couple that he revealed himself in his lifetime when, instead of carrying his usual basketload on the top of his head, he walked past them with the basket floating above him as he passed.[101] There were, then, several rumoured versions of a life in circulation. In contrast to the *Sketch*'s

assertions of the Arabness of the saint, the 'official' *Gazetteer* – and probably also popular – account of Pēdrō Shāh's life as a Portuguese sailor presented a symbolic possibility of self-transformation and fluid community
boundaries, a city of ambiguity and self-fashioning for the marketplace.
But this was not the Bombay of 'Abd al-Karīm's *Sketch*. For him and others like him, already alarmed by the threat to Bombay's Muslims posed
by Christian missionary firms and the Āryā Samāj's campaign of *shuddhī*,
or 'reversion' to Hinduism, the story of an ambiguously Christian Muslim
saint was advertized as a compromised brand.[102] If Bombay was active in
developing the Pan-Islamism or Modernism of men such as Jamāl al-dīn
al-Afghānī and Sir Sayyid Ahmad Khān, in the *Sketch*'s re-affirmation of
Muslim ethnic hierarchies we see how in the early twentieth century many
of the city's Muslims used shrine firms to promote an inegalitarian Islam
whose followers were ranked in accordance with their genealogical background. In the absence of further evidence it is impossible to judge which
of the two rival accounts best reflects historical fact, and so the biographical controversy surrounding Pēdrō Shāh is best seen as illustrating tensions
over maintaining community boundaries in a cosmopolitan marketplace.
Here were not signs of a unified global Islam, but reminders of the ethnic
and community bonds that separated the city's many different Muslims.

These communitarian tensions found further expression in the most
detailed narrative found in the *Sketch*. This was concerned with events
in the year 1903 rather than with the more distant past of the saint's
purported life. The account concerned the construction, and subsequent
collapse, of Sita Rām Building.[103] A multi-storey edifice directly in front
of Pēdrō Shāh's shrine, the Sita Ram Building was completed in 1903,
and funded by the eponymous Hindu entrepreneur Sītā Rām and his
Parsi business partner, Rustamji Kā'ūsjī. Here was cosmopolitanism in
its capitalist guise. The partners' problems began when a drinking establishment, the Windsor Bar, was established in the building's D-block.
Soon there were people gathering there day and night, including large
numbers of drunken and noisy Europeans (particularly soldiers and sailors, the *Sketch*'s author noted) who in true British fashion seem to have
become especially rowdy around closing time. The problem of drunken
Europeans roaming the streets by night had been raised as early as 1816
in the Persian *Jān-e Bombā'ī*, whose Muslim author complained about
them at length; almost a century later European drunkenness remained
a faultline in the city's moral economy.[104] Even when the caretaker of
Pēdrō Shāh's shrine lodged a complaint with the police superintendent,
nothing was done to curb the raucous boozing across the road. But if

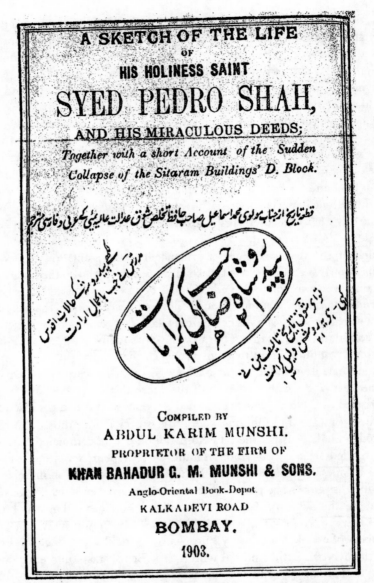

FIGURE 8. Salacious sainthood: Bilingual title of Pēdrō Shāh's journalistic hagiography (1903)

the police would not intervene, then the saint would. And so, the *Sketch* announced, on the night of 31 May 1903 the whole D-block of Sita Ram Building collapsed.[105] While five people were crushed in the rubble, other patrons of the bar managed to escape and were taken injured to hospital. According to the *Sketch*, the exact timing of the collapse was a sign of God's mercy, for the many upper storeys of the building were empty at that hour and so the casualties were mercifully few in number and limited to the Windsor barflies. One of the fortunate few was Sita Rām's Scottish manager, Charles Stewart, who dramatically recounted to the *Sketch*'s author 'Abd al-Karīm how he had managed to dash out of the bar just in the nick of time. Quite aside from the loss of life, between the two of them Sitā Rām and Rustamji Kā'ūsji lost almost 20,000 rupees that they had invested in the building. To make matters worse, when Bombay's chief of police and coroner arrived at the scene, the decision was taken to prosecute Sitā Rām, who then had to procure a barrister and team of assistants to arrange for a costly defence.

The circumstances that surrounded the spectacular collapse of Sita Ram Building echoed the many other legal struggles for private and community space that fuelled disputes in Bombay's law courts no less than in the city's streets in times of riot. Within a year of the trial of Sitā Rām, the Bombay High Court was similarly occupied with a prosecution brought by the Muslim 'Abdullāhbhā'ī Mithābhā'ī against his Hindu neighbour, Ranchod Shamji.[106] A petty neighbours' dispute in which 'Abdullāhbhā'ī claimed that his wealthier neighbour had built a large extension to his house which towered over his own home and prevented the access of air and light, the case was a smaller-scale and more mundane version of the supernatural and legal struggles against the multi-storey Sita Ram Building. To return to the trial about the latter, while the case was approaching court the unhappy Sitā Rām received even worse news that, two months after the original disaster, a fire in the remaining blocks of the Sita Ram Building had led to even more destruction. Yet when the case was finally brought before the judge, it was immediately dismissed and Sitā Rām was freed. According to 'Abd al-Karīm's *Sketch*, Sitā Rām having recognized his wrongdoings, the mercy of God and his saint Pēdrō Shāh had saved him. And so the Hindu then paid a visit to the shrine whose morals he had offended and organized a Quran recitation in gratitude. Muslim morality had won in the market of Bhindi Bazaar.

With this denouement of clear satisfaction to the Muslim promoters of Pēdrō Shāh, whose complaints had earlier been ignored by the city's policemen, we see a brief resolution to the tensions that resounded through Bombay's different moral communities. Like the other shrines of the city and its hinterland, that of Pēdrō Shāh could aid or inhibit the cosmopolitan. Just as the efforts of scores of Muslim, Christian and Hindu moralists in Bombay were jeopardized by the worldly distractions offered by the city's new experiment in urban life, so was the pious respectability of Pēdrō Shāh's shrine threatened by the ungodly patrons of the Windsor Bar across the street. In the encroachment of their moral space by the combined efforts of boozy seamen and a Hindu entrepreneur, the Muslim devotees of Pēdrō Shāh were victims of the ambiguously cosmopolitan pressures of the pluralistic religious economy.[107] But in the end, in Bhindi Bazaar at least, the economy of enchantment won out over the business in rum and beer as Sītā Rām made his symbolic investment in the rival economy of the shrine instead. Like Victorian ghost stories, the rumours of Pēdrō Shāh's miracles acted as 'potent images of the lost past – past sins, past promises, past attachments, past regrets – and could be used to confront, and exorcize, the demons of guilt and fear'.[108] And so though a Hindu, perhaps to assuage his fear of the saint, perhaps to calm the tension with his neighbours, Sītā Rām became a participant in the Muslim economy of enchantment. As with the followers of the Sufi big men of the Bombay dockyards discussed in Chapter 6, it was fear as much as love that drove people into the arms of the saints.

It is finally illuminating to compare 'Abd al-Karīm's Urdu account with an alternative version recorded in Bombay newspaper reports from the time. The Monday 1 June 1903 edition of the *Bombay Gazette* newspaper carried the story under the heading 'Fatal Collapse of a Building', with further details in a long article headed 'The Disaster at the Market' in the following day's edition. These reports closely confirm the *Sketch*'s account of the events per se, describing how 'at a quarter past ten o'clock the entire portion of the building over the Refreshment Bar suddenly came down with a crash'.[109] Further information was given concerning the rescue efforts, and the role of Bombay's fire brigade and a number of passers-by in it. Here it is the agency of the city's administrative infrastructure that is praised – that is, the modernity of the city itself rather than the Customary Islamic agency of the miraculous. Nonetheless, for all the efforts of the firemen and doctors, three European soldiers and one Parsi died. The *Gazette*'s follow-up article of 2 June 1903 contained much more detail, both on the events themselves and the background to the entire affair. It was also written in a more salaciously journalistic style. Proud of its scoop, in ironically appropriate terms the runner for the *Gazette* article declared it would 'reveal how miraculous were the escapes of some of those involved'.[110] Particularly tantalizing was the news that the firm of Messrs Heggerie, Su'zer and Co. were due to move into offices on the first floor above the bar only a day after the building's collapse.[111] Moreover, the report continued, since the bar usually 'did prosperous business', it was unusual that there were so few people there at the time of the disaster; only two hours beforehand more than twenty-five customers had been present. Mr Stewart, the Scots bar manager who also appeared in the *Sketch*, was used to add further frisson to the story, for readers were told: 'His escape was miraculous. Hardly had he stepped onto the veranda when a roar announced the collapse of the whole block. Masonry clattered into the road from the front of the building like an avalanche.'[112]

What is interesting about the manner of the newspaper reporting is its rhetorical parallels to the supernatural narrative of the *Sketch*, whose very subtitle evoked the miracles or *karāmāt* that were central to its entire presentation of events. While it seems likely that the language of the miraculous in the *Gazette* was not used as literally and deliberately as in the Urdu text, their similarities point us towards the common origin of both documents in Bombay's popular cosmopolitan print market.[113] With its links to the emergent Victorian genres of the horror story and Penny Dreadful, the newspaper appears less as the beacon of a rational public sphere than as a monger of supernatural gossip and metaphysical inconsistencies. Printed in 1903, the bookseller 'Abd al-Karīm's *Sketch* appeared at the tail end of the greatest age of the English ghost story, an explosion of literary supernaturalism that, like the cheap-print Urdu *Sketch*, was made possible by the falling costs of printing and the spread of periodicals that also enabled Bombay's economy of print. The strange modernity of 'Abd al-Karīm's journalistic miracle text was a parallel, then, to the ghost stories perused by his English contemporaries. For what Cox and Gilbert have written of such ghost stories could equally be applied to the story of Pēdrō Shāh: 'Each story should reveal to the reader a spectacle of the returning dead, or their agents, and their actions; there must be a dramatic interaction between the living and the dead, more often than not with the intention of frightening or unsettling the reader.'[114] In their appeal to a parallel and in some cases overlapping readership, the English *Gazette* and the Urdu *Sketch* belonged to a marketplace of popular print culture in which consumer demand for the spectacular story meant there was no strict border between hagiography and journalism. The hagiographical *Sketch* presented hard evidence no less than the journalistic *Gazette* flirted with rumours of the miraculous. There was, then, a kind of cosmopolitan slippage between the languages and genres of the city's plural print market.

With their symbolism of hubris, violence and divine retribution, there is an eerie familiarity to the counter-narratives and conspiracies that surrounded the collapse of the Sita Ram Building and the demise in its ruins of the immoralists and capitalists. The combination of symbols on which both the Urdu and English accounts fed hinted at a new and now all-too-familiar modernity: the high-rise building as a totem to be celebrated or despised; the oblivion to the resentment caused by unrivalled financial success; the spectacular 'punishment' of the moral offender. Alternatively perpetuating and feeding on these fertile symbols were the print media of newspapers and pamphlets for which the events and their aftermath provided an unmissable opportunity to not only sell copy but also to capitalize, in different ways, on the rich semantic yields of catastrophe. For whether in championing the city's firemen or its angered saints, both the accounts have their distinct heroes whose loyalties represent very different visions of order and authority in the miniature world of the Bombay marketplace. Like the vampire stories of colonial East Africa that presented firemen as bloodsuckers, the rumours of Pēdrō Shāh and the Sita Ram Building repudiated the new urban morality of the boozing Britons.[115]

In terms of the historical trajectory of Muslim religious violence, what is most interesting about the Sita Ram affair is its surrender of agency to otherworldly movers. This was not the 'this-worldly Islam' often associated with Muslim modernity, but a reinvigoration of Customary Islam fuelled by a combination of popular printing and the semantic possibilities of a new urban landscape.[116] The new multi-storey buildings being constructed next to the low-rise Muslim shops of Bhindi Bazaar were not the enterprises of decent men like the Persian merchants who had funded their Irānī Mosque up the road. Instead, with their liquor outlets and loose customers, they were the neighbourhood's moral corrupters. And yet it was not a community association or street protest, but rather a long-deceased saint who intervened to save his neighbours. Even when seen through the pen of a *munshī* bookseller who was clearly as literate in English as in Urdu, the religion of the *Sketch* was unaffected by the Islam of the Anglophone Muslim Reformists whose grand Anjuman-e Islām School stood only a few hundred yards along the same street as Pēdrō Shāh's shrine. After all, civic appeals in English to the city's police and magistrates had not put a stop to the immorality of the Windsor Bar. In the end, it was the long-deceased saint who came to the rescue of the outraged Muslims of Bhindi Bazaar.

Amid the daily competition of the Bhindi Bazaar, the rumours of miracles show how the economies of semantics and morals, of commerce and religion, interpenetrated and depended on each other. Drawing on the familiar religious forms of the villages and towns from which they came, the migrant Muslim groups that settled in Bombay demanded signs of continuity in the religious productions that they consumed in the city. Through the provision of festivals or the exorcism of spirits, the city's shrine-founding entrepreneurs of enchantment supplied this continuity even as they moved it into the new world of print, train stations and tower blocks. The result was not a growing standardization of Islam, but an increasing range of religious purveyors whose productions were as diverse as the backgrounds of their consumers. In part this involved a new sphere of print, enchanted and rumoured no less than disenchanted and scriptural, producing cheap pamphlets in simple Urdu that appealed to wide sections of the urban populace. But in a context in which a new and expanding labour class had entered the cash economy, leaving its members with petty cash surpluses that allowed them to purchase a shrine's specialist services or pay for a ride at a shrine's annual fair, there had also emerged new patterns of religious consumption which fed the enchanted economy of Bombay's shrine firms. These shrines were not only places of dancing cures and entertainments; they were also places of power and punishment. And in Bombay's competitive cultic contexts, displays of saintly power became more important than ever. Spectacular feats such as the destruction of Sita Ram Building were advertisements for the saint's capacity to intervene in worldly affairs, and, announced in printed works such as 'Abd al-Karīm's *Sketch*, they promised the shrine's sure ability to deal with smaller quotidian problems brought by pilgrims. Without such proofs, the cultic economy of gifts and donations would soon dry up. With its origins in older pre-colonial rivalries, the narrative inheritance of Bombay's shrine firms was one that comprised partisan and at times chauvinist displays of power as punishment. As competition for moral no less than commercial space merged with cosmopolitan tensions of densely populated neighbourhoods, the saints found themselves presented as the supernatural arbiters of the quarrels that ensued. As the rumours of Pēdrō Shāh's role in the disaster at the market show so well, to help one person is often to hinder another. This same rule of the distribution of scarce resources thus applied to supernatural no less than material sources of power. In the estranged morality of an economy of enchantment, there were inevitably winners and losers.

3

The Enchantment of Industrial Communications

The industrialization of communication among Muslims was one of the major overall characteristics of Bombay's religious economy. Powered by the spread of cheap mass-produced paper and inexpensive iron printing-presses, Bombay's industrialization enabled the city to become the most important Muslim printing centre in the Indian Ocean. Not only did this industrialization of communications mean that the varied textual productions of Bombay's religious economy were mass-produced in a period in which printing was comparatively underdeveloped in Bombay's oceanic and continental hinterlands, it also enabled the distribution of both the textual and embodied productions of the religious economy through the export of books and holy men on the steamship networks that Bombay similarly dominated. While this was an industrially enabled pattern of reproduction and distribution, such reliance on machines and steam-power no more led to a disenchanted religiosity in Bombay than it did in mill-towns such as Manchester or Ashton-under-Lyne in the age of such ocean-going charismatics as the 'Shaker' Ann Lee and the Yorkshire prophet John Wroe, whose heaven-sent visions were filled with steam-belching engines and flying iron sky-trains.[1] With regard to Muslim contexts, the spread of printing and the acceleration of travel through the development of steamships and ocean liners have usually been associated with the emergence of Islamic Reform.[2] In contrast to the abundant literature associating the spread of modern communications with Modernist, Protestant or Pan-Islamist Islams, this chapter argues that such communications as printing and travel were neutral technologies that could be and were made use of by the full range of religious firms operating in the religious economy of a given region.[3]

For in Bombay printing was not only associated with the scriptural or legalistic productions of Reformists, but was extensively used by the impresarios of holy men, shrines and the customary Sufi brotherhood firms for whom Bombay was an important place of recruitment no less than publication. In a marketplace in which miracle-working shrines held greater shares than modernizing schools, it is perhaps unsurprising that cheap-print production should have similarly followed these market trends. While many shrine pilgrims were illiterate, the shared and loud reading culture in which Indian printing developed meant that this market created demand for a vast number of hagiographical 'story books' that had an immediate narrative appeal. The enchantment of the print marketplace therefore also had something to do with the intrinsic cultural appeal of saintly stories, which bought into popular demand for entertainment in a way that moralizing or scientific Reformist tracts never could. In terms of printing, as of the pilgrimages described in the previous chapter, the economy of enchantment thus overlapped with the economy of entertainment. But printing did not only reflect the tastes of the market; it also informed them. As such, the production of hagiographical texts that we have described should also be seen as a form of advertisement by which Customary Islamic firms attempted to shape consumer preferences by advertising the miraculous services associated with particular shrines or the holy men associated with a particular firm. If nineteenth-century developments in industrialized communications have usually been connected to a rationalizing, textualizing and disenchanting trajectory of religious change, by looking at printing and then steam travel in turn, the following pages trace a less familiar trajectory by which industrial technologies were directed towards the championing of custom over reason, of person over text, and of miraculous over mechanical agency. None of this is to deny the presence of a more familiar Muslim modernity in either Bombay or its hinterlands. But side by side with this more familiarly disenchanted modernity emerged its enchanted counterpart, in which steamships were saved by miracles, printing-presses spread their strange stories, and holy men collected the technologically enhanced rewards of such publicity in their new urban enclaves.[4]

Simply put, industrial modernity forged a set of tools which different religious firms were able to use in different ways. For uprooted workers and the ambitious friends of God who protected them, this opportunity saw the reinvigoration of an Islam that maintained and even multiplied the consolations of custom. For many Muslims whose lives were shaped by the new socio-economic conditions of the age, a Reformist Islam of scripture, science and an Allah worshipped from afar held little attraction. And so between Bombay, Baghdad, Tehran and Durban, the promoters of Customary Islam travelled, printed and marketed an altogether different Muslim response to modernity. In this oceanic market of exchanges, Bombay's sheer difference (indeed, indifference) to the architectural and social norms of the older ports with which it was connected was for its visitors at once liberating and debilitating.[5] It was a newness that lent itself to the brave new worlds of Indian nationalism, trade unionism, communal violence and Pan-Islamism, to all of the familiar manifestations of the modern. At the same time, its dizzying novelty fuelled demand for the familiar securities of custom, for the saintly intercessors and shrine rituals of an older world, even if their reproduction would be shaped by the new industrial marketplace. The producers of Reformist and Customary Islam thus responded to the same social conditions, albeit with responses marketed to Muslims at different stations in the social hierarchies created by colonialism, on the one hand, and industrialization, on the other. With Bombay forming the most important centre of both transportation and printing in the west Indian Ocean, the productions of its religious economy were able to make effective use of the new means of communication to reach audiences not only within the city but also in its oceanic and continental hinterlands. Like the mobile founders of franchise shrines and the bookseller printers of miraculous rumours examined in the previous chapter, Bombay's industrial communications were drawn into the economy of enchantment.

PRINTING ENCHANTMENT

Chapter 1 described how the innovation of printing in Indian languages became one of the most efficient marketing strategies of Bombay's Christian missionary firms. Issuing texts in their thousands in each of the city's languages, and distributing them efficiently – and often for free – in Bombay no less than Calcutta, such missionaries were important catalysts in the development of an indigenous and, more specifically, an Islamic printing industry. In response, Muslim Reformist organizations became assiduous pioneers of vernacular printing, investing in newspapers, journals and other more plainly educational forms of book production. There has been a long-standing argument that the technology of printing is inherently linked to such textualist and individualist religious forms through its potential to place scripture and the authority of its interpretation into the hands of individual believers; every man his own priest. As early as 1823 the colonial commentator Leicester Stanhope predicted that the spread of an unregulated printing industry in India would shatter the 'superstitions' of customary religious forms and the authority of *faqīrs* and Brahmans, 'for it is reasonable to contend that as free discussion produced the Reformation in Europe, so, by parity of reasoning, it may produce the same result in Asia'.[6]

It was a compelling argument, and one that has proven no less attractive for many modern scholars, particularly those working in the wake of Elizabeth Eisenstein's influential linking of printing to the Protestant Reformation in Europe.[7] It is certainly the case that from its late onset among India's Muslims around 1820, the spread of Islamic printing in India no less than the Middle East was connected to the spread of Modernist and Reformist ideas.[8] The spread of printing in nineteenth-century India has similarly been seen as coeval with the evolution of 'Protestantizing' trends towards direct access to the scriptural sources of religious knowledge and authority.[9] Now that the scriptural 'sources' of Islam were made widely available in cheap printing and increasingly in translation as well, the extra-scriptural doctrines and practices associated with Customary Islam came under attack as heretical 'innovations' (*bid'a*) with no basis in Holy Writ. By the same token, widened access to religious texts is meant to have encouraged 'individualist' forms of religiosity in which the new worshipper-as-reader took control of his or her own religious destiny, rendering redundant the saintly middlemen who had long stood between Muslims and their God.

In certain cases, the familiar equation of printing with Reform and the repeal of custom was precisely what did occur. As Stanhope envisaged, this was particularly the case with the emergence of a printed public sphere of newspapers. The great example of the press's role in religious change was the Calcutta-based Hindu Reformist Ram Mohan Roy (1774–1833), who in founding the Bengali newspaper *Samvad Kaumudi* and its Persian sibling *Mir'āt al-Akhbār* (News mirror) served as the father of Indian journalism. As in Calcutta, where the vernacular reach of Bengali dominated the growth of a cheap print industry that nonetheless included Persian and Arabic, the development of Bombay printing took place in a multi-lingual and multi-script environment. As in Calcutta again, Bombay's pioneer newspapers were closely linked to ideas of socio-religious Reform being produced in collaboration with colonial critics of Indian religions. Newspaper production as such had begun in Bombay with the foundation of the *Bombay Herald* in 1789 and the *Bombay Gazette* in 1791, with the short-lived Portuguese *Messageiro Bombayense* following in 1831.[10] The latter coincided with the rise of Bombay's earliest vernacular newspapers, the Gujarati *Chabuk* (Courier) and *Jām-e Jamshid* (Cup of Jamshid), both founded in 1830, along with the Marathi newspaper *Bombay Darpan* (*Bombay Mirror*, 1832) and the somewhat later Persian weekly *Mufarih al-Qālib* (Gladdening chatter).[11] The very existence of these newspapers was dependent on the recent industrial innovations to which Bombay lent access, for the majority of these newspapers were printed on the lithographic presses that, in avoiding the expensive and time-consuming process of setting type for every page of print, allowed news to be printed both quickly and cheaply in vernacular scripts. While pre-colonial Persian news-reports certainly existed in such cities as Delhi, the very existence of such rapidly mass-produced newspapers was a reflection of both the reproducibility of matter and acceleration of time that were enabled by industrial technology. Without the speedy printing and mass production that lithographic presses made possible, the notion of a newspaper is scarcely meaningful. Such was the diversification and expansion of the newspaper trade that by the 1890s there were no fewer than fifty-one Indian-language newspapers being published in Bombay. The city's size, and the diversity of its population, had produced a competitive and pluralistic print economy that would in turn intersect with the city's religious economy.

As the newspaper reports of the previous chapter suggest, there is good reason to doubt that this newspaper economy was fully in tune with Habermas's connection of the newspaper to the formation of a 'rational' public sphere. In any case, newspapers accounted for only one section of Muslim India's print economy. This section therefore turns away from the more familiar modernity of the newspaper to examine some of the other popular genres that printing spread through the city, and to the role of printing in the reproduction of Customary Islam for a new urban marketplace. For the nineteenth century was not only the era of the Indian newspaper, it was also the age of the printed hagiography. As the following pages show, printing was in itself a neutral technology which could be used for Reformist or Customary Islamic productions, to mass produce translations of scriptures or celebrations of saintly intercessors. If printing was inextricably linked with industrial modernity, then in response to the market it also served as a vehicle of enchantment. From the port of Bombay, this in turn brought the possibility of disseminating the textual commodities of this enchanted economy to readers in other corners of its oceanic marketplace.

With its wide reach of readers, Bombay's Muslim printing industry encompassed books in the globalizing languages of Arabic and English as well as the more restricted if similarly transnational languages of Persian and Urdu. The earliest use of Arabic printing in Bombay was made in 1802 in the form of a typographic government proclamation issued in the *Bombay Courier*.[12] Within a few decades the more adaptable lithographic printing technology had passed into Muslim hands, and by the middle of the century Bombay saw the printing of large numbers of books in Arabic, Persian and Urdu. From there they were distributed far and wide through the oceanic networks of the great port. While throughout the nineteenth century Calcutta remained India's principal publishing centre, and the North Indian towns of Lucknow and Kanpur became important publishing centres for Islamic languages, as both a printing centre and a distribution point Bombay helped initiate and expand India's commercial lead in Islamic printing through its vast oceanic hinterland. For compared to the nascent publishing stations of the Middle East, India was a much earlier and fuller developer of print capitalism, a development most vividly seen in the trade of the Hindu businessman Nawāl Kishawr ('Nawal Kishore') in printing Qurans for foreign markets in the latter part of the nineteenth century. As in Calcutta, the earlier development of printing in Indian and oceanic languages owed much to the Christian missionary firms which in Chapter 2 we have already seen publishing tracts and scripture portions in the Indian languages used in Bombay. From its very beginnings, vernacular printing was polemical and competitive, both partaking in and helping to create the wider religious economy. Then, as in other parts of India, it was with the spread of lithography rather than typography that in significant measure vernacular printing broke away from its early missionary and governmental sponsors.[13]

First and foremost, the lithographic process that enabled this expansion of Islamic printing in India was an industrial technique; and it was this that allowed the industrializing port city of Bombay to have early access to it. Having been invented in 1804 by the Bavarian comic actor Aloys Senefelder (1771–1834), lithographic printing (or 'chemical lithography', as Senefelder termed it) relied on the industrial application of new forms of scientific knowledge by way of geology and chemistry. While a map with Persian place-names was printed in Calcutta by the pioneering Asiatic Lithographic Press in 1826, Bombay's importance to Persian printing can be seen in the fact that lithography was successfully

used there to print an entire Persian text as early as 1828.[14] This was a
full four years before the first lithographic book was issued even in Iran
in 1832.[15] While Bombay's first Persian lithographic text, the *Risāla-ye
istishhādāt* of 1828 whose contents were discussed in Chapter 1, was
not a Muslim text as such, it is significant that it was printed by a Parsi
rather than a Briton and was concerned with controversy and competition between the city's different religious groups.[16] An inspection of surviving copies of the book shows that the technical venture was so early
that its printer, Mullā Firōz, had to use what appears to be watermarked
English pre-cut writing paper sourced from the colonial bureaucracy
rather than conventional reams of printing paper. Yet in being printed
four years before the first lithographic book was issued in Iran, and two
years before lithography was introduced to what would subsequently
become its greatest Indian centre in Lucknow, the *Risāla-ye istishhādāt*
marked an extremely important development in the printing of Persian
no less than Gujarati in which industrializing Bombay took centre stage.
Issued in Gujarati from one end of the book and Persian from the other,
the treatise was printed on the same lithographic press used to print the
Bombā'ī Samāchār Gujarati newspaper, so pointing to the intimate links
between religious production and commercial enterprise.

Still in advance of both Iran and North India, the three years that followed the printing of the *Risāla-ye istishhādāt* saw several more Persian
texts printed through lithography in Bombay. These included Ahmad
Ghaffarī's *Tārīkh-e Nigāristān* (printed in 1245/1829); Sikandar ibn
Muhammad's famous history of Gujarat, *Mir'āt-e Sikandarī* (printed in
1246/1831); and Muhammad Qāsim Firishta's *Tārīkh-e Firishta* (printed
in 1831).[17] While, as three of the most important works of early modern Persian historiography, these texts were all published under colonial
auspices and interests, it was the technology of printing rather than the
choice of subject matter that was to prove more important. Although
the printed colophons of the *Nigāristān* and *Mir'āt-e Sikandarī* mention the supervision of Captain George Jervis (Jārj Jarwīs), who oversaw the printing house established in Bombay under the governorship of
Mountstuart Elphinstone, and the much more accomplished edition of the
Tārīkh-e Firishta was printed at Bombay's Government College Press, the
books' colophons also record the names of the Muslim scribes or printers
whose skills brought these pioneering Persian lithographs into existence,
namely Muhammad Rizā'ī al-Hamzawī al-Musawī al-Shīrāzī and Mīrzā
Ahmad Shīrāzī. Through the exposure of such Muslims to the new technology, by the 1840s lithographic printing began to spread beyond the

colonial printing houses to printing firms established and owned by Muslims themselves.[18] As hinted in the names of Captain Jarvis's assistants, Bombay Muslims of Iranian origin were early participants in these developments. As Chapter 4 discusses in more detail, among the most important Muslim lithographic printers of Persian were the family of the Iranian 'king of books' (*malik al-kuttāb*) Muhammad Husayn-e Shīrāzī, who were active in Bombay for over half a century.

Much of Bombay's vernacular printing was carried out in the former Bread Market in the Fort district, though other printing workshops were located in the 'Indian Town' to the west and north, where many of the city's Muslims were resident and owned their businesses.[19] In the hands of outfits such as the Anglo-Persian Printing Press at 642 Frere Road in the Fort, Bombay made important ongoing contributions to Persian printing, and in the long term stood only second to Lucknow in the number of Persian lithographs it produced.[20] The market for Persian books was upheld not only by a domestic readership but also by a large overseas market in Iran, and even as far away as Central Asia.[21] As seen in more detail later in Chapters 4 and 5, Iranians were keen participants in Bombay's printing market, as both producers and consumers. Still, in the period with which this book is concerned we should not exaggerate the reach of the printed word, even in urban environments such as Bombay. In the mid-1860s there were fewer than six printers and booksellers per thousand residents of the city, a figure we might compare with the nine 'priests' (or twelve prostitutes) per thousand.[22] Embodied religion was still more familiar than textual religion, a fact that underwrote the continued 'incorporation' of the rituals and holy men of Customary Islamic firms.

Given that in demographic terms illiteracy remained the norm among Indian Muslims well into the 1900s, this is scarcely surprising. As late as 1919, having produced official statistics to demonstrate the low literacy rate among India's Muslims, the Bombay-based missionary Henry Lane-Smith could still write that Muslim 'illiteracy is the missionary's greatest enemy'.[23] But the relatively small proportion of printing-presses to residents of Bombay should not disguise the impact of these printers and their machines, both within and beyond the city. In terms of the Muslim section of the new print market, from its inception Islamic printing in Bombay was not only Persian but a multilingual and trans-regional affair, with texts being issued in Gujarati and Urdu, Arabic and Tamil, Malay and Swahili. In around 1875 the sultan of Zanzibar even imported a typographic press from Bombay to establish the first Muslim printing-house in his domains, using it to print works in Swahili as well as Arabic.[24]

Bombay was anyway already producing books in Arabic and Swahili for sale in Zanzibar on the machines of the Munshī Karīm Press, and Munshī Karīm himself kept a local agent in Zanzibar to distribute his products. Later in the century Bombay's connections with Zanzibar saw Parsi entrepreneurs from Bombay founding their own printing-presses there as well. The westerly connections of Bombay's print market even reached as far as West Africa, with works of the Nigerian mystic Muhammad ibn Muhammad al-Fulānī (d. 1155/1742) being printed in the city during the 1880s.[25] For example, al-Fulānī's Arabic talismanic and astrological manual *al-Durr al-manzun wa khulāsat al-sirr al-maktum fi 'ilm al-talāsim wa'l-nujūm* was printed in Bombay in 1885. Despite the global reach of this new economy of print, this was once again no simple expression of Modernism or Pan-Islamism, for what were printed in Bombay were al-Fulānī's works on numerology and letter magic. In Africa no less than India, Bombay printing fed into a wider economy of enchantment.

Scripturalizing Reformists were certainly busy founding their own presses and distributing their books. But they competed with a publishing industry that supplied the familiar customary religious works that people wanted to read rather than what Reformists thought they ought to read. Muslim Tamil printing (that is, Tamil in Arabic script) is a case in point, for prior to the rise of printing, Muslim hagiographical writings seem not to have existed in Tamil: the classic genre of religious enchantment emerged only with the widening of market participation that came with printing.[26] Similarly, it was only the final decades of the nineteenth century that saw the translation into Malay of Indian-printed Urdu *hikāyat* 'storybooks' of saintly deeds and conversion legends.[27] We find Bombay-printed Urdu texts being used as the basis for translations into Malay, enabling trans-oceanic exchanges to be repainted for consumption in more familiar local languages, as well as cases of Muslim religious books being printed in Bombay in Javanese.[28] Bombay Arabic texts also circulated throughout South-East Asia.[29] As the following chapters show, Bombay's impact on the new economy of print also involved exporting Persian books to Iran at one end of the ocean and Urdu books to South Africa at the other. In the same way that from the mid-nineteenth century Bombay's capitalist cosmopolitanism saw the creation of new habits of restaurant dining, so did the multiple language communities to which the city was tied fuel a new market of printing.[30]

By the time Bombay developed this commercial printing economy in the 1850s, the handful of printing centres in the Middle East were still dominated by governmental and missionary presses operating with the smaller appeal of ideological rather than market-driven products.[31] But in Bombay's marketplace, both within the city and beyond it, consumers were able to buy books that they wanted to read rather being supplied with books that they were expected to read. Although Reformist printing was part of the picture, it by no means represented the full gamut of Muslim printing. The growing number of commercial printers instead responded to the tastes of their readers in the marketplace, and for very large numbers of the reading and listening consumers of cheap vernacular print, in religious terms this meant tastes that were still informed by custom. Later chapters describe how Customary Islamic firms printed and distributed hagiographies that publicized the deeds of their founders. Propagandist and vanity hagiography was therefore also part of the picture, although it was helped by appealing to the tastes of an existing market of readers.

SOME BOOKS FROM THE BOMBAY MARKETPLACE

As with the early history of the city's newspapers, early instances of religious printing do point to the alignment of printing with 'Protestantizing' Muslim Reform. This early aspect of Bombay printing is seen through the early publication of Qurans in the city, in many cases being editions accompanied by interlinear commentaries in Urdu.[32] As early as the 1840s such works as the *Tafsīr fath al-'azīz* (Commentary on the victorious spiritual openings) were being printed, which contained the last thirty-six suras of the Quran alongside an Urdu translation of the famous Persian commentary by Shāh 'Abd al-'Azīz of Delhi (d. 1239/1824).[33] This pattern of printing 'scripture portions' was commonplace, and can be understood as a reaction to the introduction of the practice by Christian missionary firms in Bombay, who we have seen printing vast numbers of Bible portions.[34] A number of such Bible portions included interlinear translations into the languages used by the city's Muslims, such as Urdu and Gujarati, but even in this case Arabic prayers and admonitions were more commonplace than scripture as such in translation. While Bombay's printers could therefore make scripture more accessible, paving the way for the scripturalism and individualism associated with the Muslim Reformists, translations or commentaries on scripture were only a relatively small part of a larger print market. Even where Quranic verses did appear in print, it was often in the form of talismanic texts aimed at the use of scripture for apotropaic purposes. While this was printed scripture of a kind, it was not scripture intended for individual comprehension. It was rather the use of printing to multiply the customary usage of scripture for talismans. Such texts were by no means uniquely Indian productions, and nineteenth-century Egyptian printed talismanic Quran portions have been found circulating the Indian Ocean as far south as the Comoros.[35] However major a participant it was, Bombay's economy of print still operated in a larger oceanic marketplace.

Turning away from Arabic, a considerable proportion of Bombay's Persian printed books consisted of familiar classics that had for centuries enjoyed wide reception in India, such as the mystical verse of Jalāl al-dīn Rūmī (d. 672/1273) that Jāmī had famously called the Quran in Persian (*Qur'ān dar zabān-e pahlawī*). Aside from such broadly esteemed classics (which many Reformists also respected), the continued popularity in print of hagiographical and other intercessionary texts points to the way in which Customary Islam was no less empowered by print than Reform.[36] Bombay's printed contribution to Customary Islamic trends partly came by way of such 'classical' works, including hagiographies whose abundance of reprints in catalogues of early Muslim printed texts shows the scale of popular demand for such works in the late nineteenth and early twentieth centuries. Although Bombay's printers could not compete with the outputs of North Indian commercial giants such as Nawāl Kishawr of Lucknow, from mid-century onwards they still printed large numbers of classic Muslim hagiographies.[37] This process of custom reproduced in print reflected the tastes of the Muslim readership which shaped the Indian book market, a readership that was arguably more concentrated and populous than any other in the Islamic world. Even as knowledge of Persian was declining in India, this market continued to provide demand for printed Persian hagiographies well into the twentieth century. One example is the *Rashahāt-e 'ayn al-hayāt* (Sprinklings from the spring of life) of Wā'iz Kāshifī (d. 910/1504) of Herat, the classic account of the feats of the Naqshbandī saints which went through at least nine Indian editions between 1890 and 1911.[38] The great expansion in hagiographical printing was not limited to the Persian classics and encompassed most of the languages spoken by Bombay's Muslims, from Gujarati to Urdu. In turn, the success of such publishing ventures helped promote the writing of new works, and Indian lithographic editions of new hagiographical texts – dealing with non-Indian as well as Indian Sufis – appeared in large numbers during the late nineteenth and early twentieth centuries. Still, India was by no means the sole region in which this hagiographical enchantment of printing was flourishing in the early twentieth century. In the similarly modernizing port city of Beirut, Arabic hagiography was also being reinvigorated in such works as the *Jami' karāmāt al-awliyā* (Compendium of saintly miracles) of the

Naqshbandī Sufi and Qāzī of Beirut, Shaykh Yūsuf ibn Ismāʿīl al-Nabahānī (d. 1350/1931).[39] Enabled by print, in Bombay as in Beirut, these stories of miracles were not limited to Bombay's city limits, but reached out to wherever its publications were distributed. Powered by the new technologies of lithographic printing and industrialized paper production, through distributing miracle stories the printed economy of enchantment allowed a much greater magnification of the status of living holy men or customary pilgrimage shrines than was possible in the pre-industrial era.[40]

While the process of printed enchantment was in part one of the dissemination of larger numbers of lithographically mass-produced books, it also interacted with the increasing mobility of the entrepreneurial holy man himself. Here Bombay's printers were responding to the new level of movement which saw Muslims from around the Indian Ocean moving in and out of Bombay through its role as the hub of oceanic steamship routes.[41] The next chapter presents a case study of one such migrant shaykh, Safi ʿAlī Shāh, whose visits to Bombay saw him making use of the greater availability of printing technology to publish his first and most famous work. For now, let us take the example of the peculiar literary anthology entitled *Tabarrukāt-e nūrānī al-maʿrūf bih gulzār-e Gīlānī* (Radiant blessings, known as Gilani's flower garden), which consisted of a collection of multi-lingual *qasīda* poems for Sayyid Ibrāhīm Sayf al-dīn al-Qādirī Effendī, the shrine-manager and family heir of the great medieval saint of Baghdad, ʿAbd al-Qādir Jīlānī (d. 561/1166).[42] The anthology was printed in Bombay in 1912, when Sayyid Ibrāhīm visited his many followers there, who would themselves have known him through the increasing Indian pilgrimage traffic to the shrine of ʿAbd al-Qādir in Baghdad, accessed through the earliest of the steamship routes linking Bombay with Basra.[43] The text consisted of six praise-songs in Arabic, Persian and the 'commonly understood' (*ʿām fahm*) Urdu which were composed for Sayyid Ibrāhīm by Sayyid Jamīl al-Rahmān Rāshid of Delhi and the local Bombay poet Ahmad ibn Seth Hājjī Sadīq Kahtarī. In print, the poems followed an introduction which celebrated the saintly visitor in the hierarchical terms of Customary Islam – as 'his most holy honour' (*ʿālī-janāb-e taqaddus māb*) and so forth – that set the saintly friends of God apart from the ordinary run of Muslims.[44] In such works as this neglected multilingual anthology we see the appropriation of mobility and print by which the saintly intercessors reached new audiences in the cosmopolitan cities of the Indian Ocean.

While the printing practices that defended Customary Islam were multifarious, it is the hagiography that deserves special attention. Comprising the overlapping genres of the *manāqib, tazkira* and *tabaqa,* through print-ing the Muslim hagiography expanded to a degree unprecedented in his-tory, a process that we can understand as the market-driven enchantment of technology.[45] As Bombay entered its half-century of greatest influence from the 1860s, its printers began to issue a range of texts celebrating the feats of holy men both old and new. Half a century before Sayyid Ibrāhīm visited Bombay from Baghdad, the life of his celebrated ancestor 'Abd al-Qādir Jīlānī found printed voice in Bombay in Qāzī Muhammad Yūsuf's *Zayn al-majālis* (Adornment of the assembly), which extolled the miraculous deeds of the great saint in several hundred pages of verse.[46] In addition to poetry, the more common prose forms of hagiography assem-bled collections of 'advertizing' stories that could be easily remembered and transmitted in speech.

Given the cosmopolitan character of Bombay's Muslim population and of its overseas reading markets, such hagiographies appeared in a range of languages, from Arabic and Persian to Gujarati, Tamil, Urdu and Malay. One Arabic example is the *Hikāyat al-sālihīn* (Tales of the righteous) of 'Uthmān ibn 'Umar al-Kahf, printed in Bombay in 1876.[47] A classic cheap-print edition of just over a hundred lithographic pages of unbleached Indian-made paper, the text comprised a series of chapters on specific moral themes, each divided into tales (*hikāyat*) of the prophets and saints to illustrate the theme in question. Chapter 7 dealt with the miracles of the saints (*karāmat al-awliyā*), its restriction to such early Sufis as Ibrāhīm ibn Adham (d. 163/779), Junayd Baghdādī (d. 298/910) and Sahl Tustarī (d. 311/896) illustrating the fact that these customary saintly figures could still be held up as behavioural exemplars who supplemented the praxis of Muhammad.[48] In a reflection of India's largely unregulated publishing industry, the Bombay edition of *Hikāyat al-sālihīn* was an Arabic trans-lation of a Persian original, of which other editions appeared from North Indian printers a few years later. Such works were financially worth pirating. Another example of such hagiographies is Muhammad Mahdī Wāsif's *Anīs al-zākirīn* (Companion of the remembrancers), which appeared from the same Bombay press as *Hikāyat al-sālihīn* in 1871.[49] A similar cheap-print lithograph, this time in a mere twenty pages of Urdu, *Anīs al-zākirīn* con-tained stories demonstrating the wiles of Satan/Iblīs and the ways in which from Noah/Nūh and Moses/Mūsā through to Jesus/'Īsā and Muhammad, the various prophets had dealt with him. These were well-known and well-loved stories: Satan stealing onto Noah's ark on the tail of a donkey (*gadhā*), asking Moses to ask God to accept his repentance and God then demanding Satan prostrate himself on the tomb of Adam. But in the new

FIGURE 9. Lithographic enchantment: The adventures of Hātim Tā'ī (dated 1326/1908)

urban marketplace that Bombay presented, with its growing population of nominally Muslim workers divested of their traditional community structures of memory, works such as *Anīs al-zākirīn* formed an effective way of transferring religious knowledge to a migrant population detached from its former links to the village shrine or mosque. In an example of the mnemonic devices through which such writings entered the urban arena of spoken memory, each of the stories in *Anīs al-zākirīn* ended with an easily remembered couplet that encapsulated its moral message.

It was not only stories of the prophets that were printed in Bombay, and such works tapped into a larger market for entertaining stories that was also fed by collections of supernatural folktales such as those compiled in the *'Ajā'ib al-hikāyat* (Strange tales) of 1883 or the Urdu versions of the fantastic adventures of the ancient Arab hero Hātim Tā'ī, such as the *Ārā'ish-e mahfil* (Ornament of the assembly) of 1326/1908, which set dozens of stories of Hātim's escapades among the genies, *divs* and other supernatural creatures alongside delightful lithographic line-drawings.[50] More importantly, the city was also notable for publishing encomia of saintly deeds, hagiographies which variously celebrated the Muslim holy men linked to the city's brotherhood firms. Among these was the *Silsilat al-'ārifīn* (Genealogy of gnostics), a Persian hagiography of the great Iranian Sufi Shāh Ni'matullāh Walī (d. 834/1431), which appeared in Bombay in 1890, while among the most interesting new hagiographies printed in Bombay was the *Riyāz-e sūfī* (Labours of the Sufi) on the life of the Counter Reform missionary to South Africa Ghulām Muhammad 'Sūfī Sāhib' (d. 1329/1911), which was printed in Bombay for the South African market two years after his death.[51] The connections that each of these texts forged between the Bombay market and its oceanic hinterlands are discussed in detail in Chapters 4, 5 and 7.[52]

STEAMSHIPS, SAINTS AND MIRACLES

If printing has been more commonly connected to the rise of Muslim Reform, in the previous section we have seen the technology's use to reproduce books that strengthened, and indeed advertised, Customary Islamic firms and their holy men and shrines. No less important to Bombay's religious economy were the accelerated forms of travel that allowed both Reformist and Customary Islamic firms to conduct missionary itineraries and other means of distributing their message.[53] As in the case of printing, the new era of the steamship and railway has been most commonly associated with Reformist trends, particularly the sub-trend of Pan-Islamism.[54]

Once again, to some degree this was accurate. Nineteenth-century colonial administrators were understandably concerned that the vastly increased number of Indian *hajj* pilgrims enabled by Bombay's steamship routes would lead to the spread of anti-British 'Wahhabism' or other expressions of Pan-Islamist sympathy.[55] But in actual fact, the only point at which such organizations did become major players in the city's religious economy was after 1915 when the defeat of the Ottomans in the First World War led to the creation of the Khilāfat (or 'Caliphate') movement among Indian Muslims. Although Bombay's Muslims, and the communications infrastructure of Bombay more generally, did play a significant role in the Pan-Islamist Khilāfat movement, it remained predominantly a North Indian organization that in any case did not emerge until after the period with which we are concerned in this book.[56] In the period from 1840 to 1915 at least, the expansion of industrial travel created a more plural set of religious trajectories that, as in the case of printing, empowered customary forms of religious loyalty no less than novel affiliations to a globalized *umma*.

Bombay was among the earliest places in the world to see the new powers of steam put to navigational purpose, affecting not only India but Arabia and Africa no less.[57] In the 1816 *Jān-e Bombā'i*, the port was already being celebrated: lit up at night by the novelty of a lighthouse (*līt-haws*), its crowded harbour of huge regal ships (*jihāzāt-e bādshāhī*) carried in travellers of every land and race (*az har mulkī, har ajnāsī*).[58] Although the first steamship had reached Bombay from London as early as 1825, it was from 1850 that the great age of the Indian Ocean steamships was truly under way. The adoption of the screw propeller in around 1880 then allowed even larger ships to sail on smaller quantities of coal and so bring down the cost of sea travel for large numbers of ordinary people, in the Atlantic no less than the Indian Ocean. And at the heart of the Indian Ocean's shipping networks stood Bombay.[59] As the volume of steam navigation increased from the middle of the century, so did the topography of Bombay itself, seeing the massive construction of docks that included the P&O dockyards in Mazagaon, whose religious productions are explored in Chapter 6. These constructions were part of a wider set of developments that comprised a genuine communications revolution, not least when placed next to what we have seen of the spread of printing in India in the same decades. Thus the first telegraph wires linking Bombay with Calcutta were laid as early as 1854, and were in turn expanded across the ocean via a network of relay points that mirrored the coal depots of the steamships to reach the imperial centre in London.[60] A year

earlier, in 1853, Bombay also heralded a new age of industrial land travel
with the opening of Asia's first passenger-train service.[61] By 1856 the city
was driving the creation of the Great Indian Peninsular Railway, the East
Indian Railway and the Baroda and Central India Railway. For these reasons, Bombay assumed a central position in the Muslim travel itineraries
and the larger Muslim communications revolution of the nineteenth century. As one Indian resident of the city rhetorically asked in the *Bombay
Chronicle* newspaper in 1914:

> Do we not see every year how when trade is active in the busy sea-
> son people come from the south and north, especially the Pathans,
> the Afghans and others, throng[ing] to our markets? Then look at the
> number of Arab and Somali and other Mahomedan mariners, crews of
> buglows from Muscat, Makalla, Aden, Basra and Zanzibar who are to
> be seen in large numbers at our docks and more distant bunders.[62]

As noted earlier, the new networks of travel did bring the great Pan-
Islamist Jamāl al-dīn al-Afghānī to Bombay as a young man in the mid-
1850s, and in the wake of the 'Indian Mutiny' of 1857–8 British officials
were concerned about the possible implications of the increased *hajj* traffic on the spread of 'Wahhabi' or what would eventually be termed Pan-
Islamist ideas among the Muslims of India, as well as with the diseases
that pilgrims also brought home.[63] Yet such was the concern among colonial officials that regulating pilgrim shipping would also have detrimental
effects on the smooth flow of merchant vessels into Bombay that a laissez-
faire policy triumphed so as to see the number of sailboat and steamship
hājjis increase dramatically.[64] Even with regard to the flow of participants in the Mecca pilgrimage, Bombay's religious economy was characterized by deregulation. As with the influx of migrant workers brought to
Bombay by the industrializing economy at large, the greater availability
of pilgrim ships brought the problem of increasing numbers of poor pilgrims to Bombay.[65] As early as the 1850s it was reported that:

> Annually there is a large concourse here of pilgrims to Mecca, from
> Sind, the Punjab, Kashmere, Delhi, Lucknow, Peshawar, Afghanistan,
> Bengal, and other countries, Bombay being the principal port of embar-
> kation for the Red Sea. Some of these pilgrims are rich, and a large por-
> tion able to maintain themselves, but many are supported during their
> stay by Mussulman families. Again, on their return from the *Hajj*, when
> the proportion of the destitute is much greater, they are fed and clothed,
> and helped on their way to their homes. The number of pilgrims who
> arrive on their way to Mecca or Medina ranges from five hundred to a
> thousand, males and females.[66]

By the early 1900s the Indian pilgrimage traffic was supported by an effective information network by which travellers in various regions of India were able to learn how to acquire tickets for a steamship in Bombay. Often such information was given within new printed narratives, as in the case of the Urdu travelogue of Ḥāfiẓ 'Abd al-Rahmān, which recounted a tour made in 1898 – not primarily to Mecca, but to Egypt, Algeria and Turkey. Although published in Lahore, 'Abd al-Rahmān's travelogue gave its readers precise details of what they must do on stepping off the train at Bombay: how to approach the agents who sold ship tickets; how often different types of ship sailed; what the charges were for the different classes of cabin; how to arrange suitable food to carry on board ship; and by this period the important matter of how to acquire a passport.[67] Yet if colonial officials were concerned about the support that such easier Indian travel to the Middle East would lend to 'Wahhabism' or Pan-Islamism, an examination of the traffic between the modern forms of transport that enabled Bombay's flow of peoples and the stories of miracles that resounded in the steamships' wake shows how the increasing availability of steam transportation was also turned into increased pilgrim revenues and the production of printed advertisements for the shrines of the saints. At the same time, old customary routes were reinvigorated by the tread of new generations of steam pilgrims. This was as true of steam travel on land as it was at sea. The shrine of Mu'in al-dīn Chishtī (d. 633/1236) at Ajmer in Rajputana was put within reach of poor pilgrims all over India by the town's connection to the railway through Ajmer's selection as headquarters of British Rajputana. Modern technology amplified the pilgrim traffic further with the printing in simple Urdu of such cheap guidebooks as Munshī Sivanāth's *Sayr-e Ajmēr* (Journey to Ajmer), which directed pilgrims from Bombay between the train station, the grand portals of Mayo College, the cloth markets, the fancy new clock tower, and eventually the shrine itself.[68]

Like the printed side of the communications revolution, the transport side was also therefore used to empower Customary Islamic firms. As the main Indian Ocean hub for these new forms of travel, the shipping lanes of Bombay became major generators of such miraculous advertisements. This was not so much the concerted ideological attack on modern technology sometimes found in the writings of the *'ulamā* at this time.[69] On the contrary, the participants in these miraculous stories were keen consumers of the new modes of transport. What mattered was that they presented the new powers of steam, and later electricity, as secondary – and, indeed, subject – to the customary enchanted powers of the saints. This is not unlike the situation Dipesh Chakrabarty has noted in the industrial jute mills of Calcutta, where the efficient operation of machinery was seen to be dependent on the ritual sacrifice of goats with 'the factory and the power-machine ... given due place in religious ceremony'.⁷⁰ It was the enhanced appeal of these supernatural powers to the vastly increased number of sea travellers facilitated by the steamship revolution that brought about an enchantment of the new maritime technology.⁷¹

Muslim saints had for centuries acted as the supernatural protectors of travellers on the Indian Ocean. In this, seafarers reflected a wider *modus operandi* of pre-modern travel in which the supernatural insurance of saintly protection played an important role. A helpful example is seen in the overland travels of the great Ottoman admiral Sayyidī ʿAlī Raʾīs (d. 970/1563), who after the wreck of his ship off the western coast of India returned to Anatolia by land via an itinerary that was regularly punctuated with visits to the shrines of the saints. Recorded in his *Mirʾāt al-mamālik* (Mirror of the kingdoms), Sayyidī ʿAlī's journey reflected a wider pattern of customary travel in which shrines played myriad roles as hostels, staging posts, horse exchanges, markets, storehouses and tourist sites no less than as suppliers of supernatural insurance: the saint (*walī*) was the hidden governor of his own territorial fiefdom (*wilāyat*). In several cases these pilgrimages of convenience resulted in dreams in which Sayyidī ʿAlī was assured of a safe passage home.⁷² The very commonality of such customs points to the tenacious association of the saints with the Muslim experience of sea travel. The shrine of Shaykh Makhdūm ʿAlī on the edge of Bombay that was described in Chapter 2 grew in importance in the nineteenth century through the increase in the number of travellers requiring his intercessionary protection. As a result, the year 1875 saw the composition of a new Arabic hagiography entitled *Zamīr al-insān* (Most scrupulous of men).⁷³ The main narrative sections of the text comprised an account of Shaykh Makhdūm's meeting with the 'green man' Khizr (*malāqāt al-khidhr*) and the miracles (*khawāraqa*) he wrought in both childhood and adulthood.⁷⁴ The saint's maritime associations were here apparent. Given that we have seen how Khizr was himself the universal patron of seafarers, his meeting with the more local saintly sea patron Shaykh Makhdūm is particularly apposite. In turn, *Zamīr al-insān* advertized how Shaykh Makhdūm protected merchants (*al-tujjār*) and rescued foundering ships (*markab*) by guiding them safely into port at Mahim, where by the time of the book's writing his shrine stood overlooking the coast.⁷⁵ As the years passed, further stories began to spread in advertisement of the shrine's powers. Miraculous narratives recorded in later sources depict the saint helping Hindu merchants recover cargoes lost at sea and aiding a poor local boy in a contest to complete the *hajj* more quickly than a wealthy Arab trader who owned his own ship.[76] Clearly, such shrines offered desirable services to sea-travellers. In a reflection of the oceanic reach of such patterns of religious productivity, the movement of large numbers of Indian merchants and pilgrims between India, Mecca and Singapore in the nineteenth century led to the foundation in Singapore of a similar franchise shrine to the great patron of Tamil Muslim seafarers Shāh al-Hamīd of Nagore.[77]

The increasing availability of sea travel to ordinary Indian Muslims in the nineteenth century brought about a corresponding increase in the demand for miraculous protection on the ocean. While the number of mobile Indian Muslims certainly increased during the last decades of the nineteenth century, for most of the pilgrims this mobility was not accompanied by any increase in the comforts of travel. As one unsympathetic observer described the appearance of a sailing-ship of returning *hājjīs* entering Bombay harbour in the 1870s:

> We found that a dhow which had just returned from Jeddah was discharging pilgrims from the sacred shrines of Mecca and Medina into a numerous squadron of felucca-rigged jollyboats. Veiled women, attenuated boys, reverend and bearded men were piled up in these native crafts as uncomfortably as a shipwrecked crew in a lifeboat. Most rueful did they look, most vilely did they smell, travel-stained and inexpressibly dirty were they.[78]

It was amid these circumstances of cheaper but correspondingly incommodious sea journeys that the demand for supernatural protection grew in tandem with the number of Muslims set upon the waves for the first time in their lives by the more competitive economy of Indian Ocean travel. This was no less the case for travellers on steamships as it was for those on the older sailing-boats, as the Yorkshire sailor Jack Keane (1854–1937) found when travelling third class in 1877 on a steamship bearing Indian pilgrims back from Mecca to Bombay. While the ship stowed 50 wealthy pilgrims 'first class' in the cabin, there were another 1,300 stowed third class on the main and lower decks. Keane's description of their on-board conditions gives us a vivid picture of the circumstances of fear and discomfort that stoked the demand for seaborne miracles:

> When I state that these were all huddled together, men, women, and children, indiscriminately, and were so put to it for space that there literally was not room for all to lie down at the same time, it will be

understood why, to many of the pilgrims, the sea voyage has greater terrors than the land journey. During our passage of twenty-one days to Bombay, not a day passed without its death; and on one fine morning three corpses were dragged up from the foul lower-deck, out of the midst of a reeking throng of penned-up human beings.[79]

It is little wonder that the *hajj* became internationally recognized as one of the principal vectors of the global cholera epidemics of the late nineteenth and early twentieth centuries, adding further to the anxiety of embarking on the overcrowded steamships. Fuelled by such conditions as the century progressed, miracle stories therefore continued to circulate and to take on new forms in Bombay, adapting themselves to the new conditions of travel or absorbing elements of the colonial experience to add to the prestige of the saint in question. In Chapter 7 we will hear an account of cholera-vanishing miracles on the steamer to South Africa. The scale of these miraculous rumours occasionally combined with their intrinsic fascination to cross over into the English-medium press. In 1926 another such account appeared in the *Times of India* with reference to the *hajj* carried out from Bombay in 1903 by the Muslim holy woman, Bābā Jān (d. 1931) of Poona in the Bombay Presidency. In a strange meeting of miracles and machines, the report described how during a terrible storm on the journey from Bombay to the Red Sea, 'she saved the steamer from being dashed to pieces after all the passengers, including the European ones, had promised to garland the grave of the Holy Prophet'.[80] Given that Bābā Jān had previously spent several years living rough on the streets of Bombay, the *Times* report was an ironical inversion of the usual social hierarchy of newspaper reporting, placing a street beggar in the news columns beside the great and good of empire. In other cases, such stories of enchanted travel found expression in the new spate of hagiographies that we have seen flourished in the era of print.

A series of similar narratives is preserved in *A'zam al-karāmāt* (Greatest of miracles), an early twentieth-century Urdu printed hagiography of Bābā Jān's contemporary, Banē Miyān (d. 1339/1921), a former colonial soldier turned *faqīr* residing in Aurangabad to the east of Bombay. Here miraculous intervention was described in more vivid terms than the sober prose of the *Times of India*. According to *A'zam al-karāmāt*, when a storm hit his steamship on his way to perform the *hajj*, a devotee named Hasan al-dīn was saved by resorting to the customary technique of 'picturing' (*tasawwur*) Banē Miyān.[81] Here was a practical outcome of the doctrines of intercession and rituals of 'picturing the shaykh' (*tasawwur-e shaykh*) described in Chapter 6 being taught in Bombay by such preachers as Habīb 'Alī Shāh, whose own lodge was conveniently located beside the P&O dockyard in Bombay's Mazagaon quarter. Reflecting the story associated with the shrine of Shaykh Makhdūm of Bombay, another narrative in *A'zam al-karāmāt* described Banē Miyān miraculously finding the money for a poor devotee to complete the *hajj*, so by miracle connecting Customary Islam to the basic tenets of the faith in a way that also echoes the wider attempts of Customary and particularly Counter Reform leaders to bolster their productions with the moral support of *sharī'a*.[82] Such pauper pilgrims, who often left Bombay with no funds for return from – or even maintenance during – their travels, were considered a serious problem by both colonial and Muslim authorities. The saint's prediction of the permanent limp that the follower later sustained after falling from his camel on the desert road between the steamboats' arrival point at Jidda and the holy city of Medina is also a reminder of the hazards that the *hajj* still involved in 1900.[83] Elsewhere, *A'zam al-karāmāt* passed on the report of a man who in 1884 claimed to have come across twenty-five Indian soldiers of the Hyderabad Contingent who were visiting to make an offering at the shrine of Afzal Shāh Biyābānī (d. 1273/1856), way inland from Bombay at Qazipeth to the north of Hyderabad (albeit right beside the railway track laid in the 1860s). The soldiers described how their ship had been caught in a storm on the way to Jidda. When the ship started to sink, and the captain told the passengers that all was lost, they too prayed to Banē Miyān to intercede for them, and five minutes later he promptly appeared in the waves, supporting the keel of the steamship on his shoulder. When the English captain demanded to know who this *diwāna* (madman) was, in a mixing of customary Muslim and colonial terminology the soldiers replied that he was their 'Sufi master padre' or *pīr pādrī*.[84] In the oral versions of the story that are still current at the saint's shrine in Aurangabad, Banē Miyān is presented as having proven his presence at the scene by displaying a great bruise on his shoulder where he had carried the ship.[85] The image of the bearded old man bearing the iron hulk of a steamship on his shoulder is a potent icon indeed.

In the decades either side of 1900 such stories were a common feature of the cheap-print hagiographical works issued in Bombay and sold at its shrines, fairs and markets. These were not free-floating and rootless tales, but printed advertisements for the powers and services of particular shrines or holy men associated with them. As such, the advertisements played an important part in the religious economy of the Indian Ocean, and their increasing production and distribution was a sign of the growing

FIGURE 10. The ocean industrialized: A steamship in Bombay harbour, *c.* 1890

competitiveness of the unregulated religious marketplace. Such talk of economy is not to rob the stories of their moral purpose; indeed, Customary Islam was so successful precisely because of its ability to link its moral imperatives to attractive products (miracles) advertised through efficient means of distribution (cheap print). In this respect, it is worth making a parallel between the way in which stories of miraculous seaborne rescues formed the turning-points of conversion narratives among not only the Customary Islamic organizations of the Indian Ocean but also among the Evangelicals and Methodists of the Atlantic a century earlier.[86] Relying on the familiar wonders of the customary universe, such narrative advertisements swayed people into following holy men and their religious firms and entering the moral communities which they created in turn.

Muslim travellers were wise to seek out such forms of supernatural insurance, for sea travel in the steam age was still fraught with a good many dangers. Much of the nineteenth- and early twentieth-century pilgrim traffic crossed the ocean in boats in which European merchants would not even have trusted their goods, let alone their families. Paradoxically, as the nineteenth century wore on and ocean steamer and then liner technology improved, the conditions of safety and comfort for thousands of *hājjīs* declined. As time passed and new types of ship were built, merchants sold on an increasing number of the first- and second-generation steamers and obsolete sailing boats to small-time navigation companies that carried on an unscrupulous trade in squeezing too many 'pious natives' above and below the decks of their coal-burning rust buckets. A full storm on one of these still small *hajj* sailboats or steamers could be terrifying indeed, and besides featuring in the many printed saintly stories of the period, in 1900 such circumstances also formed the premise for Joseph Conrad's *Lord Jim*, in whose contrastingly disenchanted world a crew of European drunkards desert their steamship's cargo of Muslim pilgrims after a mid-storm collision at sea. Whether for Conrad or the Indian sailors of the period, for those who had tasted them, the terrors of the journey lingered long in the imagination. As more and more of these older ships entered the third- and fourth-hand market, creating a competitive market in ferrying pilgrims across the ocean, prices were driven down, creating a dual incentive for more Indian Muslims to make the *hajj* and for the low-budget *hājjīs* to be crammed onto any old vessel. Many of the steamers that serviced the lower end of the pilgrim market were not only less than seaworthy, but were in their cramped and unsanitary conditions ripe environments for the diseases such as cholera that also circulated the ocean and its pilgrim routes with greater rapidity than ever.[87] If in response the period saw the proliferation of cholera stations and quarantine regulations in ports under British control, for anyone unfortunate enough to be trapped on a quarantined ship the prospects were bleak and terrifying. It is scarcely surprising, then, that alongside the tale of the sinking steamer, the other great hagiographical theme of the period was that of the holy man rescuing pilgrims from the onboard epidemic of cholera. An accolade attributed to scores of Muslim saints and their shrine firms as the nineteenth century progressed, it also featured prominently in the 1912 Urdu printed hagiography of the Bombay oceanic missionary Ghulām Muhammad 'Sūfī Sāhib' discussed in Chapter 7.[88]

Further examples of the maritime miracle are seen in other Bombay hagiographies of the period. The *Silsilat al-'ārifīn*, a Persian biography of Shāh Ni'matullāh Walī, which we have already seen being printed in Bombay in 1307/1890, contained a classic example. A group of merchants were sailing in the Sea of Oman when their ship began to sink: when they fired an 'arrow of prayer' (*tīr-e du'ā*) towards Shāh Ni'matullāh's distant shrine a man suddenly appeared in the waves and dragged the boat by its guideropes to the safety of the shore.[89] Another version of the story is found in a lithographic *Majmū'a* (Compendium) of stories about Shāh Wajīh al-dīn 'Alawī (d. 998/1589) of Ahmadabad that was printed in Bombay in the early 1900s in a parallel Urdu/Persian edition. Among the numerous miracle services of Wajīh al-dīn that are described in the *Majmū'a* we find another version of the sea-rescue story, in which a man from Gujarat decided to make the *hajj*, and gave up his home and goods before carrying out a gift-giving pilgrimage to Wajih al-dīn's shrine en route to his embarkation point in Bombay.[90] Later, after successfully reaching the holy land, while he was solemnly sweeping the earth around the tomb of the Prophet in Medina, the thought passed through his mind that he should visit a Sufi in Syria of whom he had recently heard. Just then a voice boomed from the Prophet's grave, telling him that he had not yet even begun to discover the depths of Wajih al-dīn's wisdom and commanding him to return to India instead. However, on the return journey his ship sailed dangerously close to a mountain looming out of the water and, seeing this, his fellow passengers all began to weep and wail. Fortunately the pilgrim must have listened carefully to the Sufi impressarios of the day, for when the mountain appeared he had the presence of mind to focus his 'concentration' (*tawwajuh*) on Wajih al-dīn and so summon his miraculous intercession. The dénouement of the tale unfolded as the passengers all felt the sensation of someone lifting the foundering ship from the waves and hurling it beyond the mountain to safety. In its emphasis on 'brand' loyalty to the shrine and the reward of intercession, the narrative illustrated a central theme of Customary Islam that was coming under Reformist competitive threat at this time, while acting as an advertisement for the services of Wajih al-dīn's shrine in a period of intense internecine competition between different firms. The traveller's near decision to turn to a shrine in Syria instead of Wajih al-dīn from back home underlines this new degree of religious competition provided by the increasing number of Indians travelling beyond their home towns and villages to experience a wider world of spiritual alternatives. In a society that still placed great weight on familial and ethnic descent, particularly on descent from Arab *sayyid* lineages, other expressions of the defence of the saints are found in the genealogical charters (*nasab-nāma*) that were issued with great frequency in the later nineteenth century, as in a rhymed *masnawī* version written for Wajih al-dīn around 1860, or the 1848 Persian genealogical guide to saintly biographies entitled *Mukhbir al-awliyā* (Reports on God's friends), which included an account of Wajih al-dīn's family lineage and teachers.[91] In such ways, older shrine firms used brand pedigree against newer competitors.

Nor were such enchanted maritime texts composed only in the Indian vernaculars. Hagiographies celebrating seaborne miracles also appeared in the language usually associated with the modernist 'Anglo' Reformists such as Sir Sayyid Ahmad Khān or his Bombay associate Badr al-dīn Tayyibjī: English. An example is the anonymous *Life* of Khwāja Sayyid Matʿā al-dīn printed in Bombay in 1922.[92] The hereditary saint whose family shrine was in Mangrol in the Surat district of the Bombay Presidency, Sayyid Mat'ā al-dīn was one of the many entrepreneurial shaykhs who relocated to Bombay in the nineteenth century, his own move a reflection of the establishment of other Gujarati franchise shrine firms described in Chapter 2. Recounted in Mat'ā al-dīn's hagiography is an account of how a group of sailors of the Kharva caste were sailing down the coast from Bhavnagar to Bombay when their boat was hit by a storm.[93] 'In the hour of their danger they remembered their Pir and vowed an offering of Rs.200', the text explained, adding that 'the storm abated and when the sailors landed at Bombay they went with the offering to the Pir's quarters'.[94] The services of the holy man in offering supernatural protection for his followers are abundantly clear from the anecdote, services for which payment was demanded no less than it was by other big men in the city who offered more criminal forms of 'protection'. As seen with regard to Bombay's dock and mill workers in Chapter 6, such assurances of protection lay at the heart of the continued appeal of custom amid the technologies of the industrial era. Nonetheless, the flow of financial resources was two-way, and other stories served to advertise how even simple emotional investments in such-and-such a holy man could result in solidly material dividends. The early twentieth-century Persian biographical collection *Tarā'iq al-haqā'iq*, for example, describes how a poor woman travelling by boat from Bombay approached the Iranian merchant and Sufi Hājjī Sayyid 'Alī Āghā'ī Mazandarānī for help on board ship, explaining that her husband had gone missing and that she was now penniless. When the Hājjī discovered that her husband had died in a market in Bombay, he used his influence to collect 5,000 rupees for her from the shopkeepers and have it deposited in a bank.[95] These shaykhs were men of influence, supernatural and otherwise, and to approach them was a sensible way of getting things done.

There was of course another dimension to the marketplace popularity of such stories. In the case of printed books like the *Majmū'a*, it is clear that the publishers of such hagiographical chapbooks aimed to provide a kind of licit entertainment to an audience brought up on such tales of wonder. If the proliferation of such tales was partly a reflection of the growing number of Indians experiencing the ocean for the terrifying first time, it was also a reflection of the competitive print culture which sought to commodify the imaginative leitmotifs of the age. Not quite Penny Dreadfuls, the cheap hagiographical story books are best paralleled by the pious missionary adventure books that also typified the Victorian print world, books such as Jessie Page's popular hagiography of a heroic British 'sailor and saint'.[96] Termed 'tales' (*hikāyat*), the narrative voice of the storyteller is

apparent throughout the *Majmū'a* discussed above. Without such entice-
ments, the printers, booksellers and chapmen who dealt in these unpreten-
tious pamphlets would presumably have found few customers. Embedded
in such forms of entertainment, the stories of the miraculous deliverance
from the waves helped echo and give shape to fears and perceptions of
travel in the popular imagination. But their very existence in print is also
testament to the market connections forged between Customary Islam
and the new era of commercial printing in which spectacular tales helped
not only advertise a particular shaykh or shrine but also to sell books for
those interested in printing them. Nonetheless, it is important to grasp the
rhetoric of factuality in such narratives, for in them we hear authentic if
marginalized modern voices of the experience of Indian Ocean travel, and
of the sense of danger that even in the era of the iron steamship caused
travellers to place their faith in the blessed flesh and bone of the saints on
dry land. Even on *hajj*, the orientation of Customary Islam anchored primarily to Indian *terra firma* rather than solely to the Quranic Arabia of the
Reformists was strong enough to make pilgrims call on the patron saints
of the steamships rather than on the Prophet or God to whose scriptural
geography they were travelling.

Before beginning their journeys, travellers aboard even the most
modern steamships would often pay a visit to make cash offerings at one
of the shrines along the Bombay seaboard, such as those of Makhdūm 'Alī
or Hājjī 'Alī. Before beginning his rail journey to Bombay and thence by
steamer to Europe, even the Hyderabadi modernizer Mīr Lā'īq 'Alī Khān
Sālār Jang II sought the blessings of the Prophet's son-in-law 'Alī by making a pilgrimage to the shrine known as Mawla 'Alī.[97] Despite seeking the
Mawla's blessing, once safely en route Sālār Jang indulged his fascination
with all things modern that Bombay afforded, even going to the lengths
of staying in a hotel that was built entirely of iron.[98] Sailing from Bombay
aboard the steamer *Peshawar*, he and his Hyderabadi companions made a
careful inspection of the engine room, where they quizzed its Indian engineer; every day Sālār Jang recorded all this in his elegant Persian prose,
even the speed of the ship transcribed in English 'miles per hour'.[99] On his
safe return to India in 1305/1888 Sālār Jang printed the Persian account
of his travels in Bombay rather than his home city of Hyderabad.

Other sea journeys involved even stranger traffic between religious custom and modern transportation. In 1293/1876 the Bohra Ismā'īlī scholar
Muhammad 'Alī al-Hamdānī (d. 1315/1898) set out from India to tour
the west Indian Ocean and Mediterranean in search of the Hidden Imam,
whom he was convinced had just revealed himself.[100] Before his exhausted

return to India in 1305/1887, he searched in vain for the living prophet who alone embodied the secret knowledge of the universe. In 1911 the North Indian Sufi missionary Khwāja Hasan Nizāmī (1878–1955) set sail from Bombay on his own voyage to discover the wider world of Islam by travelling to Egypt, Iraq and the Hijaz in imitation of his celebrated modernist friend, Shiblī Nu'manī (d. 1332/1914).[101] But even this was no straightforward expression of Pan-Islamism and, troubled by the relentless swell of the ocean, in his travel diary Khwāja Hasan likened the rhythm of the waves to the Sufi breathing meditation of *pās-e anfās*.[102] Thinking these thoughts aboard an Austrian ocean liner, Khwāja Hasan's journey encapsulates the strange currents of modernity that washed into Bombay. Not only did this new era of travel promote tales or experiences of enchantment, through both increasing the number of travellers and mechanizing the distribution of their stories in print, it amplified and empowered them. In such ways, no less than the power of printing, the power of steam was called to the service of the saints and the shrine and brotherhood firms they represented.

4

Exports for an Iranian Marketplace

BOMBAY AND THE RELIGIOUS ECONOMY OF IRAN

The migration of Iranians to India forms one of the great themes in the religious history of both India and Iran. But while these interchanges are common enough knowledge with regard to the pre-modern period, their continuity – and, indeed, acceleration – through the nineteenth century has been neglected.[1] From the early nineteenth century, India was key to the development of Iran's diplomatic contacts with the wider world and Iranian relations with Britain were brokered through the exchange of ambassadors with Calcutta as much as London.[2] In the opening years of the nineteenth century, the ill-fated voyage to India of the resident of Bushire, Hājjī Muhammad Khalīl, on behalf of the Iranian ruler Fath 'Alī Shāh began this round of diplomatic exchanges with India, and soon led to the establishment of a permanent Iranian consul in Bombay.[3] These diplomatic relations, and the founding of the consulate in Bombay, were a reflection of the expansion of trade between the two regions.[4] We must look first, then, at the trade connections that underwrote Bombay's connections with Iran. Recent scholarship has begun to draw attention to the persistency of mercantile connections between Indian and Iranian merchants in the nineteenth century.[5] The old Iranian trading town of Kerman, for example, maintained a growing population of Indian merchants throughout the century, while the renewed ties between the Zoroastrians of Yazd and their Parsi co-religionists in Bombay assured the presence of a wealthy contingent of Indian merchants in Yazd as well. As the century progressed, Bombay increasingly became the commercial focus for the traditional trading towns of central and southern Iran.

In 1830 Bombay's total trade with Iran amounted to 350,000 rupees, but by 1859 the annual trade in horses alone had risen to 2,625,000 rupees, and this trend continued as the century progressed.[6] By 1865 the number of Iranians officially registered as residing in Bombay reached 1,639 persons, though we can be fairly sure that a good many more unofficial residents escaped the eyes of the city's officials.[7]

As Bombay's commercial importance grew, and its Iranian community with it, its importance for Iran in social and religious terms similarly expanded. This chapter traces Bombay's interactions with this Iranian community through the production of religious forms for the 'export market' in Iran. Once again, diversity – and, indeed, diversification – were the key to this increasing level of production, both in terms of the range of religious groups involved (Parsi and Bahā'ī as well as Muslim) and in terms of the distinct types of religious production. Though Bombay was extremely important in the production and export of Reform to Iran – from Parsi Zoroastrian Reformism to the Pan-Islamism of the early Iranian visitor Jamāl al-dīn 'al-Afghānī' – it was also extremely important in the re-production and empowerment of the hierarchical and enchanted productions of Customary Islam by way of the Sufi holy men who circulated between Iran and Bombay in considerable numbers. Bombay played an important role in the gradual splintering of the substantial monopoly that the Shi'i 'ulamā had maintained over the religious economy of Iran since the early 1600s. While the ways in which Iranian Sufi brotherhood firms experienced and made use of Bombay varied, echoing the cosmopolitan and anti-cosmopolitan possibilities of the shrine firms studied in Chapter 2, a case study of the travelogue of the most important Iranian Sufi of the late nineteenth century affords a first-hand sense of the operation of Bombay's economy of enchantment. Before turning towards these Muslim entrepreneurs, let us look first at the larger context of Iranian religious production in Bombay.

By the mid-nineteenth century Bombay's ruling class comprised prominent Parsi Zoroastrian merchants who were becoming increasingly conscious of their 'Iranian' identity, a development which was linked in part to the renewal of their contact with Iran through exports of trade and Zoroastrian missionary Reform. Bombay's great Parsi families were among the city's most important civic patrons and were early pioneers of modern education in Iran, as with the schools previously founded by Sir Jamshetjee Jeejeebhoy (1783–1859), which pre-dated Bombay's first Muslim Anglo-Mohammedan schools by several decades.[8] Turning to their originally liturgical Avestan and Pahlavi 'scriptures' in new and

axiomatically 'Protestant' Reformist ways, the city's Parsi elite also under-
took a reform of their own religious heritage.⁹ Several such Parsis also
joined the colonial government in a programme of municipal improve-
ments that lent Bombay a physiognomy fitting its elevated place in Indian
Ocean trade.¹⁰ Like the Muslim Modernists discussed in Chapter 1 they
funded schools and libraries, hospitals and factories, laying the foundations of the city's 'progress', a notion which in the terminology of *taraqqī*
(progress) Bombay's Parsis helped export to Iran. As greater numbers of
Iranian Muslims began to visit Bombay, they took a strange pride in their
non-Muslim overseas Persian ('Parsi') compatriots. Enabling this was a distinct feature of the Parsi renaissance by way of an increased interest in their
Iranian heritage, resulting in the publication of works in Persian on this
subject and the renewal of direct Zoroastrian religious contact with Iran.
Like the earlier Christian and later Muslim firms, the new Parsi *anjuman*s
dispatched their own missionaries to Iran to reacquaint their co-religionists
with what they considered the true version of their faith, making use of
Bombay's printers and trade networks to disseminate their message.

After centuries of quietist minoritarianism, from around 1850 the
Parsis joined the new religious marketplace as they debated the possibility of attracting Indian converts to their religion.¹¹ However, they
quickly realized that an easier market for their new religious productions
lay across the ocean in Iran, whose trading cities had over the previous
decades been laid open to Bombay's more material productions. Bombay-
based Parsi religious firms such as the Persian Zoroastrian Amelioration
Fund (founded in 1854) sent instructors to distribute their new Reformist
Zoroastrianism to their notional co-religionists in Iran. These instructors
brought funds collected in Bombay to establish franchises of their new
institutions in Bombay, founding the first modern schools in Iran. In the
Anjuman-e Zartushtiyān of Yazd (founded in 1858), modelled on the new
Zoroastrian *anjuman*s of Bombay, they also founded one of the earliest
modern donation and fee funded Iranian associations.¹² The most famous
of these mobile exporters of the new Zoroastrianism was the Bombay
Parsi Manikjī Limjī Hatāria (1813–90), who, like his Muslim counterparts discussed below, would describe his religious journeys between
Bombay and Iran in a missionary travelogue, *Risāla-ye tarjama-ye izhār-e
siyāhat-e Īrān* (Descriptive treatise on the performance of a journey to
Iran), printed in Bombay in 1280/1863. Manikjī's export mission was very
much a part of the larger religious economy developing in Bombay, and
his first journey from Bombay to Iran in 1854 was even undertaken in the
company of two Christian missionaries.¹³ Operating in the trading towns

of southern Iran, where the last Zoroastrians survived in miserable conditions, through the series of initiatives that began in the 1850s, Bombay and its Parsi religious firms laid some of the earliest seeds of modernization in provincial Iran. Funded by Parsis who comprised some of the wealthiest businessmen in Bombay, from the middle of the nineteenth century Parsi Zoroastrian Reformist firms were able to render great changes in the lives and social status of their co-religionists in Iran, transforming them from forgotten village peasants into educated urban merchants and, ultimately, technocrats. Originating in Bombay, this re-empowerment of the rituals of a Zoroastrian priesthood and the education of their followers would lend Zoroastrianism a social profile sufficiently high to reach the consciousness of their Muslim fellow countrymen and, by the early twentieth century, fed into the reimagination of Zoroastrianism as the 'national' religion of Iran. Through a combining of its characteristic market trends of custom and reform, Bombay's religious economy was in substantial part responsible for reproducing an ancient religion for the modern age.

Such was the financial weight behind Bombay Parsi support for Iranian Zoroastrians that in 1882, with British diplomatic help, they managed to bring about the abolition of the centuries-old *jizya* (poll-tax) levied on Iran's religious minorities, with Bombay's Parsi merchants promising the Iranian ruler, Nāsir al-dīn Shāh, that they would 'buy out' the *jizya* by covering the revenue loss from their own purses.[14] The shah's official *firmān* announcing the abolition was translated and proudly reprinted in the *Bombay Gazette*.[15] The abolition of the *jizya* not only represented a demotion of the status of *sharī'a*; it also removed one of the principal legal obstacles preventing the emergence of a more liberal religious economy in Iran as in Bombay that would in time register in the nation's consciousness through the constitutional movement of the early 1900s. By this time, Bombay's Parsis had helped found fourteen modern schools for their fellow Zoroastrians in Iran, bringing many of their students to Bombay for higher studies.[16] Such philanthropy came at a cost, and Bombay's Parsi missionaries such as Manikji expected Iran's Zoroastrians to reject many of the religious customs that they found offensive, particularly those involving dancing, music and the consumption of alcohol, for which no warrant could be found in the Avestan texts being printed for the first time in Bombay and newly configured as 'scripture'.[17] Reproduced in the distant towns of Iran by Bombay's Parsi exporters was a reformed Zoroastrianism that in echoing the characteristics of such Muslim Reformists as Badr al-dīn Tayyibji was a characteristic product of the Reformist trend of the Bombay marketplace. Buoyant on the wealth of trade, the reach of Bombay's Parsi Reformists thus stretched far across the ocean into the inland towns of the Iranian plateau. As we see below, the same connections were also exploited by Customary Islamic firms associated with Bombay's Iranian Muslim diaspora.

Reformist Zoroastrian firms were by no means the sole agents of greater pluralization in the religious economy of nineteenth-century Iran. Shifts within Iranian society also reared a range of other new religious productions, of which the Bābī and, ultimately, Bahā'ī movements are the best known. As early as the 1840s, Sayyid 'Alī Muhammad Shīrāzī's self-declaration as the Bāb (from *bāb*, 'gateway') reached Bombay, prompting the allegiance of the major early Bābī impresario, the Indian Muslim Sayyid Basīr, who subsequently set off from Bombay to travel through Iran on behalf of his new master.[18] In another of the characteristically enchanted productions of Bombay's marketplace, in his proselytizing tours of the towns of Iran, Sayyid Basīr attracted followers to the Bāb by his regular performance of miracles (*khwāriq-e 'ādāt*) before being executed by Iranian officials in around 1851.[19] While Iran's rulers, and the Shi'i clerical hierarchy with which the religiously monopolistic Iranian state had managed an uneasy alliance since the Safavid era, attempted to suppress these new religious productions (most visibly in their execution of the Bāb himself in 1850), they were ultimately thwarted by the religious flows that moved in and out of Iran through the region's interaction with a larger oceanic religious economy. Sayyid Basīr was by no means the sole Bābī link to Bombay, and from the early 1850s a series of the Bāb's merchant followers established themselves in Bombay, including members of the prominent Bābī Afnān family, who registered their trading company under the name of 'Messrs. Haji Sayed Mirza and Mirza Mahmood Co.'.[20] As the parallel Bābī religious 'firm' was gradually transformed under the leadership of Bahā'ullāh, from Bombay these Bābī merchants used the wealth they gathered from their trade in the city to become major patrons of early Bahā'ī religious productivity, not least in around 1880 by founding the Nāsirī Press that would serve in Bombay as the foundational Bahā'ī publishing and propaganda firm.[21]

While these Iranian religious flows also moved in other directions towards Russia and the Ottoman Empire, the concern here is with Bombay. For these purposes, it is notable that the three major players in the pluralization of the Muslim section of Iran's religious economy – namely the Bābīs, Bahā'īs and the Ni'matullāhī Sufis – were all closely linked to Bombay. For in addition to the movement of Zoroastrians between Bombay and Iran, during the second half of the century Bombay became a notable centre for Bahā'ī activities, as after the Afnān family refugees from Iran gathered there in increasing numbers and the Bābis already established in the city chose to follow Bahā'ullāh as the Bāb's successor.[22] It is no coincidence that Bahā'ullāh drew many of his early followers from the same Iranian religious consumers in the trading towns of central Iran who were also drawn to the Ni'matullāhi Sufi brotherhood, for in merchant towns connected to Bombay was a religious market being drawn into Bombay's orbit. In a textual sense at least, early Bahā'ism was a product of the Bombay religious economy, for it was there that the writings of Bahā'ullāh were first published and distributed. Both of Bahā'ullāh's main works, which comprised the foundational scriptures of the new Bahā'i faith, were first published in Bombay. These were the Persian texts *Kitāb-e yaqin* (Book of certainty), first printed in Bombay by the city's Nāsiri Press in 1299/1882; *Kitāb-e mubin* (Book of revelation), printed in Bombay in 1308/1890; and the subsequent Arabic *Kitāb al-aqdas* (Holiest book), first printed there in 1314/1896.[23] With Nāsir al-din Shāh having established a censor system over book production inside Iran, and Bahā'ullāh himself imprisoned in exile by the Ottoman authorities, the liberal and wide-reaching religious economy of Bombay offered a key opportunity for Bahā'ullāh, who along with the Āghā Khān was the most effective Iranian religious entrepreneur of the nineteenth century. Such was the centrality of Bombay to the printed production and distribution of Bahā'ullāh's message that he dispatched his younger son, Mirzā Muhammad 'Ali, to Bombay to help prepare his father's writings for publication.[24] The founder of the Nāsiri Press, Mirzā Ibrāhim, was in turn the son of the Bāb's brother-in-law.[25] As Chapter 5 makes clear, as a highly effective trans-regional 'family firm' centred on the person and writings of a father and his sons, between Iran, Bombay and the wider world beyond them, in structural, organizational and productive terms the Bahā'i religious firm held very much in common with the family-centred activities of Bahā'ullāh's fellow Iranian exile the Āghā Khān and his impresario sons. If it was in Iran that the divine effulgence of the Bāb and Bahā'ullāh had been manifested in flesh, it was in Bombay that their personal charisma was transformed into industrially mass-produced books that could reach a wider international religious marketplace.

The shared knowledge of Persian, and perhaps even a common sense of being Iranian, at times drew these different entrepreneurs together into mutually productive collaborations, pointing to the way in which the religious economy could be at times collaborative as well as competitive. The personal secretary of the Zoroastrian Reformist exporter Manikji was a noted Bahā'i scholar, for example, while, as seen below, Iranian Muslim travellers also had dealings with the Parsis of Bombay

and the Ismāʿīlī Āghā Khān hosted a range of Iranian Niʿmatullāhī Sufis
and Pan-Islamists in his Bombay mansion. With its blend of messianism
and reason, of nineteenth-century liberalism and older ideas of incarna-
tionism, the productions of the Bahāʾullāh family firm combined many
of the dual possibilities of the Muslim religious economy charted in
this book. By locating merchants in Bombay and printing there some of
their foundational works, the early Bahāʾī proselytizers used the same
strategies as their Zoroastrian and Muslim counterparts, harnessing the
transnational resources available to them in Bombay to reshape and
pluralize the religious economy back home in Iran. Another example is
found in the *Risāla-ye siyāsiyya* (Treatise on politics) written by ʿAbd
al-Bahā, the Bahāʾī leader and son of Bahāʾullāh, in around 1892 in
response to the Tobacco Revolt in Iran, which was published in Bombay
by the Dutt Prasad Press on 1 Muharram 1314 (12 June 1896).[26] In
making what Juan Cole has called 'the strongest case for the separation of religion and state ever made in a Middle Eastern context', in its
virulent anti-clericalism the text escaped the ruler Nāsir al-dīn Shāh's
state censor in Iran through being printed in Bombay and distributed
through its wide commercial networks. Like the other books printed
for the Iranian market discussed below, the *Risāla-ye siyāsiyya* in this
way made its incremental contribution to a pluralization of the Iranian
religious economy by demanding a more 'liberal' religious marketplace through the removal of the state-sponsored monopoly of the Shiʿī
clerical *ulamā*.[27]

   However, while Zoroastrians, Bābīs and Bahāʾīs operated from Bombay,
the larger number of Iranians in residence there were Shiʿi Muslims.
Through the growth of Shiʿi Sufi brotherhood firms, the nineteenth century also saw a pluralization of the religious forms available to Iranian
Muslims. Bombay played a central role in this development as well. Like
the city's other Muslims, Iranian Muslims formed their own distinct community, possessing their own mosque and *husayniyya* so as to worship
apart from Indian and Sunni Muslims. In this, they fit into the pattern of
Muslim divisiveness seen in Chapters 1 and 2, the very pattern that would
lead Reformists such as al-Afghānī and Badr al-dīn Tayyibji to call for
their collective solidarity as Muslims. Like the Parsis, Bombay's Iranian
Muslims principally comprised a merchant community who were especially involved in the trading of textiles, horses, dried fruits and opium
between the Iranian port of Bushire and Bombay.[28] Writing of his journey between the two ports in 1867, Reverend James Paterson described
carpets being manufactured in Bushire for export to Bombay and noted

how the Iranian port had been 'colonized by Arabs' involved in the ocean trade.[29] Nonetheless, the merchant elite of inland cities such as Shiraz and Isfahan were central to the Indian Ocean trade, and with two distinctive and wealthy 'Iranian' Parsi and Muslim communities already resident in Bombay, as the century wore on many other Iranians decided to leave the economic recession of inland Iran that was itself in large part due to Bombay's industrialization, and to likewise cross the ocean from Bushire.

Linked by steamship to the port of Bushire, in the nineteenth century Bombay thus provided thousands of Iranian labour exiles and merchants with their most accessible experience of technological modernity. Bombay introduced Iranians to trains after steamships, as well as modern industrial methods and a cosmopolitanism that was alien to the culturally homogeneous towns of the Iranian plateau. As we see below in the travelogues written by Iranian Sufi entrepreneurs, Bombay could alternatively be experienced as a domain of industrial production or miraculous intervention, a place to at once seek social and technical novelties or tap into the resources of freshly empowered custom. Such movement had important consequences, consequences that were ultimately more significant for Iran than they were for India. The emergence in Bombay of a more liberal economy based on intensified competition between different religious groups was not confined to the city itself. Indeed, the very importance of Bombay for Iranian social and religious history in the nineteenth century is that the city's religious products were regularly exported to the towns and cities of Iran through the circulation of members of transnational religious firms. Ultimately, these connections to the freer religious market of Bombay were to result in major realignments in the religious economy of Iran itself through the export to Iran of both Reformist and Customary Islamic productions forged in the Bombay marketplace. Having surveyed the Parsi and Bahā'ī context, the focus of this and the next chapter is on Iranian Muslim interactions with Bombay, which were in both cases circulatory interactions, involving repeated movements between the two sites. In showing how central Bombay was to the making of careers as highly successful charismatic holy men, both chapters argue that as products of Bombay's religious economy these entrepreneurial holy men contributed no less than the city's Parsis and Bahā'īs to a diversification of the religious economy of Iran itself.[39] Of special importance was the city's role in marketing the affiliation to the Sufi *murshid* as an alternative model of religious authority to the monopoly of the Shi'i clerical class. In this way, through their interactions with a wealthy Iranian merchant community in

Bombay, newly 'manufactured' Sufi shaykhs and brotherhood firms helped pluralize the religious economy of Iran.

IRANIAN SUFIS ON THE BOMBAY STEAMSHIPS

By the 1860s, for travellers arriving in Bombay from the chief Iranian port of embarkation in Bushire, the contrast between their points of departure and arrival was stunning: to disembark in Bombay was to enter a new and distinctly modern environment. As nineteenth-century travellers between the two ports remarked, in monolithic basalt or carefully whitewashed plaster, Bombay's seaward public face could scarcely offer the traveller a greater contrast to the mud-brick fortress and date-palm shacks of Bushire.[31] This new urban environment in Bombay offered many nineteenth-century Iranians a heightened renewal of the opportunities for trade, refuge and writing that the Muslim courts of pre-colonial India had in earlier centuries. The conditions for these opportunities were radically altered by the mechanical and social changes of the 1800s. It was precisely these conditions – enhanced communications, renewed trading opportunities, religious and political liberalism – that Sufi entrepreneurs moving between Iran and India were careful to make best use of. While many of the Iranians passing through Bombay were drawn there for economic reasons, whether of high commerce or deck-sweeping, other travellers to Bombay came for more explicitly religious reasons. In many cases, as with Indian Muslim travellers, these other visitors were Iranian pilgrims making the *hajj*, funnelled through Bombay en route from Bushire to Jidda and Mecca. Among these Iranian pilgrims were many Sufis, for whom Bombay became not only a place to change ships but also to build contacts with other expatriates and make use of the city's printing-presses (far better developed than those of Iran) and use its rail network to make followers in older religious centres inland, chiefly Hyderabad. In a few cases, Iranian Sufis recorded their experiences in Bombay in Persian travelogues (*safarnāma*), a genre which grew exponentially with the new travel opportunities of the nineteenth century. Before turning towards several examples of such travelogues, it is important to look more at the foundations of the 'Iranian Bombay' in which these Sufi entrepreneurs operated.

A broad sense of the importance of Bombay among Iranian Sufis may be seen from the number of people linked to the city found in the Ni'matullāhī brotherhood's history *Tarā'iq al-haqā'iq*, citing Bombay as a place of publishing and commerce as well as of more general visitation by Niʻmatullāhī Sufis and their followers.[32] The overall impression given by the text's intertwined accounts of the Iranian dervishes and merchants who passed between India and Iran in the nineteenth century is one of the remarkable interpenetration of the spheres of mysticism and commerce. It was invariably Bombay's merchants who supported visiting Sufis and put them into contact with other potential merchant investors in other cities in India or their wider oceanic diaspora, such that in terms of logistics and personnel it makes little sense to understand commercial and religious networks as separate. Reared from childhood on the same poetic culture in which Shiʻi, esoteric and erotic imagery constantly overlapped, Iranian merchants were already familiar with the ideas and idioms of the Sufis whom they sponsored. There also seems good reason to suppose that most of the Iranian Sufi initiates moving round the ocean did so primarily as merchants, leaving only the most destitute or the most successful to beg or buy tickets for solely religious itineraries. There was nothing unique in this, an Iranian reflection as it was of the links between Hadhrami merchants and the Arab holy men of the ʻAydarusī and ʻAlawī brotherhood firms over even more expansive oceanic networks reaching to Singapore.[33]

If it is known from such sources as the early twentieth-century biographical compendium *Tarāʼiq al-haqāʼiq* that many such Iranian holy men visited Bombay and attempted to draw the city's Iranian investors into their religious firms, to understand how they imagined and experienced the city it is necessary to turn to the travelogues that they wrote there. The travelogues are important because they afford us a glimpse of the actual fabric of the city through the eyes of Iranian enchanters, recounting how the migrant Sufis of Iran experienced the city in all the complexity of its unfamiliar men and machines. The production of Persian travelogues or *safarnāmas* grew tremendously in the nineteenth century, and one of the key characteristics of this period of Iranian travel writing was the impact on Iranian mentalities of the technological and political modernity of the outside world. This was no less the case with religious forms of travel such as the *hajj*, for by the second half of the century the principal routes to Mecca brought pilgrims into contact with the modernity of either Bombay or Alexandria. For the future industrialist Hājj Muhammad Amīn al-Zarb the experience of European technology while performing *hajj* in 1279/1863 proved a turning-point in his career.[34] The accounts of the pilgrimages to Mecca of Sayf al-Dawla in 1279/1863 and Mīrzā Husayn Farāhānī also fall into this genre, with the latter including a description in his travelogue of the French-engineered piped water of Alexandria and its counterpart in Bombay.[35] In the pilgrimage diaries of these pious merchants it was the technological modernity of the outside world that was stressed, often in explicit comparison with the backwardness of Qājār Iran.

It was not only technological modernity that struck the consciousness of these travellers. It was also the increasingly cosmopolitan societies that industrialization and commercial capitalism were creating in the new cities of Asia and Africa. While some of the responses recorded in their travelogues were sympathetic, others registered bewilderment and distaste, seeing in the thronging proletarians only the ignorance and abasement of the vulgar masses. The impact of the cosmopolitan was further registered through attempts to coexist or compete with the different religious and cultural systems the metropolis presented. In doing so, the travellers' memoirs provide different responses to the cosmopolitan modernity of the Bombay marketplace. In the first specifically Sufi travelogue that we examine, we see below a negative response to the cosmopolitan pressures of Bombay life, one which, though aware of some details of the belief systems of other social groups that its author encountered in Bombay, saw in them only symbols of spiritual apathy and confusion.

This traveller was the Iranian writer of *Tarā'iq al-haqā'iq*, Nā'ib al-Sadr Shīrāzī (d. 1344/1926), who in the 1880s wrote an account of his travels to India and Mecca, which was first published as a lithograph in Bombay in 1306/1889.[36] Reflecting the discursive as well as practical importance of travel among the Sufis, much of the book concerned the theory rather than the act of travel. Nonetheless, Nā'ib al-Sadr did leave an account of Bombay in this Persian *hajj* diary, which serves as a valuable record of the circles in which Iranian Sufis moved in Bombay. While the diary is more interested in pieties than practicalities, amid its many high-minded digressions we catch glimpses of historical detail. Nā'ib al-Sadr described his arrival in Bombay on 24 Safar 1306 (30 October 1888), his own steamship entering the harbour at the same time as the steamship *London*, and being greeted with a welcome rally from the port cannon.[37] Reaching the dockside by a small boat (presumably one of the many plied by the harbour's Konkani Muslim sailors), he set off by carriage in search of a number of prominent Iranian merchants who lived in Bombay.[38] This connection with Bombay's traders reflected the distribution of the Ni'matullāhī brotherhood firm in Iran itself, where from the early 1800s it had spread from Hyderabad and Bombay along the caravan routes to establish branches in the key trading towns of Kerman, Isfahan and Shiraz. The investment of such maritime merchants was also key to the spread of the Chishtī brotherhood firm from Bombay to South Africa traced in Chapter 7.

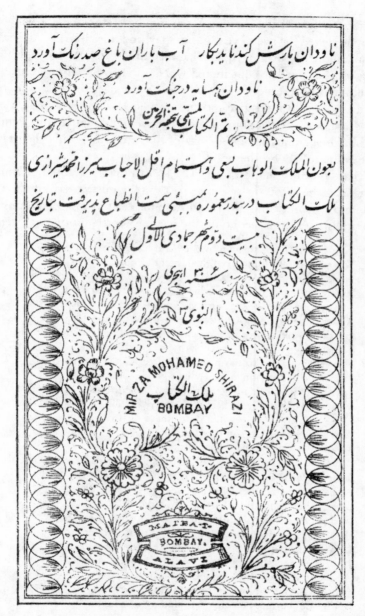

FIGURE 11. Iranian travels in print: Colophon from Nā'ib al-Sadr's travelogue (dated 1306/1889)

Later, Nā'ib al-Sadr discussed the family of the Āghā Khān, with whom he stayed for over a year in Bombay, and it is clear that the wealth the Ismā'īlī family firm of Āghā Khān acquired through the High Court ruling of 1866 further contributed to Nā'ib al-Sadr's promotion of the Ni'matullāhī brotherhood. For his part, Nā'ib al-Sadr repaid his hosts and investors with a positive account of their learning and piety, a boon in a period of anti-Ismā'īlī propaganda from the Iranian *ulamā*, while at the same time emphasizing the links of the Āghā Khāns and their family to the Ni'matullāhī brotherhood.[39]

Perhaps the most interesting part of Nā'ib al-Sadr's account of Bombay is the poem he wrote in response to the religious variety of the city's inhabitants. As one kind of Muslim response to the cosmopolitanism of the pluralistic religious economy, the poem is worth quoting *in extenso*.

> Like a hawk I was thrown by the hand of destiny
> Towards distant India from the land of Shiraz.
> None I found happy in that land of fees and prices
> Where no-one knows each other and family is unknown.
> I saw groups of crooked speakers and most curious dispositions
> All with the single thought of gathering cash and gold.
> For those souls who've gone astray people too are but a price.
> They vainly give themselves the title of good men.
> I saw them drown from tip to toe in dreaming of dirhams
> Till they could no longer tell what's good from what is bad.
> I saw in that land many groups among the Hindus
> Who always have been there and always will be too.
> One sect I saw bow down in devotion to a cow
> And another call the sun their Almighty God.
> To another side I saw a most miserable crew
> Who spend their days in pleading trees to come and save their souls.
> Then there are those who paint their foreheads like leopards
> And others and others in a thousand shapes and colours.
> One I saw washing in the urine of a bullock
> And another make ablutions in the water of the Ganges.
> Another sect was there that in the mighty age of heroes
> Left the fine land of Persia to settle far from home.
> Now their ancestry lies lost on the winds of the monsoon
> And they've every one forgotten who belongs to their own race.
> Outwardly they follow the laws of Zoroaster
> But inside they are lacking every inkling of religion.
> I saw there too a community of Jews
> Who dream of every kind of disorder that can be.
> They've all but given up on the noble way of Aaron
> And only have desire for the treasures of Qarun.
> Their hearts I saw all drowning in dreams of gold and silver

For not one can tell the difference between Friday and their Sabbath.
Of the people of Islam I saw many groups there too
But to even speak their names would be a grave disgrace.
If I were to stand before a true man of Shari'a
I'd be shamed to tell the vices I counted there among them.
I saw yet another group in that most lovely country
A filthy folk indeed whom they call the Englishmen.
With lies they have made a fool of a whole nation
And could even trick a lion into handing them a doe.
Even if it's true that their own country is well-ordered
It's outlawed there to take just a moment's time of ease.
Each and every Englishman but thinks of his own fortune
And is sweet to himself and sour to every other.
So long as his heart swells with gladness from his profits
He cares not to see the whole world is suffering losses.
I saw how chivalry is but an empty word to them
For in their lands it's loyalty that's been all but forbidden.[40]

No fascination with Bombay's liberal religious marketplace, in stilted lines that sought to echo the medieval comments of Sa'dī on the follies of the world's many peoples, this was a damning verdict on both religious pluralism and the mercantile form of government under which it flourished. Here in Persian verse was a contemporary depiction of Bombay as the marketplace of men and their religions.

Fortunately, this was not to be Nā'ib al-Sadr's last word on the city's cosmopolitanism. A few decades later he left a detailed – and more sympathetic – account of the Hindu Diwali festival in Bombay in his *Tarā'iq al-haqā'iq* that was closer in spirit to the attitudes found in the next Iranian *safarnāma* to which we turn.[41] There the pluralism of Bombay was met with far greater enthusiasm, if likewise interpreted in the metaphysical idioms of custom. This was the travelogue of Muhammad 'Alī Nā'īnī, better known as Hājjī Pīrzāda (d. 1321/1904), an initiate of the same Ni'matullāhī brotherhood firm as Nā'ib al-Sadr and the other Iranian shaykhs who visited Bombay such as Safī 'Alī Shāh.[42] Hājjī Pīrzāda's Persian account of the city dwelt in considerably more detail on his encounter with not only its non-Muslim residents but also with the technological fabric of the marketplace. Nā'ib al-Sadr was happy to merely use technology to do his travelling and print his account of it, baulking at the idea of dwelling on machines as topics of discussion. For Hājjī Pīrzāda, the new technologies that Bombay presented to him for the first time formed the mainstay of his description of the city. His travelogue similarly is rich in descriptions of his encounters with a variety of Iranian and non-Iranian residents of Bombay. Despite his affiliation to a

Ni'matullāhī shaykh, Hājjī Pīrzāda was anything but bashful in his fascination with modern novelties, and if this became most evident in his later
descriptions of Paris and London, his account of Bombay also included
enthusiastic sections on the city's ice factory as well as its industrializing
textile mills and the spectacle provided by its public zoo.[43]

Hājjī Pīrzāda's visit to Bombay was part of a long series of travels that
also took him to the Middle East and Europe. Having begun his travels
in 1858 with a journey to Istanbul in the company of his shaykh, Hājjī
Mīrzā Safā, in the mid-1880s he decided to make the *hajj* from Iran by
sailing via Bombay.[44] After first visiting Karachi, he reached Bombay via
one of the steamships that sailed between the two ports several days per
week and, like other Iranian visitors, on reaching Bombay went to stay
with the Iranian exile Āghā Khān II.[45] Like other Iranian Sufis moving
round the Indian Ocean, Hājjī Pīrzāda was reliant on the networks of
Iranian traders, and after Āghā Khān II he than stayed in Bombay with
the famous merchant 'Abd al-Husayn Amīn al-Tujjār, whom he described
as the owner of numerous fine houses and shops in the city and as a major
shareholder in four ships.[46] While Amīn al-Tujjār's hospitality to Hājjī
Pīrzāda was described gratefully in his *safarnāma*, he noted that the generosity of the great merchant was not limited to him alone. For every Friday
Amīn al-Tujjār invited Bombay's numerous Iranian *sayyid*s and *faqīr*s to
his house, where he would feed them and hand them stipends in cash. The
presence of so many Iranian holy men in Bombay was closely linked to the
existence of this wealthy class of expatriate merchant patrons and investors. In a pointer to the scale of Iranian Sufi migration to Bombay, Hājjī
Pīrzāda stressed that there was always a large number of Iranian *faqīr*s
(religious mendicants) in and around Amīn al-Tujjār's Bombay mansion.[47]
There were certainly plenty of such religious mendicants around in the city,
and even as early as the 1850s the Bombay District Benevolent Society estimated that there were around five thousand Muslim beggars in Bombay,
who were 'most active in their peregrinations, and loudest in their clamours, at those set times when liberality in almsgiving is most enjoined –
and, it must be added, is therefore most practised – by Mussulmans; such
as their holy months'.[48] An example is seen in the recollection of another
Iranian Sufi, Safi 'Alī' Shāh, stepping out of the house in which he was staying in Bombay and unexpectedly confronting a 'dervish' in the alleyway.[49]
Given the literal meaning of the term *darwīsh* as wanderer from door to
door (*dar*), this figure was probably one of the city's street dwellers, perhaps even one of the many opium-smoking Muslim beggars who later
featured in Rustom Pestanji Jehangir's survey of Bombay opium users.

Safi 'Alī recounted how the dervish demanded a gift of money, to which, not realizing that he had coins in his pockets, he replied that he had no money with him. It was only then that the dervish revealed the mystical knowledge at his disposal, reprimanding Safi 'Alī with the words, 'Say I won't give, not that you don't have money, for there are coins in your pocket right now.' He then proceeded to detail the exact number of dinars in Safi 'Alī's pocket, and, putting his hand in his pocket to check, Safi 'Alī found the dervish to be absolutely right. There were certainly many such figures in the religious marketplace. A few years before Safi 'Alī's first visit to Bombay, the methods of the city's Muslim mendicants were described in an official report in terms of an effective gift economy:

> The fukeers generally beg in the holy months, and make the most of the certain days esteemed as especially propitious for obtaining rewards in heaven by almsgiving. They, however, seize every opportunity to obtain charitable gifts. When there is rejoicing, as at weddings, they present themselves with congratulations, which are well requited. When death plunges a household in sorrow, then also the fukeer appears, and in a loud voice tenders the condolence which it would be ungracious not suitably to acknowledge.[50]

This patronage of dervishes and *faqīrs* (lit. 'poor men') was an important element in the religious economy, not least in that it was this class of persons who were most commonly associated with miracle rumours. The role of the Iranian merchant class in supporting this enchanted economy of customary holy men reflects what is seen in Chapter 7 with expatriate Indian merchants sponsoring the activities of their own community holy man, Ghulām Muhammad, in Natal.

Showing his interest in the new forms of commerce that were supporting such itinerant Sufis as himself, Hājjī Pīrzāda described in some detail the new methods of trade that he witnessed in Bombay. In a nod to the cosmopolitanism of the city's workforce, he described the system of multi-ethnic 'clerks' (*munshīs*) working for long hours in different languages, as well as the new concept of the 'office' (*afīs*) that formed the organizing principle not only of trade but also of the social activity of work itself. Moving on from matters of commerce, Hājjī Pīrzāda next recounted the characteristics of Bombay at large, an account which in reflection of the transitional modernity of the *safarnāma* genre at this time stands somewhere between the earlier Persian tradition of the urban encomium and the more recent Iranian fashion for the European travelogue epitomized by the published travel diaries of the ruler Nāsir al-dīn Shāh.[51] Although it was a somewhat less developed Bombay that Hājjī Pīrzāda's

Iranian contemporary Jamāl al-dīn 'al-Afghānī' had seen some thirty years earlier, the impact the city had on the two Iranian travellers could not have been more different. In the place of al-Afghānī's suspicion of the spread of British rule was Ḥājjī Pīrzāda's positive evaluation of English government (*dawlat-e inglīsī*). Fifteen years after Ḥājjī Pīrzāda's visit the aspiring Sufi missionary entrepreneur and musician 'Ināyat Khān (1299–1345/1882–1927) spent several months in Bombay, but he too was shocked by what he saw, pained at what he regarded as the vulgarization of Indian music and the Europeanized habits of smoking and drinking that went on during his own performance to the city's Indian merchants.[52] But he still used the city's technology to establish his own religious firm overseas.

Ḥājjī Pīrzāda's enthusiasm for the city's modernity was also expressed in his other descriptions of Bombay's infrastructure, not least the railway service that, as we see in the next chapter, his Iranian contemporaries such as Āghā Khān II used to such proselytizing effect. In addition to Bombay's horse-drawn trams, Ḥājjī Pīrzāda thus pointed to the usefulness of the 'steam carriages (*kālaska-ye bukhār*) that in Bombay they call rail and which pass through most of the streets, and which people use to travel from one quarter to another, for the length and breadth of Bombay is very great, such that houses and quarters are a long distance apart'.[53] By the time of his visit in the late 1880s, the city's pioneering rail network had spread all across India, an achievement that he saw as key to its flourishing under British rule.[54] Reflecting the industrial environment in which Chapter 6 describes the Sufi shaykh Ḥabīb 'Alī Shāh also operating in Bombay, Ḥājjī Pīrzāda next described in detail the different cotton and silk mills that existed in the city along with the various mechanized processes through which the raw materials passed before producing finished products such as lungees and turbans. He estimated the average workforce of the mills as comprising around two thousand men, women and children.[55] If Chapter 6 shows Ḥabīb 'Alī Shāh as content to simply disseminate his version of Customary Islam among the workers in these mills without openly confronting the workplace in his writings, his Sufi contemporary Ḥājjī Pīrzāda sought to confront the machines directly, and accommodate them within a new theology that still kept a place for God's saintly friends.

In continuity with the customary topics of the Persian travelogue, Ḥājjī Pīrzāda also paid attention to the flora of the city, with descriptions of Bombay's trees and climate, and how these differed even from those of tropical regions such as Iran's Mazandaran. Having spoken of the climate (*āb ū hawā*) by way of the monsoon – '*barsāt*, that is, when so much rain comes that one might say that rivers are poured on the earth from the high heavens' – he next went on to depict in detail the city's methods of water management, which by means of a vast reservoir built in the hills above the city stored rainwater to supply the individual residences of the city below. Having constructed this reservoir, he wrote, the English government had connected it to Bombay by 32 kilometres ('six *farsakhs*') of broad iron pipes, which were then connected to individual buildings, so as to even deliver water to the upper floors of six-storey houses.[56] The supply of clean and fresh water was so abundant that even the poorest people in the city had access to it; a second, even larger, reservoir, he noted, was said to contain enough water to carry Bombay through three years of drought.[57] The city's modern water system also received praise from Nā'ib al-Sadr Shīrāzī a few years later. and in the period in question such minor observations were actually dramatic.[58] For implicit in such accounts of Bombay was a comparison with Iran, where not only was the supply of water still usually dependent on the private well, but public access to water was conceived of as an act of personal charity rather than a duty of government. If the fountain (*sabīl*) and water-bearer (*saqaw*) were long emblematic of individual piety in Iran, here in Bombay the provision of water was shifted into an entirely different sphere of governmental responsibility.[59] As it was for the Zoroastrian Reformist Anjuman-e Zartushtiyān organization, in the diary of a travelling dervish Bombay served as the model of a religious and social modernity that would hopefully be exported to Iran itself.

Turning towards the religious pluralism of the Bombay marketplace that had so vexed Nā'ib al-Sadr, Hājjī Pīrzāda also wrote an account of the dress habits and religious practices of Bombay's Hindus. Whether mill-hands from the villages of the Konkan or travelling intellectuals from the cities of Iran, in Bombay Muslim migrants of all classes experienced a new vision of the world as complex, cosmopolitan and at times disorientating. Hājjī Pīrzāda's account of the plurality of Bombay's ethnic and religious groups (*tawā'if wa mazāhib*) is of interest for its attempt to conceive the new religious economy within the intellectual parameters of customary notions of God and his immanence in creation. Here he used the doctrine of *wahdat al-wujūd* that was so central to the theology of Customary Islam and which was one of the key doctrinal targets of the Reformists. Having noted that the city contained Muslims, 'Farsīs, whom we call *gebr*' (i.e. Parsi Zoroastrians), Christians and also Jews, Hājjī Pīrzāda gave special attention to Bombay's Hindus, whom he more or less correctly estimated as making up some 700,000 of its 900,000 inhabitants. As it had for an earlier generation of visitors from Central Asia as well as Iran, the 'revealing'

clothing of the Hindu women struck Ḥājjī Pīrzāda as noteworthy.[60] But his interest in the Hindus was more apologetic than prurient. Having depicted their *but-khāna* ('idol houses', as the Persian idiom had it), he went on to present a sympathetic account of Hindu theology in which the time-honoured terminology of Sufi poetry was used to render intelligible what he had learned in the marketplace of the Hindu universe.[61] The veneration of statues was not sheer idol worship, he decided, but reflected the belief that God only makes manifest (*jalwa kardan*) one of his faces (*sūrat*) at any given time. So when God manifests himself as a cow, he is worshipped by the Hindus in that form, with the same being true of his manifestations in different eras as a dog, frog, monkey, or even ogre (*dīw*).

If his choice of divine forms was a touch sensational, Ḥājjī Pīrzāda's account was nonetheless a form of positive cosmopolitanism to emerge from the marketplace as conceived through the idioms of custom. He even deflected the old charge of Hindu polytheistic *shirk* by claiming that each Hindu group worshipped just one of these gods and as such were monotheists. Ḥājjī Pīrzāda next took up the subject of the city's growing number of Hindu festivals, which were no less a production of the city's religious economy than the Muslim festivals traced in Chapter 2. This was after all the period that saw the rise in Bombay of the Ganesh-worshipping Ganpati festival as a way of mobilizing the masses in the direction of the emerging politics of Hindu nationalism.[62] But from Ḥājjī Pīrzāda the festivals received benign treatment, presented as celebrations of a particular god's birth (*ʿīd-e mawlūd*) and as such implicitly comparable to the customary Muslim celebration of Muhammad's birth, the *mawlid al-nabī*. In the same period in which the Sufi entrepreneur Ḥabīb ʿAlī Shāh was defending Bombay's celebratory deathdays of the saints, Ḥājjī Pīrzāda was by a comparative market logic using the same customary idioms of Islamic carnivalism to defend the urban celebrations of the Hindus. Moving on to the city's other religious groups, Ḥājjī Pīrzāda wrote of Bombay's Jews and their mercantile connections. Recounting with admiration the wealth of Dāʾūd Sāsān (David Sassoon, 1792–1864), whose activities stretched between Bombay, Baghdad and London, Ḥājjī Pīrzāda described his philanthropic foundation of public hospitals and schools.[63] This was followed by a lengthy and no less sympathetic comparative account of the Āghā Khān's Bombay Ismāʿīlīs, who by the 1880s were becoming the subject of theological criticism in Iran through their attempts to breach the monopoly of the Shiʿi *ʿulamā*.

In Ḥājjī Pīrzāda's appeal to Sufi terminology and concepts to make sense of the cosmopolitan otherness of Bombay's marketplace, he pointed towards the adaptability of custom as a considered response to the modern religious economy rather than the static residue of a former age. In the eyes of this itinerant dervish of the age of steam, who later dined with dons in Cambridge and discussed mystic doctrines with the young Orientalist E. G. Browne, the coexistence in the world of mechanical and divine power offered no contradiction. Allah manifested himself in the gods carried by Hindus through the streets of Bombay, while around them Englishmen built trams and ice-factories and Jews opened new kinds of hospitals for the poor. Far from retreating in the bright light of the gas lamp, in Hājjī Pīrzāda's travelogue Customary Islam found new sustenance in the wonders of the modern world, novelties and inventions which for Hājjī Pīrzāda were further proof of the inexhaustible riches of Allah's creativity. Whether in rejection or embrace, mobile Iranian Sufis were therefore quite familiar with the cosmopolitan and mechanical modernity of Bombay. Persian travelogues saw Bombay as a city of miracles as well as technological wonders, a place where a Customary Islam of pilgrimages and intercessionary shaykhs fed on the new social and technical apparatus of the era. This reinvigoration of custom – and, moreover, of customary forms of Persian Sufi organization that had previously lapsed in Iran only to survive in India – is seen most forcefully in the career of Hājjī Pīrzāda's contemporary, the greatest Iranian Sufi of the later nineteenth century: Mīrzā Hasan Safi 'Ali Shāh (d. 1316/1899). Safi 'Ali Shāh made several visits to Bombay, and in the 1890s, in recollection of his travels, wrote an account of his experiences in India in the 1860s and 1870s; we have already seen him encountering a telepathic beggar in one of Bombay's backstreets. Yet his was a more challenging and ambiguous travel narrative than that of Hājjī Pīrzāda, reluctant to depict industrial change too closely in its anxiety to present India as the great exporting warehouse of religious custom. In its blend of cliché and historical detail, and its presentation of its author's own experiences through the idioms of custom, the travelogue is the most compelling Iranian testament of the enchanted religious economy of nineteenth-century Bombay.

THE ENCHANTED ECONOMY OF SAFI 'ALI SHĀH

The case of Hājjī Pīrzāda shows how the travelogue was used to explore the intersection between customary theology of multiple divine manifestations and the Bombay religious marketplace. Attentive as he was to the pietism of the merchants who looked after their community dervishes in Bombay, Hājjī Pīrzāda was a practical man whose loyalty to the old firms of the Sufis did not prevent him from recognizing the merits of the industrial age, whether in Bombay or on his later travels in Europe. In this he stood in contrast to more critical travellers in the oceanic arena. A comparison may be made with his Zanzibari contemporary Muhammad al-Barwānī Abū Harith, whose Arabic *rihla* (travelogue) managed to celebrate the wonders of technology while being correspondingly critical of the spiritual malaise that such technical advancements had summoned among Muslims.[64] Safī ʿAlī Shāh offers a contrast with both figures. Despite belonging to the same Niʿmatullāhī brotherhood as Hājjī Pīrzāda, following the same itinerary from Iran to India, and meeting many of the same people during his stay there, he displayed a very different attitude to the marketplace in his own travel memoirs. In contrast to Abū Harith and Hājjī Pīrzāda, Safī ʿAlī made virtually no mention of modern technology, choosing to instead fetishize the customs that Bombay's economy was able to offer. For Safī ʿAlī, Bombay was a gateway to an India of holy men and miracles, and a staging-post in a trans-oceanic geography of Niʿmatullāhī shrines that stretched between Kerman in Iran and Hyderabad in India. Just as Chapter 6 shows the Hyderabadi shaykh Habīb ʿAlī Shāh spending years beside the great P&O dockyard in Bombay, his lodge literally yards from the Mazagaon rail tracks, and yet making no reference to the new age of steam in his writings, so was Safī ʿAlī able to spend four years in Bombay alongside the first train services and industrial manufactories in Asia and not let a slither of this modernity enter his picture of India as the bastion of custom. In contrast to other Persian travelogues of the period, Safī ʿAlī's memoir did not present him as going home to Iran importing the intellectual arsenal of modernity, but instead as returning with the blessing and authority born of immersion in the Indian fountains of custom.

In 1251/1835 Safī ʿAlī had been born in Isfahan into a merchant family, and on this basis it may reasonably be assumed that training in commercial matters formed the foundation of his early education.[65] Like his exact contemporary and fellow Isfahani, the great merchant and travel diarist Hājj Muhammad Hasan Amīn al-Zarb (1250/3–1316/1834/7–98), Safī ʿAlī probably attended a *maktab* school in Isfahan to acquire the skills in literacy required for a mercantile career.[66] Certainly, his later travelogue presented him as familiar with the mechanisms of oceanic trade, not least in terms of the *barāt* payment orders used to transfer cash across the ocean.[67] Whatever his connections with his family business during the 1860s, living in Isfahan, Kerman and Yazd he could not have remained unaware of the changes that shifts in oceanic trading patterns were having on Iranian society. By 1850 there were already as many as fifty shops in Yazd dealing solely in British goods from India, and ten British subjects

(Hindu merchants from Sind in the Bombay Presidency) engaged in trade there.[68] From the 1850s the import of British and British-Indian goods (textiles in particular) began to have profound effects on the Iranian economy, and Manchester and then Bombay cottons became a common sight in the great Isfahan bazaar in his home city. The domestic handicrafts industry was collapsing in the face of these machine-made imports, such that in Kashan and Yazd the main traditional industry of hand-loom silk-weaving virtually disappeared. In Yazd the silk mills were turned into opium gardens, and from the early 1860s opium began to dominate the export trade. As cities with their roles in the trading chain between Bushire and Bombay, and with growing communities of British Indian merchants, while Safi 'Ali was in Kerman and Yazd the fact that Bombay was the source of these changes can scarcely have gone unnoticed.[69] While little is known of Safi 'Ali's own mercantile activities, given his background, itinerary and the familiarity with merchant activities that surfaces in his writings, there is reason to believe that mysticism and commerce overlapped in his career, as in those of his contemporaries, so fitting with the larger overlap between the religious and commercial economies of the Indian Ocean.

Like many others of his mercantile background in this period, Safi 'Ali became enamoured of the Sufi life at an early age. At the age of around twenty he travelled to Shiraz to be initiated by the leading Ni'matullahi master Rahmat 'Ali Shah (d. 1278/1861), part of the second generation of distributors of the brotherhood firm that had been reintroduced to Iran from Hyderabad and Bombay in the early 1800s. Rahmat 'Ali had also developed such close relations with the Agha Khan in Mahallat in the 1830s before the latter migrated to India that even after Rahmat 'Ali's death the Agha Khan regularly sent money from Bombay for the upkeep of his tomb in Shiraz in Iran.[70] Even at the inception of his career, Safi 'Ali was therefore tied into the network of mercantile and religious exchanges that from around 1800 connected the towns of central Iran with Bombay. Indeed, from 1860 he spent three years in Yazd in the same years that the Bombay Parsi missionary Manikji Hataria was exporting Bombay's religious Reformism to its Zoroastrians. Safi 'Ali then moved for a shorter period to Kerman, a merchant city also being brought into Bombay's commercial hinterland in this period, before making the first of three journeys to Bombay in 1280/1864. His ability to make several other journeys to Bombay in the late 1860s and early 1870s is testament to the itinerant possibilities of the steamship era.[71]

By the time of his first journey, the steamship network that had been developing in the Indian Ocean since the 1830s was, as it were, in full steam.[72] Ships regularly sailed between Bombay and the southern Iranian ports of Bandar 'Abbas and, particularly, Bushire, from where Safi 'Ali himself departed. In the year of his first Indian journey in 1864, the ships operated by the British Indian Steam Navigation Company were sufficiently regular as to warrant daily advertisements listed under the image of a steamship on the front page of the *Bombay Gazette* newspaper: 'Steam to the Persian Gulf' under the sure command of Captain Taunton.[73] Nor was Safi 'Ali the only participant in the Bombay religious market to make use of this route, for in addition to the other Iranians who sailed from Bushire to Bombay, the same route also carried European missionaries between Bombay and Iran, so pointing towards the common role of Christian firms in both regions' religious economies. One of these was the celebrated missionary Reverend Joseph Wolff (1795–1862), who travelled to Bombay in 1833 at the end of a preaching tour of Iran. Hosted in Bombay by the SMS representative, John Wilson, Wolff lectured to large assemblies of Muslims and Hindus gathered in the hall of the recently opened neo-classical town hall.[74] Closer to the time of Safi 'Ali's own journey, in 1867 Reverend James Paterson sailed from Bushire on the steamship *Martaban* with the aim of preaching to the mariners who passed through the port of Bombay.[75] Paterson's motive is remarkably close to what we are told of the official purpose behind Safi 'Ali's first journey there in 1864 on the instructions of the Ni'matullāhī shaykh Munawwar 'Ali Shāh: as a trusted representative (*mu'taminī*) sent to ensure that the 'students of India' (*tālibān-e hind*) linked to the brotherhood were properly directed.[76] Indeed, we even hear talk of the motive for the journey as being a 'rebellion' (*sarkashī*) among the Ni'matullāhī firm's disciples in India, placing Safi 'Ali into a position of asserting control over a transoceanic constituency that Chapter 5 shows repeated in the activities of Safi 'Ali's own friend, the Āghā Khān.[77]

Safi 'Ali's Persian account of his early life and travels was purportedly written down according to his own words by his younger brother and deputy, Āghā Rizā Huzūr 'Ali (better known as Shams al-'Urafā), and has only recently been published.[78] Along with this account there also exists a short biography of Safi 'Ali that was published in his own lifetime, in 1308/1890, in the Iranian journal *Sharaf*, a kind of society magazine which featured portraits of nobles and statesmen accompanied by their biographies.[79] Like other producers of Customary Islam, Safi 'Ali appeared in the characteristically modern genre of the printed journal. It is on the *Sharaf* article and his dictated travel memoirs that the following discussions are based, though these accounts are also confirmed in outline by the version given in Nā'ib al-Sadr's early twentieth-century *Tarā'iq al-haqā'iq*.[80] Travelling in

FIGURE 12. The Sufi as celebrity: Lithograph of Safī ʿAlī Shāh (d. 1899) in *Sharaf* magazine

the 1860s and 1870s, it was not as part of an imperial geography that Safi
'Ali understood his travels, but rather as an experience of an enchanted
oceanic geography tied together by the shrines of the Ni'matullāhi saints
in India and Iran and the steamship pilgrims who travelled between them.
In order to appreciate this connected geography it is necessary to recount
something of the history of the Ni'matullāhi brotherhood. Founded by
Shāh Ni'matullāh Wali (d. 834/1431), such was the latter's fame that during his own lifetime members of his family were brought from Iran to
settle in the Indian city of Bidar to the north of Hyderabad.[81] Close to the
Bahmani sultans who had summoned them to Bidar, when the brotherhood firm was suppressed in Iran under the clerical purges of the middle
Safavid period, it survived through the Indian branch established by Shāh
Ni'matullāh's son, Shāh Khalīlullāh.[82] After a three-hundred-year 'exile' in
the territories of what was by this point the Nizam's state of Hyderabad,
in the last years of the eighteenth century the Sufi emissaries of this Indian
Ni'matullāhi franchise reintroduced the Sufi brotherhoods to Iran. There
they found a hostile reception from the monopolistic Shi'i 'ulamā, but
nevertheless in the 1780s and 1790s the Indian Ni'matullāhi impressario Ma'sūm 'Ali Shāh managed to build up a considerable merchant
following across the cities of central Iran such that by the mid-nineteenth
century a Sufi revival was well under way.[83] As other Indian Sufis followed in Ma'sūm 'Ali's wake, and as Iranian 'converts' began to spread
the Ni'matullāhi brotherhood firm through local religious markets opening up in towns all across Iran, the late nineteenth and early twentieth
centuries saw imported customary firms flourish in Iran after centuries
of the state-sponsored suppression of Sufi shaykhs as competitors of the
'ulamā. Shi'i state-sponsored regulation of the Iranian religious economy
was therefore being shaken by Sufi no less than Christian missions, by
Zoroastrians as well as Bahā'īs, all of whom had links with Bombay.

Despite this success, the Sufis' position was often precarious and, in
India as in Iran, they were surrounded by numerous rivals and detractors
in the Indian Ocean's competitive religious economy. While influential
Sufi shaykhs did find powerful investors, their doctrines and charismatic
persons competed with the Shi'i 'ulamā, and were to remain controversial throughout Safi 'Ali's career. Nonetheless, for much of the first fifteen
years of Safi 'Ali's life, the royal patronage of Muhammad Shāh Qājār
(r. 1250–64/1834–48) had ensured Ni'matullāhi entrepreneurs a protected
place in the Iranian market from which to propagate their doctrines.
The fame and franchises of the Ni'matullāhi impressarios subsequently
spread widely in the trading cities of central Iran. But by the 1860s, when

Safī 'Alī set off for India, the Ni'matullāhī position in the religious economy of Iran was again precarious, with Shi'i clerics attempting – with
state support – to reimpose their monopoly over Muslim religious production. Like other Iranian Sufis of the period, Safī Alī realized that richer
resources and better opportunities could be found in India, not least
from the Iranian 'court-in-exile' surrounding the Āghā Khān in Bombay.
Safī Alī's journey to India therefore partly drew on the early modern
history of Shaykh Khalīlullāh, Bidar and, by the way of the Bahmani
sultans, the shrine itineraries through which they connected Iran and
India in Ni'matullāhī eyes. But after centuries of the abeyance of those
brief early modern interactions, it was the nineteenth-century revival of
these exchanges, through the cheaper travel opportunities afforded by
Bombay's steamship networks and the presence there of Āghā Khān and
a rich cohort of Iranian merchants, that re-established and substantially
reinvented this oceanic network of religious exchange.

Though enabled by new networks of steamships and merchants, Safī
'Alī's presentation of his travels drew on customary idioms describing
visions of dead saints and commands of living shaykhs. The accounts of
his travels in the nineteenth-century journal *Sharaf* and the early twentieth-century Ni'matullāhī history *Tarā'iq al-haqā'iq* describe how Safī
'Alī left Isfahan aged twenty (that is, around 1271/1854) to seek out the
celebrated holy man and preceptor of the Āghā Khān, Rahmat 'Alī Shāh,
in Shiraz.[84] Safī 'Alī's travelogue makes it clear that for him the geography in which he moved was not one governed by the capitalist archons of
Bombay, but a space instead organized round the shrines of the saints and
the presence of their living representatives. The itinerary that he trod was
as enchanted geography made meaningful through supernatural experiences at its nodes in the shrines of the holy dead.

Two decades after Safī 'Alī's visit to the shrine of Shāh Ni'matullāh at
Mahan in south-eastern Iran the British consul there, Percy Sykes, observed
fine shawls covering the sepulchre and a pair of black buck horns adorn-
ing the walls that had been brought from India by visiting pilgrims travelling the same route as Safī 'Alī in the opposite direction.[85] Moving on
from the shrine of Shāh Ni'matullāh at Mahan, Safī 'Alī broke his journey to India in the Omani port of Muscat, where most of the Bombay–
Bushire steamships refuelled. In view of his account of spending eleven
days almost starving there in a ruined *takiyya* (dervish lodge) outside the
port, it seems likely that he had to disembark there because he was unable
to afford a through-passage to Bombay. Echoes of this journey are heard
in a story of another Iranian Sufi, recounted in early twentieth-century

Bombay, concerning Mīrzā Muhammad Husayn Sabzawārī, who decided
to make the journey to Bombay after inspiration from the 'hidden world'
(*ghayb*).[86] But the stops along the route were many – Muscat, Karachi,
Porbandar – and though Mīrzā Muhammad was in the habit of exploring
each of them, on likewise landing on the Arabian peninsula at Muscat he
was warned that the locals turned foreigners into lambs and roasted them
on spits for their supper. Though probably a joke, the anecdote does give
us a sense of the strangeness of even the Muslim sections of the ocean
journey in a period in which Pan-Islamism was by no means the automatic
response to the greater opportunities of steam travel. After eleven days of
pecuniary misfortunes in Muscat, for his part Safi 'Ali had the good fortune
to find a ship in port whose captain was a disciple of the Ni'matullāhī
shaykh Mast 'Ali Shāh, having met the latter on a journey to Mecca a few
years earlier.[87] Given that steamship captains were invariably Europeans
at this time, the mention of this presumably Muslim captain suggests that
it was a more traditional vessel on which Safi 'Ali made this portion of his
journey rather than the *Semiramis*, which was the main steamship operating the direct Muscat–Bombay passage in the year of Safi 'Ali's journey
in 1864.[88] More significantly, the help from the fellow Ni'matullāhī captain
points to the practical benefits that could be accrued by entering a transnational Sufi firm. Such practical services can be compared to the self-help
societies that sprang up elsewhere in the nineteenth century, a perspective
seen again in Chapter 6 in services offered by other Sufi organizations
amid the poverty of Bombay's dock and mill workers.

With the help of the Ni'matullāhī captain, Safi 'Ali crossed the Arabian
Sea to Bombay, and on arriving there set out to find the house of his
acquaintance Mīrzā Shafi', one of the sons of the exiled Iranian notable
and fellow Ni'matullāhī supporter Āghā Khān I.[89] On reaching the Āghā
Khān's house, he was greeted by an Iranian servant from the Āghā Khān's
home town of Mahallat, who with traditional hospitality brought the
guest a water pipe, which Safi 'Ali sat smoking until the head of the house
returned. Unfortunately, Mīrzā Shafi' seems not to have recognized Safi
'Ali, whose sense of honour overcame his evident needs so as to force him
to leave the house and seek accommodation elsewhere. Asking a stranger
where Iranians usually stayed in Bombay, he was given directions to the
Iranian mosque, but on getting there found it to be in poor condition. As
in Muscat a few weeks earlier, once again Safi 'Ali was down on his luck.
If this time there was no 'brother-under-the-master' (*barādar-e pīr*) from
the same brotherhood firm to help him, he was no less fortunate to run
into an Iranian from his home province of Fars, who owned a gold shop

FIGURE 13. Shiraz overseas: Iranian Mosque (founded 1858), Dongri, Bombay

opposite the Iranian mosque in the market which remains the heart of
Bombay's Shi'i quarter to this day. In a city of strangers, such common
origins were important resources for social networking, and the gold
merchant offered to host Safi 'Ali for the night. The next morning the
merchant informed him about a small house on the mosque's property
that was part of its charitable *waqf* endowment and had a tenant who
was leaving that very day, adding that he could arrange for the newcomer
to take over the tenancy. Glad to have found a compatriot in the anonym-
ity of the industrializing city, Safi 'Ali accepted the offer and moved into
the house beside the mosque.

The mosque in which Safi 'Ali stayed was the Īrānī Masjid, located in
Bombay's Dongri quarter. Completed in 1274/1858 and positioned at the
heart of the city's Iranian quarter, the 'Iranian mosque' was architecturally quite distinct from the other mosques of the city, being designed in the
Iranian style, with a walled courtyard with a rectangular pool and a low
pillared prayer hall at the far end.[90] The gateway and the mosque building
proper were embellished with bright polychrome tiles brought from Iran
in the period of the great Qājār revival of ceramic decoration. The source
of this patronage was the Iranian merchant Hājj Muhammad Husayn

Shīrāzī who, as holder of the semi-formal office of *malik al-tujjār* (king of the merchants) among Bombay's Iranian community, was expected to disseminate charity to such pious causes. Indeed, the mosque became one of the city's most important places for celebrating Muharram (whose month-long meetings in turn provided another outlet for merchant charity), while one side of the courtyard was bordered by residential rooms for the poor: it was presumably in one of these that Safi 'Alī lodged. In finding a residence at the mosque, he thus fitted into the wider picture of the city's Iranian merchants providing for their dervish compatriots who regularly reached Bombay, so channelling their profits into the customary religious productions associated with such Sufis.

Soon after moving into the mosque property Safi 'Alī met his intended host, Mīrzā Shafi', though he recalled how the meeting quickly ended in a falling out. It was only later that night when the Mīrzā's son became violently ill that he realized the advantages of being in the favour of a holy man such as Safi 'Alī. Regretting his earlier actions, the Mīrzā set out to find him, begging Safi 'Alī to come and recite Shi'i prayers in the hope of healing the child. He agreed, and on his performing the ritual the child's eyes opened and he sat up, mysteriously healed. Delighted at this turn of events, the boy's parents offered Safi 'Alī the proper recompense for his intercession by way of a plate of gold coins and a symbolic bowl of barley sugar (*nabāt*). The anecdote is very revealing of the activities – and, indeed, the economy – of the itinerant holy men such as Safi 'Alī who moved between Iran and Bombay, pointing to the customary practices of healing and intercession by which such Sufis earned their living. But, in its hint that the child's sickness was retribution for his father's insult to the holy man earlier in the day, as Safi 'Alī recounted it the story also points towards the darker side of such supernatural powers. Found in scores of similar stories of offended saints, it helps explain both the reverence in which such men were held by their followers and the contempt with which they were regarded by their Reformist critics, for whom such dervishes were little better than callous frauds. But amidst an economy of almsgiving on which hundreds of professional religious beggars depended for their living, and a small group of wealthy Muslims who supported it with their charity, the old ways were maintained by customary patterns of pious exchange that were re-empowered by the wealth divergence of a new capitalistic economy. Whether it was at the recovery or the death of a member of a family of means, Bombay's Muslim mendicants were always there to demand the righteous financial recompense for their prayers. In the words of a popular expression recorded in the Bombay marketplace a few years before Safi 'Ali's arrival, 'When a Mussulman dies ... the family suffer two calamities: first, some loved one is lost; then a large sum of money must be spent – for they are obliged to give *Kairat* [*khayrat*], or alms, and to incur expenses which often they can ill afford, merely to keep up their name and character.'[91]

In line with this economy of pious – and occasionally miraculous – exchanges, having healed the child, Safi 'Ali's own fortunes then took a turn for the better. Three days later the Āghā Khān's son and future successor Āghā 'Alī Shāh sent a carriage to collect him from his poor-man's lodgings at the Irāni Masjid.[92] Entering the circle of the Āghā Khān – Bombay's greatest patron of expatriate Iranian Sufis – Safi 'Ali began a relationship with the family that would define the rest of his stay in India and his departure from it four years later. Like the other Iranian travellers to Bombay seen earlier in this chapter, Safi 'Alī became a personal guest of the Āghā Khān while becoming increasingly close to his son, the future Āghā Khān II. Safi 'Alī recounted several anecdotes in which the Āghā Khān and his heir featured. One of these describes one of the parties given by the Āghā Khān at his Bombay mansion in Mazagaon to celebrate the month of Ramazan.[93] Safi 'Alī was 'shown lots of kindness' by the Āghā Khān during the gathering, and impressed him so much with his religious learning that the Āghā Khān sent him a purse containing 110 gold *ashrafi*s (coins), a clear admission of the Āghā Khān's lavish investment in the Sufis he hosted in Bombay, helping explain the attraction of the city to the Iranian Sufis who travelled there. In other anecdotes Safi 'Alī described being in the company of the Āghā Khān during a visit to Poona and with his heir Āghā 'Alī Shāh in Surat, both towns in the Bombay Presidency with Ismā'īlī merchant populations investing in the Āghā Khān's own family religious firm. The claim has a ring of credibility in view of the fact that the Āghā Khāns were building a palace in Poona at this time and that Āghā 'Alī Shāh was making proselytizing journeys to the Ismā'īlī communities of Gujarat and Sind from the 1860s onwards. Persian sources also describe other Iranian Sufis, such as Muhammad Hasan Sabzawārī, making the journey from Bombay to Poona by train.[94] *Tarā'iq al-haqā'iq* describes the train journeys of the Iranian Sufi and merchant Āghā Muhammad Hasan Shīrāzī, who moved back and forth between Bombay and Hyderabad, and then to Bangalore and the rest of southern India, a tour that, its Iranian recounter noted, were it not for the railway would have taken two years instead of five months.[95] Given that Surat was only absorbed into the Bombay Presidency in 1803, and Poona in 1817, the geography of Safi 'Alī's journeys was that of Bombay's industrialized travel links to the towns of its continental market hinterland. Making use of these new communications, Safi ʿAlī and the Āghā Khāns were making missionary tours to disseminate allegiance to their religious firms and so collect the tithes that came with such allegiance.

When Safi ʿAlī finally left Bombay, his departure for Mecca was prompted by a meeting he had with a *yogi* outside the Bombay Presidency port of Surat. Safi ʿAlī explained to the *yogi* that he had not been able to make his arrangements for the *hajj*, and so had to wait another whole year before he could depart. The *yogi* enigmatically assured him that all of his arrangements would be made if he left immediately. When he reached Bombay the Āghā Khān's heir informed him that a ship was due to depart for Jidda the next morning. Safi ʿAlī described the Āghā Khān's wife personally preparing his belongings and having them brought to him in the company of fourteen servants, with whom he eventually boarded ship, perhaps in the P&O docks near the Mazagaon home of the Āghā Khān. Travelling in such style, the departure of Safi ʿAlī and his new servants reflected the arrival in Bombay of the Qādirī saint of Baghdad Sayyid Ibrāhīm Sayf al-dīn, which was seen greeted in Chapter 3 by a collection of praise-poems. The pomp and circumstance of such grand Sufi sea journeys was sufficiently noticeable to attract the criticism of other Indian shaykhs of the period. In his early twentieth-century *Shamāmat al-ambar* (The amber-perfumed pastille), Sayyid Wāris Hasan (d. 1355/1936) scoffed at 'how many and various are the items of comfort and relaxation that are assembled and then carried on the journey' and described himself boarding ship to cross the Indian Ocean with nothing more than his prayer beads (*tasbih*), loincloth (*lungī*) and trust in God (*tawakkul*).[96] Safi ʿAlī by contrast seems to have been one of the comfortable travellers of the steamship age, if not quite one of the strolling, smoking and game-playing passengers described in the Persian travelogue of the Hyderabadi notable Mīr Lāʾiq ʿAlī Khān Sālār Jang as present on his steamer out of Bombay in 1888.[97] Despite the generosity of the Āghā Khān's family, Safi ʿAlī finished the narrative by pointing out that all this was in fact due to the mystical help – the *nafas*, literally the 'breath' – of the *yogi* who had predicted it.[98] Yet it was of course an outcome of the intertwinings of the commercial and religious economy of Bombay.

PRINTING ONE'S WAY TO PROMINENCE

Between its *yogis* and steamships, Bombay's religious economy enabled Safi ʿAlī to access the resources that helped build his reputation before returning to Iran in the late 1860s. Here no less important than his relationship with the Āghā Khān was Safi ʿAli's publication in Bombay of his first work, *Zubdat al-asrār* (The essence of secrets), in 1289/1872. In a clear indication of the links of his patrons, the Āghā Khān's family, to Bombay's business in Persian publishing, in 1278/1861 Āghā Khān I himself published his memoirs in Bombay, a full decade before Safi ʿAli issued his *Zubdat al-asrār* there. We know that the Bombay printing ensured the book's distribution across the ocean, not least because Safi ʿAli himself described how it was soon being read in Baghdad, so spreading his claims to religious authority from Bombay to Iraq. Numerous lithographic editions of the *Masnawi* of Rūmi were published in Bombay from the 1260s/1840s onwards, and it was against this background that Safi ʿAli's own imitative *masnawi* poem, *Zubdat al-asrār*, was published.[99] As Juan Cole has noted of the role of Bombay printing in the career of the Iranian Pan-Islamist Abū'l Hasan Mīrzā Shaykh al-Ra'īs during the 1890s, 'the way in which publishing his memoirs, poetry and essays in British India helped create for Shaykh al-Rais a sort of celebrity in Iran points to the growing impact of printing and lithography at this time'.[100] With Safi ʿAli's book too, this was made possible by the Muslim investment in industrialized printing in Bombay that, given the relatively undeveloped state of publishing in Iran itself, was all the more useful in making celebrity.

At the economic heart of the Indian Ocean in Bombay, the existence of a transnational Persian printing industry thus allowed Safi ʿAli to publish and distribute a work that would make his name as a shaykh in direct contact with God. Like the other charismatic shaykhs being empowered by print, he emerged as a mediator figure for the Niʿmatullāhi brotherhood firm which during his lifetime came to place great brand emphasis on the intercession of the master and the practice of 'picturing the shaykh' (*tasawwur-e shaykh*), the spread of which is seen in Chapter 6 to be connected to the increasing number of photographic or lithographic portraits of Muslim holy men that characterized this period. In his recollection of his interview with the pre-eminent Twelver Shiʿite cleric (*marjaʿ-ye taqlīd*) Shaykh Murtazā, Safi ʿAli recalled how the latter had said in Iraq that he had read *Zubdat al-asrār* and found it a good but difficult book (even his fellow Niʿmatullāhi Nā'ib al-Sadr Shīrāzī commented that it needed to read again and again to be understood).[101] In a defence and promotion of the truth-claims he made in *Zubdat al-asrār*, Safi ʿAli replied that the difficulty came from the fact that he had written it in a state of ecstasy (*jazba*), during which the reins of authorship were out of his control. With its repeated evocation of the imagery of the ocean (*bahr*) and its waves (*amwāj*), *Zubdat al-asrār* was an appropriation of the semantic power of the high seas to depict the vast oceans of knowledge that swayed within the soul of the 'friend of God'.[102] This was by no means the only Sufi text to use the experience of sea travel for poetic inspiration, and on the other side of the ocean an extensive body of mystical literature was developing in Malay which drew even more explicitly on the imagery of sea journeys.[103] Inspiration aside, on a more practical level, Safi 'Ali candidly noted that *Zubdat al-asrār* had only been published with the help in Bombay of Āghā 'Ali Shāh, the future Āghā Khān II, 'whom God', he asserted, 'had made a friend of mine'.[104]

Here Safi 'Ali participated in a larger economy of Iranian book production in Bombay which, in a period when printing was still undeveloped in Iran itself, formed one of the most important ways in which Bombay's industrial religious economy impacted the largely preindustrial religious market in Iran. While other Indian centres of Persian publishing existed in such inland cities as Lucknow, none could compete with the port of Bombay for the logistical simplicity of exporting books to Iran. As a result, from early after its inception, Bombay's Persian printing industry developed in connection with this oceanic market and the demands of its readers.[105] While the lithographic books themselves form the main evidence, we occasionally hear references to their publishers. One Persian biographical collection, for example, described Khātim Mīrzā Ahmad, who was born in Fars in 1232/1817, as the son of an Iranian poet who had earlier spent a decade in India as panegyrist to the Nizams of Hyderabad. In 1266/1850 Khātim Mīrzā had also travelled to Bombay and spent a year there, where he learned to print and succeeded in putting out an edition of the *Masnawī* of Rūmī, because copies of even this most famous of Persian poems were hard to come by in Iran.[106] A longer-lasting role in the development of Bombay's Persian publishing industry was played by Mīrzā Muhammad Shīrāzī (b. 1269/1852).[107] In 1868 this entrepreneur from Shiraz opened one of Bombay's most important Persian bookstores and publishing houses. In the following years he published new editions of various classical works, such as Dawlatshāh Samarqandī's *Tazkirat al-shu'arā* (Recollections of the poets), as well as several commemorative writings of his own concerning female poets and history. Shipped to markets in Iran, these Bombay-printed classics had a large impact there, in the case of one 1849 Bombay illustrated *Shāhnāma* even inspiring architectural reproductions of its lithographic illustrations in stucco sculptures in the Iranian port at Bandar-e Tahiri.[108] Another printing entrepreneur, Hājjī Muhammad Ibrāhīm Shīrāzī, travelled from Iran to Bombay and spent years preparing the manuscripts of well-known books in a form suitable for printing. However, after losing his fortune when his cargo went down with a ship, he was forced to move to Hyderabad and become a teacher of Persian.[109] For publishing, as for religious entrepreneurs, the Bombay economy was volatile and competitive.

Amid this oceanic Persian printing industry, Reformist books were also published in Bombay. As noted earlier, the most famous of all Iranian Reformists, Jamāl al-dīn 'al-Afghānī' (1254–1314/1838–97), spent time among the Iranian exiles of Bombay, and it was there around 1273/1857 that he first came into contact with Europeans and learned of their domination of a Muslim society, which would become the main topic of his career.[110] Between 1296/1879 and 1299/1882 on a second visit to Bombay (and from there to Hyderabad), he wrote and published in Persian the first of his writings, including his major work *Haqīqat-e mazhab-e naychari wa bayān-e hāl-e naychariyān* (Truth about natural religion and the condition of the naturalists), written in echoes of the competitive plural market of Islams in rejection of the pro-scientific doctrines of Sayyid Ahmad Khān. While it was first published as a lithograph in Hyderabad in 1298/1881, a second edition soon followed in Bombay, from where it was distributed more effectively as yet another production of the city's religious economy.[111]

However, as Chapter 3 described, Bombay was more important as a producer of books that appealed to the Customary Islamic trends in the market. This was no less the case with regard to the Iranian stake in Bombay's economy of printing. One of the most significant texts to be published in Bombay in this respect was *Sawānih al-ayyām fi mushāhadāt al-a'wām*, better known as *Silsilat al-'ārifīn* (Genealogy of gnostics), which was printed there in 1307/1890.[112] *Silsilat al-'ārifīn* is interesting in several ways, not least as a textual echo of the links we are seeing between Bombay and the Ni'matullāhī Sufi revival in Iran. The published text was an unattributed near copy of a long section from book three of the *Jāmi'-ye Mufīdī*, a history of the Iranian city of Yazd that had been completed in 1099/1679 by Muhammad Mufīd Mustawfī Yazdī, who had himself borrowed much of the material from an earlier hagiography of the Ni'matullāhī shaykhs by Mawlānā Sun'ullāh.[113] Printed in Bombay without attribution as an original work bearing its own name of *Silsilat al-'ārifīn* rather than its author's original title, the book reflected the commercially unregulated character of Bombay's book market, in which bookseller-printers frequently reissued books piecemeal, amalgamated or however else they thought they could sell them. Commercial strategies aside, the contents of the text itself reflected the rise in hagiographical printing seen in Chapter 3 and point to the role of Iranians within it. *Silsilat al-'ārifīn* consisted of a biography of Shāh Ni'matullāh Walī (d. 834/1431), the founder of the eponymous Sufi

brotherhood whose shrine at Mahan, outside Kerman in Iran, formed the
principal pilgrimage site of his followers right into the twentieth century.
As a product of the late Safavid period, one of the purposes of the original
text was to solve the long-standing problem of the relation of ordinarily
Sunni Sufis to the Shi'i norms of Iran. Thus Shāh Ni'matullāh was seen
piously visiting the key Shi'i holy sites in Iraq and Mashhad, which took
the place of the pilgrimages to saintly shrines that usually featured in such
Sufi hagiographies, while even his miracles (such as leaping into a well
in Hilla to replenish its water) contained echoes of older Shi'i imamog-
raphy.[114] But in being printed and reproduced in late nineteenth-century
Bombay, the text entered the market of this later period.

When, as in other customary forms of hagiography, Shāh Ni'matullāh
was presented as having a precociously learned and miracle-working childhood, like the stories of other 'mother-born saints' (*mādar-zād awliyā*),
he supported the Customary Islamic notion of an existential hierarchy of
men that stood in clear contrast to the Reformist ideal of a horizontally
'democratic' community of Muslim believers.[115] The very practices that
the saint was described as performing – such as the graveside meditation
(*kashf-e qubūr*) through which power and inspiration were sought from
the dead – acted in turn in the marketplace as a hagiographical promotion of the customary rituals that Reformists condemned as idolatrous.[116]
In the late nineteenth century, when the revival of Sufi firms' influence in
Iran had created a marketplace and print culture that was no less polemical than in India, *Silsilat al-'ārifin* served as a rejoinder that stressed the
Ni'matullāhīs' Shi'i credentials by describing Shāh Ni'matullāh making
pilgrimages to the Shi'i holy sites of Najaf and Karbala.[117] In partaking
from Bombay in a debate in distant Iran, in this respect the book bore
much in common with Bombay's role in Iranian political exile literature. On a wider level, *Silsilat al-'ārifin* served in the religious economy
to publicize the awesome powers of the saints associated with brotherhood firms, reminding readers through narrative examples of the reasons
they might repair to the living saints of their own times. The miraculous examples provided in the text were often dramatic, and we have
already seen one in Chapter 3 when Shāh Ni'matullāh was connected
with the rescue of a sinking merchant ship.[118] Other stories were no less
dramatic. When wandering through Egypt in search of the source of the
Nile, Shāh Ni'matullāh came across a village that had been decimated by
a pride of giant lions that had dragged to their den most of the village's
menfolk. Unperturbed even as he approached the lair of lions 'who were
so fearsome that even Leo would not dare to face them at dawn', Shāh

Ni'matullāh looked at them with an angry glance and commanded them
to cease oppressing the people of the village. Acquiescing, they fell to
his feet like cats and bowed before him.[119] In another instance, the saint
astounded a sceptical follower by turning a rock into a ruby.[120] During
the same journeys, when Shāh Ni'matullāh was lost, one of his holy
ancestors (again the customary emphasis on family lineage) appeared in
a dream to guide him through the Sahara.[121]

Clearly, the powers of such friends of God were something to be reck-
oned with and, with the appearance of the stories in print, at the end of the
nineteenth century more people could read them than ever. Given the rise
of the Ni'matullāhī brotherhood firm in Iran at this time, like the other
Ni'matullāhī texts published in Bombay, *Silsilat al-'ārifīn* points to the
important role of the city's book market in this transoceanic promoting
of Sufi authority that affected the religious economy of Iran. It also points
again to the role of entertainment in the religious economy. For, in a sense,
Silsilat al-'ārifīn was a storybook of enchanted travels in exotic lands, of
the journeys of the saintly hero through Persia and Turkestan, through
Egypt in search of the source of the Nile and to the holy earth of Karbala
and Mecca. As a book of adventures, *Silsilat al-'ārifīn* can also therefore be
seen as part of the explosion of travel writing that accompanied the new
mobility of the nineteenth century. For though comprising miracle stories,
its tales of Shāh Ni'matullāh were in large part tales of the adventures that
befell him on his travels. Travelling to Mecca, Hilla, Baghdad and Egypt,
where he searched for the source of the Nile, in *Silsilat al-'ārifīn* Shāh
Ni'matullāh appeared as an enchanted version of Alexander the Great as
known from the 'Sikandar' romances of Persian tradition.

Though written a few centuries earlier, in its publication in 1890
in Bombay, a time and a place where thousands of Muslims annually
embarked on pilgrimage to the same places described in its pages, *Silsilat
al-'ārifīn* can be seen as part of the wider literature of miraculous travel
that flourished in the marketplace in this period. We can imagine the
appeal of its stories, entertaining and yet pious, to pilgrims squeezed
on the cramped decks of steamers that plied the route between Bombay
and Jidda. If Chapter 3 described new miracles occurring at sea through
the growth of the *hajj* in the nineteenth and early twentieth centuries,
then here was another side of the same increasing production of miracle stories, with tales being recited on board the ships sailing to Mecca,
and perhaps in the ports of southern Iran as well. For travellers setting
out from Bombay on their own journeys, or even for the sedentary
citizens of the great port city, the popularity of such an enchanted text

is understandable. The sheer entertainment value of books such as that of the adventures of Shāh Niʿmatullāh maintained the profile in the marketplace of Customary Islam and its brotherhoods and saints above the legalizing disenchantment of their Reformist competitors.

5

The Making of a Neo-Ismāʿilism

THE ĀGHĀ KHĀNS AND THEIR NEO-ISMĀʿILISM

Among the many Iranian exiles attracted to Bombay was the most important figure to leave Iran for India during the nineteenth century. This was the would-be leader of the disconnected Ismāʿili Shiʿi Muslims of India and Iran: Āghā Khān I (d. 1298/1881) of Mahallat in central Iran.[1] Before moving into exile in India, Āghā Khān I had served Iran's Qājār rulers as governor of the southern frontier province of Kerman, and was more widely regarded as a provincial notable and soldier than a religious figure. The last chapter showed how Iranian Sufis such as Safi ʿAli Shāh, sponsored by the wealthy Iranian merchants who settled in Bombay and making use of the city's printing and travel opportunities to spread their authority, were able to use Bombay as a platform for their extraordinary leap to prominence in Iran in the second half of the nineteenth century. By similar means, after settling in Bombay in 1848, Āghā Khān I was able to use the city's communication, mercantile and administrative facilities to expand his authority over nominal Ismāʿilis to a degree without precedent in history. As with Sufi entrepreneurs, in the career of the Āghā Khān and his sons and successors, Bombay's religious economy was put to the service of an expansive mission for an Islam of living intercessors and the miraculous powers lent them by their proximity to God. The new status the first two Āghā Khāns acquired in Bombay involved the reinvention of what in Iran at least was a model of authority that had been dormant for centuries. If the Āghā Khāns were ultimately more successful in the Indian marketplace by bringing more Indian than Iranian Muslims under their sway, the new-found prominence that Bombay afforded them

155

triggered widespread fears and discussions among Iranian Shi'i clerics as to the veracity of the Āghā Khāns' claims to be the living point of contact with God. Even if the Āghā Khāns would only capture a limited portion of the religious marketplace in Iran, the very fact of their well-publicized entry to it shook the complacency of the old monopolists. Like Parsi Zoroastrians, Bahā'īs and Sufis, from Bombay the Ismā'īlī Āghā Khāns helped pluralize the religious economy of Iran as well as India.

In the decades after the arrival there of Āghā Khān I in 1848, Bombay became the new focus for the disparate Ismā'īlī communities that, like the Zoroastrians and Twelver Shi'ites, had long been dispersed throughout oceanic India and Iran. As products of an older period of less efficiently connected diasporas, their reconnection in the age of the steamship was not without its problems. In large part, the Āghā Khān's centralizing initiative was enabled by the industrializing travel networks that Bombay's Sufis were also exploiting, such that his heir Āghā 'Alī Shāh was able to visit the various Ismā'īlī communities of the subcontinent and connect them to their new religious centre – or, rather, person – in Bombay. In a logistical sense, it was a mission that was near-identical to that of the city's Parsi and Christian firms. In his intellectual contours, what Āghā Khān I and his heir achieved had nothing in common with the rationalizing Reformism of such contemporaries as Sayyid Ahmad Khān. On the contrary, theirs was a hierarchical religious production in which religious knowledge and salvation were found not in the community – still less in books, or even a scripture accessible through education – but in obedience and fealty to a charismatic holy man, an imam in perpetual contact with Allah. While Ismā'īlism is conventionally regarded as a stable religious formation passed down through an ancient pedigree of familial imams, the following pages argue that the prominence and characteristics of the Āghā Khāns' 'family firm' were very much a product of the religious economy of nineteenth-century Bombay.

Almost six hundred years since the fall of the last Iranian Ismā'īlī stronghold of Alamut, by 1800 the Ismā'īlī imamate had long slipped into provincial obscurity. Aside from occasional positions at court, the descendants of the imams lived such quiet lives that it is questionable whether the imamate had continued to operate through the centuries in any socially meaningful form. Even Vladimir Ivanow, the most important early European academic involved in the sponsored scholarly recovery of evidence for the Āghā Khāns' claims, casuistically admitted that 'to survive six hundred years of "underground" existence … their Imams were usually living in the guise of Sufic shaykhs'.[2] It is certainly the case that by the time Āghā Khān I's ancestors re-entered the historical record in the late eighteenth century, they were so closely associated with the Iranian revival of the Ni'matullāhī Sufis that was coming out of India that several of the direct ancestors of Āghā Khān I were initiated as disciples (*murīds*) of the Ni'matullāhi brotherhood.[3] Such dependence on the greater market recognition of Sufi rather than distinctly Isma'ili charisma stands awkwardly with the Āghā Khāns' subsequent claim to be the authoritative imams of the age in their own right with no need for such sub-contracted charisma. Yet before the move of Āghā Khān I to Bombay, the Iranian Qājār rulers Fath 'Alī Shāh (r. 1797–1834) and particularly Muhammad Shāh (r. 1834–48) viewed him as the provincial notable that in social terms he effectively was, and as such incorporated him into their fragile bureaucratic order. It was the shah who gave him the court title of Āghā Khān by which he and his descendants would become known. During the 1840s Āghā Khān I then made a failed attempt to overthrow the Qājār crown, and in the early 1840s used his troops to support the British in Afghanistan. Moving eastward into Sind in time to help with the British conquest in 1843, Āghā Khān I won enough merit in official British eyes to be given sanctuary from his former master, the shah of Iran. After a short period in Bombay in 1844 and a longer spell in Calcutta, at the end of 1848 he came to Bombay, where we have already seen a larger community of Iranian merchants and exiles developing. In 1852 he was followed by his son and heir Āghā 'Alī Shāh (d. 1302/1885), the future Āghā Khān II.

In the words of one colonial biographer, Āghā Khān I was first and foremost 'a brave and courageous soldier and leader of men'.[4] Even if he was not a major producer of religious teachings, it is clear that over the decades that followed his exile the Āghā Khān used the various opportunities that Bombay presented to 'reinvent' the customary authority of his ancestors around himself. Even if the problematic proposition that during six centuries of obscurity the Isma'ili imamate had somehow survived intact in Iran is accepted (a position that a century of sympathetic 'recovery' scholarship has tried hard to bolster) it is still clear that the Āghā Khān's Bombay years represented the most important turning point in Isma'ili history since the fall of the fortress of Alamut in 1256. In order to recognize rather than gloss over the discontinuity of Isma'ili history in the manner of many scholarly apologetics, it therefore makes sense to speak of the Āghā Khān and his sons as the modern producers of a 'Neo-Isma'ilism'. For centuries the various communities that had emerged from the efforts of Isma'ili teachers in the Middle Ages had developed their own distinct religious practices and had lived in isolation from their

supposed imams, many not even realizing that an imam still even existed.[5] With the relocation of Āghā Khān I to Bombay all this changed, setting in motion a determined missionary marketing campaign led by the
Āghā Khān and his sons to convince the various theoretically 'Ismāʿīlī'
groups in India and overseas that he was the true imam to whom they
owed not only allegiance but regular tithes as well. This process places
Āghā Khān I and his successor Āghā Khān II among the other Muslim
religious entrepreneurs in Bombay, and their Neo-Ismāʿīlism among the
other enchanted productions of its religious economy.

As such, the Āghā Khān's agenda followed a parallel pattern to the
assertion of personal charismatic authority by the Iranian and Indian
Sufi missions of the same period.[6] During its shadowy lost centuries in
provincial Iran, the Ismāʿīlī imams came to adapt much of the terminology, doctrines and rituals of the Sufis. These entanglements were still
ongoing by the start of the nineteenth century: the forty-second Ismāʿīlī
imam, Abūʾl Hasan Baylirbaygī (d. 1206/1792), was even initiated as a
disciple of the Niʿmatullāhī master Muzaffar ʿAlī Shāh and buried in a
Niʿmatullāhī shrine on his death.[7] Even Āghā Khān I seems to have been
initiated as a follower of the leading Niʿmatullāhī master, Mast ʿAlī Shāh
(d. 1253/1853).[8] Between the 1850s and early 1900s the first three Āghā
Khāns and their families played host in Bombay to numerous visitors
from Iran, including many of the leading figures of the Niʿmatullāhī Sufi
revival we have seen taking place between Iran and India. One such figure
was Safī ʿAlī Shāh, who has already been seen publishing his first book in
Bombay with the Āghā Khān's help. Nāʾib al-Sadr Shīrāzī (d. 1344/1926),
the Sufi redactor of the history of the Niʿmatullāhī order entitled *Tarāʾiq
al-haqāʾiq*, also stayed in Bombay for a year with the family of Āghā
Khān I in 1298/1881. Nāʾib al-Sadr claimed that when Āghā Khān II
was desperate for a male heir, he wrote from Bombay to the Niʿmatullāhī
master Munawwar ʿAlī Shāh to ask for an intercessionary prayer for
the birth of a son, which Mast ʿAlī successfully provided.[9] Āghā Khān I
patronized a good many other Niʿmatullāhī Sufis who also stayed with
him in Bombay, including Hājjī Pīrzāda, who in recompense was seen
in the last chapter speaking in defence of the Ismāʿīlīs in his account of
his travels. Even Reformist figures accepted the hospitality of his family,
and in the early 1890s Abūʾl Hasan Mīrzā Shaykh al-Raʾīs (d. 1920)
published his *Ittihād-e Islām* (Unity of Islam), one of the first Persian
works on Pan-Islamism, while staying as a guest in Bombay of Āghā
Khān II.[10] Nor was the family's hospitality limited to Muslim visitors: in
around 1292/1875 the great Bahāʾī missionary Jamāl Effendī (d. 1898)

also visited the future Āghā Khān II in Bombay, before following the latter's example by setting off on his own proselytizing journeys through
South-East Asia, powered again by the city's steam routes.[11] These links
with such figures are sufficiently clear to place the Āghā Khāns into
Bombay's larger economy of religious transactions – and, more specifically, into its Iranian export section.

As eventually the most prominent and probably most wealthy Iranian
resident in Bombay, Āghā Khān I won prominence in the eyes of Iranians
back home. His great mansion in the Mazagaon quarter became a centre
for the annual Muharram celebrations for the city's Twelver Shi'ites as
well as its smaller Isma'ili community.[12] Given the earlier political ambi-
tions and Sufi initiation of Āghā Khān I in Iran, his mansion in Mazagaon
was therefore at once the house of the living imam, an Iranian Sufi lodge
and a court in exile. From this grand house in the Mazagaon dock district, Āghā Khān I and his heir Āghā Khān II were well placed to dis-
patch and receive travellers from across their oceanic domain. Bombay
afforded their rise to power, a possibility afforded not merely by the city's
communications technology but also as a centre for the new social technology of the mission. The renewed contacts between the first two Āghā
Khāns and the nominal 'Isma'ilis' of Gujarat and Sind set in motion an
intensive missionary marketing programme. This was centred on the con-
solidation of their personal authority as the imam of what was emerging
as a trans-oceanic Isma'ili community centred on Bombay, but dispersed,
and indeed expanding, through an oceanic hinterland that soon included
East Africa no less than Iran.[13] The new authority afforded by the opportunities of Bombay lent Āghā Khān I and his son a degree of social prominence that brought respectability in British eyes as well. By 1870 Āghā
Khān I was hosting the Duke of Edinburgh on his visit to India, and he
received the Prince of Wales (the future Edward VII) during his Indian
tour in 1875.[14] Being located in the main port of entry to India thus
helped the Āghā Khāns receive British no less than the Iranian visitors we
have seen above. By 1880 Āghā Khān II was appointed to the Bombay
Imperial Legislative Council.

Concealed behind the implicit modernity of this appointment was the
Āghā Khāns' connection to the paradoxical modernity of enchantment. For
on his death in 1298/1881, Āghā Khān I contributed to the enchantment
of Bombay's urban geography described in Chapter 2 by burial in a large
new shrine. In his *Hidayat al-mu'minin al-talibin* (Advice to the faithful
seekers) the Isma'ili missionary Fida'i Khurāsānī (d. 1342/1923) recounted
a strange tale about the selection of the site and Āghā Khān's burial there

that he had heard from the Ni'matullāhī dervish Hājjī Mashhad Husayn Khurāsānī.[15] According to Mashhad Husayn, one day in Bombay he and the Āghā Khān were in a garden that belonged to a Hindu when the Āghā Khān hit the head of his staff on the ground and cryptically declared, 'This is the fruit of long misfortune (*āfat-e tāmdār*) but now it has receptivity (*qābiliyyat*).'[16] When Āghā Khān I died in Jumāda I/April 1298/1881, everyone was expecting him to be buried in a Shi'i holy city such as Karbala or Najaf, and not in the 'bed of thorns and jungle (*khāristān wa jangalistān*) of India'. So, Mashhad Husayn recounted, everyone was surprised when they learned that the Āghā Khān had ordered several shiploads of earth to be brought to Bombay from Karbala and spread in the garden where he had doffed his staff that day. Remembering the event and seeing how the dusty garden had now become a rose bed, Mashhad Husayn realized that when the Āghā Khān had said the garden had 'nobility' (*sharāfat*), he was making a prediction.

Near the Āghā Khān's residence in the Mazagaon dock district, the garden was no mere bed of roses but the building site of a grand mausoleum built to house his blessed corpse. The mausoleum (which still stands to this day) was built of sandstone and white marble, with the finest stone shipped from Iran.[17] Three pairs of gates, resplendent with hammered silver, led into the chamber; a screen of delicately carved marble, embellished with gold fittings, surrounded the sarcophagus; a great dome hovered ninety feet above the stucco reliefs of the surrounding walls. Adding to the enchanted topography of the industrial dockyards the area surrounding the shrine was renamed Hasanabad in his honour. Connecting Āghā Khān I to the larger market demand for Customary Islam and shrines of holy men, present with Mashhad Husayn and the other mourners at Āghā Khān's funeral at the mausoleum was the migrant Sufi Nā'ib al-Sadr Shīrāzī, who directly participated in the burial ceremony.[18] Like the shrines seen in Chapter 2 that emerged through the migration to the city of other Muslim groups, the mausoleum of Āghā Khān I was designed in the customary style of the courtly *dargāh*s of the Muslim saints. It too became a centre of pilgrimage for his Indian and Iranian followers, a practice that had more in common with the Customary Islam of the broader marketplace than with the Ismā'īlī theological principle that the living imam mattered more than dead ones.[19] A few hundred yards away, English gals from the Home Counties stepped off the ships of the P&O 'fishing fleet'. Dreaming of husbands in the Indian Civil Service, they were little aware that near at hand lay the shrine of the imam of the age, offering supernatural grace to answer all desires.

FIGURE 14. Mausoleum of the Ismāʿīlī imam Āghā Khān I (d. 1881), Mazagaon, Bombay

NEO-ISMĀʿĪLISM AS REPRODUCED CUSTOM

In the introduction we have seen how as the products of a plural marketplace, Customary Islamic religious firms typically acquired some of the characteristics of their competitors. In their defence of customary practices they were themselves involved in the larger process of religious change that the reproduction of custom in changing historical circumstances inevitably brought with it. Custom was not static, and its reproduction was typically accompanied by a parallel (and legitimizing) emphasis on certain formalities of religious law. This formula – of promoting certain

customs at the same time as repressing others – can be likewise seen in the
careers of Āghā Khān I and his sons. For soon after his arrival in Bombay,
Āghā Khān I began to demand changes to the customary practices of the
Indian Khōjas, who were nominally his Ismāʿīlī followers.²⁰ He objected to
customary laws on the inheritance rights of daughters, urging for their right
in a share of property. He urged greater participation in Muharram mourning gatherings and promoted the regular performance of formal worship.²¹
In 1861 he, like other Iranian exiles, made use of Bombay's Persian printing
industry to publish his autobiographical *ʿIbrat-afzā*, something that given
his earlier rebellion against the shah would have been all but impossible in
Iran itself in a period that saw the adoption there of a system of state cen-
sorship. An admonishing and moralizing work that echoed the writings of
Bombay's Sufis from the same period, issued from the publishing market
of Bombay, *ʿIbrat-afzā* represented one of the major public steps in Āghā
Khān's recreation of a public image from soldier to imam.²²

From what evidence has survived, it is Āghā Khān's sons and grandsons who appear as the main intellectual and logistical promoters of
Neo-Ismāʿīlism. To borrow a phrase from Peter Brown's discussion
of the saint-makers of Christian Late Antiquity, it would not be too
great a vulgarization to regard the sons and grandsons as their grand/
father's 'impresario'. Building on the *ʿIbrat-afzā*, after their relocation to
Bombay the sons began a programme of missionary outreach on behalf
of the Āghā Khān aimed at bringing as many Bohra and Khōja Muslims
(and possibly Iranian Shiʿi Muslims as well) under the aegis of the Āghā
Khān's protection as the imam of the age. In Bombay, Āghā Khān I's
son Āghā ʿAlī Shāh (later Āghā Khān II) was specially trained for the
purpose, and Āghā Khān I had 'learned and pious mullahs ... specially
brought from Persia and Arabia' to teach his son Arabic and Persian,
as well as a familiarity with the metaphysical and moralistic literature
that Chapters 6 and 7 show was also important to the making in the
marketplace of Sufi Counter Reform.²³ While a later section will look
at the proselytizing journeys that Āghā ʿAlī Shāh made on his father's
behalf, at this point it is important to grasp something of the ideology
of Neo-Ismāʿīlism through examining the Ismāʿīlī *summa theologica*
written by Āghā ʿAlī Shāh's eldest son, Shihāb al-dīn Shāh Husaynī.
Although he had been educated and raised to succeed his father as imam,
Shihāb al-dīn was prevented from doing so by his premature death in
May 1885 (Rajab 1302), a few months before his father (who was by
then Āghā Khān II) also died, leaving Shihāb al-dīn's infant brother to
succeed as Āghā Khān III.²⁴ Nonetheless, having been raised in Bombay

as the Ismā'īlī heir apparent, Shihāb al-dīn's writings offer us the clearest picture of the Neo-Ismā'īlī 'product' as it was taking shape in the
Bombay of the 1870s and 1880s. In a period of Ismā'īlī history for
which primary sources are notoriously hard to come by, Shihāb al-dīn's
writings therefore offer us the closest record available as to the 'official' message of the Āghā Khān family firm in the years during which
it sought to capture a part of the religious marketplace of Bombay's
oceanic hinterland.

The text in question is Shihāb al-dīn's Persian *Risāla dar haqīqat-e dīn*
(Treatise on religious truth).[25] Given the fact that the *Risāla* allows us to
compare the ideological contours of the Āghā Khān firm with those of the
other holy men who made their careers in the city in the same years, its
most striking general element is its resort to the vocabulary and concepts
of the Sufis.[26] The implications of this very rarely cited document are that
Neo-Ismā'īlism emerged as part of the larger pluralizing production of
Customary Islamic forms in which Sufi organizations also participated.
Contrary to the familiar historiographical picture, the Āghā Khāns did
not appear in Bombay as the heirs to an ancient and unbroken tradition
of distinctively Ismā'īlī thought, but were instead part of the enchanted
corner of a larger religious marketplace in which other Iranians also participated in similarly oceanic fashion.

In the form of the Āghā Khān, the living imam offered a distinct alternative to either Sufi or clerical models of leadership. It was this form
of 'product separation' that formed the only major distinction between
Shihāb al-dīn's text and the writings of Iranian Sufis of the period. As
such an important differentiator from its rivals, the point was reiter-
ated in Shihāb al-dīn's *Risāla*: 'Man must have in this world a leader
(*pīshwā*) ... [and] to be obedient to one person only';[27] 'Brother, obedience (*itā'at*) is the same thing as devotion (*'ibādat*), and devotion is the
basis of the religious knowledge (*ma'rifat*)';[28] 'He who does not know his
Imam, does not know God (*ān ke imām-e khōd-rā nashanākht, khodā-ra
nashanākhta-ast*)';[29] 'He, the Guide (*rāhnumā*), comes with all the fea-
tures of an ordinary man.'[30] In fact, it was not so much the idea of a
sole leader that was unique, for the Sufi printed 'advertisements' of the
time shared this.[31] What distinguished Neo-Ismā'īlī writings was rather
the identity of this figure as the lineal family descendant of the sixth
imam, Ismā'īl ibn Ja'far (d. 138/755), in the form of Āghā Khān I. As
with Bombay's other Customary Islamic religious firms, this message
was exported to the city's oceanic marketplace. For, like other successful
'firms' in Bombay, the Neo-Ismā'īlīs adapted the missionary techniques

of the city's Christians that were so important to the creation of a competitive religious economy. Like other Muslim firms, they clothed these
new practices in customary terminology: the neo-Ismāʿīlī *dāʿī* (messenger)
and *muʿallim* (instructor) emanating from the Bombay of the nineteenth
century were very much a re-production of custom.

The Āghā Khāns operated in no less a circulatory pattern than the
Iranian Sufi impressarios who also appeared in Bombay, leading brotherhood firms that did not merely relocate to Bombay but from their
outpost there were exported back to their former homeland in an
industrially quickened version of the classic pattern of oceanic circulation. An example is Muhammad ibn Zayn al-ʿĀbidīn Khurāsānī (d.
1342/1923), known by the pen-name Fidāʾī (Faithful). Born in a north-
eastern Iranian village in 1266/1850, between 1896 and 1906 Fidāʾī
made three journeys to Bombay to see Āghā Khān III, and from India
was appointed as *muʿallim* (instructor) to the Ismāʿīlīs back in Iran.[32]
He was highly successful in capturing the Iranian market for the Āghā
Khāns in Bombay: according to the doyen of Ismāʿīlī historians, Farhad
Daftary, 'By the time of Fidāʾī Khurāsānī's death in 1342/1923, Agha
Khan III had established his authority over the Persian community.'[33]
In Fidāʾī's writings lay a powerful recreation of Ismāʿīlī history as an
unbroken lineage of teachings passed down through the centuries by the
living imams, to be spread in Iran by himself in the closing years of the
nineteenth century, a picture iterated in his history of the Ismāʿīlī community at large.[34] For Fidāʾī's *Hidāyat al-muʾminīn al-tālibīn* (Advice to
the faithful seekers) presented an overview of Ismāʿīlī history *en somme*,
with a particular focus on two ages of Ismāʿīlī greatness: the era of the
Ismāʿīlī Fātimid sultans of Cairo; and the lifetime of Āghā Khān I. A dis-
organized and rambling text, *Hidāyat al-muʾminīn* was in some senses
a distinctly modern text, constructing an intellectual history of major
trends in Ismāʿīlī theology and the great minds who represented them. It
discussed the rise of Nuqtawī-type numerological doctrines; the preaching tours of Nāsir Khusrow; the age of the 'old man of the mountains'
Hasan-e Sabāh; the feats of the great Fātimid rulers of Egypt and Syria;
and the schisms that emerged on the death of the 'Abbāsid caliph al-
Mustansir, in 487/1094.[35] Given the reappearance of Ismāʿīlism in the
Bombay of the mid-1800s after centuries of provincial obscurity, in its
attempt to piece together the missing links between Bombay's latter-day
Āghā Khāns and the Fātimid caliphs of eleventh-century Cairo, *Hidāyat
al-muʾminīn* formed the connection in the intellectual lineage between the
impresarios of Āghā Khān I and the many twentieth-century European

scholars patronized for their sympathetic excavations of the same lost centuries. For the long isolated and impoverished Ismāʿīlī villagers of the mountains and plains of eastern Iran to whom Fidāʾī was sent from Bombay to minister, the *Hidāyat al-muʾminīn* produced a historical narrative that not only reminded them of a past age of Ismāʿīlī grandeur, but also of their present obligations to an imam who was very much alive. In this dual purpose of galvanizing the historical identity of a distinct Muslim community with its own version of Islam and reaffirming their ties to a charismatic leader, *Hidāyat al-muʾminīn* was a product of the same forces seen above in the genealogical family histories promoted by saintly shrine firms and below leading to the writing of defensive self-histories for Bombay's Bohra Ismāʿīlīs. As a work of the historical reinvigoration of a minority community identity, the text's production between Bombay and the villages of Iran renders it a counterpart to the works on the glory of the pre-Islamic rulers of Iran produced for Iran's demoralized Zoroastrians by their wealthy Parsi brethren, a product of the same intellectual workshops in Bombay. For all its neglect by modern scholars of the Ismāʿīlīs, in its reproduction and distribution to Iran of reinvigorated custom and a charisma-based family religious firm, *Hidāyat al-muʾminīn* was not only a quintessential Neo-Ismāʿīlī text but a classic product of Bombay's religious economy.

This is seen all the more in the *Hidāyat al-muʾminīn*'s detailed account of the career of Āghā Khān I. This text presents a perspective on his life that is quite out of step with the modernist Ismāʿīlism promoted after the permanent move of his grandson, Āghā Khān III, to Europe after 1910, an Ismāʿīlism that subsequently emerged in a quite different arena to Bombay Islam.[36] Like other printed products of Bombay's marketplace, *Hidāyat al-muʾminīn* presented Āghā Khān I in the clothes of the customary holy man. Its lengthy biographical section on the imam was dedicated to stories of 'miracles and wonders' (*karāmāt wa khāriq-e ʿādāt*) that belonged to a supernatural service repertoire shared with saints such as Wajīh al-dīn and Shāh Niʿmatullāh, whose hagiographies Chapter 2 described being printed in Bombay and appealing to large sections of its population.[37] However, what is most striking about the stories in *Hidāyat al-muʾminīn* is their precision: these are less the stock-in-trade of formulaic rumour than closely observed anecdotes that fit neatly with the known details of Āghā Khān's life. There are many details, for example, of his dealings with the court of Fath ʿAlī Shāh Qājār before his exile in India; of his movements through Sind and negotiations with the British government; and of his later proselytizing tours from Bombay into Gujarat whose 'revertist' logic echoed the attempts by the Bombay-founded Āryā Samāj firm to convert Gujarat's Muslims 'back' to newly manufactured Hindu customs.[38] These anecdotes give a measure of the imam as he was presented by his ocean-crossing impresario, Fidā'ī Khurāsānī. One story described an episode when Āghā Khān I travelled in the company of a group of followers from Bombay to Kathiawar, an agency of the Bombay Presidency in peninsular Gujarat.[39] Fidā'ī decorated it with plenty of incidental detail, such as about how in the town of Rajkot (the headquarters of the British political agent) the party fell into the company of a British 'party (*majlis*), or as the English call it, a "durbar"' and travelled with them until they reached the region of Broach.[40] There, the Āghā Khān and his party began hunting, an activity which in the manner of the classic Persian nobleman and the newer British sportsman the text presented the imam as having been passionate about since his youth.[41] Just then the Āghā Khān was warned not to kill the favoured hunters' quarry, the gazelle (*āhū*), because it was worshipped by the local Hindus, who would cause trouble if they heard of such killing.[42] And so the next day, when the party set off again, the Āghā Khān forbade his followers to use their guns. The day passed until, just as they were approaching their stopping place, the party entered a ravine where they spotted a herd of gazelles, and, to everyone's surprise, the Āghā Khān asked for his gun and bagged five of them with one cracking shot. After 'rendering them halal' (that is, slitting their throats while repeating the ritual formula), he then hid the bodies before the party recommenced its journey. When they reached the fort where they had intended to stay, they found the gate locked and the headman of the local Hindus angry and refusing to sell them food. On hearing this, from the tent that had been set up for him in the shade, the Āghā Khān summoned the headman, who a few hours later turned up with his followers and sat before the imam in accordance with their habit. Taking offence at the posture of their sitting, the Āghā Khān declared them 'very impolite' (*khaylī bī-adab*) and it took one of his local followers to explain that they were only simple countryfolk who meant him no offence. All the same, the Āghā Khān demanded of the headman the reason for his locking of the fortress gate and refusal to sell them food, and went on to say that if the reason was his killing of the gazelles, then the Hindus should know that he hadn't wanted to kill them, but had only done so because their appointed time (*ajal*) had come. Just then, everyone saw one of the male gazelles separate itself from its dead companions, scamper into the Āghā Khān's tent and lie down under his cot. Summoning the gazelle before him, the Āghā Khān then stroked its head and antlers, and told it to go back to the wild: when he set it down on the ground the whole assembly saw the dead gazelle obey his command and skip away into the plains. On seeing this unmistakable miracle (*karāmat*), all of the Hindus gathered there at once pronounced the profession of Muslim faith and 'entered the religion of Islam' (*bih dīn-e islām dar āmadand*). When, after staying as their guest in the fortress for three days, the Āghā Khān again set off on his travels and left one of his companions in charge of his new followers to teach them the 'way of obedience' (*rāh-e dīn*), a franchise was successfully established in the provinces. Throughout the tale the Āghā Khān was presented in the guise of the miraculous holy man of custom. No spiritually democratic *primus inter pares*, like the supernatural 'big men' described in the Bombay dockyards in Chapter 6, even by the standards of the religiously aristocratic, the Āghā Khān appeared as haughty. (At one point in the anecdote he even cursed a disciple with the swear word *pedar-sukhta* ('son of a hell-burned father'), a rare sight in period Persian prose).[43] More importantly, the story demonstrated the way in which miracles remained essential to the gathering of new followers: in the Gujarati hinterland of the Bombay marketplace from which the imam was travelling, enchantment remained at the centre of the religious economy.

Other stories in *Hidāyat al-mu'minīn* concerned the activities of the Āghā Khān in Bombay itself, as in one that Fidā'ī heard from Rāwī Mūsā ibn Muhammad Khurāsānī.[44] The latter described how one day a group of the Āghā Khān's followers brought a dying child before him, and asked him to show mercy on the child's parents. Displeased at the request, the Āghā Khān declared, 'Do you think I am Jesus Christ to bring the dead back to life?' (A pointer perhaps to the awareness of Christian competition in Bombay?) Even so, he agreed to pray for the child's recovery, while urging his followers not to make such requests in the future. And so he asked a midwife who was the spouse of one of his shopkeeper disciples to fetch some almond oil (*rowghan-e bādām*) and ox-tongue flowers (*gul-e gaw-zabān*), and drop the former in the child's nose and the latter in his mouth. As soon as the midwife dripped the oil in the child's eyes, who was now as good as dead, he started to sneeze and show signs of life. Three days later Rāwī Mūsā reported seeing the boy hale and hearty and back in the company of his parents. Pointing us back to the economic rewards that were always a factor in the larger economy of enchantment, Fidā'ī then noted how the grateful parents presented the Āghā Khān with generous offerings (*nazar*). Such services and payments were central to the transactions that underwrote the religious economy.

Like the other miracle texts we have seen in previous chapters supporting the hierarchical status of God's saintly friends, Fidā'ī's *Hidāyat al-mu'minīn* was a classic product of Bombay's religious marketplace. Even in the moments in which we hear Āghā Khān complaining about the demands made on him, Fidā'ī's text shows us that the economy was shaped by demand no less than supply; and one had to supply such services to be a successful player.[45] But the Āghā Khān and his heirs were distinct in marketing themselves as a specific 'brand' type of charismatic leader, not mere 'friends of God' like the Sufis, but unique imams of the age. It is in the verses of Fidā'ī's Persian *Masnawī-ye nigāristān* (Poem of the picture gallery) that we find the most distilled statement of this Neo-Ismā'īlī mission:

> He is the *imām* of the time,
> the guide and comforter,
> the protector of his followers,
> whether young or old.
> Like the sun in the sky,
> he is manifest in the world.[46]

Lest the objection be raised that the Ismā'īlīs had no need to compete with other firms since they already had the 'automatic' following of other 'Ismā'īlīs', it is important to reiterate the fact that, in the decades after the arrival of Āghā Khān I in Bombay, such a following in the pluralistic market was far from automatic. Having lived for centuries without any contact with a living imam, most of the nominally Ismā'īlī or Ismā'īlī-derived groups around the Indian Ocean very much needed convincing that the responsibilities involved in following and supporting a living imam such as Āghā Khān I and his heirs was worthwhile. It is worth remembering that Bombay was also a place where books upholding traditional Twelver Shi'i models of the imamate were published, such as with the printing of *Āyāt al-wilāya* (Signs of vicegerency') from the press of another Bombay-based Iranian exile, Mīrzā Muhammad. If anything, the Neo-Ismā'īlī attempt to capture the following of a notionally pre-existent community (or market share) of believers most closely resembles the marketing strategies of the Ārya Samāj, and the Hebraicizing Christian missionaries to the notionally Jewish Cochin Jews and Bene Israel community of Bombay's hinterland.

The economy's competitive context appears also repeatedly in Shihāb al-dīn's *Risāla* discussed above, warning the listener away from the other religious leaders in the marketplace. 'My friend, listen to what the real

Leader (*rah-namā*) says, and never disobey his orders; do not permit the tricksters and thieves to fool you – they are nothing but thieves ... Why then should you follow them, who are like beasts or imbeciles, and why should you not follow the Perfect Man (*insān-e kāmil*).'[47] Even in its most intensely pejorative moments, Shihāb al-dīn's *Risāla* used a familiar customary vocabulary of 'perfect men' to describe the Āghā Khān, who even though theoretically drawing on his own legitimacy as a direct blood descendant of the Prophet's son-in-law was placed into the more familiar shoes of the Sufi saints who were better known in the Indian marketplace. While Ismā'īlī intellectual historians might offer their own internal explanations for such cross-pollinations of vocabulary, in the context in which the *Risāla* was composed, the logic of the market to co-opt the terminology and claims of one's rivals made competitive sense. The confused bustle of Bombay's bazaars also made its presence felt in the text, as Shihāb al-dīn returned repeatedly to the image of the cheated crowd: 'It is the devil who mixes with the crowd, which is as stupid as a calf, cheats them and destroys their faith.'[48] This competitive context also manifested itself in the text's demotion of the emphasis and display of formal legalistic piety that characterized some competing Muslim firms. Thus, Shihāb al-dīn warned, 'Do not permit yourself to be cheated by those who ostentatiously pray much or talk about fasting.'[49] Nonetheless, as we see in the next section, several 'Ismā'īlī' groups decided that the responsibilities (financial no less than moral) of accepting the Āghā Khāns' leadership were not worthwhile. In view of the larger argument of *Bombay Islam*, what these respective struggles to project or reject the Āghā Khāns' claim to be the living imam demonstrate is that Neo-Ismā'īlism was very much a participant in the competitive religious economy produced by the cosmopolitan and communicational modernity of Bombay.

If Shihāb al-dīn's *Risāla* was primarily characterized by its promotion of the status of his father the Āghā Khān as imam, like other Customary Islamic productions of the economy, the writings of the Neo-Ismā'īlīs surrounded their charismatic claims by moralizing statements on correct behaviour. Proper attention to fasting, praying and 'the discharge of one's ordinary (*zāhirī*) duties (*a'māl*)' were therefore recommended (not to do so would be a gift to their opponents), but stated as being inadequate on their own for salvation in the absence of loyalty to the true imam.[50] Like other Customary Islamic family firms, Neo-Ismā'īlism was also defined by an anti-egalitarian emphasis on genealogy. As seen in the demotion of displays of public piety, this

was no firm recognizing either salvation or authority through the performance of works alone. While, depending on their proximity to the
ideas of Reformist groups, different Sufi brotherhood firms emphasized
genealogical links of either an initiatic or familial kind, Neo-Ismāʿilism
defended the doctrine of blood genealogy and appointment (*wasiyya*)
by one's father as the sole basis for leadership as *imām*. This was very
much a family firm.

Here was no Reformist meritocracy of authority acquired through the
accomplishments of piety or learning. In the words of Shihāb al-dīn,

> Ordinary people whose duty is only to obey the command of God have
> no capacity to act as they wish or to elect [as their leader] any one whom
> they want, disregarding the real one. Leadership ... is a matter of the
> greatest possible importance, which cannot be left to the decision of the
> mob ... Therefore the meaning of *'itrat*, or the [rightful] successors,
> belongs only to the legitimately appointed successors ... who rightfully,
> from father to son, have inherited their rank of leader.[51]

In such ways Shihāb al-dīn returned repeatedly to his central theme:
recognition and obedience to the imam, his own father the Āghā Khān.
Texts such as Shihāb al-dīn's *Risāla* give a clear sense that at this point
Neo-Ismāʿilism was no global 'world religion', but very much a family
affair in a competitive religious market. Like such other transnational
family enterprises as those of the Jewish Sassoons and the Parsi Tatas,
by operating out of Bombay the Āghā Khān family acquired the connections and capital required to go global within a few generations. Little
surprise, then, that like the patriarchs of the Sassoon and Tata families,
at the turn of the century Shihāb al-dīn's younger brother, Āghā Khān III,
left Bombay for the larger opportunities of Europe.[52]

REJECTING THE IMAM: ISMĀʿĪLĪ COMPETITION AND PLURALIZATION

Neo-Ismāʿilism was a characteristic product of Bombay's economy of
enchantment: in its centralizing and missionary agenda; in its promotion
of an intercessionary holy man; in its use of print, rail and steamship;
and in its appeal to a genealogical lineage of charismatic authority. It
is important to point to the commonalities between the activities of the
first two Āghā Khāns and the Sufi blessed men of the period, who also
made use of the opportunities that Bombay afforded. For if Ismāʿilī history has usually been written as a seamless narrative connecting medieval
Fātimid Egypt with the global Ismāʿilism of the twentieth century, what

this model misses is the key period of transformation and reinvention that occurred in nineteenth-century Bombay.

In the case of the Ismā'īlī imams no less than the Ni'matullāhī shaykhs, Bombay played a central role in circulating and proselytizing a hierarchical and intercessionary person-centred Islam around the Iranian and Indian communities of the Indian Ocean. Through the discussions of Iranian activities over the past two chapters we have seen how Bombay's marketplace was not only confined to India and its Muslims, but reached out across the ocean to other peoples as well. We have seen Iranians experiencing and appropriating elements of Bombay's religious economy in a range of ways: from commerce, law and printing to proselytizing, exile and religious renewal. From influential figures such as the Āghā Khāns and Safī 'Alī Shāh to lesser-known men such as Ḥājjī Pīrzāda and Nā'ib al-Sadr Shīrāzī, in one way or another each of these Iranian migrants made use of Bombay's modernity, technological or social. In some cases, such as the adoption of new commercial techniques or the use of colonial law, these adoptions are familiar enough to our picture of the nineteenth-century Indian Ocean. In other cases, such as miraculous travel, shrine foundation and hagiographical printing, Iranian interaction with Bombay points towards a more complex picture of modernity. And it is this less familiar, enchanted modernity that this book has emphasized. What should be clear, though, is that the holy men and miracles, and the texts and organizations that celebrated them, were not merely the survivals of pre-modernity, but were instead reproductions of customary forms of Islam powered by the new apparatus of the age.

Yet like any other entrants to the marketplace, the Āghā Khān and his sons quickly found themselves facing competition. Such was the intensity of conflict between the different groups that the Āghā Khān tried to bring together under his leadership that dispute even led to murder.[53] As noted previously, India's notionally Ismā'īlī communities had lived for centuries with little or no contact with their imams, and for many the prospect of suddenly finding themselves subject to the legal and moral rulings of a living authoritarian master was an unappealing and expensive one. Again, the religious struggles among Bombay's Ismā'īlīs in the middle of the century are best understood through the model of economy. Through the movement of their members to the cosmopolitan and industrializing environment of Bombay, what had previously been reasonably coherent local communities of Khōja and Bohra Ismā'īlī merchants began to splinter in response to the dissonance between their customary lifeways and alternative options glimpsed in the market metropolis. As the coherence of old community

ways began to unravel, a range of new trends and religious firms appeared
among the Khōjas and Bohras, who struggled to compete with the well-
funded and coherent market articulations brought by the entry to India
of the transnational family firm of the Āghā Khāns. One of these new religious productions was the centralized model of community and religious
authority offered by the Āghā Khān himself; but as the local religious firms
responded, and entrepreneurs repackaged or rejected custom among the
Khōjas and Bohras, the Āghā Khāns became only one option. Ismaʿili productivity was therefore also on the increase in Bombay.

Prior to Āghā Khān I's arrival, Bombay had for decades been attracting members of the old Khōja and Bohra trading communities of Gujarat,
and among them there emerged market religious demands and entrepreneurial responses quite distinct from what was offered by the Āghā Khān.
The new firms that emerged among Bombay's Bohra Ismaʿilis are discussed in a separate section below; for now it is sufficient to note that
the rival competition offered by their own customary leaders was strong
enough for them to reject the Āghā Khān's advances. But even the Khōjas
among whom the Āghā Khān would ultimately find his greatest number
of followers developed a pluralizing sub-economy of religious productions. Not least among these was what historians have labelled the Khōja
Reform movement.[54] As early as the 1830s, led by their *shethiyya* merchant elite, a number of Bombay Khōjas had begun to reject their former
rituals and community forms and attend the city's main Sunni mosque
instead. Emerging among such members of Bombay's wealthy Khōja
comprador class as Habīb Ibrāhīm and Dāyā Muhammad, this Khōja
Reform firm had much in common with the Modernist wing of the Sunni
Muslim Reformists discussed in Chapter 1. Using journals and newspapers to spread their ideas, the Khōja Reformists placed 'modern' English
education at a high premium, laying particular emphasis on the education of Khōja women, who were encouraged to reject their customary
clothing and jewellery and learn to speak a bookish 'standard' Gujarati.[55]
Caste-like customs that separated Khōjas from 'fellow Muslim' citizens
were regarded as backward and, in a response to the attacks of Christian
missionaries including Reverend John Wilson, Khōja Reformists began
to question outright the hierarchical notion of loyalty to an imam who
claimed perfect knowledge as the base of his authority.[56] In the cosmopolitan market setting, the polemics and interactions were multidirectional.

As wealthy successful businessmen, it was this comprador section of
the Khōja community that voiced the greatest objections when Āghā Khān

I began to demand that regular tithes be collected for him from each of the Khōjas' community worship houses (*jamā'at-khāna*). In a reflection of the role of print in the religious economy, a printed-pamphlet war broke out between the two firms, leading to the production of closer iterations of the differentiated positions of Āghā Khān I and the Reformists – the familiar pattern, then, of competition producing diversification.[57] It was this competition that ultimately resulted in the famous 'Aga Khan Case' of 1866, in which the genealogical claims of Āghā Khān I to be the direct heir of the Isma'īli imams of the Middle Ages were fought for and won in the neo-Gothic chambers of the Bombay High Court.[58] His resort to colonial law to prove his right to collect tithes based on a genealogically transmitted metaphysical status points to the ways in which Bombay provided access to modern administrative institutions for the empowerment of reinvented and reproduced custom. But even though Agha Khān I won the case, the final outcome of the competition between him and the Khōjas' merchant elite firm was a permanent divide in the community, with different opponents rejecting the Āghā Khān to form new Twelver Shi'i and Sunni Khōja communities. Far from creating a standardizing uniform Isma'īli Islam, the characteristic expression of Bombay's religious marketplace therefore led to the creation of a series of new ways of being a Khōja Muslim.

Nonetheless, Āghā Khān I was still extremely successful, and those Khōja individuals and institutions who did not join the dissenters' firms found themselves drawn into a new enchanted economy based on regular 'donations' to the imam. In less than two decades after setting up in Bombay in 1848, in the Aga Khan Case of 1866 the Āghā Khān acquired the rights to an income from previously disconnected 'Isma'īli' communities and institutions, including a large number of shrines long regarded as being the tombs of Sufi rather than Isma'īli saints. The Āghā Khān was not the only religious entrepreneur involved in such attempts to use 'proofs' of genealogical descent to claim control of the revenues of pilgrimage sites in the Bombay Presidency. A decade after the Aga Khan Case, the Hindu Pattana Prabhu community attempted to use colonial law in a long-standing dispute to control the Bhuleshwar temple in Bombay and other sites around the Presidency, also appealing to the Bombay High Court and printing a partisan Marathi–English history of their 'true' orgins and thereby just claims.[59] Such court rulings were an example of governmental intervention in an otherwise liberal economy of religious competition, and though rare they were nonetheless effective forms of market regulation. The court ruling in the Āghā Khān's favour lent both legitimacy and

legality to his endeavours by declaring him the rightful hereditary leader
of India's 'Ismā'īlī' Khōjas and so granting him control of their communal
property all across India, from prayer-houses to pilgrimage shrines and
burial grounds.⁶⁹ The great wealth that would turn him and his sons into
a regular fixture at the Western India Turf Club was built on an income
derived from merchant donations and a shrine economy of customary pilgrimage. Through the authoritative intervention of legal decree that gave
official sanction to the Āghā Khān's genealogical claims, the theology and
social structure of the previously disparate and local forms of Ismā'īlī life
were quickly transformed in an oceanic marketplace that would eventually
connect Bombay with a wealthy Ismā'īlī diaspora in Iran, Sind, Gujarat,
East Africa, Singapore and Burma. Following the successes of his father
in putting the family firm on a new industrialized setting, much of the
career of Āghā Khān II was spent in building contacts with this 'Ismā'īlī'
merchant diaspora. On steamships and trains, from Bombay and the city's
younger sibling of Karachi in the northern Bombay Presidency, the second
Āghā Khān expanded his stake in the 'Ismā'īlī' section of a religious economy of oceanic proportions.

It would be a mistake to present the entry of the first two Āghā Khāns
into the Bombay religious economy as an outright success. For Ismā'īlīs
no less than other kinds of Muslims, Bombay remained a marketplace in
which various versions of faith, community and leadership were on offer.
In moving to Bombay, Āghā Khān I triggered an intensification rather
than a reduction of this competition. Even after calling in the 'market
regulators' of the colonial state in the Aga Khan Case to declare him the
legal and legitimate heir to the Ismā'īlī imamate, for all his success, at
the end of his lifetime there remained thousands of Ismā'īlīs who refused
to accept his leadership and the rejection of their own customs that this
involved. In addition to the new Reformist firm of the Khōjas, these rejec-
tors belonged mainly to the Bohra Ismā'īlī community. In clinging to their
own lineage of leaders who had been on Indian soil for centuries, these
Bohras entered into fierce disputes with the impresario of the Āghā Khāns
that lasted until Āghā Khān III finally left Bombay for Europe in the early
1900s. The larger pattern to be observed is that the cosmopolitan coming together of notionally similar Ismā'īlī Muslims created by the smaller
world of the nineteenth century did not create a widespread vision of Pan-
Islamic unity, but rather an intensified recognition of difference among
'fellow' Muslims. Ismā'īlīs became more aware of one another, but those
new interactions produced increased difference and competition as much
as unification around an imported imam.

The appeal and subsequent reproduction of custom in this unsettling context can be seen in a self-history of the Bohra community written in Bombay a year after the arrival of Āghā Khān I. Completed by Hājjī Salāh al-dīn Ārāʾī on 7 Safar 1265 (2 January 1849), *Risālat al-tarjamat al-zāhira li firqatī Bohrat al-bāhira* (Expository treatise on the sect of the maritime Bohras) reproduced in new form the customary vision of Bohra history.[61] Written in Arabic with an interlinear translation into Persian to maximize its distribution in the marketplace, the *Risālat al-tarjama* was a self-conscious apology for Bohra custom that sought to demonstrate the Islamic foundations of the Bohras' 'pure religion' (*dīn-e pāk*).[62] In the face of attacks from their critics, it explained that the Bohras keep the fast (*sawm*), follow the commands of the Quran and Sunna (*yaʿmulūn bāʾl-kitāb waʾl-sunna*), stick to the 'path and customs' of the Sunna and never leave its way.[63] As seen in the introduction to *Bombay Islam*, in a competitive marketplace the reproduction of custom inevitably involved a degree of self-modification, reforming custom in the very moment of its reproduction. A market is after all a place of negotiation.

After describing the structure of Bohra leadership, and clarifying its patterns of hereditary or non-hereditary succession in implicit contrast to the leadership of the Khōja Ismāʿilis and their Āghā Khān, Hājjī Salāh al-dīn went on to recount the story of the founder of the Bohra community.[64] Reaching back to an earlier age when the appearance of a holy man from across the ocean was less commonplace, this was the aetiological legend of the 'man from Yemen' (*rijal min al-yaman*).[65] No ordinary seafarer, this ʿAbd Allāh al-ʿĀbid was a 'saint among saints and godfearer among godfearers' (*walī min al-awliyāʾ wa taqī min al-taqiyyāʾ*), who centuries earlier had set foot on Indian soil at the port of Cambay in Gujarat.[66] There he met the Indian ancestors of the Bohra community, Kākā Kīlā and his wife Kākī Kīli, who were farming land that lacked water. In colloquial voice, Hājjī Salāh al-dīn described the farmers' request to the stranger that he provide them with water, and, leading the stranger to a well, Kākā Kīlā showed him that it was far distant from their lands and the water brackish. On seeing this, ʿAbd Allāh al-ʿĀbid threw an arrow into the well, which struck a stone at the bottom and let clear water flow in plenty.[67] At this, Kākā Kīlā and his wife converted to the faith of ʿAbd Allāh, promising to reject (*tark*) their own religion (*dīn*).[68] In turn, the people of the nearby towns were no less impressed by ʿAbd Allāh al-ʿĀbid's performance of wonders (*ʿajāʾib*), and so their headman (*sardār*) was converted as well.[69] ʿAbd Allāh also set about demonstrating the false beliefs of the surrounding idol-worshippers. Showing the impotence of a great iron elephant worshipped by a local king and his subjects, 'Abd Allāh proved that the idol was merely silent stone until he then commanded it to speak himself; the king understood that his old ways were wicked idolatry (*shirk wa kharāb*).[70] Taking the Muslim name Mawlānā Sayf al-dīn, in time the converted king was succeeded by his son, Ya'qūb, and so on through a lineage that reached to Zayn al-dīn, the leader of the Bohras at the time of the tract's writing.[71] Hājjī Salāh al-dīn then linked Bohra practices to wider forms of Customary Islam, describing the grave (*qabr*) of 'Abd Allāh al-'Ābid in Cambay and the pilgrimages (*ziyāra*) regularly made to it.[72] Linking Bohra practice still closer with Customary Islamic lineages of esoteric knowledge, he explained how 'Abd Allāh al-'Ābid's knowledge had originated with the Prophet's companion Salmān the Persian, and was handed down through Bohra leaders to the present day in 1849.[73] Rounding up his aetiological history, Hājjī Salāh al-dīn explained that the name Bohra meant merchant, 'for the people of Gujarat say *bohra* for a merchant and worker'.[74]

The *Risālat al-tarjama* offered its explanations of Bohra identity in reaction to the cosmopolitan marketplace of Muslims unknown to one another and critical of each other's Islam. The text's very existence is proof of the lack of mutual knowledge between the different Muslim groups moving to Bombay: the author's intention was of linguistic outreach by choosing Arabic and Persian for its bilingual text rather than the Gujarati of the Bohras themselves. Given the choice of languages, its intended audiences were probably the Arab and Iranian merchants with whom the Bohras were trading in Bombay, merchant groups which included followers of Āghā Khān. In being written a year after the arrival in Bombay of Āghā Khān I, the text was also an apologetic reaction to the polemical marketplace, specifically to the corner of it in which the followers of the Āghā Khān stood criticizing the Bohras as the followers of false imams. In these ways, the text fits into a larger pattern in which the increasing encounters between different Muslim communities brought about by the cosmopolitan forces of capital rendered no simple surrender to religious uniformity but a defensive reproduction of custom through the writing of new community histories such as the *Risālat al-tarjama*. In a period better known for the creation of such familiarly 'modern' histories as those of Sir Sayyid Ahmad Khān and Sayyid Amīr 'Alī, Bombay's religious economy also reproduced the enchanted historiography of custom. The newness of this textual productivity is seen in the fact that the period saw many community histories and customary practices being

written down, and in many cases printed, for the first time. The customary historical vision of the Bohras was thus reproduced in even fuller form
in the three volumes of *Mawsim-e bahār fi akhbār al-tāhirīn al-akhyār*
(The season of spring in account of the pure and pious) written in the
1880s and 1890s by Muhammad ʿAlī ibn Mullā Jīwābhāʾī (d. 1315–16/
1897–9).[75] Again, religious firms sought the prestige of lineage and history.

Even as such texts as the *Risālat al-tarjama* and *Mawsim-e bahār*
defended the genealogies and legends of the Bohra customary leaders,
they did so in response to internal ruptures in the community as much as
attacks from outside. Under the pluralizing pressures of Bombay's religious economy, even such small Muslim communities as the Bohras produced new versions of faith and practice as much as they reproduced
older forms, and the last years of the century saw a Bohra Reformism gain
a place in the marketplace.[76] Built on the commercial profits of Bombay,
the Reformist firm was headed by the Bohra merchant Sir Adamjee
Peerbhoy (1846–1913), who first made his fortune as a contractor to the
Indian army and finished his career as Justice of the Peace and Sheriff of
Bombay. Built on such wealth, the firm led the founding of hostels for
Bohras making the *hajj* alongside an orphanage, a hospital and dozens of
modern schools.[77] Attempting to draw on the wealth of his followers in
Bombay during the same years, the older family firm of the forty-eighth
Bohra *dāʿī*, Sayyidnā ʿAbd al-Husayn Husām al-dīn (d. 1308/1891), also
introduced a new form of Bohra Islam. Urging his followers to reject
their customary beliefs in ghosts and vampires and follow a purer version of Islam,[78] in protecting the hereditary authority of the *dāʿī* against
the Bohra Reformists' critique of their venality, Husām al-dīn ultimately
reflected the larger market appeal of Customary Islam. Here again was
the same pattern of religious fragmentation accompanied by the use of
new resources to reinstate the authority of hereditary holy men. The
range of religious productions, both Customary and Reformist, that were
generated in response to the entry of a diverse range of Ismāʿīlī Muslims,
Gujarati and Iranian, Bohra and Khōja, presents a model of the Muslim
religious economy in miniature. Even as the Bohras debated whether to
follow this or that leader, the fact remained that Bombay presented a
range of blessed men whom they might choose to follow. The previous
pages have shown how this range of leaders and services on offer in the
Bombay marketplace was supplied by not only migration from within
India itself, but also from overseas in Iran. Whether as the imam of the
Ismāʿīlīs or the cosmic *qutb* axis of the Sufis, the firms founded by traffic

of holy men between Bombay and Iran in the nineteenth century shared the same product characteristics of divine immanence, personal intercession and charismatic authority. Theirs were enchanted bodies that were circulated and celebrated as never before through the trains and steamships, and vicariously the printing-presses, to which Bombay lent easy access.

6

A Theology for the Mills and Dockya

ON THE TRAIL OF THE MIGRANT WORKER

While the last two chapters examined the maritime dimensions of the religious economy by way of Iranian migration to Bombay, the following pages turn towards the religious entrepreneurs and consumers who entered the market from the city's continental hinterlands. An essential element of this pattern of demand and supply was the migrant Muslim workforce from Hyderabad and the Konkan who from the 1860s made up the largest proportion of the city's Muslim workforce. Working in Bombay's textile mills and dockyards, these migrants constituted the new social entity that was a Muslim industrial labour force. Through tracing the teachings of one of the religious 'patrons' of these workers and connecting his doctrines to the conditions of workers' lives, this chapter examines how, in a religious economy in which labourers formed an important part, the reproduction of custom acted as a successful response to the social change of industrialization. Bereft of the support networks of their village homes, and at the bottom of the social hierarchy of the industrial metropolis, migrant workers found themselves in greater need than ever of patrons and protectors. This socially driven demand in turn helped fuel a particular type of religious production by way of a theology and brotherhood of intercession that placed the miraculous powers of the holy man at the service of the uprooted labourers who pledged allegiance as his disciples. As the following pages show, for his followers among the migrant workers in the mills and docks of Bombay, the Hyderabadi Sufi Habīb 'Alī Shāh (d. 1323/1906) represented a comfortably familiar supplier of religious services by means of which the special 'friends' (awliyā)

of God could intercede for their migrant protégés. As a religious entrepreneur responding to the new proletarian demand in the Bombay marketplace, Habīb 'Alī was himself also a migrant to the city from the old
Muslim centre of Hyderabad, his shift to Bombay echoing the migrations
of similar entrepreneurs seen in earlier chapters relocating from Gujarat
and Iran. While Habīb 'Alī's emphasis on the doctrine of intercession of a
hierarchy of saints was the antithesis of the levelling theologies of Islamic
Reform, its vertical organization and theological vision was also a strong
contrast with the trade unionism sought by Indian labour historians of
the period. To trace the appeal to Bombay's workforce of custom, intercession and hierarchical brotherhoods is therefore not only to unravel
the operations of the religious economy, but also to peer into the cultural
foundations of the labour economy.

In view of the thesis that the rural cultural heritage of Bombay's industrial workforce was in constantly changing interaction with urban life,
this is not to say that labourers existed in a state of cultural stagnation,
relying on a customary culture imported wholesale from their villages.[1]
On the contrary, as participants in the religious economy, even in aligning
themselves to service providers who seemed to reflect their existing religious preferences, workers found their Customary Islam was changed in
the very act of its reproduction. This reproduction of Muslim custom also
reflected the apparent paradox of the reinvention of Hindu caste practices
in industrial labour conditions in colonial Bengal.[2] It is a paradox that
this chapter explains by showing the continued appeal of a worldview in
which the embodied divine interface or *barzakh* of the living 'friend of
God' was seen to be able to manipulate the world from behind the scenes.
For a new urban workforce, uprooted from their ancestral communities
and shunted to the pell-mell of a metropolis whose networks were impossible to fathom, a theology of intercession held evident attraction. Since
to turn to the shaykh was to draw the protection of the Prophet himself,
for a dockyard and cotton mill congregation bereft of other forms of
support, such a theology held the promise of much-needed patronage.
Besides the mills and dockyards, the brotherhood firm of the Hyderabadi
migrant Habīb 'Alī and others like him were reproducing custom for the
labourers who were an important element of the religious market. The
following pages turn first to these proletarian small-time players in the
economy of enchantment, before later sections of the chapter examine
the religious productions that their demand was to fuel in Bombay, partly
at least by importing holy men from their home regions in the continental
hinterland of the religious economy.

On the eastern borders of the Bombay Presidency lay the princely state of Hyderabad. An international Muslim centre in its own right during the nineteenth century, Hyderabad's own expanding religious productivity was partly enabled by its connection with the oceanic travel hub of Bombay, and from the 1870s Bombay became increasingly important for Hyderabadi Muslims, both elite and subaltern.[3] The combination of economic growth in Bombay and stagnation in Hyderabad led to a steady flow of emigration to Bombay, while the city's amenities also attracted Hyderabadis of means. During the 1870s and 1890s catastrophic famines pushed large numbers of peasants out of the Hyderabad Deccan and into Bombay. For the most part, then, Hyderabad's Muslim migrants were from the poorer sectors of society, pushed out by the decline of inland trade through the middle years of the nineteenth century and then by the catastrophic famines that stretched into the 1910s.[4] Like the rural migrants from the Konkan discussed below, many Hyderabadi Muslims found work among the city's mills and dockyards.[5] A good sense of the occupations Hyderabadi Muslims found in Bombay can be gleaned from a survey the lives of Bombay's opium users carried out in the 1880s, which recorded autobiographical statements made by dozens of Hyderabadi migrants. One was Wāhid Ahmad 'Alī, who earned his living in Bombay as a fortune-teller; another was Farīd Bakhsh Muhammad of Aurangabad, who worked in Bombay as a cabman; his fellow Aurangabadi Qamr al-dīn Muhammad 'Īsā worked in an opium tavern. Then there was Ya'qūb Muhammad Husayn of Hyderabad who worked in Bombay as a bricklayer, while Sāmān Khudā Bakhsh and Sayyid Husayn 'Alī sold finger rings and horses and Faqīr Muhammad Shaykh Muhammad worked for the P&O Company as a fireman in the docks.[6]

Aside from this migrant labour class, members of the Hyderabadi elite also visited the city. For them Bombay became a worldly resort to which they could travel by train to enjoy diversions and commodities unavailable in Hyderabad itself. The Nizam's prime minister Sir Sālar Jang (1829–83) made his first tour outside Hyderabad by visiting Bombay in the company of the Resident at the Nizam's court, C. B. Saunders (1821–88), travelling by road from Hyderabad to Gulbarga, from where they were able to complete the journey by train.[7] A few years later Sir Sālar Jang's son, Mīr Lā'iq 'Alī Khān Sālar Jang II (1868–89), penned a baroque Persian travelogue in which he recounted how he stayed in the completely iron-built Watson's Hotel in Bombay. From there he boarded a steamer that he praised for connecting India more easily with England, so bringing to Bombay the 'progress' (taraqqī) of such technological

discoveries as 'electric power' (*quwwat-e alaktrīk*), the classical timbre
of his prose creaking beneath the weight of the new world it described.[8]
Again, for Hyderabadis for Iranian travellers, Bombay was the gateway
to industrial modernity, a transition symbolized for Lā'iq 'Alī Khān by the
futuristic folly of a cast-iron hotel that had been made in England after
the designs of Rowland Mason Ordish (1824–86) and shipped for assembly in Bombay between 1867 and 1869. As the century progressed, other
members of the Hyderabadi elite bought property in Bombay, cementing
its role as Hyderabad's window to the world, enabling Reformists such
as Jamāl al-dīn 'al-Afghānī' and Customary Islamic figures such as Habīb
'Alī Shāh to move easily between the two cities, connecting the religious
economies of the two regions together no less than migrant labourers
connected their financial economies. Positioned between the movement
of Hyderabad's courtiers and labourers, members of Hyderabad's religious class followed in the footsteps of their compatriots, as has already
been seen in the case of Bombay's other Muslim communities. Relocated
in the larger marketplace, they were able to spread their teachings among
fellow Hyderabadis while using the prestige of their association with
the *dār al-islām* of Hyderabad to gain a wider following among other
Muslim groups. As it did for the Āghā Khān and Safī 'Alī Shāh, residence
in Bombay offered possibilities for proselytization beyond the city's labour
force, since as in the case of Iran Bombay's flourishing Muslim publishing
industry dwarfed that of Hyderabad, and its rail and steamship routes
offered opportunities for distributive proselytization that Hyderabad could
not match. These opportunities were seized by Hyderabad Reformist and
Customary Islamic firms, such that reformists such as Nawwāb Muhsin
al-Mulk travelled from Hyderabad to preach to the Muslims of Bombay
at the same time that Hyderabad's Sufis also visited or relocated to the
larger marketplace. As with Iran, the impact of Bombay could also be
felt in the territories of Hyderabad itself, with the economies of religion
and capital at times intertwined. An example was seen in the early 1900s
in Aurangabad, just beyond the eastern edge of the Bombay Presidency,
when a Muslim entrepreneur imported textile machinery from Bombay
to open a silk mill whose profits were then poured into the religious productions of the Hyderabad Sufi Mu'īn Allāh Shāh (d. 1345/1926) and his
preaching tours of the urban mills and the surrounding countryside.[9]

In addition to Hyderabadis, the period from the 1870s to the 1910s also
saw the large-scale migration of Konkani Muslims to Bombay.[10] The Konkan
coastline ran south of Bombay and, along with the inland Marathi-speaking
regions to the east of Bombay, formed the main source of cheap labour for

the city's expanding industries. By the turn of the twentieth century even the single Konkani district of Ratnagiri had come to be regarded as 'the great recruiting ground of the Bombay Presidency'.[11] While there were 71,000 people resident in Bombay who in 1872 were registered as born in Ratnagiri District, by 1901 the figure had more than doubled to 145,000.[12] Konkani Muslims gradually became the largest segment of Bombay's Muslim population, despite the fact that their low-status occupations has left them on the margins of the historical record. As well as working as lascars aboard ships travelling in and out of the port, many Konkani Muslims worked as stevedores and messengers in the Bombay dockyards, while a large proportion worked in the city's cotton mills and foundries.[13] Descriptions from the period give some sense of their conditions at work in the mills: 'the labouring natives, stripped to the waist, aided the ascent of the fluffy substance into the main building through the exhauster. At eight boilers, flaring and steaming, the Moslem firemen lustily stirred blocks of Cardiff coal with tongs and fire-irons of English manufacture.'[14] This is not to say that Konkani Muslims were any more without their elites in Bombay than were Hyderabadis. This middle class of respectable Konkani Muslims belonged to an earlier wave of migrants, and scarcely interacted with the mass of labour migrants that moved from the Konkan from the late 1860s. The Konkan's long history of commerce enabled a number of mercantile families to successfully shift their operations to Bombay, and their wealth was at times channelled into religious firms of various kinds. The Konkani patrician class included several of the leading Reformists discussed in Chapter 1, as well as the Rōghē family, responsible for founding the city's Jami' Mosque, and the Mōrghē family, which from the late eighteenth century onwards held the hereditary post of Qāzī Muslim judge of Bombay.[15] Re-founded in 1802 and located in the heart of the city, the city's oldest Jami' Mosque was also managed by a Konkani director (*nazīr*) and a board of twelve other Konkani Muslims.

Even so, common Konkani roots did not attract Konkani labourers to the productions of such Reformists, and the following pages turn to the success of the Hyderabadi Sufi Habīb 'Alī Shāh among both Hyderabadi and Konkani Muslims in Bombay. Many of these Konkani and Hyderabadi migrants found work in the vast dockyards of Bombay's Mazagaon quarter. Replete with several old Catholic churches, Mazagaon was originally a Portuguese settlement that lay several miles beyond the original British districts on Bombay Island. However, in the mid-1860s Mazagaon began to change shape as the Peninsular & Oriental (P&O) shipping company bought most of the land there to build the city's largest and most modern docks through the grand engineering of land reclamation.[16] Mazagaon was in any case located only a few miles away from the main Bombay harbour, and newspaper reports from the 1860s suggest that, like any other port district, Mazagaon had its fair share of social problems. Alongside the consequences of seasonal and irregular labour, the newspapers point to regular outbreaks of violence among sailors there. The port was frequently a place of drunkenness and disorder. A report from July 1864 described a fight aboard the Parsi merchantman *Jamshetjee Family* in which the attacker, in liquor, threatened to eat his victim's liver for breakfast.[17] The following month a Scottish vagrant called James Douglas assaulted the Indian fireman of a P&O steamship in Mazagaon. Both cases were handled by the Mazagaon police office, which included Muslim constables such as Nazar 'Alī Murād 'Alī, who was praised in the court proceedings for his diligence.[18]

The concentration of capital that the docks and warehouses brought to Mazagaon soon meant that the area around the P&O's new dockyard became a focus for the textile industry. By 1870 some ten mills had opened there, a figure that would increase a full seven-fold in the next twenty years. The presence of so many mills gave this part of Bombay the new capitalist society that would set it apart from that of Hyderabad and other older cities. While much of Mazagaon's population was made up of mill hands, to the south of the Victoria Road that dissected Mazagaon were large bungalows occupied by Europeans and a clique of wealthy Indians.[19] It also attracted wealthy Iranians, including the Āghā Khān, whose own palace was located there. Nevertheless, with so many mills offering work, a large settlement of Konkani Muslims also developed in Mazagaon, working typically as firemen or oilmen among the heaving new machinery of the weaving and spinning mills.[20] Aith its industrializing turmoil of new social relations, Mazagaon reflected other Indian sites such as the famous jute factory districts of Calcutta.[21] As the greatest dockyard on the western coast of India, its competitive influx of workers also in many ways had much in common with the situation across the ocean in Mombasa, where casual migrant labourers were similarly prey to the gang leader *sergan*s who dominated the recruitment of workers.[22] Bombay stood at the centre of this wider oceanic work culture, and there too entry for migrant Konkanis and Hyderabadis into the dockyard labour market was mediated through the influential job contractors known as *sarang*s or *toliwalla*s, just as mill work could only be gained through the *muqaddam*s whom it was frequently necessary to bribe.[23] It was from among the new urban society of migrant casual labourers created contemporaneously on both sides of the Indian Ocean that the Hyderabadi Sufi Habīb 'Alī found many of his followers, including his most famous disciple, Ghulām Muhammad, whose own export mission to Indian labourers in Africa is explored in Chapter 7.

In the hands of this Hyderabadi migrant, both Konkani and Hyderabadi labourers found a supernatural patron whose largesse was more appealing than the schools and books of the Reformists. The content of Habīb 'Alī's preaching for this market of labourers can be reconstructed from his surviving manuscripts, and it is to these works that the following pages turn.

A MISSIONARY TO THE WORKING MEN

Habīb 'Alī Shāh was born in Hyderabad into a notable *nawwābī* family with long-standing connections to the Nizams' court.[24] Born in 1236/1821, he spent much of his youth in the company of his own and his father's preceptor, Hāfiz 'Alī Shāh of Khayrabad (d. 1266/1850).[25] Despite his relocation to Bombay some time after 1860, Habīb 'Alī maintained his connections with Hyderabad as well as the North Indian *qasba* towns of his master, making use of Bombay's rail network to make the kind of journeys that in his youth in the 1830s still involved considerable danger. An account in his lithographic biography *Manāqib al-habībīn* (Feats of the beloveds) records in colourful detail his scrapes with wild animals in the jungle-side roads of central India during one such youthful journey.[26] In the years after his move to Bombay he collected a large circle of followers, particularly in the dockyard district of Mazagaon. Among the earliest of these followers was Muhammad Mungī, a Konkani port foreman who lived a few doors away from the house in which Habīb 'Alī settled near the Dockyard Road train station; Mungī became one of his leading disciples and impressario 'deputies' (*khulafā*).[27] Over the following years many of Habīb 'Alī's other followers were drawn from the manual labourers of the dockyards.[28] In his deliberate self-transformation from a *nawwāb* born to courtly privilege to a preacher among the urban proletariat, Habīb 'Alī typified the new kind of downward social mobility that laid the ground for the emergence of the fully fledged Muslim missionary firms that entered India's other religious markets in the early twentieth century. As with any successful firm, location was all-important, and Habīb 'Alī was wise to establish his home-cum-*khanaqah* conveniently near to the Mazagaon dockyards and less than a minute's walk from the Dockyard Road railway station that carried workers to the dockyards. This also connected both him and his followers to the pan-Indian rail network by which they were able to distribute the master's religious productions. During his decades in the city, Habīb 'Alī's brotherhood firm attracted a large number of followers from among whom he selected a small number as his deputies (khulafā), dispatching them by rail to different parts of India, including Ajmer, Poona, Peshawar and Ahmadabad, as well as by steamship to South Africa and Syria, presumably from the P&O docks less than a mile away from his khanaqah. His circle of disciples also drew on the merchant community settled around his khanaqah beside the dockyards. We thus hear the story of the Bombay Muslim businessman Qamar al-dīn, who shortly after becoming Habīb 'Alī's disciple lost all of his wealth through a commercial mishap. When Qamar al-dīn was finally at the point of complete destitution, Habīb 'Alī taught him how to write talismans for the curing of illnesses and possession by genies, in this way allowing Qamar al-dīn to earn a new living through providing services in the religious economy.[29] In this poignant little tale, custom can be seen triumphing over the commercial capitalism on which the story of Bombay has long been built. In such ways Habīb 'Alī mediated between the spiritual and economic lives of his fellowship.

A lengthy account of the master's last days, the events of his funeral in Bombay and his posthumous train journey forms the subject of another text written by his disciple Ghulām 'Alī Shāh shortly after his death.[30] This text, Habīb al-wisāl (Death of the beloved), describes how in the days before his death Habīb 'Alī had entered a state of overwhelming mystical absorption (istighrāq) on a train journey from the saintly pilgrimage centre of Gulbarga in the south of Hyderabad State, a city which was also one of the main railheads linking Hyderabad with Bombay. Having been carried back to his lodge by a disciple upon his return to Bombay, Habīb 'Alī died there a few days later among the stevedores and mill hands.

While it has not been possible to trace a definitive record of Habīb 'Alī's funeral procession in non-hagiographical sources, on 5 February 1906 the Bombay Gazette newspaper did relate how the body of what it described as a Muslim merchant called 'Seyyid Koja Abiballi' was specially transported to his home city of Hyderabad by train from Bombay's Victoria Terminus. Since the newspaper was printed later on the same day that the Manāqib al-habībīn described Habīb 'Alī's body being transported for burial, it seems possible that this 'Abiballi' was the Sufi in question, the titles 'Seyyid' (sayyid) and 'Koja' (khwāja) being common terms of respect used for religious notables such as Habīb 'Alī. As for the garbled name of Abiballi, this can only make sense when read as Habīb 'Alī. The report claimed that this figure was aged 109, whereas Habīb 'Alī would have been only eighty-five (eighty-seven in lunar years), but it is possible that the reported age was as confused as the name, not least given the regular penchant for exaggeration that surrounded the lives of India's holy men and the likelihood that the reporter relied on members of the funeral crowd for information. If the newspaper report did refer to Habīb 'Alī, his designation as a merchant would sit well with his decision to settle right beside the dockyard at Mazagaon and echo the Āghā Khāns' links with Iranian merchants. Other newspaper reports of the period in which Habīb 'Alī settled in Bombay do refer to the presence of Hyderabadi merchants in Mazagaon. A report from October 1864 referred to the mercantile activities of the Hyderabadi prime minister Sālār Jung, which shows that the court elite of Habīb 'Alī's class were not averse to soiling their hands with trade in Bombay.[31] Contemporary oral traditions at his shrine in Hyderabad and among his descendants in Bombay also connect Habīb 'Alī to the company of Bombay's merchants, and he would certainly not have been the first merchant Sufi in the Indian Ocean. His Yemeni contemporary Ahmad ibn Abī Bakr ibn Sumayt (1861–1925) was able to spread his Sufi firm while travelling as a merchant on the new steamships that crossed the ocean.[32]

At two minutes past nine on the morning of 6 Zī'l-hijja 1323 (1 February 1906) Habīb 'Alī died. The precision of this time to the 'minute' (minat) recorded in the Manāqib al-habībīn was itself testament to the new consciousness of time introduced by the factory clock and the train timetable.[33] According to this text and the later biography Zikr-e Habīb, a few days later, on 10 Zī'l-hijja (5 February), his body was transported to his ancestral home of Hyderabad by train.[34] In accordance with the rules of sharī'a his body was dispatched to Hyderabad for burial the day after his death. In line with local forms of custom, the water used for the ghusl ablution of his body was collected and sent to his followers in the villages of the Konkan. Then the coffin was carried through the streets of Bombay from his house in Mazagaon to the city's Friday Mosque (itself run by a Konkani committee) for the funeral prayer. From there it was carried to the Victoria Terminus station, from where it was to be delivered to Hyderabad. A great procession apparently followed the bier through the city, the coffin itself escorted by a guard of honour drawn from the majzūb ecstatics who slept in the streets of the industrial city. Due to the size of the crowd that had gathered, just before reaching the Victoria Terminus's palace of steam power the coffin was set down in the shrine of the 'Portuguese Muslim' Pēdrō Shāh, which bordered the pavement en route to the station. After a dispute with the railway officials, who initially insisted that all coffins had to be placed in the goods wagons rather than the passenger carriages, the officials backed down, wary of upsetting the crowd in the heyday of the Bombay riot. In comparison to the processions of the Delhi Durbar of 1903 just a few years earlier, when the Duke of Connaught had likewise crossed through Bombay to board a train at the Victoria Terminus, here was an altogether different procession whose ceremonial guards were not the splendid liverymen of an aristocratic empire but a motley parade of ragged *faqīrs* and working men. Unlike the Āghā Khān, Habīb 'Alī was not to create a new shrine in Bombay, but rather in Hyderabad, where he was buried in his old family compound. Locked into its narrow alleyway behind the Dockyard Road railway station, the small building in which he had taught and lived in Bombay had no land for a mausoleum to be built on, and so in death he escaped the crowded port for the feudal pastures of his forefathers. Like the erstwhile Bombayite Safi 'Alī Shāh in his mausoleum in Tehran, the sacred geography of Bombay Islam reached far and wide.

In his move to Bombay, Habīb 'Alī reflected a larger trend of religious entrepreneurs from all around the region making visits or extended residences in Bombay. As noted, this followed the patterns of labour movement from the city's hinterlands. Since these workers had very little holiday, often unable to return to their villages for years on end, a pattern emerged of their ancestral shaykhs coming to the city to meet them instead. These were not simple acts of benevolence, and shaykhs needed their followers as much as their followers needed them. Besides, as was the case with Habīb 'Alī, residence in Bombay also brought the possibility of attracting an entirely new following from among dislocated labourers who had lost touch with the religious guardians of their village lives. Given that in moving to the city their followers entered the cash economy, there was also money involved in such entrepreneurial visits to Bombay. A case in point is the holy descendents of Pīr Yūsuf al-dīn of Mundra in Gujarat, the Qādirī Sufi founder of the Memon community firm or *jamā'at*, who would regularly visit their followers in Bombay to gather a customary 'subscription' known as *kheda*.[35] Another example of this pattern is seen in the career of the Chishtī Sufi master Khwāja Sayyid Mat'ā al-dīn, the hereditary saint of Mangrol in the Surat district of the Bombay Presidency.[36] A biography printed in Bombay in 1922 told how Sayyid Mat'ā al-dīn visited the city after 'his disciples who were living in Bombay and who had been unable to pay a visit to him for a long time sent some representatives to him with a request that he should pay a visit to Bombay'.[37] The text described a proletarian constituency that closely reflected that of Habīb 'Alī, for Sayyid

Mat'ā al-dīn's old disciples were mainly oil-pressers and of these 'thousands of men used to visit him' while he was in Bombay.[38] There, among the trains and factories, the mobile saint of Mangrol 'performed various miracles'.[39] Offerings were granted in return.

Even Habīb 'Alī's death and funeral were echoed in the death of Sayyid Mat'ā al-dīn. Although Mat'ā al-dīn died and was buried in Bombay, he had promised his other followers that he would be buried in the hereditary shrine of his forefathers back in Mangrol. His Bombay-printed hagiography tells a strange tale of the events that followed this breaking of his word that saw him absorbed for eternity in the soil of the Bombay marketplace. For so determined was the saint to honour his word that he appeared to a disciple in a dream and instructed her to disinter his body from its grave in Bombay and bring his remains back to Mangrol. Unfortunately for her, the saint's dreamtime wishes met with rather more tangible objectors in Bombay among the city's Konkani Muslims, whose objections to the opening of a shaykh's grave were so vociferous that 'a breach of the peace being apprehended, the police with European officers appeared on the scene'.[40] The disciple decided to explain her motives to the policemen in the following words: 'I have had a vision and so I am here to act according to the saint's instructions. If you don't believe in it, open the grave and let us see if the body is in a removable condition; if so permit me to take it away; if not let it remain here.'[41] When the policemen agreed, and the Konkanis were forced to relent, the grave was finally opened: from it there rose the sweetest of odours, but there was no body to be seen. Not to be deterred, the faithful disciple took off her veil and laid it in the grave and prayed to her master to make himself visible. When she lifted the veil from the earth, there lay the uncorrupted body of her master, 'with beads of perspiration on the forehead, a smile on the face and hair and beard a little grown'.[42] The text recounted that both the Konkanis and Europeans present were 'stupefied with amazement [and] when this tale spread abroad the whole of Bombay turned out to have a look at the saint'.[43] The story tells us a good deal about the ways in which the deaths of Bombay's holy men were treated by their followers, echoing the spectacle seen around the funeral of Habīb 'Alī. In being transmitted in a printed pamphlet in the English language, the very medium by which the rumour of Mat'ā al-dīn's miraculous cadaver was distributed points again towards the cosmopolitan character of the Bombay marketplace.

From the heart of Bombay's industrial district Habīb 'Alī Shāh for his part led a transnational brotherhood firm for the reproduction and distribution of customary practices among a new class of industrial Muslim

workers. In his writings Habīb 'Alī elaborated an intellectual defence of
the Customary Islam of saintly mediators and miracles, a defence that
was built round an ontological notion of a chain of being connecting man
to God through the medium of Muhammad and his saintly representatives on earth. Habīb 'Alī's success enabled him to create from Mazagaon
an organization of 'missionary' deputies (*khulafā*) spanning the Bombay
Presidency, Punjab, Hyderabad, Syria and South Africa. From his
khanaqah in the Bombay dockyards he was able to distribute his teachings to new audiences across the oceanic and continental hinterland's of
Bombay's religious marketplace. As part of his firm's diffuse network of
proselytizers, Habīb 'Alī's leading disciple Ghulām Muhammad – also
known as Sūfi Sāhib ('Soofie Saheb') – belonged to the Konkani community, but under his master's guidance eventually left Bombay to settle
among the indentured Indian labourers in Natal and expand his master's firm. In Habīb 'Alī's career it is therefore possible to place Bombay
at the heart of an expansive religious firm which distributed its rituals,
organizations and doctrines into the farthest reaches of the city's religious
economy in South Africa.

CUSTOMARY ISLAM IN THE MARKET OF LABOUR

Before turning to the content of Habīb 'Alī's teachings, it is important to
recall the competitive context in which his activities took place. Habīb
'Alī's movement to the Mazagaon port district was part of a larger entry
of rival firms into the religious marketplace that also saw the spread of
Christian missionaries among the mill and dock workers. Around the time
of Habīb 'Alī's arrival the Mazagaon docks were being supplied with the
sermons of Reverend James Paterson, for example, who in the late 1860s
'preach[ed] the Gospel ... to the captains, engineers, and mariners constantly coming and going to that port'.[44] The works of Muslim preachers such as Habīb 'Alī were parallel products supplied to the indigenous
participants of the same religious market. Some ten of Habīb 'Alī Shāh's
books are known, in which he reproduced customs and created doctrines
that would appeal to his industrial constituency.[45] Works such as *Habīb
al-awrād* (Beloved of litanies) present a detailed picture of the rituals that
he produced for this market. *Habīb al-awrād* emphasized not only the
outward performance of the five daily prayers, but also described a far
larger repertoire of supererogatory litanies and prayer forms to be performed on specific days and times of the year.[46] Often these private rituals
were extremely ornate, and it would not be too far off the mark to say

that they would have taken up all of the practitioner's spare time: performed around the dockyards, they would certainly have kept the faithful away from the district's less elevating entertainments. Given that works such as Habīb 'Alī's *Habīb al-tālibīn* (Beloved of the students) and *Habīb al-barāzikh* (Beloved of the isthmuses)do not appear to have been printed during his lifetime, it seems fair to suggest that their circulation in written form was fairly limited. Even so, to overstate the importance of written texts and their access through reading is to misunderstand the methods of vocal readings and spoken knowledge transmission that had for centuries characterized Customary Islam.

Although literacy and access to cheap and often vernacular printed books increased in the last decades of the nineteenth century, literacy remained very much a minority skill among India's Muslims. Census statistics from 1911 show that in Hyderabad literacy remained as low as twenty-eight per thousand persons, and even in Bombay reached only a figure of seventy per thousand.[47] These statistics were echoed throughout India, to the extent that Christian missionaries came to realize that their methods of large-scale tract printing were still leaving massive numbers of Muslims beyond their reach. This was a problem faced by any missionary firm, Christian or Muslim, that emphasized individual access to and understanding of holy writ. Evidently, these social conditions of mass illiteracy favoured certain types of religious praxis and missionary activity over others such that the Protestantizing champions of *sola scriptura* would find inevitably little success compared to proponents of spoken word and ritual. Again, the Muslim religious economy was massively disposed towards the non-scriptural productions of Customary Islam by way of shrines, rituals, holy persons and spoken words. It is within this oral section of the market that Habīb 'Alī should be placed, and his success was ultimately based on the spoken forms of instruction, the ritual meditations and the emphasis on his own intercessionary person for which Bombay's demographic explosion of uneducated Muslim labourers offered such demand. In his *Habīb al-barāzikh* Habīb 'Alī thus described a variety of meditation rituals known as *zikr* and *murāqaba*. Other meditational practices that Habīb 'Alī taught his followers were described in *Habīb al-in'ām*, an early twentieth century printed work by his follower Ahmad 'Alī Shāh Chishtī which collated the spoken 'guidance' or *irshādāt* publicly preached by Habīb 'Alī himself.

The supernatural practices that *Habīb al-in'ām* described were straightforwardly instrumental, suggesting the popular and simple techniques that Habīb 'Alī taught a wider number of followers. In this, the text resembles Habīb 'Alī's own *Habīb al-awrād*, which recommended and detailed

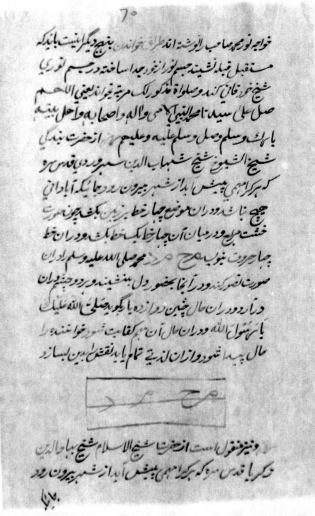

FIGURE 15. Manuscript page from *Habīb al-barāzikh* in Habīb 'Alī Shāh's own hand

supererogatory prayers and litanies (*awrād*) to piously fill the worker's spare time.[48] The instructions in *Habīb al-in'ām* for one such exercise ('*amal*) recounted the proper cycle of prayers and incantations necessary to bring the practitioner a dream of the Prophet Muhammad. Against Reformist market criticism of the practice, its legitimacy was assured by a claim that it was based on the Prophet's own instructions.[49] In another case, a set of chants (wird) was recommended with the claim that they gave the practitioner help at the point of death and assured entry to paradise. These, and a series of rituals appropriate to burial and graveside visits, were legitimized through the citation of Hadith and the sanction of such medieval saintly authorities as Qutb al-dīn Bakhtiyār Kākī and Shāh Kalīm Allāh of Delhi.[50] Central to the practices described in the Habīb al-in'ām was the genealogical tree (shajara) of the saints that connected the disciple through his master to a saintly chain of being that reached back to the Prophet Muhammad. A much longer set of instructions in the book was described for those in any form of dire need, an echo of the supernatural services seen associated with Bombay's shrine firms in Chapter 2. The performer should begin with the cry of taking refuge in God (ā'wz bi'llāh), before singing the ritual praise of the Prophet (durūd) seventy times, next reciting the Quranic chapter Yā-Sīn, then reciting the praise genealogy (shajara) of the Chishtī line of saints and so on.[51] Even in abbreviated form (that is, just saying 'repeat the shajara' rather than actually reciting the shajara in full) these instructions filled some nine pages of manuscript, which would have to be committed to memory before being performed. Elsewhere in the text Habīb 'Alī advised his followers to repeat another formula no less than 125,000 times![52] In such complicated but nontheless instrumental rituals can be seen the interaction between metaphysical theory and the needs of ordinary life that bound the shaykhs to the quotidian demands of their followers. Fortunately, those unable or unwilling to memorize such lengthy incantations could also copy the magic square (naqsha) provided in the next section of the text, which contained the numerical distillate of the shajara's names through using the talismanic powers of numerology (abjad).[53] Here Habīb 'Alī 's teachings fit neatly into the market demand for magical and occult manuals that was so characteristic a feature of nineteenth-century Urdu printing in Bombay and elsewhere.

An interesting parallel example from Bombay of the reproduction of the occult meditational genre in the economy of print was Awrād-e ihsānī (Litanies of spiritual beauty), which was issued in a cheap lithographic edition in 1873.[54] Over the course of forty-four pages, Awrād-e ihsānī offered the reader instructions in a set of over fifty zikr meditations, prayers and Quranic invocations, many of them to be performed at very specific points of the ritual calendar. Thus on the night of 'Ashūra, that is the tenth of Muharram, shortly before dawn, the practitioner should perform four series (ruk'at) of prostrations with Ayat al-Kursī (the Throne Verse) and Sūrat Ikhlās (Sincerity, chapter 112 of the Quran) repeated three times each for every ruk'at, before then reciting Sūrat Ikhlās a hundred times.[55]

If this was performed properly, then all of the practitioner's sins would be forgiven. Other rituals were even more complex, such as a technique for after the sunset prayer which required the repetition of several longer Quranic chapters a hundred times each.[56] As in the teachings of Habīb ʿAlī, the exercises in *Awrād-e ihsānī* gained their legitimacy from being recommended by the great shaykhs of the past, in the case of the latter technique no lesser figures than a pairing of the great medieval overseas Sufis ʿAbd al-Qādir Jīlānī and Shihāb al-dīn Suhrawardī. Given the industrializing context in which such texts were issued, what is particularly interesting is their treatment of time. For in a city whose timescape was dominated by the mechanical time of factory clocks and ship and train timetables, here were attempts to reinstate time that was not only sacred but was also explicitly Islamic, a chronological counterbalance then to E. P. Thompson's picture of the factory worker's submission to clock time.[57] A similar temporal schizophrenia afflicted Hindu workers in Calcutta in this period, torn between the ticking seconds of clock time and the mythopoeic rhythms of the Kali Yuga.[58] Obedience to industrial time might offer steady employment, but attuning oneself to the cosmic tempo of Islamic time offered much greater rewards, ranging from the promise of paradise to the acquisition of occult powers in the present world. Issued by the modern technology of lithographic, and in some cases steam-powered printing, works such as *Awrād-e ihsānī* attempted to use industrial technology to bring about a re-enchantment of time itself.

Such printed works as *Awrād-e ihsānī* and the *Habīb al-inʿām* that contained Habīb ʿAlī's own occult rituals placed the enchanted 'secrets' (*asrār*) that set the Sufis apart from their Reformist rivals on the public book market. Another example of this distributive printing of the powers of enchantment was issued in handy pocket-size format. This was the *Asrār-e darwēsh* (Secrets of the dervish).[59] Printed in 1898, the booklet seems to have been written as a guidebook for those wishing to set themselves up as Sufi entrepreneurs in their own right but who wished to avoid the trouble of initiation and gradual training at a pace dictated by a living master. It consisted of instructions on a similar series of practices – prayers, visualization techniques, breathing exercises – to those that appeared in Habīb ʿAlī's works; techniques, moreover, that its author claimed could be employed for worldly ends. This was not a Sufism of metaphysical theory, but rather its market expression as medicine, prognostication and amulet-making, all techniques that could of course be adapted for profit-making enterprises. For our present purposes, what is most interesting about the *Asrār-e darwēsh* is the section it contains on breathing techniques, a section underpinned by a short theoretical excursus on the connections between breath and the wider universe. More minimal and convenient than the complex and time-consuming exercises of *Awrād-e ihsānī*, these were a series of simple breathing techniques that could accompany very specific real-life circumstances. In effect, dangerous or otherwise risky situations and activities should be met by breathing through different nostrils or towards different parts of the body. The many and varied situations in which the power of breath could be so employed included the purchase of a horse or camel; the receipt of gold jewellery or a gift of new clothes (presumably to avoid the evil eye); and the search for lost property. Accompanied by simple instructions to breathe in certain directions or through one or the other nostril, the numerous other eventualities in which the reader was advised to resort to the power of breath ranged from the quotidian (learning whether one was pregnant with a boy-child or ensuring a safe journey in given directions of the compass) to the extraordinary (meeting a king or expecting an armed invasion).[60] The image that this suggests, of dock and factory workers entering altered states of consciousness and power through the performance of these lengthy orisons and meditations, is in fact one that echoes the more recent ethnographic picture of the spread of spirit-possession cults among female Muslim factory workers in Malaysia.[61]

With its apparatus of police and law courts, Bombay offered dangers as well as opportunities to such merchants of anti-scientific agency. The time of Habīb 'Alī's arrival in Bombay saw the prosecution of a 'Mahomedan Quack doctor' called Sayyid La'l Burhānshāh in the same port district of Mazagaon in which Habīb 'Alī settled. The Sayyid's customary diagnosis had injured his patients, and so he found himself called before the district magistrate and charged with fraud and negligence; not all Muslim entrepreneurs were successful in their service-providing.[62] If, as part of its deregulation of the religious economy, the colonial state did not restrain the sales of what it considered 'religious' (that is, non-political) services in the way it regulated the economy of medicine, there were still potential dangers from other Muslims rather than the state in issuing books of such instructions in print. There was the danger that the reader might choose to learn the ritual and meditation techniques from the book alone, and bypass the customary requirement of performing such practices under the guidance of a living shaykh, so leaving the brotherhood firm to set up as a rival. For firm leaders such as Habīb 'Alī, who passionately defended the authority and mediational centrality of the shaykh in his teachings, such an idea was anathema. Nonetheless, it was an option that was made feasible by the loss of control of teachings and techniques that resulted from the transition of religious knowledge from the controllable realm of manuscript circulation to the open market of print. Although religious firms (including Habīb ʿAlī's own followers) attempted to beat the print market by controlling the printing and distribution of their own texts as manuscripts, other text-producers in the period were more willing to sell the 'secrets' of the Sufis in the printed marketplace. By finding expression in printed books available on the open book market, even the enchanted powers that fuelled the demand for Customary Islam could become part of a 'do-it-yourself' ritual economy that used the purchased text to bypass the shaykhs themselves. Ironically, the various uses to which Chapter 3 showed print being put also allowed the ritual quest for occult powers to itself be 'Protestantized' as the expression of a religious individualism that allowed the religious consumer to skip the time-consuming and often expensive relationship with the firm of the living master by the simpler purchase of a book. Living among the highest concentration of Muslim printers in the west Indian Ocean, in its threat to undermine his own centrality to the distribution of his ritual productions, this was a danger that perhaps explains Habīb ʿAlī's reluctance to issue his own writings in print, and to preserve them instead in the more controllable distribution of spoken word and manuscript.

BOLTING THEOLOGY TO THE FACTORY FLOOR

To understand the success of brotherhood firms such as Habīb ʿAlī's in the religious economy it is necessary to address the central aspect of their teachings: their self-presentation as living intermediaries capable of transmitting the power of God to their humble followers on the factory floor. It is this theology of intercession (*tawassul, shafāʿ*) that stands at the centre of their popularity and explains their appeal to the disenfranchised constituencies created by industrialization.[63] Habīb ʿAlī was by no means alone in his promotion of intercession against Reformist critique, and the founder of the Barelwi *madrasa* firm, Ahmad Rizā Khān (d. 1339/1921), also wrote extensively in its defence.[64] However, this section attempts to link this theological debate to the social contexts that provided it with demand in a market of diverse religious productions. To do so, it is necessary to turn first towards an elucidation of the theology itself. The key to this theology of intercession was the model of lineage and charismatic succession, for the Sufi shaykhs stood in a line of 'apostolic succession' that connected them through their own chain (*silsila*) of masters to the charismatic power of the Prophet Muhammad. Although none of these chains ever attained the monopolistic market status of the Catholic Church, in the formality of their organization the Sufi brotherhood firms did possess Church-like hierarchies and structures, forms of religious organization that in the case of some Sufi firms (such as the renascent Ni'matullāhīs in nineteenth-century Bombay and Iran) did manage to dominate large geographical regions for themselves. It was for good reason that Sufis spoke of their exclusive geographical (or market) 'zone of supremacy' (wilāyat), a notion that cropped up regularly in Habīb 'Alī's writings.

In line with the importance of this hierarchical model of organization, Habīb 'Alī began his Habīb al-tālibīn and Habīb al-barāzikh by identifying himself, as author, as a shaykh in the lineage of Hāfiz 'Alī Shāh and through him the heir to Sulaymān Tawnsawī (d. 1267/1851), Mawlānā Fakhr al-dīn of Delhi (d. 1199/1785) and his father Nizām al-dīn of Aurangabad (d. 1142/1729). By the nineteenth century this lineage of Chishtī masters spread across Punjab, the United Provinces and Delhi, to even count the spiritual master of the last Mughal emperor among its members.[65] It was the prestige and fame of this genealogy that Habīb 'Alī attempted to draw upon in Bombay, connecting himself and his productions to a well-established older 'brand'. In the opening lines of Habīb al-tālibīn he thus identified himself as one of the inner circle (halqa bih-gūshān, literally 'ear-ringed [servants]') of Hāfiz 'Alī of Khayrabad, who had specifically asked him to compose the book 'for the pocket of the seekers (tālibīn)'.[66] Following on from this summoning of the authority of the initiatic chain, Habīb 'Alī laid out his purpose as being to instruct his audience in the real nature of faith (īmān) and God-fearing piety (taqwā) and the importance of mystical 'passing away' (fanā) and 'survival' (baqā). He then went on to discuss the connection between Divine Reality (haqq) and the Prophet, and thence between the Prophet and the Sufi shaykh who represented him on earth.[67] In a theological sense, this was the familiar customary doctrine of the great chain of being, connecting God with the primordial light of Muhammad (nūr muhammadī) and thence to God's saintly friends on earth. But from a sociological perspective, Habīb 'Alī was attempting to defend the institution of Sufi leadership and the brotherhood firm that was coming under attack from other players in the marketplace.

For this reason, like other Sufi writers of the period Habīb 'Alī also had to defend the doctrine of intercession (tawassul) by which the Prophet, and in turn shaykhs such as Habīb 'Alī himself, were the necessary intermediaries between man and God.[68] No salvation, no miracle or act of grace, was possible except through the hands of such intercessionary shaykhs, the saintly middlemen in the economy of enchantment.

Tawassul or 'intercession' was a doctrine whose legitimacy was sought in the Quran and Hadith.[69] In one of its most famous scriptural citations, the notion of seeking a 'medium' or 'means' (*wasīla*) of coming close to God is found in the Quran's Table chapter (Sūrat al-Mā'ida):

> O ye who believe, be mindful of your duty to Allah and seek out ways (wasīla) of approach unto Him and strive in His way that you may prosper.[70]

Over centuries of rumination, which included the elaboration of the model of a cosmic chain of being mentioned above, it was into this ambiguous notion of an intermediary 'means' of coming close to God that the Sufi masters placed themselves and their own masters in turn. Having done this in the opening section of *Habīb al-tālibīn*, in the second section Habīb 'Alī summarized the theology of intercession by developing the idea of the two 'faces' or 'aspects' (*sūrat*) of Muhammad. One of these aspects was turned so as to face the world and the other turned to face away from it, with the face of Muhammad that was turned towards the exoteric (*zāhir*) world made manifest in the *sharī'a*. In the days of old when Muhammad was physically present in the world, Habīb 'Alī explained, there was no need for the help of a shaykh intermediary such as himself. But since the Prophet was no longer physically present, people needed the help of an intercessionary master. Whoever is in an intermediary position with the Prophet – such as a shaykh – could then pour blessing upon others.[71] In this way, the social institution of the Sufi shaykh found support in the market from a metaphysical doctrine of intercession through which the shaykh was able to mediate with the Prophet, who would in turn mediate with God. Between the Muslim mill hand in Bombay and his God stood Habīb 'Alī, assuring him that there was no other route to the blessings of God's favour.

These ideas were developed further in Habīb 'Alī's *Habīb al-barāzikh*, the eponymous theme of which was the doctrine of the human interface or isthmus (*barzakh*) between man and God.[72] This was often explained through the image of an isthmus between two seas, a recollection of the Quranic metaphor of the 'meeting of the two oceans' (*majma' al-bah-rayn*, Quran XVIII: 60). According to Habīb 'Alī there were two kinds of interface, which he labelled as the major interface (*barzakh-e kabīrī*) and the minor interface (*barzakh-e saghīrī*).[73] While the major interface was the Prophet Muhammad, the minor interface was the living Sufi shaykh. Thus, for the Muslim who wished to reach God with his prayers, it was necessary to clasp the hands of such a living human interface between human and divine worlds – in practice, by grasping the hand of a shaykh in the ritual pledge of allegiance (*bay'at*) to his brotherhood. Even though Muhammad was obviously in closer communion with God, Habīb 'Alī went on, with his external aspect (*zāhir*) manifesting the divine attributes (*safāt-e haqq*) and his inner aspect (*bātin*) the divine essence (*zāt-e haqq*), it was impossible to immediately achieve direct contact with Muhammad, whom Habīb 'Alī presented as too ontologically removed from ordinary humans like his followers to be reached by individual effort.[74] Here there came a simple metaphor that surely echoed the oral tenor of Habīb 'Alī's preaching: just as an ant cannot walk all around the Ka'ba on its own but must climb upon the foot of a pigeon in order to make its circumambulation, so does the ordinary human need to attach himself to a guide (*rahbar*) to make the journey towards God. Pushing his point further, Habīb 'Alī reminded his followers that in order to be made perfect, even Muhammad had needed the angel Gabriel. Given the minimal level of formal education of most of his followers, Habīb 'Alī found it expedient to reiterate certain themes through easily memorizable doggerel:

> Chū mumkin nīst raftan bī dalīl
> bibāyad Mustafā-ra Jabra'īl
> §
> It's just not possible to go with no guide:
> Muhammad had Gabriel there by his side.

By the same token, he explained, it was impossible for the ordinary Muslim to reach paradise without the help of a guiding shaykh, who was himself the 'minor interface' (*barzakh-e saghīrī*) who would rescue his humbler protégés. Indeed, such was the centrality of the shaykh to the cosmic order that he was himself the living manifestation of Divine Reality (*mazhar-e haqq*)! Like the miracle stories and printed hagiographies of Chapter 3, here the success of rituals of enchantment in the religious economy can also be connected with new forms of mechanical reproduction. For this reason, the key practice that Habīb 'Alī expounded was the ritual of 'picturing the shaykh' (*tasawwur-e shaykh*) as intermediary. This practice required the follower to form a mental image of his master and meditate on it through the use of a range of visualization techniques accompanied by the ritual repetition of sacred formulae.[75] This was not to be considered a part-time pursuit, since the follower should endeavour to never allow himself to be 'empty' of his master's image by allowing his attention or affections to drift elsewhere.[76] An important new means for the rapid spread of the 'picturing the shaykh' ritual in the late nineteenth century was the emergence of cheap photography. Photographic technology had first reached Bombay in the early 1850s, with two daguerrotypists being listed in the *Bombay Almanac* for 1853 and a photographic society (which included Indian members) being founded a year later.[77] By the late 1850s Bombay businessmen such as Hurrychund Chintamon were establishing studios specializing in the formal studio portraits that religious entrepreneurs also favoured. Such photographs enabled disciples to carry the image of their master, which could be used as either a meditational aid for the *tasawwur-e shaykh* ritual or a talismanic device to call on the shaykh in times of need. For as the accounts of seaborne miracles in Chapter 3 showed, the focusing of 'attention' (*tawajjuh*) on the shaykh's image summoned his miraculous intercession. By the early twentieth century, the carrying of shaykhs' photographs for such purposes was no less common among Iranian followers of the Ni'matullāhī shaykhs, while in distant West Africa the photographic image of shaykh Amadou Bamba M'Backe (d. 1346/1927) would become the definitive ritual object of his Senegalese followers.[78]

Like other religious entrepreneurs of the period (including Safi 'Alī Shāh and the Āghā Khān) Habīb 'Alī similarly made use of several Bombay photographic studios. Treasured by his followers, these photographs have survived to the present day. The spread of photography also aided the reproduction of other aspects of custom: its adoption into Muslim marriage arrangements, for example, allowed visual assessment of the possible spouse without breaking the customary ban on meeting outside wedlock. Like the other new technologies at work in Bombay, photography could empower different parties, including women. A few years after Habīb 'Alī's death, a Christian missionary reported from Bombay that 'in a local Urdu paper a few months ago, I was astonished to see an ishtihar [advertisement] by a Moslem damsel wanting a husband, asking for the photo and other particulars of the suitor to be sent to the mushtahire [advertisor], care of the editor'.[79] Looking beyond India, a more significant example of new photographic practices was the widespread dissemination in the late nineteenth century of chromolithographic postcards of a photograph of a beautiful Algerian youth taken to be the picture of the Prophet Muhammad.[80] If a question mark hangs over the precise date at which photography intertwined with the ritual of 'picturing the shaykh' in Bombay, as in the use of printing discussed in Chapter 3, the absorption of photography into the strategies of firms competing in the religious economy points to the same pattern of the enchantment of technology.

FIGURE 16. Devotional photograph of the dockyard Sufi preacher Habīb 'Alī Shāh (d. 1906)

INTERCESSION IN THE MARKETPLACE

If the previous pages have outlined the theology and rituals that Habīb 'Alī distributed in the dockyards, the following pages interpret their appeal in this labourers' corner of the marketplace. The theory and practice of the *tasawwur-e shaykh* ritual can first be understood in terms of the importance lent to intercession (*tawassul*) as the ideological basis of institutions of Sufi leadership that were facing competition from a range of alternatives between which the religious consumer could choose.

Not least among these alternatives, the similar marketing strategy of personal legal emulation (*taqlīd-e shakhsī*) was promoted by the Reformist *madrasa* firm at Deoband through which every Muslim was encouraged to choose an individual legal scholar (*ʿālim*) and model his behaviour after his example.[81] Although Deoband's stake in the Bombay marketplace was limited, the availability of 'do-it-yourself' cheap-print handbooks on religious practice meant that living Sufi shaykhs were no longer the sole means of accessing the powers or salvation that intercession brokered. Habīb ʿAlī's *Habīb al-inʿām* therefore formed a compromise with the popular Urdu occult manuals, providing similar kinds of 'licit magic' but welding them to the master–disciple institution of the brotherhood firm through the centrality of the genealogical *shajara* and the pledge of loyalty to the shaykh that its ritual repetition involved. The same attempt to seal the bonds between producer and consumer, shaykh and disciple, can be seen in *Habīb al-tālibīn*, where the reader was constantly reminded that the devotion to the shaykh that brought blessing and salvation required loyalty and obedience to the shaykh. The lexicon used to describe this relationship was based on the wholesale appropriation of kinship relations. In terminology of decorum, respect and obedience, the relationship between master and disciple paralleled the norms of behaviour between father and son, transposing the duties, affection and loyalty a son owed his father onto his Sufi shaykh or *pīr* (literally 'elder'). The washing of shoes and kissing of the shaykh's foot (*qadambūsī*) described in Habīb ʿAlī's writings had strong echoes of filial loyalty, while the kin-based sociability of the *pīr-bhāī* ('under the old brother man') by which fellow disciples were encouraged to think of one another further illustrates the brotherhood firm's semantic co-option of kinship.[82]

Anecdotes from Habīb ʿAlī's hagiography *Manāqib al-habībīn* illustrate the ways in which the 'parallel family' the firm offered to its followers could be of practical use in industrializing urban India. One anecdote described the long train journey undertaken between Bombay and Delhi by one of Habīb ʿAlī's followers from the latter city. The traveller was making this journey across India alone (an undertaking that would itself have voiced an implicit sense of danger to Indian readers) when en route he came down with a sickness that left him drifting in and out of consciousness. To make matters worse, the itinerary he had chosen required a number of train changes to travel via Hyderabad. At one point the traveller woke to find himself in a completely empty rail carriage; the train had stopped at a station but he had no idea which one it was. Sick, lost and alone in the middle of India, he was relieved when a stranger appeared, whom he asked where he was. Falling into conversation with the stranger, the lost traveller learned that the stranger was in the service of a 'big man' sitting further along in the first-class carriage. When the stranger learned that the sick traveller was hoping to pass through Hyderabad to visit his shaykh Ḥabīb ʿAlī, he suddenly dashed off the train and along the platform. Returning from the first-class carriage, he then exchanged the lost traveller's ticket and assured him that he and his master in the first-class carriage would see the lost traveller safely to Hyderabad. On eventually reaching Hyderabad, the lost traveller learned that his first-class benefactor was a fellow disciple of Ḥabīb ʿAlī. He had been rescued because the rich man sitting further along the train was his 'brother under the master' (pīr-bhāī) in the same religious firm.[83]

Though the new pan-Indian railway made travel far easier than before, the story illustrates the fact that rail travel did not rid travellers of the sense of danger and insecurity they felt in being far from their homes and supporting networks of kin. The rail traveller might no longer face the dangers of wild animals and bandits, but to be alone among unfamiliar Indians with whom one had no 'connections' (rishtadārī) was worry enough in itself. Here at a 'national' level lay parallels to the tensions of cosmopolitan interactions seen in Bombay's Iranian travelogues and shrine histories. The railways and the neighbourhoods of hotels and the drifting and transient populations that surrounded every significant station in India were the operating grounds for a whole range of tricksters, robbers, false friends and confidence men who were the heirs to the roadside 'thugs' of the pre-rail era. Sick and lost in the middle of India, the predicament of the traveller in the story was that he had no 'connections' with anyone he could trust until he was rescued by a representative of the expanded surrogate family based around Ḥabīb ʿAlī, who presided over his charges with his miraculous gaze. Here was the practical expression of the doctrine of intercession found in Ḥabīb ʿAlī's teachings, the kind of rescue that his many humbler followers hoped to receive in similar moments of crisis.

Other anecdotes from Manāqib al-habībīn recount incidents in which, while more spectacularly supernatural, Ḥabīb ʿAlī's intercession was directed towards similarly mundane perils in this age of industrialized movement. Many of these narrative advertisements focused on other pitfalls of travel. One disciple was miraculously rescued from a tiger when lost in the jungle surrounding Bombay; another invoked Ḥabīb ʿAlī when the steamship (āgbūt, literally 'fire ship') on which he was travelling ran into danger.[84] In all such situations, the emergency ritual procedure

recommended remained the same: call out, 'O, Shaykh Muhammad Habīb
'Alī, be present! O, Shaykh Muhammad Habīb 'Alī, I am in your refuge!'
(*Yā Shaykh Muhammad Habīb 'Alī hāzir bāsh! Yā Shaykh Muhammad
Habīb 'Alī dar panāh-e tū am!*). In cheap-print Urdu, here was a neat
and simple ritual production aimed at an abundant market of displaced
Muslim labourers. For the Konkani Muslims sailing in and out of the
docks at Mazagaon through the industrialization of their old maritime
trade, Habīb 'Alī was clearly a useful man to know – or, better still, to be
'connected' to by a pledge of mutual allegiance. Parallels can be found in
the 'conditions and culture' of Calcutta jute mill workers of the period,
for the widespread notions and practices of 'inequality' to which Dipesh
Chakrabarty has drawn attention were no less present among the mill
workers of Calcutta than Bombay.[85] On one level this was a question of
the larger formations of caste or caste-like community structure, but it
also filtered through to the quotidian practices of the workplace in both
cities where the *sardār* or *muqaddam* labour contractor loomed large in
labourers' lives, not least through the physical violence and bribery that
the contractor exacted on them. Seen in this light, Sufi brotherhood firms
begin to look like reproductions of customary associations for a portion
of the marketplace not served by the voluntary and charitable associations founded by Bombay's Reformist middle class.

Such protection, however, came at a price. Shaykhs such as Habīb
'Alī expected the cultivation of self-discipline in return for their protec-
tive intercession, a theme echoed repeatedly in the moral admonitions
of Habīb 'Alī's writings, admonitions which particularly concerned the
behaviour of his lower-class fellowship at the shrine festivals seen flourishing in Bombay in Chapter 2.[86] Since moral sentiments are best cultivated
by example, *Habīb al-tālibīn* recounted stories about how the misdeeds
of disciples brought an inevitable comeuppance through the supernatural authority of the paternalist shaykh. This image of the shaykh as
paterfamilias acted as the nexus through which Sufi firms interacted with
consumers in the marketplace around them. For in nineteenth-century
Bombay, as elsewhere in India, the Sufi shaykh operated both literally and
figuratively as a godfather. He was the 'big man' to whom children were
taken at birth to receive the miraculous blessing with which came the
promise of lifelong 'protection' (*himāyat*) in reward for lifelong loyalty
to the brotherhood firm. Like the mobster, that other production of the
industrializing city, the shaykh sat at the hub of a wide-reaching network
of allegiances to people who each owed him loyalty for the protection he
offered them. In the words of a more recent Indian Sufi disciple,

The *pir* [master] is like a father. He looks after all aspects of the *murid*'s life, both his spiritual welfare and physical welfare. The *pir* will take away the worldly difficulties of the *murid* [disciple] through his prayers. If he wants success, wealth, etc, the *pir* will give it to him.[87]

This relationship needs to be seen in the context of Bombay labour conditions, for in economic terms the lives of the migrant labourers who formed so many of Habīb 'Alī's followers were dominated by the 'jobber' labour contractor (variously known as a *sardār* or *muqaddam* in the mills or a *toliwalla* or *sarang* in the docks) who acted as middlemen between employers and workers. The relationship between worker and jobber was one of client and patron and, as a result of the influence this gave the jobbers, they were feared and powerful figures in Bombay's workers' neighbourhoods.[88] Amid a labour culture dominated by such hierarchical relationships, intercessionary shaykhs such as Habīb 'Alī found an easy – and, in a sense, ready-made – position. One of Habīb 'Alī's most influential followers in the Mazagaon dockyards was Muhammad Mungī, whose occupation was precisely that of a jobber for the dockyards and, according to the oral tradition of Habīb 'Alī's family, Mungī would often find jobs for Habīb 'Alī's poorer followers in the dockyards.[89] In similar terms, Chapter 3 recounted how after a widow asked the Iranian holy man Sayyid 'Alī Āghā'ī Mazandarānī for help, the shaykh drummed up a subscription of 5,000 rupees from the merchants in the Bombay bazaar where her husband had died.[90] The result of such Sufi big men's intercession was as material as it was metaphysical.

With a theology predicating an entire universe governed by such client–patron relations, in which, like a metaphysical jobber, the shaykh mediated between his dockyard disciples and the riches of God and his Prophet atop the cosmic chain of command, Habīb 'Alī fitted neatly into wider structures of socio-economic relations in the industrial city. This was not unique to Bombay and, in their reproduction of inequality, the ideology and rituals produced by Habīb 'Alī's firm echoed the spread during the same years of spirit-summoning cults among North Indian labourers in Bihar. As these cults spread among both landowners and their workers, 'ritual practices associated with spirit cults not only bore the imprint of caste hierarchy but also became instruments for articulating and securing social hierarchy'.[91] As a *sharīf* Muslim of the Hyderabadi aristocracy teaching rural migrant workers to beg for the intercession of similarly *sharīf*-born holy men, Habīb 'Alī thus reproduced a customary social hierarchy for a new industrial marketplace. From this perspective, the contrast between Customary Islamic brotherhoods and the trade unions

that also emerged among Bombay's labourers around 1900 appears more
clear. For as with the spirit protectors sought by agricultural labourers in
Bihar, what many of Bombay's workers sought was not a bureaucratic
union but a patron blessed with supernatural agency. As living patrons
who were more tangible but no less potent than the ghosts of Bihar, intercessionary shaykhs such as Habīb 'Alī held understandable appeal to their
labour constituents, whatever the hierarchical trade-off in social relations
that membership of their brotherhoods required. In this way, the success
of brotherhood firms such as Habīb 'Alī's in the religious economy was
tied to the wider workplace economy of their clients. These developments
in the lives of rural and small-town migrants to Bombay reflected the way
Sicilian peasants were dragged into a new global economy through the
industrial boom in sulphur and the naval trade in lemons that saw the
first Mafia firms emerge during the 1870s.[92] Based on oaths of initiation,
secrecy and loyalty, and organized through infiltrating and imitating the
structures and norms of kinship, in their social formation the early Mafia
associations had much in common with the Sufi firms of industrializing
India. Whether through the idioms of Sicilian *omerta* or Indian *adab*, both
sets of firms also promoted strong moral codes. We can only speculate as
to whether Habīb 'Alī's relations with his poorer clients also involved the
forms of financial patronage associated with the Sicilian 'godfathers', but
descriptions in his biography of wealthy merchants among his followers
suggests that connecting his poorer and wealthier clients together did-
indeed take place. Other evidence shows this was certainly the kind of
service expected of South Asian Sufi shaykhs.[93]

For Calcutta, Chakrabarty has similarly pointed to parallels between
the gangster (*goonda*) and labour contractor (*sardār*) in terms of behaviour and status.[94] But while the *goonda* ultimately had little legitimacy
for his authority, 'the respect that the *sardār* commanded had roots in
certain other aspects of the culture to which both the *sardār* and the
worker belonged. It derived from a precapitalist culture with a strong
emphasis on religion, community, kinship, language, and other, similar loyalties.'[95] The same could be said of the authority commanded by
shaykhs such as Habīb 'Alī Shāh, whose success in the market was deeply
rooted in the inegalitarian traditions of labourers to whom he preached.
Both Sufi and contractor were understood as giving 'commands' (*hukum*)
that brooked no dissent and so, whether in the daytime commands of the
sardār in the factory and the *toliwalla* in the dockyard or in the behavioural edicts issued by Habīb 'Alī in the evenings at his meeting house, a
common pattern was at work of the reproduction in the industrial city

of pre-capitalist modes of social domination.[96] As with the labour contractor, whose 'bribes' and 'extortions' found legitimacy through being
termed 'introductions' (*salāmī*), 'offerings' (*bakhshīsh*) or simply 'custom'
(*dastūrī*), the authority of the shaykh had easy appeal to a market of
Indian labourers in the industrial age.[97]

7

Bombay Islam in the Ocean's Southern City

A MISSIONARY MARKETPLACE IN NATAL

In the course of the nineteenth century, Bombay developed numerous connections with the new port city of Durban on the southern reaches of the African continent. The traffic between the two ports has usually been framed in the familiar terms of colonialism and modernity, a role in which the transit of political forms – of imperialism or nationalism, of the apparatus of empire or new democratic associations – has loomed largest. Imperial careers certainly played a large part in trans-ocean exchanges, whether in the elevated ranks of such personnel as Henry Bartle Frere (1815–84), sometime Governor of Bombay and High Commissioner for Southern Africa, or the humbler offices of Sikh and Pathan sepoys in the policing of British Africa.[1] The key example of the anti-colonial side of the same modern coinage is the founding of the Indian National Congress in Bombay in 1885 and its echo across the ocean in the establishment of the Natal Indian Congress in Durban in 1894. The most famous figure to connect the two movements was Mohandas Gandhi, who departed India through Bombay on his journey to South Africa. Having helped found the Natal Indian Congress, at the end of this book's period it was at Bombay's Apollo Bunder that Gandhi disembarked in 1915 to join in the struggles of its Indian sibling.[2] Yet the travels of the young lawyer between Bombay and Durban were part of a larger traffic between the two ports that included religious no less than secular transactions. Like Gandhi's own transformation from a barrister into a *mahatma* celebrated in miracle tales that spread through a circuit of train stations, this was a modernity that functioned through acts of enchantment no less than

the cold prose of constitutions.[3] It is towards the reach of Bombay's religious economy in Africa that this chapter turns, moving to the southern reaches of Bombay's oceanic hinterland to trace the exports there
of its religious firms. For in the second half of the nineteenth century
the same forces that created a competitive religious economy in Bombay
were also at work in Natal, whose cosmopolitan and uprooted population offered expanding markets for a wide array of missionary firms. As
the religious dimension of the great scramble for Africa in which Muslim
entrepreneurs were no less active than their Christian counterparts, as in
other regions of the continent many such missionary societies targeted
black Africans. But with the emergence of a large Indian community,
Natal also tempted missionaries with the familiar quarry of Indians on
whom the effectiveness of their proselytizing had already been tested in
the subcontinent. Around the displaced communities in Natal, of whom
Indians formed only one example, there developed a missionary marketplace in which Hindu and Muslim organizations operated alongside their
Christian competitors. As part of an oceanic religious economy, many
of South Africa's Christian missions were transferred from India rather
than exported directly from Britain, manned by missionaries who had
been trained in India and Ceylon, from where after moving to Africa they
received financial support in addition to that from the colonial centre in
Britain. In this way, the Christian firms should also be located among the
new pattern of more varied and competitive religious production that circulated the Indian Ocean and in which Bombay played a central role.

Echoing the catalytic impact of Christian missions on Muslim religious
productivity prior to the arrival of Muslim and Hindu firms in Bombay,
Natal received a disproportionately high number of Christian missions
devoted to its Indian population.[4] With their funding and methods
already in place from India, and with their long-standing contact with the
low castes who made up much of the indentured workforce in Natal, the
Christian missions were swift in their pursuit of the shiploads of indentured labourers. In Durban as in Bombay, the Christian missionaries were
well ahead of their competitors, establishing the first school for Indian
children in Natal as early as 1867, and by the early 1870s several more
mission schools and other charitable institutions.[5] As in Bombay again,
Hindu and Muslim religious firms were slower in their outreach to the
new proletarians, a reflection of the newness of the idea of Hindu and
Muslim religious professionals pandering to the poorest and, in terms
of traditional prestige, the least rewarding sectors of Indian society. But,
once established, the Hindu and Muslim competition proved effective,

and the swift success of their own missions led to serious concern among the Christian organizations that had by 1900 dominated the Natal religious marketplace for several decades.[6] So it was that in the early twentieth century members of such neo-Hindu missionary firms as the Āryā Samāj began to travel to Natal in the wake of the British missionary societies, with an eye to the nominal 'Hindus' among the region's labour force. Although the Āryā Samāj had been founded in Bombay in 1875, it took until 1908 for their representative Swāmī Shankarānandajī Māhārāj to arrive in Durban and preach the society's principles. This same period saw the entry among the Natal indentured class of Ghulām Muhammad 'Sūfī Sāhib' (d. 1329/1911), the franchise representative of Habīb ʿAlī Shāh, whose dockyard theology was explored in the last chapter.[7] Ghulām Muhammad's career comprised the export of a brotherhood firm reared among the poor and displaced in Bombay's dockyards to the similar port setting of Durban.[8] For all his energy and independence, Ghulām Muhammad remained only one player in a larger market in which he had to compete with rival firms promoting other versions of Islam, including the spread from Bombay of adherence to the Āghā Khān.[9]

Like his master before him, Ghulām Muhammad responded to market transformations through the conditions of labour. He produced carnivals, processions and customary shrine practices for an originally rural Muslim workforce, while at the same time promoting an intercessionary theology stressing the soteriological role of the shaykh. Like Habīb ʿAlī in Bombay, Ghulām Muhammad represented the novelty of missionary outreach to new labouring groups, in his case by way of indentured labourers rather than mill and dock workers. As such, his project was part of a panoceanic process of drawing the people of the countryside into the urban marketplaces of the new religious economy. Ghulām Muhammad was by no means the only Indian Sufi to make use of the expanded opportunities of travel afforded by Bombay's infrastructure of travel. In 1910, fifteen years after Ghulām Muhammad sailed from Bombay to Durban, another determined Sufi entrepreneur left Bombay destined for New York.[10] Like Ghulām Muhammad, ʿInāyat Khān (1299–1345/1882–1927) was a disciple of a Hyderabadi shaykh, Abū Hāshim al-Madanī (d. 1325/1907), who, like his exact contemporary Habīb ʿAlī Shāh, instructed him to distribute his teachings overseas.[11] From his home city of Baroda, which had been connected to Bombay since the laying of its earliest major railway, Bombay's infrastructure had allowed ʿInāyat Khān to travel regularly between Baroda, Bombay and Hyderabad, moving on the same rail network that was seen used by the followers of Habīb ʿAlī Shāh in

Chapter 6. Having first been pained by what he saw as the vulgarity of Bombay's 'Westernization', 'Ināyat Khān eventually used Bombay's very modernity to travel to New York, and from there access the vast religious marketplace that few Muslims had reached in the New World.

A MUSLIM RELIGIOUS MARKET IN SOUTH AFRICA

The earliest Muslim community in the territories of what would in 1910 become the Union of South Africa emerged around the Cape under the Dutch East India Company, through the deporting of political exiles from the Indonesian archipelago and the settling of slaves of African, Indonesian and Indian origin.[12] Despite the distinct origins of the 'Malay' Muslims of the Cape from the community of Indian Muslims that developed in Natal from the 1860s, common patterns are nonetheless apparent in the transformation of their religious life around 1900. Through intermarriage with African women by the middle of the nineteenth century, what had been a dispirited and fractured Muslim population of political exiles and former slaves from the Dutch Empire had developed into a new and coherent community concentrated in the district of Cape Town known as Bo-Kaap.[13] The coming of British government to the Cape brought new possibilities for its Muslims, who from 1804 were granted religious freedom they had not possessed under Dutch rule. As in Bombay, the removal of overt state regulation of religious activity was an important enabling factor in the development of a more competitive religious economy. But if Muslim worship was now unrestricted, during the first half of the nineteenth century the institutions to support it were relatively rudimentary, and the only mosques in the Bo-Kaap consisted of informally adapted houses or shops.[14] South Africa offered a ripe, underdeveloped market for religious firms and entrepreneurs from elsewhere.

One such intervention in the South African market was the dispatching of the Ottoman Kurdish Reformist Abū Bakr Effendī (d. 1297/1880) from Istanbul to Cape Town in 1862.[15] Sent by the Ottoman government at the suggestion of a European diplomat, with his formal education at the famous *madrasa* at Shahrazur, Abū Bakr was keen to promote the formal observance of *sharī'a* among the Cape Muslims. Unfortunately, his education in and subsequent promotion of Hanafi law was to cause problems, for the Cape Muslims' own sense of the Law was based on the Shāfi'ī rite of their Malay ancestors. Despite the controversies, Abū Bakr achieved his greatest influence through his composition of *Bayān al-dīn* (Exposition of the faith), a lengthy text printed in 'Muslim-Afrikaans' (that is, Afrikaans in the Arabic script) on the regulations of *shariʿa* and interspersed with the author's commentary. As part of the larger oceanic movement of printed books described in Chapter 3, the text was published in Istanbul in 1873 and shipped in bulk for distribution in Cape Town.[16] With his connections to the translation of scriptural and legalistic works into vernacular print, Abū Bakr reflected the production methods of Reformist Islams in Bombay. In doing so, Abū Bakr contributed to the pluralization of South African religious productions afforded by new steamship and print communications. This pattern of increasing religious production was reflected in Natal, where in the 1880s and 1890s the religious lives of Indian agricultural labourers were transformed through the migration of Muslim missionaries and the foundation of an Islamic urban geography of religious franchise institutions. However, in the case of Ghulām Muhammad, it was a Customary Islam that was promoted which maintained a role for the shrines and saints that Abū Bakr hoped to stamp out. As in Bombay, demand fed the marketplace.

Unlike at the Cape, the introduction of Islam to Natal came through the migration of indentured labourers from India during the 1860s, with a second, larger, movement following from the 1870s onwards.[17] Between 1860 and 1911 over 150,000 Indian labourers arrived in Natal.[18] The greatest proportion of these early migrants was shipped from Madras, with between 7 and 10 per cent of the first shipments between 1860 and 1868 being classified as Muslims.[19] With shipments of labourers also arriving from Calcutta, the activities of the up-country middlemen responsible for enlisting labourers meant that the Indian indentured workers who arrived in Natal were socially variegated. While the limited data on individual labourers preserved in the 'Ships Lists' does show regional concentrations of recruitment, indenture cut across the kin and caste networks by which the Indian peasantry of the nineteenth century organized and identified itself.[20]

As the twentieth century approached, the economy of Natal expanded greatly, through not only the sugar plantations that the original indentured labourers had been sent to cultivate, but also through the opening of the diamond fields and other mines around Johannesburg and the Transvaal. As Durban's port became arguably the most developed in Africa, its genteel esplanade lined with tea shops and hotels, the city began more and more to resemble Bombay. From the 1880s a key role in this transformation of Durban's economy and society was played by the Ismaʿīlī and Sunni 'Arab' merchants from the Bombay Presidency regions of Gujarat and the Konkan who established branches of their trading houses in Natal in connection with their larger outposts in Bombay.[21] It was one such Muslim merchant, Abū Bakr Amod Jhavery, who in 1893 was famously responsible for bringing Gandhi to Natal to represent him in a business dispute with his brother.[22] Such was the scale of immigration of the 'Passenger Indians' such as Gandhi who represented the next generation of Indians that by the early 1890s the opposition of white traders led to discriminatory laws against Indian merchants. Aside from the banning of Indian representation from the Natal legislature which provoked Gandhi and his mercantile friends to form the Natal Indian Congress in 1894, it was the Immigration Restriction Act (Natal) of 1897 that was most effective in controlling the immigration of petty merchants and other small- and medium-scale economic migrants from India.[23] Other laws, such as the 1897 Natal Dealers' Licences Act (No. 18), restricted Indian trading and land purchasing. Nonetheless, indentured immigration continued unabated until 1911, maintaining a steady flow of peasant migration from India in the period with which *Bombay Islam* is concerned. Since most of these labourers chose to stay on in Natal after their indenture expired, even by the early 1870s a sub-community had emerged of formerly indentured 'free Indians'. Many of them chose to buy small plots of land in Durban's rural hinterland, and by 1884 there were already 2,000 Indian freeholders settled within two miles of Durban borough.[24] Alongside these new freeholders, ongoing indentured migration ensured that the influx of an Indian merchant elite – some of whom controlled vast international businesses and possessed great fortunes by any standards – remained a small proportion of Natal's overall Indian population, albeit one that is seen below having considerable influence in the religious economy through patronizing the activities of Ghulām Muhammad among their poorer Muslim cousins.[25]

While numerous historians have traced the formation and dissolution of the Indian communities in eastern and southern Africa, the lack of primary source material has meant that 'voices' from written sources in Indian languages have been almost entirely absent from such work. While extremely rare, such sources do exist and, in addition to the Urdu hagiography of Ghulām Muhammad discussed below, an Urdu travelogue from the same period lends a more intimate sense of the immigrants' perceptions of Africa. With its accounts of the African peoples and unfamiliar flora and fauna of British East Africa, the travelogue suggests the strangeness of Africa for the Indian settlers who moved there in the same period as Natal's settlement.[26] Written in 1901, the *Safarnāma-ye Ūgandā wa Mumbāsā* (Travelogue on Uganda and Mombasa) began with a survey of

East Africa's history which, as in such texts as the hagiography of Pēdrō Shāh published a year earlier in Bombay, sought to present an Islamic aetiology for the region. Showing the common concerns of travel, historical and hagiographical texts, like the presentation of Natal in the hagiography of Ghulām Muhammad discussed below, the *Safarnāma-ye Ūgandā wa Mumbāsā* pictured East Africa before Muslim settlement as a land of jungles with 'no government (*saltanat*), judges (*qāzi*), lawyers (*muftī*) or law (*qānūn*)'.[27] While fully aware of the rise of British power and administration in East Africa, the author nonetheless emphasized the much earlier activities of Muslim immigrants in originally civilizing the 'wild and blood-drinking (*wahshī aur khūnkhwār*)' African peoples of the region.[28] Yet after stressing the foundational role of pre-colonial Muslim settlers, the author went on to celebrate the achievements of British law and order and the affection in which the new rulers were held by all sections of East Africa's population.[29] What is most striking about the travelogue is therefore its vision of the opening up and 'taming' of East Africa as a joint Muslim and British project in which the Indian Muslim settlers for whom the author was writing played the central teleological role as the zenith of this long-term Anglo-Muslim project. In view of its intended readership of would-be Indian Muslim travellers from Bombay, much of the central portion of the text was devoted to practically minded information on the infrastructure, peoples and economy of Mombasa and Uganda. Yet the region's Islamic credentials never slipped from view, with detailed descriptions of Mombasa's mosques featuring next to accounts of its modern bridges, waterfront and newspapers.[30] Although this chapter focuses on the case of South Africa, the travelogue's discussions of the passage through Bombay of Islam, settlers and even Urdu have bearings on the history of East Africa in this period.

Just as Indian Muslim settlers in East Africa conceived their new environment through the historical and religious discursive frameworks of Urdu, in Natal the uprooted labourers also drew on older customary idioms – of ritual and entertainment no less than language – to help their home-making in distant Africa. As with the wide market appeal of recognizable custom in Bombay, the use of such customary idioms also helped create new forms of sociability for early migrants who other than their conditions of labour often had little in common to identify with. In these quintessentially modern conditions of deracination and displacement, like the rural migrant labour force of Bombay itself, the indentured labourers of Natal found solace in religious productions directed towards their conditions, a process that echoed the emphasis on a long-term and inclusively

'Islamic' (rather than caste- or region-based) community in East Africa in the *Safarnāma-ye Ūgandā wa Mumbāsā*. Despite the arrival in Natal of small numbers of black 'Zanzibari' migrants, the Muslim marketplace that emerged there was of overwhelmingly Indian origin. Indeed, the Zanzibar Muslims (many of them escaped or manumitted slaves) were officially classified as 'Indians'.[31] Drawn as the majority of the first gen-eration of Natal Indians were from the rural peasantry, like so many of the labour migrants to Bombay, their religious culture held much in common with the Customary Islam of the Tamil and Bengali countryside from which they originated. As in Bombay, mass rural migration into a cosmopolitan urban environment helped fuel a religious economy in Natal with strong cultural ties to the Indian subcontinent. Although few survive from the first generation, oral folk songs composed originally in the period of indenture reflect the collision of cultures experienced by Indians finding themselves a minority in a society of Zulus, Britons and other immigrants, a society no less cosmopolitan than the Bombay of Habīb 'Alī Shāh. The quick shedding of the ways of the village that sim-ilarly characterized Hyderabadi and Konkani migrant life in Bombay is echoed in these Natal Indian folk songs:

> *Tu chal jā pagadandī*
> *... Pahire ultā sārī*
> *Tū chōr diye kuwalā ke chāl.*
> §
> You go out walking down the roads
> ... And wear your sari back-to-front
> You've abandoned family traditions.[32]

These anxieties about the exilic loss of custom would in turn create demand for the religious forms of the homeland, demand which was met with the arrival from Bombay of Ghulām Muhammad.

EXPANDING THE FRANCHISE

The family brotherhood firm that Ghulām Muhammad established in Natal was an export from Bombay's religious economy into a larger oce-anic market. Like the Gujarati entrepreneurs seen in Chapter 2 establish-ing franchise shrines in Bombay, as a deputy (*khalīfa*) in Habīb 'Alī Shāh's firm, Ghulām Muhammad established an African franchise of his master's brotherhood. He was helped in this by the 'accreditations' that were pub-licized of his close connection to the master in Bombay, ultimately through the printing of an Urdu biography of Ghulām Muhammad in Bombay for distribution in Natal.³³ According to this Bombay-printed *Riyāz-e sūfī* (Labours of the Sufi), Ghulām Muhammad was born in 1269/1852 in Ibrahimpatan, a small ocean port in the Ratnagiri District of the Konkan coast of the Bombay Presidency.³⁴ From his family archive it is also known that Ghulām Muhammad claimed to be of Arabian descent, for this was testified to in a genealogical certificate (*shajara*) demonstrating his belonging to a long line of Muslim scholars and judges (*qāzī*). Such Arabian ancestries were commonplace among the Muslims of the Konkan, and the small ports of the Konkan littoral were able to maintain their centuries-old trading and pilgrimage links with the Arabian peninsula well into the colonial period. In his move to Bombay, and then Durban, Ghulām Muhammad's itinerary echoed that of his master Habīb 'Alī from Hyderabad to Bombay, with older religious centres providing religious entrepreneurs to the new urban markets. In placing him as a member of the *ashraf* (noble) birth-line among India's Muslims, Ghulām Muhammad's 'Arab' ethnicity served to place him on equal terms with the new middle class of Indian Muslim merchants in Natal, who likewise considered themselves as Arab traders with roots in Arabia and branches all round the ocean, not only in India.³⁵ Their investment followed. Just as Habīb 'Alī was a Hyderabadi notable preaching to the mill hand, Ghulām Muhammad was a *sharīf* Indian 'Arab' preaching to the indentured labourer. In Natal Ghulām Muhammad addressed himself mainly to fellow Konkani Muslims, on the one hand, and Muslim indentured labourers, on the other. Although more of Natal's indentured Muslims were from Tamil-speaking regions of India than Hyderabad, they were known in Natal as *Hydrabadee*.³⁶ Among the Konkanis and 'Hyderabadis', even in South Africa Ghulām Muhammad worked among a remarkably similar group of religious consumers to those whose loyalties his master had cultivated among Hyderabadi and Konkani migrants to Bombay.

Ghulām Muhammad's own relocation from his home town to Bombay in the early 1890s reflected this larger migration of Konkani Muslims to the urban labour markets. Like Ghulām Muhammad's own subsequent sea journeys, the occupations of many migrants in the Bombay docks and shipping lines represented a pattern of continuity with pre-modern Konkani Muslim life: the sea was as familiar to the Konkani working man as it was to the new missionaries who emerged from their community. In its connections to overseas travel, Ghulām Muhammad's career bore certain echoes of that of his fellow Konkani Muslim Sardār 'Abd al-Haqq (1853–96), who similarly left the Konkan as a young man, before entering the Hyderabad civil service and later travelling to London as the Agent of the Hyderabad State Railways. In the years before Ghulām Muhammad's death in 1329/1911, many other Konkani Muslims followed the new itineraries of empire by migrating to Natal as well as to the Transvaal and the Cape Colony.[37] In line with these larger movements of Konkani Muslims, a few years after he became Habīb 'Alī's disciple in 1895, Ghulām Muhammad left Bombay aboard the steamship *Hoosen* to distribute allegiance to his master's firm among the new Indian markets in Natal. However, Ghulām Muhammad's own journey reflected less the sea-crossings of the indentured than the travels of the 'Passenger Indians' who had been setting up Muslim business in Durban as a result of the spread of cheap screw-propelled ocean-liner travel in the 1880s. The steamships on which he sailed on his several subsequent journeys between India and Natal – the *Umzinto XI* and *Hoosen* – were those used by Indian merchants of the 'Passenger' class. Announcements and recommendations for these ships featured in the advertising section of the Durban *Indian Opinion* newspaper founded by Gandhi and supported by a merchant readership, part of an industrial infrastructure of travel of which Ghulām Muhammad was able to take advantage.

According to *Riyāz-e sūfī*, Ghulām Muhammad was specifically instructed to go to South Africa by Habīb 'Alī in order to spread 'the light of Islam and encourage people to keep the commands of God and the Prophet'.[38] While such hagiographical allocations of motive should be read with caution, this sense of deliberate purpose rings true in a period characterized by increased competition, production and distribution by Bombay's religious firms. By 1909, when the Certificate of Domicile with which Ghulām Muhammad was eventually issued recorded his profession as 'priest',[39] he was by no means the only professional Muslim 'priest' working or seeking work in Natal, and his success overshadowed the failures of many other Muslim entrepreneurs eager to establish themselves in Durban. Colonial law did occasionally intervene in the religious market and, as in the case of Āghā Khān I in Bombay, this could work to the advantage of particular Muslim players. In Ghulām Muhammad's case, this was seen in the way in which immigration regulations limited the 'supply' or migration of Muslim entrepreneurs to the Natal marketplace. An article in Durban's *Indian Opinion* from 1911, for example, described how 'a Moulvi or Mahomedan priest' was denied permission to land in Durban, despite having the money to pay the required deposit of £10 on arrival.[40] In response to local Muslim criticism of this refusal, the immigration officer claimed that there were already five such 'Mahomedan priests' staying in Durban under the visiting pass scheme alone. If by

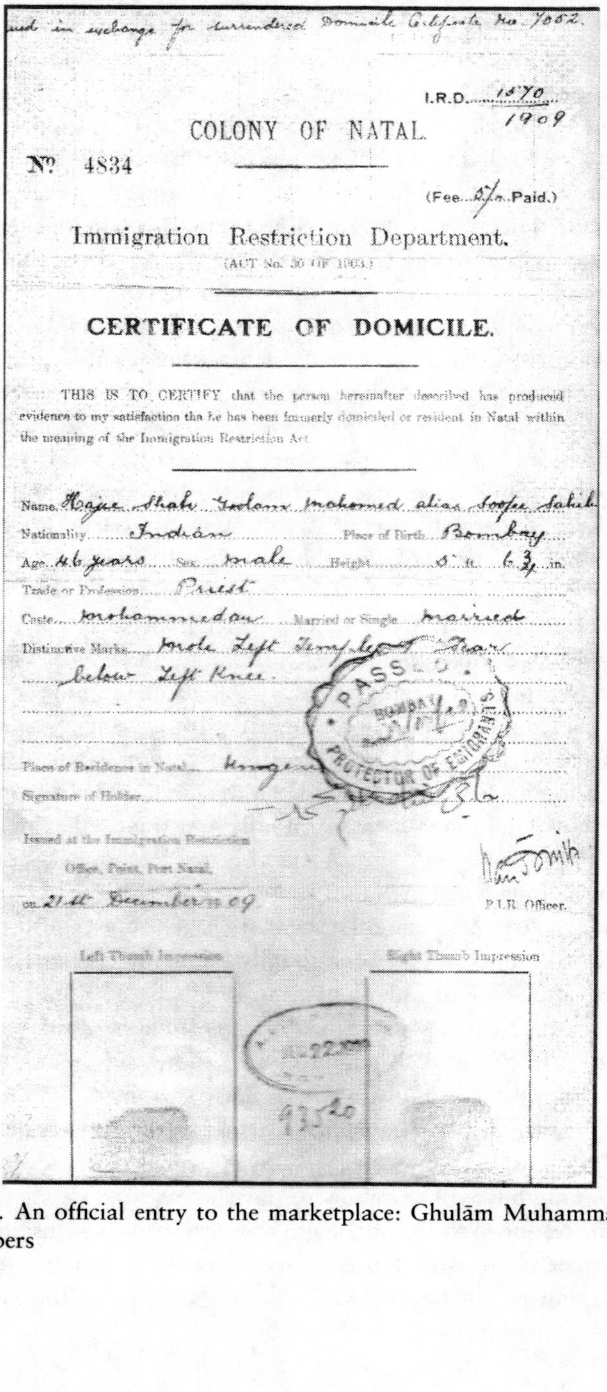

ued in exchange for surrendered Domicile Certificate No. 7052.

I.R.D. 1570
1909

COLONY OF NATAL.

Nº 4834

(Fee 5/- Paid.)

Immigration Restriction Department.
(ACT No. 30 OF 1903.)

CERTIFICATE OF DOMICILE.

THIS IS TO CERTIFY that the person hereinafter described has produced evidence to my satisfaction tha he has been formerly domiciled or resident in Natal within the meaning of the Immigration Restriction Act.

Name. Hajee Shah Goolam Mahomed alias Soofee Sahib
Nationality Indian Place of Birth Bombay
Age 46 years Sex male Height 5 ft. 6¾ in.
Trade or Profession Priest
Caste Mohammedan Married or Single married
Distinctive Marks Mole Left Temple & Scar below Left Knee.

PASSED BOMBAY PROTECTOR OF EMIGRANTS

Place of Residence in Natal Umgeni
Signature of Holder

Issued at the Immigration Restriction Office, Point, Port Natal,
on 21st December 1909

P.I.R. Officer.

Left Thumb Impression | Right Thumb Impression

FIGURE 17. An official entry to the marketplace: Ghulām Muhammad's immigration papers no means a monopoly, such an oligopoly was good enough for Ghulām Muhammad. Even so, entry to Durban was not in itself an assurance of success there, and although Ghulām Muhammad was allowed to land on his first journey of 1895, his attempts to gain a following and investors were unsuccessful on this initial expedition. He was to return to India several times over the next fifteen years, in classic migrant strategy persuading other male members of his extended family to join his firm and support his overseas venture.[41]

Although over time Ghulām Muhammad would prove to be the most influential religious entrepreneur among Natal's Muslims, he was by no means the earliest figure to found Muslim religious firms in the colony. While no information survives on the religious practices of the first Muslim indentured migrants in the 1860s and 1870s, it seems likely that prayers were offered in sugar-cane fields and dormitories before the foundation of Natal's first mosques. It was not until some twenty years after the arrival of the first indentured Indian Muslims that the earliest formal site of Muslim worship emerged with the establishment of the Friday mosque in Durban's Grey Street in 1881. This was six years after the founding of the earliest recorded Hindu temple in Durban, located in the Magazine Barracks in Durban's dockyards.[42] The mosque came about when a small brick building on Grey Street was purchased in 1880 by the Memon merchant and subsequent employer of Gandhi, Abū Bakr Amod Jhavery (d. 1304/1887) for the sum of £115 for use as a mosque.[43] The establishment of the Grey Street Mosque occurred in the same decade in which formal mosque construction began in Cape Town with the relaxation of building restrictions for the Cape's non-Christian communities. The activities of the immigrant Muslim and Hindu missionaries can be seen as a response to the liberalization of South Africa's religious marketplace that occurred in the 1880s and 1890s. Although the initial plot purchased on Durban's Grey Street for the mosque was a small one – measuring only six by four metres – it lay at the heart of the commercial district in which the new Indian trading class was establishing itself, and just a few minutes' walk away from Abū Bakr Amod's own shop. As a result of the donations of other merchants, in 1884 the original mosque was demolished and rebuilt, before being twice extended again in 1903 and 1905.[44] As such, the founding of the Grey Street Mosque was a direct result of the arrival in Durban of the Indian Muslim 'Passenger' merchant investors. Nonetheless, the first decades of the mosque's history saw its antechambers echoing with disputes as rival Muslim groups sought to establish their control of a place of worship founded by Indian members of the same

Memon merchant community seen in Chapter 1 building mosques and schools in Bombay.[45] By the 1890s the mosque was riddled with disputes between those maintaining the Memons' Customary Islamic affiliation and donation to saintly shrines (particularly of 'Abd al-Qādir in Baghdad) and Reformists who exported from India the critique that such customs were nothing more than a wasteful borrowing from Hindus.[46] As in Bombay, the many Muslim groups brought together in Durban generated religious competition as older local socio-religious hierarchies clashed in the cosmopolitan arena of the port city. This was seen in the struggle to control the Grey Street Mosque, which saw the reproduction of a religious economy that had already formed in Bombay as different parties competed in the promotion of an increasingly diverse array of religious productions.

Ghulām Muhammad represented the next stage in this process. In April 1896, a few months after his arrival in Durban, he bought a plot of land at Umgeni, part of the Riverside area on the northern outskirts of the city. There, just near the ocean, he built the first mosque, *khanaqah* and *madrasa* of the many that he and his followers would found in the next three decades. The area that he chose to settle closely followed the trajectory of earlier Indian immigration, for over the previous two decades the region around the River Umgeni to the north of Durban had been extensively settled by former indentured labourers.[47] By the mid-1890s the smallholders' success began to attract other Indians to the region, and the social profile of the Riverside area began to change, seeing the establishment of Indian workshops and trading outlets in addition to the farmsteads.[48] By the time of Ghulām Muhammad's arrival in 1895 much of the logistical and legal apparatus for his venture was therefore already in place through the enterprise of the pioneer indentured labourers and merchants. In this respect, the legal means by which Ghulām Muhammad founded his complex at Umgeni are particularly revealing. Although in a transoceanic relocating of the shrine legends of the Bombay Presidency described in Chapter 2, the account given in *Riyāz-e sūfī* of Ghulām Muhammad's arrival and foundation of a mosque at Umgeni depicted him stamping out Hindu idol worship and ousting a fearsome monster, the picture that emerges from more bureaucratic documentation is quite different.[49] The Deed of Sale that acting as a lawyer Gandhi oversaw for Ghulām Muhammad's initial land purchase at Riverside records the agreed price for the land as £185.[50] Despite the public image of custom with which Ghulām Muhammad's firm surrounded itself, each of his outposts was founded on the commercial bedrock of colonial property law.

After the initial land purchase, he subsequently employed the English lawyers J. P. Calder & Calder Conveyancers to establish the legal mechanisms by which the foundation and management of his mosques, shrines and *madrasa*s could be achieved through the Common Law of Trusts.[51] Here his strategy reflected that of the Mēmon founders of the Grey Street Mosque a decade earlier, who in 1891 established the Natal Porbander Trust to ensure that control of the mosque and its associated properties remained in the religious firm of a small number of Mēmon families.[52] The fact that this trust was a copy of the earlier Porbander Trust founded in 1884 in the eponymous port in the Bombay Presidency shows how Muslim religious firms in South Africa were founded through an extension of legal and organizational mechanisms previously developed in greater Bombay. The centrality of kinship to these institutional religious productions also points to the way in which the religious as much as the commercial economy operated on the family business model, with Ghulām Muhammad in Durban no less than Āghā Khān in Bombay. In the legal paperwork that established his firm in South Africa, Ghulām Muhammad thus inserted legal clauses to ensure that ultimate control over these institutions should remain with his family, who by the same token to warrant their trusteeship had to work in the service of Islam.

Like the European missionaries with whom he competed, Ghulām Muhammad used these institutions to supply basic amenities as much as metaphysics to his labouring clientele. As well as a medical dispensary and *madrasa* lessons for poor Muslim children, he founded an orphanage for the children of the many labourers whose lives were cut short through overwork. Charitable donations were collected for medicines which were made up in a dispensary at the Umgeni complex and for the proper burial of poor Muslims in the cemetery he also founded.[53] Echoing the dockyard following of his master in Bombay, a number of lascars and other Muslim sailors were also buried there over the years; among them was Shaykh Bilal Hasan (d. 1336/1918), the ship steward of *HMS Trent*. Another means of helping the labourers was the refuge nicknamed the *mawlī khāna* ('house of the good-for-nothing'). It was intended as a shelter for the homeless *mawlī*s, effectively meaning *gānjā* (cannabis) smokers, though toddy drinkers were probably also admitted. The scale of *gānjā* use among the indentured found an echo in mournful Durban folksongs in Bhojpuri dialect of a type known as 'Riverside songs' due to their association with performers in the area where Ghulām Muhammad and his formerly indentured neighbours dwelt.

Gānjā pī ke sāiyā āwē
Jhagharā macchāwēlā
Jab ham kucchū bōlē
§
My husband comes home high on *gānjā*
And raises havoc.
Should I say something?[54]

Ghulām Muhammad also established a *madrasa* for the distribution of the intercessionary theology of his master, Habīb 'Alī. Competition was present here too in Natal's diversifying religious economy, and Ghulām Muhammad was by no means the sole Indian Muslim involved in the establishment of such schools. In other Indian settlements, members of the merchant class were investing in schools and mosques and appointing their own *mawlwī* religious instructors, just as they had previously founded the Grey Street Mosque in Durban in 1881. In 1912 the Muslim merchants of the inland Natal trading station of Nottingham Road took it upon themselves to establish a *madrasa* behind 'Shop No. 1' to educate their children, bringing a certain Munshī Jamāl al-Qādirī from India to act as teacher.[55] However, Ghulām Muhammad's *madrasas* formed a self-conscious Counter Reform to both these local rituals and to the Anglo-Hindustani Schools promoted in Bombay by his fellow Konkani and Reformist namesake, Ghulām Muhammad Munshī.[56] More importantly, his activities reflected a larger pattern of distribution by Sufi brotherhood firms around the Indian Ocean that was as important to Africa as to India. The same years thus saw Ghulām Muhammad's Egyptian contemporary Muhammad al-Dandarāwī (d. 1328/1910), the heir of the Moroccan Sufi Ahmad ibn Idrīs (d. 1253/1837), enter the Indian Ocean via the Suez Canal to expand into Somalia.[57] In both eastern and southern Africa, Customary Islamic firms responded effectively to the social changes of the Indian Ocean in the age of expanding capitalism.[58]

Between 1904 and 1905 Ghulām Muhammad expanded his franchise by founding several more mosques and *madrasas* in other districts of Durban. His second outpost, at Westville (around ten miles west of central Durban), reflected the character of his first. Like Umgeni, when Ghulām Muhammad arrived Westville was an agricultural settlement on Durban's periphery that was just being connected to the urban economy. Westville's early settlers were Germans involved in the cotton trade, but by the time Ghulām Muhammad established himself there the area was also becoming the home to wealthier Indian market gardeners who had served out their indenture.[59] The mosque established at Springfield two years later

in 1906 was similarly located among a community of former indentured labourers, a class of self-bettering religious consumers with a little
more cash at their disposal than in their days of indenture.[60] By 1910
Ghulām Muhammad had founded branches of his original Umgeni complex in Cape Town, Tongaat, Springfield, Ladysmith, Pietermaritzburg
and Kenville, all under the leadership of his sons or kinsmen.[61] In these
towns Ghulām Muhammad was again no first-generation pioneer, and
as in Durban he also followed the movement of Indian merchants. Most
of the Indian migrants moving to the new towns of the Natal interior or
the Transvaal were small-time traders who were following the expansion
of the mining industry and the railway in South Africa to set up shop.[62]
Although Indians began to arrive in Pietermaritzburg in the Midlands
of Natal as early as 1863, Indian Muslims did not start to settle there
until around 1890.[63] Ghulām Muhammad established his mosque in
Pietermaritzburg two decades later, in 1909, by which time the Indian
population had reached almost seven thousand.[64] The mosques and
*madrasa*s he founded in the uplands of Natal – at Springfield, Ladysmith
and Kenville – were similarly connected to the secondary migration of
Indian traders. In the Transvaal, for example, as early as 1870 a mar-
quee tent had been erected to serve as a mosque among the other min-
ers' shanties in Johannesburg, with a proper mosque built on the site
in 1888, which again preceded Ghulām Muhammad's expansion to the
area by several decades.[65] The mosque Ghulām Muhammad founded in
Cape Town in 1903 reflected this pattern, being set up in the wake of
the migration to the Cape of Muslim merchants from his home Indian
region of the Konkan; his brother-in-law, 'Abd al-Latīf (d. 1334/1916),
was appointed as its head.[66] Here was an Indian reflection of the kin-
based strategies of Chinese migrants in the east Indian Ocean.[67] Through
his family brotherhood firm in the economy of enchantment, Ghulām
Muhammad repeated on a smaller scale what the family of the Āghā
Khān had accomplished in Bombay a few decades earlier.

Ghulām Muhammad was not always successful, and his most ambitious venture was a failure. Having established himself so effectively in the
South African marketplace, he attempted to connect his outposts in Africa
with a *madrasa* he hoped to establish in his home town in the Konkan
region of the Bombay Presidency, so cementing the connections he had
made between the Durban and Bombay markets. The plan took shape
some time after the death of his master Habīb 'Alī, in 1906, when Ghulām
Muhammad travelled back from Durban to pay a visit to his master's tomb
in Hyderabad.[68] Instead of travelling directly back to Durban, Ghulām

Muhammad returned to the port of Kalyan in the Konkan. According to the biographical *Riyāz-e sūfi*, he bought a plot of land there which he established as a *waqf* endowment for the foundation of a mosque and *madrasa* from which to spread Habīb 'Alī's teachings.[69] According to the Census of India of 1901, a few years before Ghulām Muhammad's visit the population of Kalyan stood at nearly 11,000, among whom was a large Muslim community chiefly involved in the rice-husking industry and so in similarly agricultural activities to the indentured Muslims of Natal.[70] The *madrasa* at Kalyan was envisaged as a partner to those he had already established in Natal, intended to facilitate the exchange of students between India and Natal in the pursuit of a theology emphasizing intercession and custom. Once again, other Bombay entrepreneurs were already active in the area, and around the same time, having already founded a large *madrasa* on New Kazi Street in Bombay, the Konkani notable Muhammad Hasan Muqba opened a *madrasa* for girls in his own neighbouring hometown of Ratnagiri.[71] But shortly before Ghulām Muhammad's *madrasa* was completed, news came by telegraph from South Africa that the father of his deputy and brother-in-law 'Abd al-Latīf had died, and as a result he had to return to Natal. The momentum was lost, and Ghulām Muhammad's plan to tie Natal into a formal pedagogic network spanning both sides of the ocean was to remain incomplete.[72]

Amid his failures and successes, Ghulām Muhammad was clearly not the sole supplier of Islam to the Natal Muslims, and his Customary Islam was not the only Islam on offer in its marketplace. The Reformist Anjuman-e Ishā'at al-Islām (Society for the propagation of Islam) was also active among Natal's indentured Muslims and, in the person of Dīn Faqīr Yūsuf, Ghulām Muhammad faced an especially well-qualified competitor. Born in Durban to indentured parents in 1879, Faqīr Yūsuf was a founder member of the Natal wing of the Anjuman-e Ishā'at al-Islām that Chapter 1 described as active in Bombay at the same time. In 1899 Faqīr Yūsuf managed to find colonial investment for his mission by being employed as an interpreter in Durban's prison and later law court.[73] This connection to the colonial state served him well, and when the disputes for control of the city's central mosque in Grey Street resulted in outside intervention he was nominated by the solicitors Doull & Stuart as the mosque's trustee. Many of Durban's former indentured and otherwise working-class 'Hydrabadee' Muslims saw such appointments as a threat to their own customary religious practices, 'because the control of mosques meant the power to impose traditions, beliefs and practices as hegemonic'.[74] If Faqīr Yūsuf's entry to the prison and mosque shows how the modern apparatus of the state at times intervened in the religious economy on behalf of Reformists, the following section shows how Ghulām Muhammad responded by creating alternative institutions appealing to the market demand for enchantment.

A GEOGRAPHY OF AFRICAN ENCHANTMENT

Among such competitors as Faqīr Yūsuf, Ghulām Muhammad's ties to a Customary Islam of saints and shrines lent him potential advantages in a religious market of indentured rural migrants, the same class of people whose migration to Bombay had stimulated the development of the shrine firms discussed in Chapter 2. Responding to this demand, in what was ultimately his most successful venture Ghulām Muhammad and his family established parallel shrine franchises in Durban by first constructing a shrine and then teaching the rituals to accompany them. Given that even more than Bombay, Durban lacked an existing sacred geography bequeathed by an earlier Muslim presence, it was in this that Ghulām Muhammad showed his greatest entrepreneurial flair – first by identifying a recently deceased labourer as an unnoticed saint, and second by promoting in Durban the Muharram carnivals that were so important a feature of Bombay labour culture. According to the rumours preserved by his followers, on his arrival in Durban Ghulām Muhammad realized through a dream that an obscure indentured labourer called Shaykh Ahmad was one of the hidden 'friends of God' (*awliyā allāh*). Whether he also knew of the dead labourer from conversations with other Durban Indians, who remembered Shaykh Ahmad as a wandering beggar in the Grey Street market, remains uncertain.[75] Shaykh Ahmad had died only a year earlier in 1312/1894, allowing Ghulām Muhammad to locate his pauper's grave and build a simple platform to mark the spot, and subsequently construct a wood-and-iron shelter above the grave that within eight years of Ghulām Muhammad's own death was replaced in 1919 by a domed mausoleum in the style of the shrines of India.[76] A well-chosen spot it was, for the platform and subsequent mausoleum that Ghulām Muhammad established over Shaykh Ahmad's grave was not only a few minutes walk from the city's central mosque on Grey Street, in which he was never able to gain a foothold, but also right behind Durban's main market. As with the shrine to 'Abd al-Rahmān we earlier saw established in Bombay's bazaar a few years later, in terms of attracting a following this was prime cultic property. Gathering income from the pious donations of the marketmen, the original rough shelter that he constructed was eventually replaced by an arched and domed reproduction of the saintly shrines of India. Like the insignia of all successful franchises, the deliberate modelling of the shrine enabled it to buy into an easily recognizable 'brand' with immediate appeal to the Indians of the nearby market. The appearance of the shrine echoed in Muslim form the wider architectural traffic between Durban and Bombay seen in the commonalities in the official built environment of colonial offices and public buildings in the two ports.[77]

Who Shaykh Ahmad actually was is obscure in the early sources from Ghulām Muhammad's circle. He appears as a mysterious and somewhat marginal figure in the earliest Urdu source, *Riyāz-e sūfī*, where he is only mentioned in the familiar hagiographical role of predicting Ghulām Muhammad's arrival in Durban.[78] According to the oral tradition transmitted by Ghulām Muhammad's followers, Shaykh Ahmad had sailed from Madras as part of the earliest shipment of labourers and arrived in Durban on the *Truro* in November 1860 to work in the sugar-cane fields at Tongaat.[79] In line with the customary 'ancestor saints' found all round the Indian Ocean, the story emphasized Shaykh Ahmad's role as a community founder or settler-saint among the earliest Muslim migrants to Natal.[80] However, the passenger manifest or Ship List for the *Truro* does not contain the name of any indentured passenger by the name of Shaykh Ahmad.[81] There is listed the name of a sixteen-year-old female passenger 'Ameena Bee' (Amīna Bī), who registered a 'Sheik Ahmed' as her father.[82] Given that several generations of the same family often moved into indenture together and listed related labourers in Natal as their next of kin, this suggests some measure of fact in the rumoured account. This seems to be supported by documentation of an indentured Indian Muslim from Masulipatam listed as 'Sheik Ahmed' who disembarked in Durban a month later in December 1860 from the *Lord George Bentinc*. Although this was not the *Truro*, the *Lord George Bentinc* was one of the first generation of indentured ships and arrived only slightly later than the emblematic 'first Indian ship', the *Truro*.[83] At this time 'Sheik Ahmed' was twenty-four years of age, which means that by the time of the death in Durban of the former labourer of the same name in 1895 he would have been around fifty-nine years old. While its historicity cannot be established with certainty, the story of a former indentured labourer spending his last years wandering and begging around the market and mosque on Grey Street reflects what is known about the poorest Natal Indians in the late nineteenth century, a state of affairs to which the colonial government responded by passing a Vagrant Law to limit the movements of this drifter underclass. Although over the fifty-one-year period in which the indenture programme was in operation, seven other labourers by the name of 'Sheik Ahmed' appear among the thousands of other indentured Indians in the Ship Lists, the labourer aboard the *Lord George Bentinc* fits most closely with the dates described in the story of Shaykh Ahmad, the labourer who became a hobo and who upon his death was recognized as a saint. Apart from recording the height of this 'Sheik Ahmed' as five foot nine (relatively tall by the standards of his shipmates), the name of his father (simply 'Abdool'), and his registered home of the port of Masulipatam on the eastern coast of India, nothing is recorded of him in the Ships List data by way of distinguishing marks (such as the facial pox marks recorded for so many of the indentured) or the employer to whom he was contracted. There is a certain poignancy in the biographical obscurity of the working man buried beneath the dome in the Brook Street cemetery, a monument of the unknown labourer.

Whether or not the man buried in the grave in actuality was this 'Sheik Ahmed' who sailed on the *Lord George Bentinc*, Ghulām Muhammad's efforts ensured that the grave was quickly transformed into a place of pilgrimage. Miracle stories were spread about the dead man's powers and the cult that Ghulām Muhammad established there reproduced the rituals of saint veneration and financial gift-giving that were so central to the teachings of his master in Bombay. For now that he was custodian of a shrine, Ghulām Muhammad could promote the festival of the death anniversary (*'urs*) that his master had written about in such detail. As in Bombay, a key part of the *'urs* festival was the musical concert that held great attraction for the urban masses. Here, Ghulām Muhammad reflected the strategies of that other Indian Sufi entrepreneur, 'Ināyat Khān, whose own travels also began in Bombay. Sailing to New York and eventually California in the early 1900s, 'Ināyat Khān made the same use of custom as Ghulām Muhammad in Natal, drawing followers through the attraction of the Sufi musical performance.[84] While Reformists shunned the religious use of music, by promoting customary musical rituals (*mahfil-e samā'*) their competitors held a considerable advantage.

Ghulām Muhammad next constructed another mausoleum in Durban – apparently intended for Habīb 'Alī, but destined, in the event, for himself. By the time of his death in 1911 Ghulām Muhammad's following was extensive, and his obituary in the *Natal Mercury* on 1 July 1911 described large numbers of merchants as well as labourers among the hundreds at his funeral.[85] After his death, his family promoted his own *'urs* festival at the mausoleum he had himself built, enabling even in death the continuity of the family firm. Here for the Muslim worker was a kind of licit entertainment on the 'holy day' of the *'urs*. Like the boxing-rings of British labour groups, the *'urs* fairs contained a rough appeal to their audience, with photographs from the 1912 *'urs* initiated at Ghulām Muhammad's own shrine showing black 'Zanzibari' Muslims performing the self-mutilating sword-and-skewer displays known as *ratiep*.[86]

It was in response to the instigation of Ghulām Muhammad's *'urs* that the biography *Riyāz-e sūfī* was printed in Bombay in 1331/1913, containing a long appendix of Urdu litanies that allowed it to serve as a prayer book for the congregation around his tomb. After the biographical section, the second half of *Riyāz-e sūfī* consisted of Urdu *na'at* and *munāqib*, prayer songs addressed to the Prophet and to Habīb 'Alī and Ghulām Muhammad as his intercessionary heirs.[87] *Riyāz-e sūfī* also supplied a whole repertoire of hymns to accompany the ceremonies of the procession (*jālūs*), the rubbing of sandalwood into the tomb (*sandalmālī*) and the laying of the 'flower blanket' (*phūlūn kī chādar*).[88] Each of the ritual stages in the festival's symbolic creation of a marriage bed for the saint and his divine bride (*'arūs*) was directed to the fealty to the shaykhs that tied Durban Indians to Ghulām Muhammad's family firm and prompted their donations. Here in simple songs printed for Durban Muslims in Bombay was a liturgical echo of the theological principles of intercession that featured in the writings of Ghulām Muhammad's teacher in Bombay. In this way hagiographical narrative ritual song, labour migration and Bombay's lithographic print industry were all partners in the success of Ghulām Muhammad's firm.

Along with the *'urs* of Shaykh Ahmad, during his lifetime Ghulām Muhammad had also promoted other aspects of Customary Islam that were familiar to the Konkani and Tamil Indian consumers in Natal's religious marketplace, particularly the celebration of Muharram, replete with processions from his Umgeni complex bearing the customary decorated standard (*'alam*) and coffin (*ta'ziya*) of the martyred Husayn.[89] His promotion of Muharram occurred in competition with the city's Hindu *kavadī* processions, which he was concerned that the city's Muslims were joining.[90] As with the *'urs*, Ghulām Muhammad was thus able to draw on the new urban needs for distraction and entertainment with the aim of channelling boredom into binding discipleship. The style of Muharram procession that Ghulām Muhammad promoted closely reflected those of Bombay, with the glittering symbolic coffin carried for hours until its final deposition in the Umgeni River. With their African drummers and sword-swallowing *faqīrs*, the processions were an echo of the customary processions of the Afro-Indian *nawwābs* of Janjira to the *'urs* of Makhdūm 'Alī in Bombay, where the *nawwāb* and his African-descended retainers marched behind bands

FIGURE 18. Advertisement for Durban ʿurs festival in Urdu and Gujarati (1912)

of tumblers, drummers and chest-slashers.[91] For all the lessons Ghulām Muhammad had learned from his master Habīb 'Alī about the importance of proper decorum (*adab*) on such occasions, in a district of Durban that was still heavily populated by Indian agricultural workers the processions frequently ended in raucous shambles. But where the shaykh's control failed, the state waded in, and the Durban constabulary served to bolster his moral orchestrations. The pattern was again reflected in Bombay, and in 1913 Bombay's Muharram processions were effectively prohibited by the Police Commissioner S. M. Edwardes, a regulation enforced by armed soldiers, who finished up shooting illegal celebrants.[92]

AN AFTERLIFE IN PRINT

When Ghulām Muhammad died, his family in Durban sponsored the printing in Bombay of his hagiography, *Riyāz-e sūfi*, a production of the Bombay marketplace that would consolidate his family firm's stake in the smaller and connected religious economy of Natal. Building on the enchanted print industry seen in Chapter 3, here was a transoceanic hagiography produced for an overseas market. Printed in Bombay in 1913, for all its enchanted characteristics, *Riyāz-e sūfi* was still a product of a competitive religious economy. Amid the printing of many such hagiographical chap-books, the tales of Ghulām Muhammad were but one voice in a clamour of tales carried into the port of Bombay by the hustle-bustle of travellers. In this market of stories, *Riyāz-e sūfi* would need more than the flourishes of miraculous convention to promote Ghulām Muhammad's fame. So the character of the stories in the text was adapted in response to these competitive demands, spicing older Indian narratives with the newer flavours of Africa to appeal to the new Indian consumers of Durban. While continuing to rely on the familiar appeal of certain customary tropes, its account of Ghulām Muhammad's arrival in Africa echoed the more plural religious economy that had spread through the Indian Ocean during his lifetime.

After the model of the Christian missionaries and their Reformist Muslim acolytes, in *Riyāz-e sūfi* Ghulām Muhammad's purpose in coming to South Africa was explicitly presented as 'establishing the light of Islam and stamping out disbelief (*kufr*)'. Magnifying his role in the moral no less than the miraculous economy, before Ghulām Muhammad arrived, the text claimed, Natal's Muslims were effectively 'unacquainted' (*nā-āshnā*) with the basic rules of Islam.[93] If the resemblance to the rhetoric of European missions to Africa is striking, given the competitive marketplace that Ghulām Muhammad entered in Natal this is not surprising. However, the most effective way in which *Riyāz-e sūfī* competed in this market was through the section it devoted to the miracles Ghulām Muhammad performed in Natal. While the text boldly claimed that he performed literally thousands of miracles, the author demurred that there was only space to recount a few of the most special ones. The first of these reflected the maritime miracles seen in Chapter 3 being reinvigorated in this period of increasing ocean travel through the printing in Bombay of miraculous chap-books. According to *Riyāz-e sūfī*, a few days out of port from Bombay to Durban, cholera (*hayza*) broke out on board ship. Terrified at what at the height of the global cholera epidemic of the 1890s was a dreaded prospect, the passengers turned to Ghulām Muhammad for 'refuge' (*iltijā*). Resorting to a technique that was central to the service repertoire of custom, Ghulām Muhammad asked to be brought some water and, reciting from the Quran, blew on it before then passing the 'breathed water' around the passengers to drink. Consequently, each of them remained immune to the disease for the duration of the journey.[94] Here was not only a customary miracle on the decks of the steamship, but an effective printed endorsement of the kinds of miraculous services still available at the holy man's shrine in Durban. While miracles of this kind were familiar enough in a period of expanding Indian migration to Natal, the locus of the tale in a book that was itself shipped there from Bombay was fitting, for this was a journey that was approached with much apprehension. Echoing the anxieties of train travel among the stories printed about Habīb 'Alī in Bombay, among the text's readers in Natal the story would have stirred vivid memories of their own sea crossing. Similar miracles were associated with Habīb 'Alī himself. In one of these tales, Habīb 'Alī is said to have issued a warning to a merchant not to set sail, but the advice was ignored, and when, as Habīb 'Alī had foreseen, the ship sank, the saint was forced to supernaturally rescue him from the waves. Back on dry land, at the moment of rescue Habīb 'Alī's sleeve was seen dripping with seawater.[95] As a book printed for an overseas market, *Riyāz-e sūfī* represented the reproduction and export of such stories from the religious market of Bombay to its smaller sibling in Durban.

Another miracle recorded in *Riyāz-e sūfī* more vividly relocated the Indian imagery of religious competition to its new overseas setting. The story recounted how when Ghulām Muhammad arrived in Natal, he chose to settle in a neighbourhood near to the harbour (a strategy that reflected that of Habīb 'Alī locating himself in the Mazagaon dockyards).[96] However, a Hindu temple had already been built there

by earlier settlers, and opposite the temple was a rock beneath which
lived a fearful *izhdihā*. Since in Urdu the term *izhdihā* can refer to both
a python and a dragon, it is unclear which meaning was intended, and it
seems a certain ambiguity was deliberate in order to summon the dangerous exoticism of the new African environment.[97] A decade earlier, the
Urdu travelogue *Safarnāma-ye Ūgandā wa Mumbāsā* had already ended
its account of East Africa with a detailed and exoticizing description
of such strange creatures as the giraffe (*jirāf*), zebra (*zībrā*), rhinoceros
(*gīndā* or *gorg-shīr*, literally 'wolf-lion') and ostrich (*shutar-murgh*, literally 'camel-bird').[98] As to the *izhdihā* itself, an illustration printed around
this time in the Bombay Urdu lithographic edition of the travels and
adventures of Hātim Tā'ī gives a visual sense of the appearance of such
a creature in the popular imagination. Whatever the precise zootomy of
the beast that Ghulām Muhammad confronted, by the time he arrived
in Durban the Hindu worshippers in the temple were so petrified that
they were unable to leave for their homes. Seeing him arrive, the Hindus'
priest ran up to him and with clasped hands described the *izhdihā* and
the worshippers' predicament, begging the Muslim holy man for help.
Feeling pity, Ghulām Muhammad walked over to the *izhdihā*'s cave and
shouted: '*Bhā'ī*, brother, you will have to leave here now, because the
bearer of Gharīb Nawāz's flag has come!' On hearing this invocation of
the great Muslim saint of Ajmer in India, the creature quit its lair, headed
straight to the sea, and disappeared in the waves. Naturally, everyone was
amazed and, having witnessed what was clearly a great miracle (*i'jāz*),
the priest made all of the property and buildings of the temple over to
Ghulām Muhammad and left. The story ended by explaining that it was
on this land that Ghulām Muhammad founded his first mosque, and
nearby the *madrasa* and shrine in which he was later buried. Written in
Bombay at a time when the Āryā Samāj was expanding from Bombay
into Natal to win the support of 'lapsed' Hindus and Muslims, *Riyāz-e
sūfī* presented as a supernatural envisioning of the communal market
rivalries seen in the miraculous role of Pēdrō Shāh in the collapse of the
Hindu-owned bar in the Sita Ram Building in Chapter 2. Amid the rising
price of property, the competition for community space and the entrepreneurial requirement to set up shop in these twin cities on either side of the
ocean, the forces of the competitive economy found expression in tales of
miraculous land-grabbing, expulsion and defeat. Natal's Indians would
no longer go to the temple firm whose gods had failed to save them from
the monster, but turn as they had in the story to the superior services of
Ghulām Muhammad, who had in any case acquired the very property of

نگلنا اژدها کا حاتم کو

FIGURE 19. Enter the dragon: Bombay-printed lithographic drawing of an *izhdiha* (1908)

their temple.[99] In its reproduction of older tropes, the story exported the old stories of Muslim saints conquering idolatrous and demonic spaces that we earlier saw imported to the Bombay marketplace from older shrine towns of the hinterland. Just as Hājjī Malang conquered the monstrous glowing-headed goddess from the property that would become his own shrine in Ghulām Muhammad's home town of Kalyan, so in Durban did Ghulām Muhammad expel the dragon from the place where he would be buried in turn. Not only the saintly architecture of Bombay, but also its narrative and imaginative trappings were being reproduced by Bombay's religious firms for export to South Africa.

Conclusions

Writing in Bombay around 1890, the colonial administrator James Douglas recounted tales of former times, when, far from hearth and home, spirits of the Anglo-Saxon dead warned friends and family of impending danger or rescue in supernatural ways that were strongly reminiscent of Muslim seaborne miracle stories heard in previous chapters.[1] All such stories, and the anxieties that fed them, were products of circumstances that fed religious demand. But near the century's end Douglas was convinced that Bombay could no longer harbour such fantasies:

> The utility of these ghostly exhibitions has been altogether superseded by the introduction of the electric telegraph. Fed and nourished by the nervous excitement about friends in far-off countries, from whom they were separated by stormy oceans and arid deserts, the devotees of this religion – for it was a religion – gave up their belief as soon as it was found possible to communicate with individuals instantaneously on the other side of the world. The truth is, the electric telegraph has flashed this class of spirits out of existence.[2]

Like other Victorian champions of scientific progress and the rational utility of technology, Douglas saw in the industrializing city around him an arena of disenchantment, an urban workshop for the dismembering of old religions and customs. Such attitudes have weathered surprisingly well: Thompsonian Methodism and the occasional study of plebeian Liverpudlian séances aside, the nineteenth-century city continues to be policed by the historiographical heirs of Bentham and Weber. But far from flushing out the old ways into the tide of history, the previous chapters have shown how with its printers, factories and steamships the industrial age instead placed more religious 'consumers' into situations on the high seas or in the threatening metropolis which fuelled demand for the old saints and miracles no less than its technologies supplied entrepreneurs with new means to reproduce and distribute these enchanted products and services. For many of its Muslims, especially among the labouring classes, Bombay's industrialization was inseparable from the enchantment of its mills, stations and dockyards by the providers of religious services that ranged from supernatural medicines to social support networks and licit entertainments. If *Bombay Islam* is a Muslim story, it is part of a larger one of an industrialization that in its many locations fuelled new forms of religious productivity. By the side of James Douglas we might sit his American contemporary Mark Twain, who in two essays from 1878 and 1895 likewise recounted incidents of supernatural communications between family and friends and the possibility of cultivating such communications through a 'phrenophone'.[3] But for Twain, these supernatural incidents were neither subjugated to nor separate from the times in which he lived; they were, in his fitting phrase, acts of 'mental telegraphy'.[4] There is ultimately no better example of the ways in which Victorian technologies were generative of new forms of enchantment than in the development of the very word 'telepathy', first attested in 1882, as the religious and semantic by-product of 'telegraphy'.

Through the successful adaption of new technologies (social, mechanical or commercial) Bombay's religious entrepreneurs were thus able to respond to the demands of a large and diverse urban populace through the distribution mechanisms of missionary organization, steam power and print capitalism. Through such a 'domestication' of what were initially colonial or Christian technologies, even the ideological impact of empire was diluted to leave its technologies at the service of more indigenous cultural productions, a process symbolized in the printed stories of Muslim saints lifting steamships on their shoulders.[5] In showing that, even when confronting one another in the same market, Customary Islamic firms were more successful than either their colonial or Reformist rivals, *Bombay Islam* presents a picture of Muslim 'conservatism' that is at odds with more familiar images of an age of modernizing reform. The conservative market appeal of custom did not mean that Islam stood still. As the previous chapters have shown, the re-producers of custom were canny entrepreneurs operating in the new religious economy created by industrial urban life. The ongoing economy of this adaptive conservatism helps explain why even today tens of millions of Muslims in India, Pakistan and elsewhere retain their allegiance to the 'tested products' of a Customary

Islam of holy men, miracles and shrines. This suggests in turn that, outside the bureaucratic and comprador classes most exposed to European ideas in the long nineteenth century, the colonial impact on Muslim religious forms was considerably less than has often been imagined. If the old economy of feudal land grants and peasant clienteles that supported the religious economy of pre-colonial Islam in India was gone, the industrial cities provided opportunities for customary firms operating in a newly industrialized economy of religious production and consumption.

By closing its survey in 1915, *Bombay Islam* deliberately stops at the moment at which proponents of Muslim nationalism or Pan-Islamism did become significant players among Bombay's Muslim market through such organizations as the Muslim League and the Khilāfat movement. But despite their projections backwards in time, such homogenizing trends were more products of the twentieth than the nineteenth century.[6] By closing off a distinct time period between around 1840 and 1915 it has been possible to see the religious productions of the period in their own terms, and not those of later globalizing or nationalizing moments. The city described here was one with a pluralistic and competitive religious economy, which reared Reformist firms promoting Quranic scripture and English education no less than family firms of charismatic itinerant holy men and nocturnal possession services in dockyard mausoleums. Not only a city of the 'progress' (*taraqqī*) of the Muslim Modernists, Bombay was also a space of the enchantment (*hayrat*) generated as the religious response to industrial and commercial growth as social processes. In the industrial cosmopolis of the west Indian Ocean, Bombay's different Muslims did not collapse themselves into a coherent or unified community based on either nation or religion. Instead, they participated in a pluralizing religious economy which drove the increasing production of a variety of Islams by a spectrum of new migrant entrepreneurs and relocated firms that ranged from modernist associations to the brotherhoods of custom. Seen against this background, the appeal after 1915 of discourses of unified communities of religion and/or nation appears not as an innately 'modern' trajectory towards homogeneity, but as a *reaction* to a prior process of pluralizing religious productivity shaped by the specific historical condition of the industrializing and globalizing nineteenth century.[7]

In order to explain the modern persistence of enchantment, the previous chapters have made a case for seeing Bombay as both a crucial factory and market for an Islam that while neither disenchanted nor otherwise 'Protestant' was no less a product of the nineteenth and early twentieth centuries than its better-known Reformist and Modernist competitors.

While no claim is made here of providing a complete picture, the previous chapters have sought to uncover a different urban history from the familiar tropes of factory conditions, trade unionism and amelioration societies that have long dominated the historiography. In view of the problems that have long vexed Indian labour history, whether in Bombay or Durban, the stake of the Indian workers in an economy of religious enchantment helps explain the continuity of the 'traditional' hierarchical social relations that the rise of industrial labour was once seen as challenging.[8] As a production of hierarchical social and workplace environments, Customary Islam offered no democracy of souls such as that promised by the middle-class Reformists. By showing how a hierarchical conscience of patrons and intercessors was perpetuated by the metaphysical visions of workplace preachers and the miraculous interventions of popular printing, *Bombay Islam* explains the absence of an egalitarian ethic among Indian workers that once so perplexed the heirs of E. P. Thompson. Placing the religious consumption patterns of Muslim labourers into the context of a larger religious economy on both sides of the Indian Ocean shows how workers' lives were shaped by the reproductions of religious customs and services that ultimately drew demand from the conditions of workers' lives.

Through the cosmopolitan port of Bombay, India not only continued to operate in older transnational networks such as those connecting it with Iran, but also established new networks connecting it with such unfamiliar regions as South Africa, routes for both the import and export of concrete religion by way of 'firms' promoting charismatic persons, books or practices.[9] Although enabled by what were originally by-products of colonial communication requirements by way of steamship routes, ultimately these Muslim firms expanded according to the demands of a Muslim passenger traffic that moved beyond the territories of empire into Iran and the Hijaz. Whether in terms of relocated population markets or industrialized communication networks, the transformative effects of empire – and Bombay as their urban embodiment – provided resources which various kinds of religious entrepreneur were quick to make use of. It is striking here that the most successful Muslim entrepreneurs examined in the previous chapters migrated to Bombay from beyond the formal geography of British rule, whether from overseas in Iran or from inland in Hyderabad. Here on the ocean's edge was a distinct trajectory of religious development from that which emerged in the better-documented townscapes of northern India, and one whose diversity – indeed, its increasing diversification – was a reflection of the range of religious producers and consumers from within and without the oceanic boundaries of India. In the period of Bombay's greatest influence, this 'oceanic' as much as 'imperial' India played an increasingly important role in a maritime marketplace that, as older pre-colonial culture routes were serviced by the steamship, was expanded rather than diminished by the opportunities of empire.

The development of Bombay's religious economy enables us to place India into the development of a larger oceanic economy of Muslim religious exchange whose growth in the nineteenth century led to an increase of religious production and consumption between East Africa, Arabia and South-East Asia no less than between India, Iran and South Africa.[10] While these oceanic patterns of religious exchange were by no means invented in this period, they were radically transformed by the development of new industrial sites of the production of religion (whether the missionary firm or the printing-press) and the consumption of religion (whether by industrial labourers or exiled indenture markets). These transformations in the overall economy of religious transactions placed Bombay at the centre of the newly industrialized oceanic marketplace, whereas it had scarcely even featured in the pre-industrialized religious economy of the period before the mid-nineteenth century. On a larger global and comparative scale, these developments reflect the production and dissemination of new Christianities in the Atlantic marketplace, not least through the parallel nexus of labour migration, printing, 'providential' supernaturalism and empire that witnessed the oceanic expansion of Methodism, Mormonism and Spiritualism in the same period.[11] Like the steamship travels of New York's Spiritualist missionaries to England's industrial north or the trans-oceanic printing operations of expansive American Mormons in Liverpool, the rise of Bombay as a centre of Muslim religious production was part of a larger global moment in which industrialization shifted the configurations of older economies of religious supply and demand. This enabled former sites of religious consumption (of Islam in India or Christianity in America) to become centres of production and export to their former overseas suppliers, whether in England or Iran, while at the same time finding new and unexpected markets (Mormonism in Denmark or Customary Islam in South Africa) on the crest of the new waves of steam communications, printing and labour migration.

In the economy of Muslim religious exchanges with which this book is concerned, this traffic of holy men and books, of doctrines and ritual services, saw Bombay emerge in its own right as a site for the production and reproduction of a dizzying 'product range' of Islams, each forced to distinguish itself from its competitors by alternative strategies of representing newness or custom, reason or charisma. The success and scale of Bombay's religious economy were enhanced by its location as the nodal point of 'pre-colonial' and 'colonial' networks. From this position as commercial and technological centre of the west Indian Ocean, Bombay did not simply import religious products, firms and entrepreneurs from its continental and maritime hinterlands, but re-produced and re-exported them with the distinct stamp of its own marketplace. The manner in which Bombay was able to reproduce custom in response to the demands of new urban consumers (particularly merchant and labour groups) and the opportunities of new production and distribution mechanisms helps explain why, despite the transformations of modernity, the Customary Islam of saints, miracles and shrines continues to flourish throughout South Asia and the Indian Ocean to this day, even if the place of Bombay within it has long diminished. Even in the nineteenth century oceanic epicentre of industrial modernity, Customary Islam did more than simply stand still and survive. Through the technological adoptions of its purveyors and their successful outreach to both the displaced communities of the metropolis and the less developed religious economies of such places as South Africa and Iran, the consolations of custom were reproduced in ways that responded to the new experiences and anxieties of the age.[12] From a Neo-Ismāʻīlism based on regular communications with a living imam to the towerblock-shattering miracles of the moral protector of Muslim shopkeepers, the varied religious products and services that this book has collected in a metaphorical aisle marked Customary Islam were each the result of successful firms' opportunistic adaptations to a new religious economy born from the transformations of empire, industry and capital.

This brings us to the model of the religious economy that has been used to frame the interaction of these different 'producers' and 'consumers' of the variable productions of Islam. The previous chapters have argued that Bombay's economic, demographic and more broadly industrial expansion after 1840 enabled the creation of a new kind of religious economy that was more pluralistic, competitive and productive than its pre-industrial predecessors. What was new about this marketplace was, first, the number and diversity of participants interacting on both the supply and demand sides as a result of the new merchant and labour communities attracted to Bombay by the cosmopolitan pull of capital. Second, fed by acts of comparison no less than consumption of religious products and services, increasing religious productivity was accompanied by an intensified degree of competition for a stake in an increasingly polemical market in which not only Muslims but Hindus, Christians, Jews and Parsis also inspected, compared and critiqued the religious productions of others. The introduction to this book argued that the development of this 'liberal' economy of religious exchange had several enabling factors. The first of these was the official agenda and mentality of colonial governance, for just as a laissez-faire ideology afforded the emergence of powerful Gujarati industrialists and Iranian merchants, so did a parallel policy of official non-interference in religious affairs enable local entrepreneurs to create a competitive religious economy in which, despite certain advantages, colonial Christian players were ultimately less successful than religious firms with a better sense of local demand.

However, the pluralizing forces of the religious economy should not be framed in the familiar dichotomy of the colonial and indigenous, for the usefulness of the market model is the way it highlights the perpetual transactions of the borrowing and adaptation of technologies and techniques between all players in the market, as well as the places it provided to new firms (such as Reformist *anjumans*) and old firms (such as Sufi brotherhoods) or to local entrepreneurs and more distant migrants from the oceanic hinterlands of the main Bombay marketplace. In the background lay the arrival from around 1820 of the Christian missionary firms which, though winning few converts, were highly influential catalysts of the new market through introducing a new social apparatus of 'the mission' which in practical no less than conceptual terms enabled new patterns of the production and distribution no less than the 'exchangeability' of religion. The fierce new polemics that missionary firms introduced to the economy through their investment in vernacular printing and the organizational innovations that ranged from subscriber revenues to proletarian outreach were all quickly (and more successfully) adopted by the other firms that entered the city over the following decades. Rather than seeing these multidirectional polemics through a dichotomous model of 'dialogue', *Bombay Islam* has attempted to show that the model of religious economy provides a clearer conceptual framework for dealing with the multiplicity of religious competitors that emerged in the nineteenth century and the webs of interaction that linked them. The logic and thereby the usefulness of the marketplace model is precisely the sense of complexity and contingency of interactions that it proposes: neither dichotomized nor dialogical, the marketplace is typified by the cacophony of multiple players. To adopt this model does not involve the reduction of religion to materialistic forms of exchange. Many of the 'products' and 'services' on offer in Bombay and its hinterlands had no clear financial value (though many clearly did). The usefulness of the economistic model is rather the way in which it allows us to track the social life of Islam as a set of exchanges and interactions between specific parties – between notional 'suppliers' and 'consumers' – whose cultural tastes and social relationships shape the characteristics and fortunes of any religious production under scrutiny. In turn, the language of production gives life to the category of Islam as a ritual and discursive mine of deployable resources used for specific individual or collective purposes rather than as a set of static 'traditions' that once founded are passively handed down until they become 'reformed' in a decisive 'modern' epoch.

Conceiving Bombay as the market for a range of Muslim productions shaped in response to demand driven by the social conditions of specific consumer groups enables us to move beyond Weberian analyses seeking axiomatically 'modern' or 'Protestant' forms of Islam. We can thereby make sense of the survival – and even expansion – of the enchanted religious productions that this book has grouped together as Customary Islam. In place of the singular trajectory of Weberian sociology,[13] the market model shows how the many different Muslims of Bombay's Indian Ocean demanded a corresponding range of different religious products and services and, though 'individualist', 'Protestant' or 'disenchanted' forms appealed to a certain stratum of society, even in the oceanic engine room of industrial and capitalistic change, the greater proportion of market demand was for firms promoting intercessionary holy men and their miraculous services. This demand in turn laid the basis of an economy of enchantment which, through travelling holy men, entrepreneurial shrine founders and printed books, was distributed to the far corners of an oceanic marketplace in which Bombay became the largest urban player. The market conceived here was not limited to Bombay itself, but was oceanic in scope, its traffic and exchanges in different degrees affecting many regions of the west Indian Ocean and ultimately involving new forms of Hindu, Zoroastrian, Jewish and Christian religious productivity no less than Muslim. By way of example, earlier chapters looked at South Africa and Iran, where the second half of the nineteenth century witnessed an unprecedented availability of new religious products and the social ramifications incumbent on such pluralism. However, the analysis might alternatively have traced the foundations of the first Hindu temples in Zanzibar by Bombay Presidency traders or the role of Bombay in the creation of a satellite religious marketplace in Aden. The point has not been to claim all of these developments as being 'made in

Bombay', and the development of a more plural religious economy in each of these other sites was influenced by local as much as oceanic factors. Instead, what the previous chapters have argued is that between around 1840 and 1915 Bombay emerged as the most competitive and productive single urban marketplace in a larger oceanic economy of religious transactions, and that such was its centrality to its oceanic and continental markets that its opportunities of demand and supply inevitably had an impact on the smaller and less developed religious marketplaces in such places as South Africa and Iran.

Ultimately, this holistic model of a religious economy based on countless interactions helps explain why certain forms of what has usually been termed 'traditional', 'popular' or 'mystical' Islam avoided the disenchantment of a Weberian modernity to not only survive but expand in the modern era.[14] It also helps redress the misinterpreted trajectory of Islam in the modern world that has posited a diminishing of diverse 'local' Islams under the hegemony of the 'Protestant', 'disenchanted', 'uniform' or 'globalized' forms of an apparently standardized Islam.[15] What is suggested by the experience of Bombay's oceanic marketplace is that in creating a liberally competitive and efficiently productive economy of religious exchange, in the absence of state religious monopolies, modernization enables the ritual, organizational, material and ideological productions of a dizzying range of Muslim religious firms whose visions, whether rationalizing or enchanting, answer to the needs of the heterogeneous Muslims of an uneven world. The bewildering array of Islams ready for inspection and comparison in the global market of the twenty-first century represents the expansion of the same forces that gave shape to Bombay Islam.

Notes

Introduction

1. 'Fatal Collapse of a Building', *Bombay Gazette* newspaper, Monday 1 June 1903.

2. L. Barrow, *Independent Spirits: Spiritualism and English Plebeians, 1850–1910* (London: Routledge & Kegan Paul, 1986); N. S. Green, 'Breathing in India, c. 1890', *Modern Asian Studies* 42, 2–3 (2008); P. van der Veer, *Imperial Encounters: Religion and Modernity in India and Britain* (Princeton: Princeton University Press, 2001); and L. White, *Speaking with Vampires: Rumor and History in Colonial Africa* (Berkeley: University of California Press, 2000).

3. D. Hempton, *Methodism: Empire of the Spirit* (New Haven: Yale University Press, 2005); S. J. Stein, *Communities of Dissent: A History of Alternative Religions in America* (Oxford: Oxford University Press, 2003); and M. Tromp, *Altered States: Sex, Nation, Drugs, and Self-Transformation in Victorian Spiritualism* (Albany: State University of New York Press, 2006).

4. M. Dossal, *Imperial Designs and Indian Realities: The Planning of Bombay City, 1845–1875* (Delhi: Oxford University Press, 1991); S. Patel and A. Thorner (eds.), *Bombay: Mosaic of Modern Culture* (Delhi: Oxford University Press, 1995). For the only notable monographic studies of Bombay's Muslims see sections of C. Dobbin, *Urban Leadership in Western India: Politics and Communities in Bombay City, 1840–1885* (Oxford: Oxford University Press, 1972); and J. Masselos, *The City in Action: Bombay Struggles for Power* (Delhi: Oxford University Press, 2007).

5. On the industrialization of travel see S. Searight, *Steaming East: The Forging of Steamship and Rail Links between Europe and Asia* (London: The Bodley Head, 1991); and D. Thorner, *Investment in Empire: British Railway and Steam Shipping Enterprise in India 1825–1849* (Philadelphia: University of Pennsylvania Press, 1950).

6. F. Cooper, *On the African Waterfront: Urban Disorder and the Transformation of Work in Colonial Mombasa* (New Haven: Yale University Press, 1987); A. Larguèche, 'The City and the Sea: Evolving Forms of Mediterranean

Cosmopolitanism in Tunis, 1700–1881', in J. Clancy-Smith (ed.), *North Africa, Islam, and the Mediterranean World: From the Almoravids to the Algerian War* (London: Frank Cass, 2001); T. Mitchell, *Colonising Egypt* (Cambridge: Cambridge University Press, 1988); L. Tarazi Fawaz, *Merchants and Migrants in Nineteenth-Century Beirut* (Cambridge, MA: Harvard University Press, 1983); and L. Tarazi Fawaz and C. A. Bayly (eds.), *Modernity and Culture: From the Mediterranean to the Indian Ocean* (New York: Columbia University Press, 2002). For one recent exception see S. Bose, *A Hundred Horizons: The Indian Ocean in the Age of Global Empire* (Cambridge, MA: Harvard University Press, 2006).

7. M. C. Low, 'Empire and the Hajj: Pilgrims, Plagues, and Pan-Islam under British Surveillance, 1865–1908', *International Journal of Middle East Studies* 40, 2 (2008); F. E. Peters, *The Hajj: The Muslim Pilgrimage to Mecca and the Holy Places* (Princeton: Princeton University Press, 1994), chapter 6.

8. On Muslim maritime cosmopolitanism elsewhere in this period see E. A. Alpers, 'Muqdisho in the Nineteenth Century: A Regional Perspective', *Journal of African History* 24, 4 (1983); M. Bazin (ed.), *Métropoles et Métropolisation*, special edition of *Cahiers d'études sur la Méditerranée orientale et le monde turco-iranien* 24 (1997); Larguèche, 'The City and the Sea'; and R. Ostle, 'Alexandria: A Mediterranean Cosmopolitan Center of Cultural Production', in Tarazi Fawaz and Bayly (eds.,), *Modernity and Culture.*

9. T. Albuquerque, *Urbs Prima in Indis: An Epoch in the History of Bombay, 1840–1865* (Delhi: Promilla, 1985).

10. Anonymous, *Jān-e Bombā'ī* (Calcutta: n.p., *c.* 1820), pp. 11–12.

11. Ibid., p. 37.

12. S. M. Edwardes, *By-Ways of Bombay* (Bombay: D. B. Taraporevala Sons & Co., 1912), pp. 7–10. For a similarly pluralistic description see Sir D. E. Wacha, *Shells from the Sands of Bombay, Being my Recollections and Reminiscences, 1860–1875* (Bombay: Indian Newspaper Co., 1920), p. 411, repr. from the *Bombay Chronicle* (1914).

13. N. Brenner and R. Keil (eds.), *The Global Cities Reader* (London: Routledge, 2005), p. 200. On the importance of colonial port cities, and of Bombay as an example, see A. D. King, 'Colonial Cities: Global Pivots of Change' and D. Kooiman, 'Bombay: From Fishing Village to Colonial Port City (1662–1947)', both in R. Ross and G. J. Telkamp (eds.), *Colonial Cities: Essays on Urbanism in a Colonial Context* (Leiden: Martinus Nijhoff, 1985).

14. Committee of the District Benevolent Society, 'The Native Poor of Bombay: Reports of the Committee of the District Benevolent Society, for the years 1854 and 1855; Bombay 1855 and 1856', *Bombay Quarterly Review* 4, 8 (1856), p. 263.

15. Anonymous [S. M. Edwardes], *Gazetteer of Bombay City and Island*, 3 vols. Bombay: Times Press, 1909, vol. I, pp. 164–6.

16. On the latter see M. Mohiuddin, *Muslim Communities in Medieval Konkan: 610–1900 AD* (Delhi: Sundeep Prakashan, 2002), p. 83.

17. On al-Afghani in Bombay see A. Ahmad, 'Afghānī's Indian Contacts', *Journal of the American Oriental Society* 89, 3 (1969); and N. R. Keddie, *Sayyid*

Jamāl ad-Dīn 'al-Afghānī': A Political Biography. (Berkeley: University of California Press, 1972), pp. 22–32.

18. My usage here draws on T. Asad, *Genealogies of Religion: Discipline and Reasons of Power in Christianity and Islam* (Baltimore: Johns Hopkins University Press, 1993).

19. N. Dirks, 'Annals of the Archive: Ethnographic Notes on the Sources of History', in B. Axel (ed.), *From the Margins: Historical Anthropology and its Futures* (Durham, NC: Duke University Press, 2002); S. Feierman, 'Colonizers, Scholars, and the Creation of Invisible Histories', in V. E. Bonnell and L. Hunt (eds.), *Beyond the Cultural Turn: New Directions in the Study of Society and Culture* (Berkeley: University of California Press, 1999).

20. On which see, *inter alia*, Sir Arthur Conan Doyle, *The History of Spiritualism*, 2 vols. (London: Cassel, 1926).

21. This is true of a full range of studies, from A. H. Hourani, *Arabic Thought in the Liberal Age, 1798–1939* (London: Oxford University Press, 1962); M. A. Karandikar, *Islam in India's Transition to Modernity* (Westport: Greenwood, 1969); and F. Rahman, *Islam and Modernity: Transformation of an Intellectual Tradition* (Chicago: University of Chicago Press, 1982) to more recent monographs and collections such as J. Meuleman (ed.), *Islam in the Era of Globalization: Muslim Attitudes towards Modernity and Identity* (London: RoutledgeCurzon, 2002); and B. Schaebler and L. Stenberg (eds.), *Globalization and the Muslim World: Culture, Religion, and Modernity* (Syracuse: Syracuse University Press, 2004). For a critique and exposition of the case for 'Protestant Islam' see R. Loimeier, 'Is There Something like "Protestant" Islam?', *Die Welt des Islams*, 45, 2 (2005); and F. Robinson, 'Islamic Reform and Modernities in South Asia', *Modern Asian Studies* 41, 5 (2007).

22. Cf. M. Moaddel, 'Conditions for Ideological Production: The Origins of Islamic Modernism in India, Egypt, and Iran', *Theory and Society* 30, 5 (2001) and works listed in note 19.

23. On Khilāfat activity in Bombay see G. Minault, *The Khilafat Movement: Religious Symbolism and Political Mobilization in India* (New York: Columbia University Press, 1982), pp. 34–7, 71–87, 96–105; and A. Özcan, *Pan-Islamism: Indian Muslims, the Ottomans and Britain, 1877–1924* (Leiden: Brill, 1997), chaps. 2 and 3.

24. Cf. M. Van Bruinessen and J. D. Howell (eds.), *Sufism and the Modern in Islam* (London: I. B. Tauris, 2007); and P. Werbner and H. Basu (eds.), *Embodying Charisma: Modernity, Locality, and Performance of Emotion in Sufi Cults* (London: Routledge, 1998).

25. P. J. E. Damishky, 'The Moslem Population of Bombay', *The Moslem World* 1, 2 (1911), p. 125.

26. For the clearest outlines of the theory of religious economy see R. Stark, 'From Church-Sect to Religious Economies', in P. E. Hammond (ed.), *The Sacred in a Post-Secular Age* (Berkeley: University of California Press, 1985); and the essays in L. A. Young (ed.), *Rational Choice Theory and Religion: Summary and Assessment* (New York: Routledge, 1997). For the most useful case studies see R. A. Chesnut, *Competitive Spirits: Latin America's New*

Religious Economy (Oxford: Oxford University Press, 2003); T. C. Kiong, *Rationalizing Religion: Religious Conversion, Revivalism and Competition in Singapore Society* (Leiden: Brill, 2007); H. Urban, *The Economics of Ecstasy: Tantra, Secrecy and Power in Colonial Bengal* (New York: Oxford University Press, 2001); and P. van der Veer, *Gods on Earth: The Management of Religious Experience and Identity in a North Indian Pilgrimage Centre* (London: Athlone Press, 1988).

27. R. Stark, 'Bringing Theory Back In', in Young (ed.), *Rational Choice Theory*, p. 17.

28. See e.g. M. Gaborieau, 'Criticizing the Sufis: The Debate in Early Nineteenth Century India', in F. de Jong and B. Radtke (eds.), *Islamic Mysticism Contested: 13 Centuries of Controversies and Polemics* (Leiden: E. J. Brill, 1999); B. D. Metcalf, *Islamic Revival in British India: Deoband, 1860–1900* (Princeton: Princeton University Press, 1982); H. O. Pearson, *Islamic Reform and Revival in Nineteenth Century India: The Tarīqah-i Muhammadīyah* (Delhi: Yoda Press, 2008); and U. Sanyal, *Devotional Islam and Politics in British India: Ahmad Riza Khan Barelwi and his Movement, 1870–1920* (Delhi: Oxford University Press, 1996).

29. Cf. de Jong and Radtke (eds.), Islamic Mysticism Contested; and E. Sirriyeh, *Sufis and Anti-Sufis: The Defence, Rethinking and Rejection of Sufism in the Modern World* (London: Curzon, 1999).

30. Cf. C. A. Bayly, *The Birth of the Modern World, 1780–1914: Global Connections and Comparisons* (Oxford: Blackwell, 2004), chap. 9; and O. Roy, *Globalized Islam: The Search for a New Ummah* (London: Hurst, 2004).

31. Stark, 'Bringing Theory Back In', p. 17.

32. T. R. Metcalf, *Imperial Connections: India in the Indian Ocean Arena, 1860–1920* (Berkeley: University of California Press, 2007).

33. Cf. Kiong, *Rationalizing Religion* on the religious economy of the port city of Singapore.

34. Rafiuddin Ahmed, *Times of India*, 18 February 1908, cited in J. Masselos, 'Power in the Bombay "Mohalla", 1904–15: An Initial Exploration into the World of the Indian Urban Muslim', in Masselos, *The City in Action*, p. 41. Cf. A. Jalal, 'Negotiating Colonial Modernity and Cultural Difference: Indian Muslim Conceptions of Community and Nation, *c.* 1870–1914', in Tarazi Fawaz and Bayly (eds.), *Modernity and Culture*.

35. Anonymous, *Jān-e Bombā'ī*, esp. pp. 19–42.

36. For an alternative interpretation of the results of the new Muslim individualism see F. Robinson, 'Religious Change and the Self in Muslim South Asia since 1800', *South Asia* 20, 1 (1997).

37. On the latter, see in particular Urban, *The Economics of Ecstasy*.

38. On interaction between individual and community patterns of religious consumption see C. L. Bankston, 'Rationality, Choice, and the Religious Economy: Individual and Collective Rationality in Supply and Demand', *Review of Religious Research* 45, 2 (2003).

39. Sayyid Ahmad Khan, *Selected Essays by Sir Sayyid Ahmad Khan*, trans. J. W. Wilder (Lahore: Sang-e Meel Publications, 2006), p. 43.

40. R. L. Raval, *Socio-Religious Reform Movements in Gujarat during the Nineteenth Century* (Delhi: Ess Ess Publications, 1987), chap. 3.

41. W. J. Fischel, 'Bombay in Jewish History in the Light of New Documents from the Indian Archives', *Proceedings of the American Academy for Jewish Research* 38 (1970–1); S. Manasseh, 'Religious Music Traditions of the Jewish-Babylonian Diaspora in Bombay', *Ethnomusicology Forum* 13, 1 (2004); and M. W. Numark, 'Translating Religion: British Missionaries and the Politics of Religious Knowledge in Colonial India and Bombay' (Ph.D. thesis, UCLA, 2006).

42. M. Ringer, 'Reform Transplanted: Parsi Agents of Change amongst Zoroastrians in Nineteenth-Century Iran', *Iranian Studies* 42, 4 (2009).

43. E. P. Thompson, *Customs in Common: Studies in Traditional Popular Culture* (London: Merlin Press, 1991).

44. B. D. Metcalf, 'Islam and Custom in Nineteenth-Century India: The Reformist Standard of Mauláná Thánawí's *Bihishtí Zewar*', *Contributions to Asian Studies* 17 (1982).

45. On the varying fortunes of three provincial shrines in North India in this period see C. Liebeskind, *Piety on its Knees: Three Sufi Traditions in South Asia in Modern Times* (Delhi: Oxford University Press, 1998).

46. Sanyal, *Devotional Islam.*

47. U. Sanyal, *Ahmad Riza Khan Barelwi: In the Path of the Prophet* (Oxford: Oneworld, 2005), p. 128.

48. For an excellent survey with regard to Calcutta see A. Ghosh, *Power in Print: Popular Publishing and the Politics of Language and Culture in a Colonial Society* (Delhi: Oxford University Press, 2006).

49. On the reproduction of such hierarchies in a rural context see S. M. Lyon, *An Anthropological Analysis of Local Politics and Patronage in a Pakistani Village* (Lampeter: Edwin Mellen Press, 2004).

50. E. P. Thompson, *The Making of the English Working Class* (New York: Vintage Books, 1966), chap. 5.

51. E. P. Thompson, 'Custom and Culture', in Thompson, *Customs in Common.*

52. D. Chakrabarty, *Rethinking Working-Class History: Bengal, 1890–1940* (Princeton: Princeton University Press, 1989), p. 69.

53. See e.g. R. Chandavarkar, *The Origins of Industrial Capitalism in India: Business Strategies and the Working Classes in Bombay, 1900–1940* (Cambridge: Cambridge University Press, 1994); D. Kooiman, *Bombay Textile Labour: Managers, Trade Unionists, and Officials, 1918–1939* (Delhi: Manohar Publications, 1989); and S. B. Upadhyay, *Existence, Identity, and Mobilization: The Cotton Millworkers of Bombay, 1890–1919* (Delhi: Manohar, 2004).

54. On the problem of the 'paucity of sources' see Chakrabarty, *Rethinking Working-Class History*, pp. 65–6, 114–15.

55. Cf. Bayly, *The Birth of the Modern World*; J. Cesari, 'The Hybrid and Globalized Islam of Western Europe', in Y. Samad and K. Sen (eds.), *Islam in the European Union: Transnationalism, Youth and the War on Terror* (Oxford: Oxford University Press, 2007); Robinson, 'Islamic Reform and Modernities'; and Roy, *Globalized Islam.*

56. Loimeier, 'Is There Something like "Protestant" Islam?'.
57. G. Lang and L. Ragvald, *The Rise of a Refugee God: Hong Kong's Wong Tai Sin* (Hong Kong: Oxford University Press, 1993); T. Tschacher, 'From Local Practice to Transnational Network: Saints, Shrines and Sufis among Tamil Muslims in Singapore', *Asian Journal of Social Science* 34, 2 (2006); and White, *Speaking with Vampires*.

1. Missionaries and Reformists in the Market of Islams

1. Cf. Hindu and Muslim responses to Christian missionaries in the port of Madras: see G. A. Oddie, 'Anti-Missionary Feeling and Hindu Revivalism in Madras: The Hindu Preaching and Tract Societies, *c.* 1886–1891', in F. W. Clothey (ed.), *Images of Man: Religion and Historical Process in South Asia* (Madras: New Era, 1982); and A. A. Powell, *Muslims and Missionaries in Pre-Mutiny India* (Richmond: Curzon Press, 1993).
2. M. Boyce, 'Manekji Limji Hataria in Iran', in N. D. Manochehr-Homji and M. F. Kanga (eds.), *K. R. Cama Oriental Institute Golden Jubilee Volume* (Bombay: K. R. Cama Oriental Institute, 1969); T. Naidoo, *The Arya Samaj Movement in South Africa* (Delhi: Motilal Banarsidass, 1992) and Raval, *Socio-Religious Reform Movements*.
3. N. Etherington (ed.), *Missions and Empire* (Oxford: Oxford University Press, 2005); and A. Porter, *Religion versus Empire? British Protestant Missionaries and Overseas Expansion 1700–1914* (Manchester: Manchester University Press, 2004).
4. A. M. Colton, *Gordon Hall: A Memorial* (Northampton, MA: Bridgman & Childs, 1882), chap. 1; and H. Newell, *Memoir of Mrs Harriet Newell, Wife of the Rev. Samuel Newell, Missionary to India* (New York: American Tract Society, 1828).
5. G. Hall and S. Newell, *The Conversion of the World, or, The Claims of Six Hundred Millions and the Ability and Duty of the Churches Respecting Them* (Andover, MA: American Board of Commissioners for Foreign Missions, 1818).
6. Albuquerque, *Urbs Prima in Indis*, pp. 129–30.
7. G. Smith, *The Life of John Wilson, DD, FRS, for Fifty Years Philanthropist and Scholar in the East* (London: John Murray, 1878).
8. Ibid., p. 99.
9. Ibid., p. 111.
10. John Wilson, *The Pársí Religion: As contained in the Zand-Avastá, and propounded and defended by the Zoroastrians of India and Persia, unfolded, refuted, and contrasted with Christianity* (Bombay: American Mission Press, 1843).
11. Mullā Firōz bin Mullā Kāvus, *Risāla-ye istishhādāt* (Bombay: Matba'-e Bombā'ī Samāchār, 1197/1828).
12. N. S. Green, 'Stones from Bavaria: Iranian Lithography in its Global Contexts', *Iranian Studies* 43, 3 (2010).
13. Smith, *The Life of John Wilson*, p. 113.

14. J. Wilson, *Rad'-e dīn-e musulmānī; or Refutation of Muhammadanism in Persian in Reply to Muhammad Hashim* (Bombay: Tract and Book Society, 1836); and J. Wilson, *Musulmānī dīn ka rad'iyya; or Refutation of Muhammadanism in Hindustani in Reply to Muhammad Hashim*, 2nd edn (Bombay: Tract and Book Society, 1840 [1833]). I have been unable to trace the Gujarati edition.

15. Wilson, *Musulmānī dīn kā rad'iyya*, pp. 2–12.

16. Ibid., pp. 2–14, 25–7, 39–44.

17. K. Smith Diehl, 'Lucknow Printers, 1820–1850', in N. N. Gidwani (ed.), *Comparative Librarianship: Essays in Honour of Professor D. N. Marshall* (Delhi: Vikas, 1973).

18. Wilson's response, detailing *inter alia* Muhammad Hāshim's own argument, was translated and printed in *Oriental Christian Spectator* 4 (May 1833), pp. 177–84. Thanks to Mitch Numark for this reference.

19. V. V. Gupchup, 'The Social Life of Bombay in the First Half of the Nineteenth Century, 1813–1857' (Ph.D. thesis, Bombay University, 1990), p. 275.

20. On North India see Powell, *Muslims and Missionaries*.

21. Ibid., p. 139, placing the printing of the first Persian edition of 1835 in Shusha before the Calcutta edition appeared in 1839. On Pfander's pre-Indian career see N. S. Green, 'The Trans-Colonial Opportunities of Bible Translation: Iranian Linguists between the Russian and British Empires', in Michael Dodson and Brian Hatcher (eds.), *Trans-Colonial Modernities in South Asia, 1800–1940* (London: Routledge, 2011).

22. On links between missionary polemics and such major Delhi-based Reformists as Shāh 'Abd al-'Azīz (d. 1239/1824) see Powell, *Muslims and Missionaries*, pp. 62–75.

23. *The Missionary Register for 1826* (London: Seeley, Jackson & Halliday, 1826), pp. 342–4.

24. Albuquerque, *Urbs Prima in Indis*, p. 133.

25. H. J. Smith, 'Moslem Missions in the Diocese of Bombay', *The Moslem World* 6, 1 (1916).

26. Ibid.

27. Church Missionary Society, *The Church Missionary Intelligencer*, vol. VIII (London: Church Missionary House, 1872), p. 384.

28. E. Stock, *The History of the Church Missionary Society: Its Environment, its Men and its Work*, 3 vols. (London: Church Missionary Society, 1899), vol. II, p. 534. On corresponding reactions to Parsi conversions see Wacha, *Shells from the Sands of Bombay*, pp. 647–52.

29. Church Missionary Society, *Church Missionary Intelligencer and Record*, vol. VIII (London: Church Missionary House, 1883), p. 497.

30. G. Johnson, *Provincial Politics and Indian Nationalism: Bombay and the Indian National Congress, 1880 to 1915* (Cambridge: Cambridge University Press, 1973); Kooiman, *Bombay Textile Labour*.

31. P. Kidambi, *The Making of an Indian Metropolis: Colonial Governance and Public Culture in Bombay, 1890–1920* (Aldershot: Ashgate, 2007), chaps. 6 and 7.

32. J. Habermas, *The Structural Transformation of the Public Sphere: An Inquiry into a Category of Bourgeois Society* (Cambridge, MA: MIT Press, 1989).
33. Dobbin, *Urban Leadership in Western India*, pp. 27–52. Also Kidambi, *The Making of an Indian Metropolis*, pp. 161–2.
34. Wacha, *Shells from the Sands of Bombay*, pp. 641–2.
35. Among the vast literature on this subject see D. Kopf, *British Orientalism and the Bengal Renaissance: The Dynamics of Indian Modernization, 1773–1835* (Berkeley: University of California Press, 1969).
36. For an overview of the Parsi Reform project see J. S. Palsetia, *The Parsis of India: Preservation of Identity in Bombay City* (Leiden: Brill, 2001), chap. 4; and J. S. Palsetia, 'Parsi and Hindu Traditional and Nontraditional Responses to Christian Conversion in Bombay, 1839–45', *Journal of the American Academy of Religion* 74, 3 (2006).
37. Gupchup, 'The Social Life of Bombay', p. 269, quoting J. N. Farquhar, *Modern Religious Movements in India*.
38. Dobbin, *Urban leadership in Western India*, pp. 58–65.
39. Gupchup, 'The Social Life of Bombay', pp. 268–70.
40. Ibid., pp. 272–3. On the emergence of Reformist political leaders see L. Rodrigues, 'Parsi Elite Leadership in the Politics of Western India in the Mid-Nineteenth Century', *Journal of the K. R. Cama Oriental Institute* 68 (2008).
41. Gupchup, 'The Social Life of Bombay', p. 273.
42. Albuquerque, *Urbs Prima in Indis*, p. 106.
43. J. Hinnells, 'Parsi Responses to Religious Pluralism', in H. G. Coward (ed.), *Modern Indian Responses to Religious Pluralism* (Albany: State University of New York Press, 1987).
44. Dobbin, *Urban leadership in Western India*, pp. 248–58.
45. Naidoo, *The Arya Samaj Movement*; Raval, *Socio-Religious Reform Movements*.
46. Dobbin, *Urban leadership in Western India*, p. 255.
47. For an overview of religious reform in colonial India see K. W. Jones, *Socio-Religious Reform Movements in British India* (Cambridge: Cambridge University Press, 1989).
48. On the attack on caste see Dobbin, *Urban leadership in Western India*, pp. 98–130.
49. Sayyid Shihāb al-dīn Dasnawī, *Anjuman-e Islām kē sau sāl: tārīkh ū jā'iza* (Bombay: Anjuman-e Islām, 1986). On Reformism as a 'cultural project' of Bombay's middle class see Kidambi, *The Making of an Indian Metropolis*, pp. 210–15.
50. Dasnawī, *Anjuman-e Islām*, pp. 17–18; M. Shakir, *Muslims and Indian National Congress: Badruddin Tyabji and his Times* (Delhi: Ajanta Publications, 1987); and H. B. Tyabji, *Badruddin Tyabji: A Biography* (Bombay: Thacker, 1952).
51. Tyabji, *Badruddin Tyabji*, p. 9. On the wider family experience see T. P. Wright, 'Muslim Kinship and Modernization: The Tyabji Clan of Bombay', in I. Ahmad (ed.), *Family, Kinship and Marriage among the Muslims in India* (Delhi: Manohar, 1976).

52. On experiences in England, see Tyabji, *Badruddin Tyabji*, pp. 16–23.
53. Mohiuddin, *Muslim Communities*, pp. 252–3. On his life see Dasnawī, *Anjuman-e Islām*, pp. 19–20; and G. M. Munshi, *Autobiography of Haji Ghulam Muhammad Munshi* (Bombay: Surat Mission Press, 1893).
54. For details see Sayyid Shujā'al-dīn Muhammad Rabbānī, *Selected Notices from the Newspaper Press of the Efforts made by Ghulam Muhammad Munshi to Spread Education among Mahomedans* (Bombay: Fort Mercantile Press, 1880).
55. *Native Opinion*, 20 June 1869, repr. in ibid.
56. Dasnawī, *Anjuman-e Islām*, pp. 21–2, 35.
57. Ibid., p. 20.
58. Ibid., pp. 38–9.
59. On the DPI system see C. Whitehead, *Colonial Educators: The British Indian and Colonial Education Service, 1858–1983* (London: I. B. Tauris, 2003), chap. 1.
60. Dasnawī, *Anjuman-e Islām*, pp. 29, 176.
61. Ibid.
62. Dasnawī, *Anjuman-e Islām*, p. 177.
63. Ibid., p. 28.
64. Ibid. On the formation of the *dars-e nizāmī* syllabus see F. Robinson, *The 'Ulama of Farangi Mahall and Islamic Culture in South Asia* (Delhi: Permanent Black, 2001), chaps. 2 and 3.
65. Metcalf, *Islamic Revival in British India*; M. Q. Zaman, 'Islamic Institutions of Learning: Religious Education and the Rhetoric of Reform: The Madrasa in British India and Pakistan', *Comparative Studies in Society and History* 41, 2 (1999).
66. Dasnawī, *Anjuman-e Islām*, p. 31.
67. Ibid., p. 32.
68. On the Anjuman's contacts with Sir Sayyid Ahmad Khān and Shiblī Nu'manī see ibid., pp. 16–17, 23–7; and Shaykh Farīd, 'Anjuman-e Islām Bombā'ī aur Aligarh', *Nawā-e Adab* 36 (April 1986). For claims of its Pan-Islamist character see Dobbin, *Urban leadership in Western India*, pp. 232–5.
69. Financial details drawn from Dasnawī, *Anjuman-e Islām*, p. 31; D. A. Pinder, *The Visitor's Illustrated Guide to Bombay* (Bombay: G. Claridge & Co., 1904), p. 56; and Tyabji, *Badruddin Tyabji*, pp. 88–92.
70. Dasnawī, *Anjuman-e Islām*, p. 32.
71. On the gifts and stipends ('*atiyāt aur wazīfē*) raised for other Anjuman activities, such as the founding of the Dār al-Iqāma hostel in 1901, see ibid., pp. 35–6.
72. Pinder, *Visitor's Illustrated Guide*, p. 56.
73. Dasnawī, *Anjuman-e Islām*, pp. 31–2.
74. G. Minault, *Secluded Scholars: Women's Education and Muslim Social Reform in Colonial India* (Delhi: Oxford University Press, 1998), pp. 182–7.
75. B. C. Fortna, *Imperial Classroom: Islam, the State, and Education in the Late Ottoman Empire* (Oxford: Oxford University Press, 2002).
76. Dasnawī, *Anjuman-e Islām*, p. 35, citing Badr al-dīn Tayyibjī.
77. Mohiuddin, *Muslim Communities*, p. 251.

78. Gupchup, 'The Social Life of Bombay', p. 277.

79. Mohiuddin, *Muslim Communities*, p. 126.

80. F. Hasan, '*Madāris* and the Challenges of Modernity in Colonial India', in J.-P. Hartung and H. Reifeld (eds.), *Islamic Education, Diversity and National Identity: Dini Madaris in India Post 9/11* (Delhi: Sage Publications, 2006).

81. Kidambi, *The Making of an Indian Metropolis*, p. 174.

82. On local Muslim responses to CMS activity on the eastern fringes of Bombay Presidency see N. S. Green, 'Mystical Missionaries in Hyderabad State: Mu'in Allāh Shāh and his Sufi Reform Movement', *Indian Economic and Social History Review* 41, 2 (2005).

83. A. J. P. French, 'The Problem of Islam in India (A Discussion of "Methods")', *The Moslem World* 6, 1 (1916), p. 7.

84. Mohiuddin, *Muslim Communities*, p. 118.

85. Moulavi Cheragh Ali, *The Proposed Political, Legal, and Social Reforms in the Ottoman Empire and Other Mohammadan States* (Bombay: Education Society's Press, 1883).

86. Ibid., p. ii.

87. On Muhsin al-Mulk's role in Pan Islamist politics and the Aligarh Movement see Minault, *The Khilafat Movement*, pp. 10–19.

88. Nawab Mohsin ul-Mulk, *Causes of the Decline of the Mahomedan Nation* (Bombay: Bombay Gazette Steam Printing Works, 1891), esp. pp. 30–54.

89. Ibid., p. 42.

90. S. Joshi, *Fractured Modernity: The Making of a Middle Class in Colonial North India* (Delhi: Oxford University Press, 2001), pp. 113–23.

91. Munshi 'Ali 'Umar, *Life of Mir Munshi Mohammad Hassan Muqba, J. P.* (Bombay: n.p., 1914).

92. E. Stock, 'The CMS Missions to Mohammedans', *The Moslem World* 2, 2 (1912), p. 131.

93. F. Hart, *Rahator of Bombay, the Apostle to the Marathas* (London: The Epworth Press, 1936), p. 10. See also Numark, 'Translating Religion'.

94. Hart, *Rahator of Bombay*, p. 100.

95. Mohiuddin, *Muslim Communities*, p. 240.

96. Haji Riazuddin Ahmed, *The Moslem Guide* (Bombay: Education Society's Press, 1891), unpaginated preface. The pamphlet may have been issued by the followers of Mirzā Ghulām Ahmad.

97. Revd Canon H. U. Weitbrecht, 'Reform Movements in India', in E. M. Wherry, S. M. Zwemer and C. G. Mylrea (eds.), *Islam and Missions: Being Papers Read at the Second Missionary Conference on Behalf of the Mohammedan World at Lucknow, January 23–28, 1911* (London: Fleming H. Revell Company, 1911).

98. 'Imad al-Din, *A Mohammedan Brought to Christ: Being the Autobiography of a Native Clergyman in India, Translated from the Hindustanee*, trans. Robert Clark (London: CMS House, 1874).

99. Ibid., p. 11. I have standardized the transliteration of the litanies referred to here.

2. Cosmopolitan Cults and the Economy of Miracles

1. On related effects of labour migration on domestic architecture see F. Conlon, 'Industrialization and the Housing Problem in Bombay, 1850–1940', in K. Ballhatchet and D. Taylor (eds.), *Changing South Asia: Economy and Society* (London: School of Oriental and African Studies, 1984).
2. Stark, 'From Church-Sect to Religious Economies', p. 18.
3. On labour migration and shrine foundation in the South China Sea during the same period see Lang and Ragvald, *The Rise of a Refugee God*.
4. Wacha, *Shells from the Sands of Bombay*, p. 411, reprinted from the *Bombay Chronicle* (1914).
5. On the historicity of such oral traditions see N. S. Green, 'Stories of Saints and Sultans: Re-membering History at the Sufi Shrines of Aurangabad', *Modern Asian Studies* 38, 2 (2004).
6. White, *Speaking with Vampires*, p. 312.
7. Cf. the economy of Hindu pilgrimage analysed in van der Veer, *Gods on Earth*.
8. Dossal, *Imperial Designs*.
9. Cf. Mitchell, *Colonising Egypt*; and V. T. Oldenburg, *The Making of Colonial Lucknow, 1856–1877* (Delhi: Oxford University Press, 1989).
10. For a comparative description of Bombay and Bushire during this period see W. A. Shepherd, *From Bombay to Bushire and Bussora* (London: Richard Bentley, 1857), pp. 123–63.
11. Kidambi, *The Making of an Indian Metropolis*.
12. A parallel can be found on the other side of the Indian Ocean in the saintly shrines established amid the bustling markets of colonial Singapore by Tamil Muslim migrants from South India. See Tschacher, 'From Local Practice to Transnational Network'.
13. Kidambi, *The Making of an Indian Metropolis*; and S. Sarkar, 'The City Imagined: Calcutta of the Nineteenth and Early Twentieth Centuries', in S. Sarkar, *Writing Social History* (Delhi: Oxford University Press, 1997).
14. Chakrabarty, *Rethinking Working-Class History*, chap. 6; A. de Haan, *Unsettled Settlers: Migrant Workers and Industrial Capitalism in Calcutta* (Hilversum: Verloren, 1994), pp. 167–86.
15. A. Farooqui, *Opium City: The Making of Early Victorian Bombay* (Delhi: Three Essays Collective, 2006).
16. H. Catlin-Jairazbhoy and E. A. Alpers (eds.), *Sidis and Scholars: Essays on African Indians* (Noida: Rainbow Publishers, 2004).
17. On Muharram as urban disorder see Kidambi, *The Making of an Indian Metropolis*, chap. 5; and J. Masselos, 'Change and Custom in the Format of the Bombay Mohurrum during the Nineteenth and Twentieth Centuries', *South Asia* 5, 2 (1982).
18. Rustomji Pestonji Karkaria, *The Charm of Bombay: An Anthology of Writings in Praise of the First City in India* (Bombay: D. B. Taraporevala, 1915), pp. 243–4.
19. K. Moinuddin, *A Monograph on Muharram in Hyderabad City* (Delhi: Controller of Publications, 1977).

20. J. Masselos, 'Appropriating Urban Space: Social Constructs of Bombay in the Time of the Raj', *South Asia* 14, 1 (1991).

21. F. J. Korom, *Hosay Trinidad: Muḥarram Performances in an Indo-Caribbean Diaspora* (Philadelphia: University of Pennsylvania Press, 2003).

22. Edwardes, *By-Ways of Bombay*, pp. 47–9.

23. For data on the shrines see M. Ahmed, 'Sacred Muslim Sites', in P. Rohatgi, P. Godrej and R. Mehotra (eds.), *Bombay to Mumbai: Changing Perspectives* (Mumbai: Marg Publications, 2006); Anonymous [Edwardes], *Gazetteer of Bombay City and Island*, vol. I, pp. 188–9, vol. III, pp. 300–4; S. M. Edwardes, *The Rise of Bombay: A Retrospect* (Bombay: Times of India Press, 1902), pp. 61–2; Mohiuddin, *Muslim Communities*, pp. 76–84.

24. Anonymous, *Jān-e Bombā'ī*, pp. 31–3.

25. For further discussion of such urban founder saints see N. S. Green, *Indian Sufism since the Seventeenth Century: Saints, Books and Empires in the Muslim Deccan* (London: Routledge, 2006), chap. 2.

26. On the wider applicability of this characterization see N. S. Green, 'Migrant Sufis and Sacred Space in South Asian Islam', *Contemporary South Asia* 12, 4 (2003).

27. Interview, shrine *mujāwirs*, 25.4.09. On Hadhrami soldier traffic see O. Khalidi, 'The Arabs of Hadramawt in Hyderabad: Mystics, Mercenaries and Moneylenders', in A. R. Kulakarni, M. A. Nayeem and T. R. De Souza (eds.), *Mediaeval Deccan History: Commemoration Volume in Honour of Purshottam Mahadeo Joshi* (Bombay: Popular Prakashan, 1996).

28. H. Basu, *Habshi-Sklaven, Sidi-Fakire: Muslimische Heiligenverehrung im westlichen Indien* (Berlin: Das Arabische Buch, 1995); H. Basu, 'Music and the Formation of Sidi Identity in Western India', *History Workshop Journal* 65, 1 (2008).

29. H. Basu, 'Slave, Soldier, Trader, Faqir: Fragments of African Histories in Western India', in S. de S. Jayasuriya and R. Pankhurst (eds.), *The African Diaspora in the Indian Ocean* (Trenton, NJ: Africa World Press, 2003), p. 236.

30. The shrine attendant informed me that it was 'around a hundred and twenty years old': interview, 30.4.09.

31. On local Khōja history see J. Masselos, 'The Khojas of Bombay', in I. Ahmad (ed.), *Caste and Social Stratification among Muslims in India* (Delhi: Manohar, 1978).

32. Edwardes, *By-Ways of Bombay*, p. 44.

33. Ibid.

34. Edwardes, *By-Ways of Bombay*, p. 45; Basu, *Habshi-Sklaven*.

35. On customary beliefs in black magic and its cures in Maharashtra see S. Kapur, *Witchcraft in Western India* (Hyderabad: Orient Longman, 1983), esp. chap. 9, on Muslim participation.

36. On early twentieth-century Urdu stories of other *majzūb*s see N. S. Green, 'Transgressions of a Holy Fool: A Majzub in Colonial India', in B. D. Metcalf (ed.), *Islam in South Asia in Practice* (Princeton: Princeton University Press, 2009).

37. Interview, Abdullah Wahedna, shrine of 'Abd al-Rahmān, 28.4.09.

38. M. Homāyūnī, *Tārīkh-e silsilahā-ye tarīqa-ye ni'matullāhiyya dar Īrān* (London: Bunyād-e 'Irfān-e Mawlānā, 1371/1992), p. 263.
39. P. Davis, *The Penguin Guide to the Monuments of India*, vol. II: *Islamic, Rajput and European* (London: Penguin Books, 1989), p. 447.
40. Anonymous, *Jān-e Bombā'ī*, p. 32.
41. Interview, Minhaj 'Ali, shrine of Bismillāh Shāh, 23.4.09.
42. S. M. Edwardes, *Census of India*, vol. X, pt 4: *Bombay: History* (Bombay: Times of India Press, 1901), p. 108.
43. N. S. Green, 'Who's the King of the Castle? Brahmins, Sufis and the Narrative Landscape of Daulatabad', *Contemporary South Asia* 13, 3 (2004).
44. Basu, *Habshi-Sklaven*; S. F. Dale, 'The Hadhrami Diaspora in South-Western India: The Role of the Sayyids of the Malabar Coast', in U. Freitag and W. G. Clarence-Smith (eds.), *Hadhrami Traders, Scholars, and Statesmen in the Indian Ocean, 1750s–1960s* (Leiden: Brill, 1997).
45. Munshī 'Abbās 'Alī, *Qissah-ye ghamgīn*, ed. S. C. Misra (Baroda: Maharaja Sayajirao University of Baroda, 1975), pp. 37–9.
46. Ibid., p. 77.
47. Anonymous, *Jān-e Bombā'ī*, p. 31.
48. Sayyid Ibrāhīm al-Hussayni al-Madanī, *Zamīr al-insān*, Bombay University Library, Arabic MS, vol. 56, no. 99 (paginated).
49. Ibid., p. 2. Date given in colophon.
50. Ibid., p. 3.
51. Ibid., p. 23.
52. 'Abd al-Majīd Qāzī, *Awliyā Allāh kē zinda karishmāt* (Bombay: Karīmī Press, n.d.), pp. 18–22.
53. Ibid., p. 22. For a description of such rituals in 1912 see Edwardes, *By-Ways of Bombay*, p. 80.
54. Edwardes, *By-Ways of Bombay*, p. 81.
55. Ibid.
56. P. Werbner, 'Economic Rationality and Hierarchical Gift Economies: Value and Ranking among British Pakistanis', *Man* N.S. 25 (1990); P. Werbner, '*Langar*: Pilgrimage, Sacred Exchange and Perpetual Sacrifice in a Sufi Saint's Lodge', in P. Werbner and H. Basu (eds.), *Embodying Charisma: Modernity, Locality and the Performance of Emotion in Sufi Cults* (London: Routledge, 1998).
57. W. A. Shepherd, 'Sleepy Sketches', in *Sleepy Sketches; or, How we Live and How we do not Live. From Bombay* (London: Sampson, Low, Marston, Searle & Rivington, 1877), p. 210.
58. O. Khalidi, 'Konkani Muslims: An Introduction', *Islamic Culture* 74, 1 (2000). As at many other shrines, the control of Shaykh Makhdūm's shrine was disputed, and in 1909 the Supreme Court placed the prominent Konkani notable Muhammad Hasan Muqba as trustee of its finances. See Mohiuddin, *Muslim Communities*, p. 83.
59. E. B. Reeves, *The Hidden Government: Ritual, Clientelism and Legitimation in Northern Egypt* (Salt Lake City: University of Utah Press, 1990).
60. Anonymous [Edwardes], *Gazetteer of Bombay City and Island*, vol. I, pp. 188–9, vol. III, pp. 300–14. On the flourishing of customary practices see

also R. E. Enthoven, *Gazetteer of the Bombay Presidency: Musalmans and Parsis* (Bombay: Government Central Press, 1899).

61. On Hindustani music performances, their links to prostitution and missionary perceptions of them in nineteenth-century Bombay see A. Pradhan, 'Perspectives on Performance Practice: Hindustani Music in Nineteenth and Twentieth Century Bombay (Mumbai)', *South Asia* 27, 3 (2004). On new cultures of food consumption see F. F. Conlon, 'Dining Out in Bombay', in C. A. Breckenridge (ed.), *Consuming Modernity: Public Culture in a South Asian World* (Minneapolis: University of Minnesota Press, 1995).

62. Anonymous [Edwardes], *Gazetteer of Bombay City and Island*, vol. I, p. 189.

63. Ibid., vol. III, pp. 301–4.

64. H. J. Smith, 'Mahim Fair', *Bombay Muhammadan Mission News* (15 Feb. 1902). Copy kept in file Z1, Urdu Mission Records, Bombay 1900–1903, in Papers of Revd Henry Lane-Smith (1901–38), Church Missionary Society (CMS) Collection, Unofficial Papers, Acc. 33, Special Collections Department. Birmingham University Library, UK.

65. See http://en.wikipedia.org/wiki/Bhiwandi (accessed 20 May 2009).

66. 'Abd al-Majīd Qāzī, *Awliyā Allāh*, p. 63.

67. Ibid., pp. 60, 62.

68. On such variable community conceptions of a saint's identity see also N. S. Green, 'Making a "Muslim" Saint: Writing Customary Religion in an Indian Princely State', *Comparative Studies of South Asia, Africa and the Middle East* 25, 3 (2005).

69. 'Abd al-Majīd Qāzī, *Awliyā Allāh*, p. 61.

70. Ibid., pp. 61–2.

71. N. S. Green, 'Oral Competition Narratives of Muslim and Hindu Saints in the Deccan', *Asian Folklore Studies* 63, 2 (2004).

72. Muhammad Muhyī al-dīn, *Sawānih-e hayāt-e Khwāja Shams al-dīn al-maʿrūf Khwāja Shamnā Mīrān* (n.p.: Khwāja Buk Dipō, n.d.), pp. 11–13. Staring at the sea, Shamnā Mīrān was guided to India by a visionary 'map of the way' (*rāstē kā naqsha*) that appeared before his eyes.

73. Ibid., pp. 16–17.

74. Ibid., pp. 21–3.

75. 'Abd al-Majīd Qāzī, *Awliyā Allāh*, pp. 82–3.

76. Ibid., pp. 84–5. On similar legends of riding tigers and walking walls see Green, 'Oral Competition Narratives'.

77. D. Hardiman, 'Purifying the Nation: The Arya Samaj in Gujarat, 1895–1930', *Indian Economic and Social History Review* 44, 1 (2007).

78. Edwardes, *By-Ways of Bombay*, p. 22.

79. Ibid., p. 27.

80. Ibid.

81. Basu, *Habshi-Sklaven*.

82. Edwardes, *By-Ways of Bombay*, p. 43. On African sailors see also J. Hyslop, 'Steamship Empire: Asian, African and British Sailors in the Merchant Marine c. 1880–1945', *Journal of African and Asian Studies* 44, 1 (2009). Thanks to Nir Shafir for this reference.

83. Cf. the attractions of the possession cults among Malaysian Muslim factory workers in A. Ong, *Spirits of Resistance and Capitalist Discipline: Factory Women in Malaysia* (Albany: State University of New York Press, 1987).
84. Sayyid Shujāʿ al-dīn Muhammad Rabbānī, *Sawānih-e Sayyid Mīrān ʿAlī Dātār aur karāmāt wa munāqib* (Unava: Khayrō Kitābghar, n.d.), pp. 14–15.
85. Interviews, pilgrims at shrine of Shāh Dawla Dātār, 18.4.09.
86. Interviews, pilgrims at shrine of Shāh Dawla Dātār, 18.4.09.
87. J. W. Laine, *Shivaji: Hindu King in Islamic India* (Delhi: Oxford University Press, 2003).
88. Cf. Jalal, 'Negotiating Colonial Modernity'.
89. T. Tschacher, 'Witnessing Fun: Tamil-speaking Muslims and the Imagination of Ritual in Colonial Southeast Asia', paper presented at workshop on Ritual, Caste and Colonial Discourse in South India, Heidelberg, September 2008.
90. White, *Speaking with Vampires*.
91. Anonymous, *The Mahomedan and Hindu Riots in Bombay, Aug. 1893, from the Bombay Gazette* (Bombay: Bombay Gazette, 1893). Also Masselos, 'Appropriating Urban Space'.
92. Cf. B. S. A. Yeoh, *Contesting Space: Power Relations and the Urban Built Environment in Colonial Singapore* (Kuala Lumpur: Oxford University Press, 1996).
93. ʿAbd al-Karīm Munshī, *A Sketch of the Life of His Holiness Saint Syed Pedro Shah, and His Miraculous Deeds – Pēdrō Shāh Sāhib kī Karāmāt* (Bombay: Gulzār Press, 1321/1903).
94. Ibid., pp. 2–4.
95. Ibid., pp. 4–5. On comparable counter-narratives elsewhere in India see N. S. Green, 'Shiʿism, Sufism and Sacred Space in the Deccan: Counter-Narratives of Saintly Identity in the Cult of Shah Nur', in A. Monsutti, S. Naef and F. Sabahi (eds.), *The Other Shiʿites: From the Mediterranean to Central Asia* (Berne: Peter Lang, 2007).
96. ʿAbd al-Karīm Munshī, *Sketch*, p. 4.
97. Ibid., back cover (in English), citing Edwardes, *Census of India*, vol. X, pt. 4, p. 108.
98. On such early modern European converts to Islam see N. Matar, *Turks, Moors, and Englishmen in the Age of Discovery* (New York: Columbia University Press, 1999).
99. White, *Speaking with Vampires*, p. 64.
100. The Prabhus' struggle found clearest expression in Shamrao Moroji Nayak, *A History of the Pattana Prabhus, Containing an Account of the Origin of this Caste, the Loss of their Principalities, and the Migration from Other Parts of India to Paitan, and thence Finally to Konkan* (Bombay: Family Printing Press, 1877), esp. pp. 100–13 on colonial testimony of their 'purity' of lineage. Thanks to Rosalind O'Hanlon for drawing this to my attention.
101. Interview, *mujāwir*, shrine of Pēdrō Shāh, 20.4.09.
102. Hardiman, 'Purifying the Nation'; Y. S. Sikand, 'The *Fitna* of *Irtidad*: Muslim Missionary Response to the *Shuddhi* of Arya Samaj in Early Twentieth

Century India', *Journal of Muslim Minority Affairs* 17, 1 (1997). On earlier antecedents in the Bombay region see R. O'Hanlon, 'Narratives of Penance and Purification in Western India, *c.* 1650–1850', *Journal of Hindu Studies* 2, 1 (2009).

103. 'Abd al-Karīm Munshī, *Sketch*, pp. 6–12.

104. Anonymous, *Jān-e Bombā'ī*, pp. 46–7.

105. On other acts of supernatural defence of Muslims from British mores and institutions in the early 1900s see N. S. Green, 'The *Faqīr* and the Subalterns: Mapping the Holy Man in Colonial South Asia', *Journal of Asian History* 41, 1 (2007).

106. W. W. Hunter, J. S. Cotton, R. Burn and W. S. Meyer (eds.), *Indian Law Reports (Bombay Series)* (Bombay: Government Central Press), vol. XXVIII (1904), pp. 428–31.

107. On communal rivalry for urban space as expressed in festivals and riots in early twentieth-century Bombay see Masselos, 'Appropriating Urban Space'; and in Singapore Yeoh, *Contesting Space.*

108. M. Cox and R. A. Gilbert (eds.), *Victorian Ghost Stories: An Oxford Anthology* (Oxford: Oxford University Press, 1992), p. ix.

109. 'Fatal Collapse of a Building', *Bombay Gazette*, Monday 1 June 1903. The event was also reported on in such vernacular newspapers as *Jām-e Jamshid* and *Indu-Prakāsh*, where it was used to attack the administrative efficiency of the Bombay Municipality. See *Reports on Native Newspapers Published in the Bombay Presidency for the Week Ending 6th June 1903*, Maharashtra State Archives, Bombay, Records Dept, no. 28 of 1903, L/R/5/158, pp. 27–8.

110. 'The Disaster at the Market', *Bombay Gazette*, Tuesday 2 June 1903. Further particulars, including on the beginning of the legal inquiry, were also carried in *Bombay Gazette*, Wednesday 3 June 1903.

111. I have been unable to find details on this company in such reference works as L. Carter, *Chronicles of British Business in Asia, 1850–1960* (Delhi: Manohar, 2002).

112. *Bombay Gazette*, Tuesday 2 June 1903.

113. Cf. A. Ghosh, 'Cheap Books, "Bad" Books: Contesting Print Cultures in Colonial Bengal', in A. Gupta and S. Chakravorty (eds.), *Print Areas: Book History in India* (Delhi: Permanent Black, 2004).

114. Cox and Gilbert (eds.), *Victorian Ghost Stories*, p. x. On the appearance of supernaturalism in imperial representations of Africa during the early 1900s see H. Wittenberg, 'Occult, Empire and Landscape: The Colonial Uncanny in John Buchan's African Writing', *Journal of Colonialism and Colonial History* 7, 2 (2006).

115. Like the African vampire rumours, the tales surrounding Pēdrō Shāh and the tower block 'were a way of talking about the world that both parodied the new technologies and showed the true intent behind their use': White, *Speaking with Vampires*, p. 29.

116. F. Robinson, 'Other-worldly and This-worldly Islam and the Islamic Revival', *Journal of the Royal Asiatic Society* 14, 1 (2004).

3. The Enchantment of Industrial Communications

1. E. Green, *Prophet John Wroe: Virgins, Scandals and Visions* (Stroud: Sutton, 2005); S. J. Stein, *The Shaker Experience in America: A History of the United Society of Believers* (New Haven: Yale University Press, 1992).

2. Most influentially, see F. Robinson, 'Technology and Religious Change: Islam and the Impact of Print', *Modern Asian Studies* 27, 1 (1993).

3. J. Sconce, 'Mediums and Media', in M. Sturken, D. Thomas and Sandra Ball-Rokeach (eds.), *Technological Visions: The Hopes and Fears that Shape New Technologies* (Philadelphia: Temple University Press, 2004).

4. On American parallels see J. Sconce, *Haunted Media: Electronic Presence from Telegraphy to Television* (Durham, NC: Duke University Press, 2000).

5. On the scale of Bombay's port modernization, even in relation to other British ports, see R. K. Home, *Of Planting and Planning: The Making of British Colonial Cities* (London: Taylor & Francis, 1997), chap. 3. On the 'imperial' quality of Bombay's architecture see T. R. Metcalf, *An Imperial Vision: Indian Architecture and Britain's Raj* (Oxford: Oxford University Press, 2002).

6. L. Stanhope, *Sketch of the History and Influence of the Press in British India* (London: C. Chapple, 1823), p. 160.

7. E. L. Eisenstein, *The Printing Press as an Agent of Change: Communications and Cultural Transformations in Early Modern Europe*, 2 vols. (Cambridge: Cambridge University Press, 1979).

8. See the classic study of J. Heyworth-Dunne, *An Introduction to the History of Education in Modern Egypt* (London: Luzac & Co., 1939).

9. Robinson, Technology and Religious Change.

10. Albuquerque, *Urbs Prima in Indis*, pp. 33, 37.

11. Kidambi, *The Making of an Indian Metropolis*, pp. 161–2; L. Carter, *Catalogue of Native Publications in the Bombay Presidency up to 31st December 1864* (Bombay: Education Society's Press, 1867), esp. p. 228 on Persian publications.

12. M. A. Krek, *Gazetteer of Arabic Printing* (Weston, MA: privately printed, 1977), p. 16. On the origins of Bombay printing per se see G. M. Shaw, 'The Printer of the First Book Published in Bombay', *The Library*, series 6, 1 (1979).

13. On the diffusion of lithographic printing see Green, 'Stones from Bavaria'.

14. On Calcutta printing see Graham Shaw, 'Calcutta: Birthplace of the Indian Lithographed Book', *Journal of the Printing Historical Society* 27 (1998).

15. Green, 'Stones from Bavaria'.

16. Mullā Firōz bin Mullā Kāvus, *Risāla-ye istishhādāt*.

17. Ahmad Ghaffarī, *Tārīkh-e Nigāristān* (Bombay: n.p., 1245/1829); Sikandar ibn Muhammad, *Mir'āt-e Sikandarī* (Bombay: n.p., 1246/1831); Muhammad Qāsim Firishta, *Tārīkh-e Firishta*, ed. Major-General John Briggs 'with the assistance of' Munshi Mir Kheirat Ali Khan Mushtak, 2 vols. (Bombay: Government College Press, 1831).

18. O. P. Shcheglova, 'Lithography ii: In India', in E. Yarshater (ed.), *Encyclopaedia Iranica* (New York: Biblioteca Persica Press, 2009).

19. By 1909 there were some 120 printing-presses recorded as being active in Bombay, though some of these were English presses. On Bombay's printers at the turn of the twentieth century see Anonymous [Edwardes], *Gazetteer of Bombay City and Island*, vol. III, pp. 145–7.

20. On the Bombay–Lucknow comparison see Shcheglova, 'Lithography ii: In India'.

21. On Bombay printers (the older ones identifiable by their addresses in the Fort) see L. Sambolle, *All India Press Directory* (Calcutta: Calcutta Exchange Gazette Press, 1935), pp. 55–8.

22. Anonymous, *Bombay Almanac and Directory for 1865* (Bombay: Bombay Gazette Press, 1865), p. 561.

23. H. J. Lane-Smith, 'Illiteracy among Indian Moslems', *The Moslem World* 9, 2 (1919).

24. I am grateful to Sean O'Fahey for information on printing in Zanzibar.

25. J. Hunwick, 'The Arabic Literary Tradition of Nigeria', *Research in African Literatures* 28, 3 (1997), note 3.

26. Thanks again to Torsten Tschacher for this information.

27. V. Braginsky and A. Suvorova, 'A New Wave of Indian Inspiration: Translations from Urdu in Malay Traditional Literature and Theatre', *Indonesia and the Malay World* 36, 104 (2008), pp. 117–18; Ian Proudfoot, 'Malay Books Printed in Bombay: A Report on Sources for Historical Bibliography', *Kekal Abadi* 13, 3 (1994).

28. Braginsky and Suvorova, 'A New Wave of Indian Inspiration', p. 121.

29. M. van Bruinessen, 'Kitab Kuning: Books in Arabic Script used in the Pesantren Milieu', *Bijdragen tot de Taal-, Land- en Volkenkunde* 146 (1990), pp. 230–1.

30. Conlon, 'Dining Out in Bombay'.

31. M. W. Albin (rev. N. S. Green), 'Book Publishing', in J. L. Esposito (ed.), *Oxford Encyclopaedia of the Islamic World* (Oxford: Oxford University Press, 2008).

32. S. A. Hakim Sharafuddin, *A Brief Survey of Urdu Translations of the Quran* (Bombay: Sharafuddin, 1984).

33. 'Abd al-'Azīz Dihlawī, *Tafsīr-e fath al-'azīz sīpāra-ye 'ām kī tarjama* (Bombay: Muhammadī Press, 1261/1845). This was the last section of the Quran (*sūra*s LXXVIII–CXIV) with an Urdu translation of the Persian commentary entitled *Fath al-'azīz*. Later parallels included the Urdu commentary *Tafsīr-e mujaddidī* of Ra'ūf Ahmad ibn Shu'ūr, which had been written in the Muslim princely state of Bhopal in 1248/1832. See Ra'ūf Ahmad ibn Shu'ūr Ahmad, *Tafsīr-e mujaddidī ma'rūf bih tafsīr-e ra'ūfī* (Bombay: Matba'a Haydarī, 1876).

34. See the many Marathi and Gujarati examples printed in Bombay and listed in J. F. Blumhardt, *Catalogue of the Library of the India Office* (London: Eyre & Spottiswoode, 1908), vol. II, pt. 5, pp. 101–11, 250–3.

35. S. Blanchy, 'Les texts islamiques protecteurs aux Comores: transmissions et usage', in C. Hamès (ed.), *Coran et talismans: Textes et practiques magiques en milieu musulman* (Paris: Karthala, 2007).

36. On these Bombay *masnawī*s see A. J. Arberry, *Catalogue of the Library of the India Office*, vol. II, pt 6: *Persian Books* (London: India Office, 1937), pp. 301–3.

37. O. Scheglova, 'Lithograph Versions of Persian Manuscripts of Indian Manufacture in the Nineteenth Century', *Manuscripta Orientalia* 5, 1 (1999). The scale of Persian printing in nineteenth-century India is also made clear in the bibliographic listings contained in K. Mushar, *Fihrist-e kitābhā-ye chāpī-ye fārsī az āghāz ta ākhar-e sāl-e 1345* (Tehran: Bungā-ye Tarjuma wa Nashr-e Kitāb, 1352/1974).

38. B. Abu Manneh, 'A Note on "Rashahāt-i 'Ain al-Hayat" in the Nineteenth Century', in E. Özdalga (ed.), *Naqshbandis in Western and Central Asia* (Istanbul: Swedish Research Institute in Istanbul, 1999), p. 65.

39. Shaykh Yūsuf ibn Ismā'īl al-Nabahanī al-Naqshbandī, *Jamiʿ karāmāt al-awliyā*, 2 vols. (Beirut: al-Maktaba al-Thaqafiyya, repr. 1411/1991).

40. I have adapted this notion of magnification from Chakrabarty, *Rethinking Working-Class History*, pp. 166–70.

41. On these steamship routes see Anonymous [Edwardes], *Gazetteer of Bombay City and Island*, vol. I, pp. 388–400.

42. Anonymous, *Tabarrukāt-e nūrānī al-maʿrūf ba gulzār-e Gīlānī* (Bombay: Muzafarī Steam Press, 1330/1912).

43. For observations on the large number of Indian pilgrims to the shrine of 'Abd al-Qādir at this time see L. Massignon, 'Les pélerinages populaires à Baghdad', *Revue du Monde Musulman* 6, 12 (1908), p. 650.

44. Anonymous, *Tabarrukāt-e nūrānī*, p. 2.

45. A. Gell, 'The Technology of Enchantment and the Enchantment of Technology', in J. Coote and A. Shelton (eds.), *Anthropology, Art and Aesthetics* (Oxford: Clarendon Press, 1992).

46. Qāzī Muhammad Yūsuf, *Zayn al-majālis* (Bombay: n.p., 1868; repr. 1879).

47. 'Uthmān ibn 'Umar al-Kahf, *Hikāyat al-sālihīn* (Bombay: Matba'a Haydarī, 1293/1876).

48. Ibid., pp. 32–6.

49. Muhammad Mahdī Wāsif, *Anīs al-zākirīn* (Bombay: Matba'a Haydarī, 1288/1871).

50. Anonymous, *'Ajā'ib al-hikāyat* (Bombay: n.p., 1300/1883); Anonymous, *Ārā'ish-e mahfil ya'nī qissa-e Hātim Tā'ī bā taswīr* (Bombay: Matba'a Karīmī, 1326/1908). This book's cover illustration is taken from this edition.

51. Anonymous, *Sawānih al-ayyām fī mushāhadāt al-aʿwām mawsūm bih silsilat al-'ārifīn* (Bombay: n.p., 1307/1890), repr. in J. Aubin (ed.), *Matériaux pour la biographie de Shâh Ni'matullah Walî Kermânî* (Tehran: Département d'Iranologie de l'Institut Francoiranien, 1956), pp. 133–268; Shaykh Dā'ūd bin Sulaymān, *Riyāz-e sūfī* (Bombay: Mustafā'ī Steam Press, 1331/1913).

52. Later forms of Customary Islamic printing took on the guise of the periodical or magazine, as with the Urdu *Anwar al-Quds* (Lights of holiness) published in Bombay between 1925 and 1927 by the Chishtī Sufi and confidante of Jinnāh, Muhammad Zawqī Shāh (d. 1370/1951). See C. W. Ernst, 'Ideological and Technological Transformations of Contemporary Sufism', in

M. Cooke and B. B. Lawrence (eds.), *Muslim Networks: From Hajj to Hip-hop* (Chapel Hill: University of North Carolina Press, 2005), p. 234.

53. For an overview of change in the nineteenth century Indian Ocean see M. Pearson, *The Indian Ocean* (London: Routledge, 2003), chap. 7.

54. A. Reid, 'Nineteenth Century Pan-Islam in Indonesia and Malaysia', *Journal of Asian Studies*, 26, 2 (1967).

55. Low, 'Empire and the Hajj'.

56. On Bombay as a venue for Khilāfat activity see Minault, *The Khilafat Movement*, pp. 34–7, 71–87, 96–105.

57. W. G. Clarence-Smith, 'The Rise and Fall of Hadhrami Shipping in the Indian Ocean, *c.* 1750–*c.* 1940', in D. Parkin and R. Barnes (eds.), *Ships and the Development of Maritime Technology across the Indian Ocean* (London: RoutledgeCurzon, 2002).

58. Anonymous, *Jān-e Bombā'ī*, pp. 54–5.

59. K. Desai, 'Bombay – The Gift of her Harbour', in Rohatgi *et al.* (eds.), *Bombay to Mumbai*, p. 151.

60. Wacha, *Shells from the Sands of Bombay*, p. 556. For telegraph statistics see Anonymous [Edwardes], *Gazetteer of Bombay City and Island*, vol. I, pp. 381–8. On the symbolic role of the telegraph in subsequent imperial literature see A. Worth, 'All India Becoming Tranquil: Wiring the Raj', *Journal of Colonialism and Colonial History* 9, 1 (2008).

61. For an eyewitness account of Bombay's communications revolution see Wacha, *Shells from the Sands of Bombay*, pp. 550–61, 576–86.

62. Ibid., p. 411, repr. from the *Bombay Chronicle* (1914).

63. Low, 'Empire and the Hajj'.

64. M. Harrison, 'Quarantine, Pilgrimage and Colonial Trade, 1866–1900', *Indian Economic and Social History Review* 29, 2 (1992).

65. R. Singha, 'Passport, Ticket, and India Rubber-stamp: The Problem of the Pauper Pilgrim in Colonial India (*c.* 1882–1925)', in A. Tambe and H. Fischer-Tiné (eds.), *The Limits of British Colonial Control in South Asia: Spaces of Disorder in the Indian Ocean Region* (London: Routledge, 2009).

66. Committee of the District Benevolent Society, 'The Native Poor of Bombay', p. 264.

67. Hāfiz 'Abd al-Rahmān Sāhib, *Safarnāma-e Bilād-e Islāmiyya* (Lahore: Shaykh Imām Bakhsh, repr. 1338/1919 [1322/1904]), pp. 4–14.

68. Munshī Sīvanāth, *Sayr-e Ajmēr* (Ajmer: Matba'a Printing Company, 1892).

69. For a study of one such Arabic text from the 1880s see R. Peters, 'Religious Attitudes towards Modernization in the Ottoman Empire: A Nineteenth Century Pious Text on Steamships, Factories and the Telegraph', *Die Welt des Islams* 26, 1–4 (1986).

70. Chakrabarty, *Rethinking Working-Class History*, pp. 89–90.

71. I have borrowed this phrase from Gell, 'The Technology of Enchantment'. However, see also A. Salvatore (ed.), *Muslim Traditions and Modern Techniques of Power* (Piscataway, NJ: Transaction Publishers, 2001).

72. Sidi Ali Reïs, *The Travels and Adventures of the Turkish Admiral Sidi Ali Reïs*, trans. A. Vambéry (London: Luzac, 1899), pp. 33, 84–5, 91.

73. Sayyid Ibrāhīm al-Hussayni al-Madanī, *Zamīr al-insān* (1292/1875).

74. Ibid., pp. 9–10 and 5–7, 16–22 respectively.
75. Ibid., pp. 20–2.
76. Mohammad Abdullah Mama Paro Qaisary, *The Life History of Hazrat Shaikh Makhdum Ali Paro* (Mumbai: Ghazali Typesetters, 1999), pp. 25–32.
77. Tschacher, 'From Local Practice to Transnational Network'.
78. D. Aubrey, *Letters from Bombay* (London: Remington & Co., 1884), p. 54.
79. J. F. Keane, *Six Months in the Hejaz; Being Keane's Journeys to Meccah and Medinah* (London: Ward & Downey, 1887), p. 278.
80. The reports on Bābā Jān appeared in the *Times of India* (Poona edition) on 4 and 7 September 1926. On Bābā Jān and Banē Miyān's links to the colonial soldiery see N. S. Green, *Islam and the Army in Colonial India: Sepoy Religion in the Service of Empire* (Cambridge: Cambridge University Press, 2009).
81. Muhammad Ismā'īl Khān, *A'zam al-karāmāt* (Aurangabad: Mu'īn Prēs, n.d. [c. 1921]), p. 34.
82. Ibid., pp. 70–1.
83. Low, 'Empire and the Hajj', p. 270.
84. Khān, *A'zam al-karāmāt*, pp. 72–3.
85. Interview, Seyyid Quddus, shrine of Banē Miyān, 12 December 1999.
86. Hempton, *Methodism*, chap. 3; S. O'Brien, 'A Transatlantic Community of Saints: The Great Awakening and the First Evangelical Network, 1735–1755', *American Historical Review* 91, 4 (1986); Thompson, *English Working Class*, pp. 365–6.
87. On the *hajj* and disease circulation see Low, 'Empire and the Hajj'.
88. Shaykh Dā'ūd bin Sulaymān, *Riyāz-e ṣūfī*, p. 11.
89. Aubin (ed.), *Matériaux*, Persian text, p. 168.
90. Anonymous, *Majmū'a: Hālāt-e hazrat Shāh Wajīh al-dīn 'Alawī Gujarātī* (Bombay: Matba'a-ye Shihābī, n.d.), pp. 12–15.
91. Sayyid Yahyā ibn Sayyid Husayn, *Nasabnāma-ye Shāh Wajīh al-dīn*, Asiatic Society, Bombay, MS Persian 15. I have suggested this date based on the paper and dates of the surrounding manuscripts in the same volume. Rashīd al-dīn ibn Ahmad Chishtī, *Mukhbir al-awliyā*, Asiatic Society, Bombay, MS Persian 14, fos. 70v–77v. On the long-term importance of Arab descent lineages in the Indian Ocean see E. Ho, *The Graves of Tarim: Genealogy and Mobility across the Indian Ocean* (Berkeley: University of California Press, 2006), esp. chap. 6.
92. Anonymous, *The Gadi of Mangrol and Maulana Pir Mota Miya Saheb III alias Khwaja Syed Matauddin, being a Brief Description of the Biggest Chishtiya Gadi in the Bombay Presidency and a Small Account of the Life of the Present Sajjada Nashin* (Bombay: n.p., 1922).
93. On the Kharva see R. E. Enthoven, *The Tribes and Castes of Bombay* (Bombay: Asian Educational Services, 1990), pp. 221–2.
94. Anonymous, *The Gadi of Mangrol*, p. 17.
95. Nā'ib al-Sadr Shīrāzī, *Tarā'iq al-haqā'iq*, 3 vols. (Tehran: Kitābkhāna-ye Baranī, 1339–45/1960–6), vol. III, p. 564. Interestingly, the text borrows the English term as *mārkēt*.

96. J. Page, *Captain Allen Gardiner, Sailor and Saint* (London: S. W. Partridge & Co., n.d. [1897]).

97. Mīr Lā'iq 'Alī Khān 'Imād al-Saltana [Sālār Jang II], *Safarnāma-ye 'Imād al-Saltana bih Urūpā* (Tehran: Nashr-e Pāband, 1383/2005), pp. 44, 52.

98. Ibid., p. 54.

99. Ibid., pp. 56–7.

100. I. K. Poonawala, *Biobibliography of Ismā'īlī Literature* (Malibu: Undena Publications, 1977), pp. 226–8.

101. Bose, *A Hundred Horizons*, pp. 195–202.

102. Ibid., p. 196.

4. Exports for an Iranian Marketplace

1. For a notable exception see J. R. I. Cole, 'Mirror of the World: Iranian "Orientalism" and Early 19th-Century India', *Critique: Journal of Critical Studies of Iran and the Middle East* (1996).

2. On diplomatic and economic relations see R. Greaves, 'Iranian Relations with Great Britain and British India, 1798–1921', in P. Avery, G. Hambly and C. Melville (eds.), *The Cambridge History of Iran*, vol. VII: *From Nadir Shah to the Islamic Republic* (Cambridge: Cambridge University Press, 1991); and G. G. Gilbar, 'The Opening Up of Qājār Iran: Some Economic and Social Aspects', *Bulletin of the School of Oriental and African Studies* 49, 1 (1986). Documents on Indo-Iranian connections from this period are collated in Ahmad Jalālī Farāhānī (ed.), *Asnādi az rawābit-e Īrān wa Hind dar dawra-ye Muzaffar al-Dīn Shāh Qājār* (Tehran: Daftar-e Mutāla'āt-e Siyāsī wa Bayn al-Milalī, 1997).

3. Ghulām Husayn Mīrzā Sālih (ed.), *Tārīkh-e sifārat-e Hājjī Khalīl Khān wa Muhammad Nabī Khān bih Hindūstān* (Tehran: Kavīr, 1379/2000). The original edition was printed in Bombay in 1886.

4. Cf. W. G. Clarence-Smith, 'Middle-Eastern Entrepreneurs in Southeast Asia, *c.* 1750–*c.* 1940', in I. Baghdiantz, G. Harlaftis and I. P Minoglou (eds.), *Diaspora Entrepreneurial Networks: Four Centuries of History* (London: Berg, 2004).

5. C. Markovits, *The Global World of Indian Merchants, 1750–1947* (Cambridge: Cambridge University Press, 2000).

6. M. Mohiuddin and I. K. Poonawala, 'Bombay: Persian Muslim Communities', E. Yarshater (ed.), *Encyclopaedia Iranica* (New York: Biblioteca Persica Press, 2009).

7. *Bombay Almanac and Directory for 1865* (Bombay: Bombay Gazette Press, 1865), p. 563.

8. J. R. Hinnells, 'The Flowering of Zoroastrian Benevolence: Parsi Charities in the 19th and 20th Centuries', *Acta Iranica*, series 2, 10 (1985); J. R. Hinnells, 'Parsis and British Education, 1820–1880', in J. R. Hinnells, *Zoroastrian and Parsi Studies* (Aldershot: Ashgate, 2000).

9. J. R. Hinnells, 'Changing Perceptions of Authority among Parsis in British India', in J. R. Hinnells and A. V. Williams (eds.), *Parsis in India and the Diaspora* (London: Routledge, 2007).

10. Hinnells, 'The Flowering of Zoroastrian Benevolence'.

11. M. Sharafi, 'Judging Conversion to Zoroastrianism: Behind the Scenes of the Parsi Panchayat Case (1908)', in Hinnells and Williams (eds.), *Parsis in India and the Diaspora*.

12. Boyce, 'Manekji Limji Hataria in Iran'; N. S. Green, 'The Survival of Zoroastrianism in Yazd', *Iran: Journal of Persian Studies* 38 (2000).

13. Husein of Hamadán, *The Tarikh-i-jadid: or New history of Mirza Ali Muhammad the Bab*, trans. E. G. Browne (Cambridge: The University Press, 1893), pp. xxxvii–xxxviii, footnote.

14. Ringer, 'Reform Transplanted', pp. 553–5.

15. Ibid., p. 554.

16. Ibid., p. 556.

17. Ibid., pp. 557–8.

18. Husein of Hamadán, *The Tarikh-i-jadid*, pp. 245–6.

19. S. Manuchehri, 'Historical Accounts of two Indian Babis: Sa'in Hindi and Sayyid Basir Hindi', *Research Notes in Shaykhi, Babi and Baha'i Studies* 5, 2 (2001).

20. M. Momen, 'Jamāl Effendi and the Early Spread of the Bahā'ī Faith in Asia', in J. Danesh and S. Fazel (eds.), *Search for Values: Ethics in Bahá'í Thought* (Los Angeles: Kalimat Press, 2004), pp. 162–3.

21. Ibid., p. 163.

22. J. R. I. Cole, *Modernity and the Millennium: The Genesis of the Baha'i Faith in the Nineteenth Century* (New York: Columbia University Press, 1998), pp. 41, 61–5, 81–2; Momen, 'Jamāl Effendi'.

23. C. Buck, 'The *Kitab-i iqan*: An Introduction to Baha'u'llah's Book of Certitude with Two Digital Reprints of Early Lithographs', *Occasional Papers in Shaykhi, Babi and Baha'i Studies* 2, 5 (1998); D. MacEoin, 'From Babism to Baha'ism: Problems of Militancy, Quietism and Conflation in the Construction of a Religion', *Religion* 13 (1983), footnotes 16 and 35.

24. Buck, 'The *Kitab-i iqan*'. On the censor (*sansūr*) system see P. Avery, 'Printing, the Press and Literature in Modern Iran', in Avery et al. (eds.), *From Nadir Shah to the Islamic Republic*, p. 828.

25. Momen, 'Jamāl Effendī', p. 163.

26. J. R. I. Cole, "Abdu'l-Baha's "Treatise on Leadership": Text, Translation, Commentary', *Translations in Shaykhi, Babi and Baha'i Texts* 2, 2 (1998).

27. On other Iranian proponents of the division of secular and religious authority in this period see Cole, *Modernity and the Millennium*, pp. 25–35; and M. Momen, 'The Baha'is and the Constitutional Revolution: The Case of Sari, Mazandaran, 1906–1913', *Iranian Studies* 41, 3 (2008).

28. N. M. Parveez, 'Indo-British Trade with Persia', *Imperial and Asiatic Quarterly Review*, 3rd series, 23 (1907).

29. J. G. Paterson, *From Bombay through Babylonia* (Glasgow: David Bryce & Son, n.d.), pp. 24–5.

30. For Hindu parallels see P. van der Veer, 'The Sacred as a Profession', in van der Veer, *Gods on Earth*, pp. 183–267.

31. For a comparative description of Bombay and Bushire during this period see Shepherd, *From Bombay to Bushire*, esp. pp. 123–63.

32. Nā'ib al-Sadr Shīrāzī, *Tarā'iq al-haqā'iq*, vol. III, pp. 117, 328, 373, 399, 434, 438–9, 464–6, 471, 510.
33. Ho, *The Graves of Tarim*.
34. S. Mahdavi, *For God, Mammon and Country: A Nineteenth Century Persian Merchant* (Boulder: Westview Press, 1999), pp. 48–51.
35. Sultān Muhammad Sayf al-Dawla, *Safarnāma-ye Makka*, ed. A. A. Khudāparast (Tehran: Nashr-e Nayy, 1363/1985); Mirza Husayn Farahani, *A Shi'ite Pilgrimage to Mecca (1885–1886): The Safarnāmeh of Mirzā Mohammad Hosayn Farāhāni*, ed. and trans. M. Gulzar and E. L. Daniel (Austin: University of Texas Press, 1990), p. 161.
36. Nā'ib al-Sadr Shīrāzī, *Tuhfat al-Harāmayn: Safarnāma-ye Nā'ib al-Sadr Shīrāzī dar ziyārat-e Makka wa siyāhat-e Īrān* (Tehran: Bābak, 1361/1983). The original edition was published by Bombay's 'Alawī Press in 1306/1899.
37. Ibid., p. 232.
38. Ibid., pp. 282–3.
39. Ibid., pp. 285–90.
40. Ibid., pp. 283–5, my translation.
41. Nā'ib al-Sadr Shīrāzī, *Tarā'iq al-haqā'iq*, vol. III, pp. 530–3.
42. 'Ali Mazharī, 'Hājjī Pīrzāda: Darwīsh-e Safi-zamīr', *Sūfī: Faslnāma-ye Khānaqāh-e Ni'matullāhī* 36 (1376/1997), pp. 7–16; A. Vanzan, 'Hājjī Pirzāda', in E. Yarshater (ed.), *Encyclopaedia Iranica* (New York: Biblioteca Persica Press, 2009).
43. Hājjī Muhammad 'Ali Pīrzāda, *Safarnāma-ye Hājjī Pīrzāda*, ed. Hāfiz Farmānfarmā'iyān, 2 vols. (Tehran: Dānishgāh-e Tihrān, 1342–3/1963–5), vol. I, pp. 126–8, 138. The ice factory had been founded forty years earlier, in 1843.
44. Ibid., pp. 120–42.
45. Ibid., pp. 135–6.
46. Ibid., pp. 120–2.
47. Ibid., p. 123.
48. Committee of the District Benevolent Society, 'The Native Poor of Bombay', p. 263.
49. Homāyūnī, *Tārīkh-e silsilahā*, p. 263.
50. Committee of the District Benevolent Society, 'The Native Poor of Bombay', p. 265.
51. Nāsir al-dīn Shāh, *The Diary of HM the Shah of Persia During his Tour Through Europe in AD 1873*, trans. J. W. Redhouse (Costa Mesa: Mazda, 1995).
52. E. de Jong-Keesing, *Inayat Khan: A Biography* (London and The Hague: East–West Publications, 1974), pp. 44–5.
53. Hājjī Muhammad 'Alī Pīrzāda, *Safarnāma*, vol. I, p. 124.
54. Ibid., p. 126.
55. Ibid. The word used here for factory was the *kār-khāna* familiar (and so implicitly comparable) to the traditional pre-industrial workshops still in use in Iran.
56. Hājjī Muhammad 'Alī Pīrzāda, *Safarnāma*, vol. I, pp. 124–5.
57. Ibid., p. 126.

58. Nā'ib al-Sadr Shīrāzī, *Tarā'iq al-haqā'iq*, vol. III, pp. 530–1.
59. On the religious symbolism of water in Islam see M. Lings, 'The Qoranic Symbolism of Water', *Studies in Comparative Religion* 2, 3 (1968).
60. Hājjī Muhammad 'Alī Pīrzāda, *Safarnāma*, vol. I, p. 128. For an overview of early modern Indo-Persian travellers see M. Alam and S. Subrahmanyam, *Indo-Persian Travels in the Age of Discoveries, 1400–1800* (Cambridge: Cambridge University Press, 2007). On earlier understanding of India's religions see Y. Friedmann, 'Medieval Muslim Views on Indian Religions', *Journal of the American Oriental Society* 95 (1975); and V. Minorsky, 'Gardīzī on India', in V. Minorsky, *Iranica: Twenty Articles* (Tehran: University of Tehran, 1964).
61. Hājjī Muhammad 'Alī Pīrzāda, *Safarnāma*, vol. I, pp. 129–30.
62. N. Gooptu, *The Politics of the Urban Poor in Early Twentieth-Century India* (Cambridge: Cambridge University Press, 2001).
63. Hājjī Muhammad 'Alī Pīrzāda, *Safarnāma*, vol. I, p. 131. Sassoon's death in Poona was widely reported in the Bombay press: see e.g. *Bombay Gazette*, 16 November 1864, p. 2: 'a prince and a great man has fallen'. On his career see S. Jackson, *The Sassoons* (London: Heinemann, 1968).
64. S. S. Reese, 'The Adventures of Abu Harith: Muslim Travel Writing and Navigating Modernity in Colonial East Africa', in S. S. Reese (ed.), *The Transmission of Learning in Islamic Africa* (Leiden: Brill, 2004).
65. For modern accounts of Safī 'Alī Shāh see 'A. K. Barq, *Justujū dar Ahwāl wa āsār-e Safī 'Alī Shāh* (Tehran: Intishārāt-e Ibn Sīnā, 1352/1973); N. Chahārdihī, *Sayrī dar Tasawwuf* (Tehran: Intishārāt-e 'Ishrāqī, 1361/1982), pp. 141–83; and Homāyūnī, *Tārīkh-e silsilahā*, pp. 243–334. However, see also R. Gramlich, *Die Schütischen Derwischorden Persiens*, 2 vols. (Wiesbaden: Franz Steiner, 1965), vol. I, pp. 61–4 and L. Lewisohn, 'An Introduction to the History of Modern Persian Sufism, Part I: the Ni'matullāhī Order: Persecution, Revival and Schism', *Bulletin of the School of Oriental and African Studies* 61, 3 (1998), pp. 453–6.
66. On merchant life in Qajar Iran see W. Floor, 'The Merchants (*tujjār*) in Qajar Iran', *Zeitschrift der Deutsche Morgenlandische Gesellschaft* 126 (1976); A. K. S. Lambton, 'The Case of Hāji 'Abd al-Karīm: A Study of the Role of Merchants in Mid-Nineteenth Century Iran', in C. E. Bosworth (ed.), *Iran and Islam: In Memory of the Late Vladimir Minorsky* (Edinburgh: Edinburgh University Press, 1971); and Mahdavi, *For God, Mammon and Country*.
67. Homāyūnī, *Tārīkh-e silsilahā*, p. 260. On the use of *barāt*s see Mahdavi, *For God, Mammon and Country*, pp. 41–3.
68. A. Amanat (ed.), *Cities and Trade: Consul Abbot on the Economy and Society of Iran, 1847–1866* (London: Ithaca Press, 1983), pp. 79–82 and 131–6.
69. Ibid.; Mahdavi, *For God, Mammon and Country*. On Bombay's centrality to the opium trade see A. Farooqui, 'Bombay and the Trade in Malwa Opium', in Farooqui, *Opium City*.
70. F. Daftary, *The Isma'ilis: Their History and Doctrines* (Cambridge: Cambridge University Press, 1992), p. 517.
71. For example, Nā'ib al-Sadr Shīrāzī dates one journey as occurring in 1289/1872. See Nā'ib al-Sadr Shīrāzī, *Tarā'iq al-haqā'iq*, vol. III, p. 445.

72. Searight, *Steaming East*, chap. 2.
73. *Bombay Gazette* newspaper, 6 and 16 July 1864.
74. Smith, *The Life of John Wilson*, pp. 126–7.
75. On the journey see Paterson, *From Bombay through Babylonia*, pp. 17–34.
76. Nā'ib al-Sadr Shīrāzī, *Tarā'iq al-haqā'iq*, vol. III, p. 445.
77. Ibid.
78. Homāyūnī, *Tārīkh-e silsilahā*, pp. 246–74. On Shams al-'Urafā see Nā'ib al-Sadr Shīrāzī, *Tarā'iq al-haqā'iq*, vol. III, pp. 452–4. Āghā Rizā Huzūr 'Alī Shams al-'Urafā is not to be confused with Sayyid Husayn-e Husaynī Shams al-'Urafā (d. 1353/1935).
79. *Sharaf*, issue 84 (1308/1890–1), republished in *Dawra-ye rūznāmahāī-ye sharaf wa sharāfat* (Tehran: Intishārāt-e Yasawolī Farhangsarā, n.d.). A number of years later a lightly edited version of this account was included and expanded upon by Nā'ib al-Sadr Shīrāzī (d. 1344/1926) in the Ni'matullāhī history *Tarā'iq al-haqā'iq*: see vol. III, pp. 441–7. This account has formed the basis of most subsequent summaries of Safi's life found in modern Persian and European-language works.
80. Nā'ib al-Sadr Shīrāzī, *Tarā'iq al-haqā'iq*, vol. III, pp. 441–5.
81. J. Aubin, 'De Kubahan à Bidar: la famille Ni'matullahī', *Studia Iranica* 20, 2 (1991); and W. R. Royce, 'Mir Ma'sum 'Ali Shah and the Ni'mat Allahi Revival, 1776–77 to 1796–97' (Ph.D. thesis, Princeton University, 1979).
82. N. Pourjavady and P. Lamborn-Wilson, 'The Descendants of Shāh Ni'matullāh Walī', *Islamic Culture* 48, 1 (1974). For a seventeenth-century Persian account of Khalīlullāh and his sons see J. Aubin (ed.), *Matériaux pour la biographie de Shâh Ni'matullah Walî Kermânî* (Tehran: Département d'Iranologie de l'Institut Francoiranien, 1956), Persian text, pp. 199–208.
83. Royce, 'Mir Ma'sum 'Ali Shah'.
84. *Sharaf*, issue 84 (1308/1890–1), republished in *Dawra-ye rūznāmahāī-ye sharaf wa sharāfat* and Nā'ib al-Sadr Shīrāzī, *Tarā'iq al-haqā'iq*, vol. III, p. 442.
85. P. M. Sykes, *Ten Thousand Miles in Persia, or Eight Years in Iran* (London: John Murray, 1902), p. 149.
86. Nā'ib al-Sadr Shīrāzī, *Tarā'iq al-haqā'iq*, vol. III, pp. 509–10.
87. Homāyūnī, *Tārīkh-e silsilahā*, p. 248.
88. 'Shipping Arrivals (1864)', in *Bombay Almanac and Directory for 1865* (Bombay: Bombay Gazette Press, 1865), p. 591.
89. Homāyūnī, *Tārīkh-e silsilahā*, pp. 250–3.
90. I have relied on the Persian inscription inside the mosque for this data, though a more recent inscription outside the entrance gives the date of 1276/1859–60. See also the note in Anonymous [Edwardes], *Gazetteer of Bombay City and Island*, vol. III, p. 311.
91. Committee of the District Benevolent Society, 'The Native Poor of Bombay', p. 265.
92. Homāyūnī, *Tārīkh-e silsilahā*, p. 254.
93. Ibid., pp. 263–4.
94. Nā'ib al-Sadr Shīrāzī, *Tarā'iq al-haqā'iq*, vol. III, pp. 511–12.
95. Ibid., p. 528.

96. Maulana Shah Syed Waris Hassan, *A Guide for Spiritual Aspirants* [*Shamāmat al-ambar*] (Kuala Lumpur: A. S. Noordeen, 2001), pp. 34–5.
97. Mīr Lā'īq 'Alī Khān 'Imād al-Saltana, *Safarnāma*, p. 65.
98. On this and Safi's three other supernatural *yogi* anecdotes see Homāyūnī, *Tārīkh-e silsilahā*, pp. 257–8, 258–64, 270.
99. On these Bombay *masnawīs* see Arberry, *Catalogue*, pp. 301–3.
100. J. R. I. Cole, 'The Provincial Politics of Heresy and Reform in Qajar Iran: Shaykh al-Rais in Shiraz, 1895–1902', *Comparative Studies of South Asia, Africa and the Middle East* 22, 1–2 (2002), p. 120.
101. Nā'ib al-Sadr Shīrāzī, *Tarā'iq al-haqā'iq*, vol. III, p. 445.
102. Safi 'Alī Shāh, *Zubdat al-asrār* (Tehran: Intishārāt-e Safi 'Alī Shāh, 1379s/2000).
103. V. Braginsky, 'Sufi Boat Symbolism: Problems of Origin and Evolution', *Indonesia and the Malay World* 26, 74 (1998); V. Braginsky, *And Sails the Boat Downstream: Malay Sufi Poems of the Boat* (Leiden: Publicaties van Semaian, 2007).
104. Homāyūnī, *Tārīkh-e silsilahā*, p. 244.
105. On Persian publishing in India during this period see Scheglova, 'Lithograph Versions of Persian Manuscripts'.
106. Nā'ib al-Sadr Shīrāzī, *Tarā'iq al-haqā'iq*, vol. III, p. 373.
107. Mohiuddin and Poonawala, 'Bombay: Persian Muslim Communities'.
108. J. M. Scarce, 'Bandar-e Tahiri: A Late Outpost of the Shahnama', in R. Hillenbrand (ed.), *Shahnama: The Visual Language of the Persian Book of Kings* (Aldershot: Ashgate, 2004), esp. p. 149, with reference to an 1849 Bombay *Shāhnāma* illustrated by one 'Alī Akbar.
109. Nā'ib al-Sadr Shīrāzī, *Tarā'iq al-haqā'iq*, vol. III, p. 516.
110. Keddie, *Sayyid Jamāl ad-Dīn 'al-Afghānī'*, esp. pp. 22–32; J. R. I. Cole, 'New Perspectives on Sayyid Jamal al-Din al-Afghani in Egypt', in R. Matthee and B. Baron (eds.), *Iran and Beyond: Essays in Middle Eastern History in Honor of Nikki R. Keddie* (Costa Mesa: Mazda, 2000). It has even been claimed, albeit without supporting evidence, that al-Afghānī was himself a pupil of Safi. See Chahārdihī, *Sayrī dar tasawwuf*, p. 163.
111. The book was later translated into Arabic by Muhammad 'Abduh and published in 1886 in Beirut under its better-known title of *al-Radd 'ala al-dhahriyyīn* (The refutation of the materialists).
112. The Persian text has been republished in Aubin (ed.), *Matériaux*, pp. 133–268.
113. Ibid., introduction, p. 7.
114. Ibid., Persian text, pp. 148, 169–71.
115. Ibid., Persian text, pp. 140–3.
116. Ibid., Persian text, p. 141.
117. Ibid., Persian text, pp. 148–50.
118. Ibid., Persian text, p. 168.
119. Ibid., Persian text, pp. 152–3.
120. Ibid., Persian text, pp. 157–8.
121. Ibid., Persian text, pp. 154–5.

5. The Making of a Neo-Ismāʿilism

1. N. J. Dumasia, *The Aga Khan and his Ancestors* (Bombay: Times of India Press, 1939).
2. See W. Ivanow, 'The Tombs of Some Persian Ismaili Imams', *Journal of the Bombay Branch of the Asiatic Society* NS, 14 (1938), p. 49.
3. Daftary, *The Ismaʿilis*, pp. 501–18.
4. A. S. Picklay, *The History of the Ismailis* (Bombay: Popular Printing Press, 1940), p. 80.
5. For 'exceptionally rare' evidence for contact between the imams in Iran and followers in India in the eighteenth century see Ivanow, 'The Tombs of Some Persian Ismaili Imams', pp. 57–8.
6. H. Algar, 'The Revolt of the Āghā Khān Mahallātī and the Transference of the Ismāʿīlī Imamate to India', *Studia Islamica* 29 (1969), pp. 43–69.
7. Lewisohn, 'An Introduction to the History of Modern Persian Sufism, Part I', p. 444; N. Pourjavady and P. Lamborn-Wilson, *Kings of Love: The Poetry and History of the Niʿmatullahi Sufi Order* (Tehran: The Imperial Iranian Academy of Philosophy, 1978).
8. Lewisohn, 'An Introduction to the History of Modern Persian Sufism, Part I', p. 448.
9. Nāʾib al-Sadr Shīrāzī, *Tarāʾiq al-haqāʾiq*, vol. III, p. 434.
10. Cole, 'The Provincial Politics of Heresy', pp. 119–20.
11. Momen, 'Jamāl Effendi'.
12. On Muharram celebrations in colonial Bombay see Masselos, 'Change and Custom'.
13. H. M. Amiji, 'Some Notes on Religious Dissent in Nineteenth-Century East Africa', *African Historical Studies* 4, 3 (1971); M. Boivin, *Les Ismaéliens: des communautés d'Asie du sud entre islamisation et indianisation* (Turnhout: Brepols, 1998).
14. Dumasia, *The Aga Khan and his Ancestors*, p. 61; Z. Noorally, 'The First Agha Khan and the British' (MA thesis, University of London, 1964).
15. Muhammad ibn Zayn al-ʿĀbidīn Khurāsānī Fidāʾī, *Kitāb-e tārīkh-e ismāʿīliyya, yā Hidāyat al-muʾminīn al-tālibīn*, ed. Aliksāndir Sīmiūnūf (Tehran: Intishārāt-e Asātīr, 1362/1983), pp. 173–4.
16. Ibid., p. 173.
17. Interview, shrine attendant, Mazagaon, 27.5.09.
18. Daftary, *The Ismaʿilis*, p. 507.
19. Even in 1940 the shrine was still recorded as 'being visited to this day by thousands of Ismailis'. See Picklay, *The History of the Ismailis*, p. 82.
20. Masselos, 'The Khojas of Bombay'; A. Shodhan, *A Question of Community: Religious Groups and Colonial Law* (Calcutta: Samya, 2001), pp. 85–7, 92–3.
21. Shodhan, *A Question of Community*, p. 86.
22. Muhammad Hasan al-Husaynī [Āghā Khān I], *ʿIbrat-afzā* (Bombay: n.p., 1278/1862).
23. Picklay, *The History of the Ismailis*, p. 84.
24. An alternative date of December 1884 is occasionally cited for Shihāb al-dīn's death.

25. Shihabu'd-Din Shah al-Husayni, *The True Meaning of Religion or Risala dar haqiqati din*, Persian text with English trans. W. Ivanow (Bombay: Islamic Research Association, 1933).

26. As Ivanow delicately phrased the matter in his preface, 'the author did not give up the Sufic form, or tone, of his speculations'. See ibid., p. ii.

27. Ibid., pp. 7–8 (translation), p. 12 (Persian text).

28. Ibid., p. 9 (translation), p. 15 (Persian text).

29. Ibid., p. 11 (translation), p. 18 (Persian text).

30. Ibid., p. 26 (translation), p. 36 (Persian text).

31. N. S. Green, 'Mirza Hasan Safi 'Ali Shah: A Persian Sufi in the Age of Printing', in L. Ridgeon (ed.), *Religion and Politics in Modern Iran* (London: I. B. Tauris, 2005).

32. On Fidā'ī's biography see F. Daftary, *A Short History of the Ismailis: Traditions of a Muslim Community* (Edinburgh: Edinburgh University Press, 1998), pp. 203–4; and F. M. Hunzai, *Shimmering Light: An Anthology of Isma'ili Poems* (London: Institute of Ismaili Studies/I. B.Tauris, 1997), p. 117.

33. Daftary, *A Short History of the Ismailis*, p. 204.

34. Fidā'ī, *Kitāb-e tārīkh-e ismā'īliyya*. The colophon on p. 199 records the date of the text's completion as 1328/1910.

35. Ibid., pp. 24–5, 77–80, 82–9, 57 *et passim*.

36. For an anthology and study of the writings of Āghā Khān III see M. Boivin, *La rénovation du Shîisme ismaélien en Inde et au Pakistan: d'après les écrits et les discours de Sultan Muhammad Shah Aga Khan (1902–1954)* (London: RoutledgeCurzon, 2003).

37. The terms are used repeatedly in the text, e.g. Fidā'ī, *Kitāb-e tārīkh-e ismā'īliyya*, pp. 152–5.

38. Ibid., pp. 151–4, 156–62. Cf. Hardiman, 'Purifying the Nation'.

39. Fidā'ī, *Kitāb-e tārīkh-e ismā'īliyya*, pp. 163–5.

40. Ibid., p. 163.

41. For the imam's love of hunting, and earlier no less miraculous hunting stories based around Mahallat in Iran, see ibid., pp. 152–4.

42. Given the location, the particular species of gazelle in question was probably the chinkara (*gazella bennettii*).

43. Ibid., p. 164.

44. Ibid., pp. 161–2.

45. Ibid., p. 162.

46. Hunzai, *Shimmering Light*, p. 119.

47. al-Husayni, *Risala dar haqiqati din*, p. 19 (translation), p. 27 (Persian text).

48. Ibid., p. 17 (translation), p. 25 (Persian text).

49. Ibid., p. 23 (translation), p. 32 (Persian text).

50. Ibid., *passim*, and esp. p. 23 (translation), p. 32 (Persian text).

51. Ibid., pp. 16–17 (translation), pp. 24–5 (Persian text).

52. On the final move to Europe after 1907 see Daftary, *The Isma'ilis*, p. 520. Cf. Jackson, *The Sassoons*.

53. Daftary, *The Isma'ilis*, p. 515; Shodhan, *A Question of Community*, p. 92.

54. Albuquerque, *Urbs Prima in Indis*, pp. 48–9. On the Reformist activities of this new *shethiyya* 'intelligentsia' see Dobbin, *Urban Leadership in Western India*, pp. 153–85.
55. Daftary, *The Isma'ilis*, pp. 514–16, Shodhan, *A Question of Community*, pp. 85–7, 92–3.
56. Shodhan, *A Question of Community*, p. 87.
57. Daftary, *The Isma'ilis*, p. 515.
58. On the context of the case see Dobbin, *Urban Leadership in Western India*, pp. 112–21.
59. Shamrao Moroji Nayak, *A History of the Pattana Prabhus*, esp. pp. 93–115. Thanks to Rosalind O'Hanlon for drawing this to my attention.
60. Algar, The Revolt of the Āghā Khān Mahallātī, pp. 43–69.
61. Hājjī Salāh al-dīn Ārā'ī, *Risālat al-tarjamat al-zāhira li firqatī bohrat al-bāhira*, Asiatic Society, Bombay, MS Arabic 4. The date of composition is recorded in the colophon (fo. 13v.)
62. Ibid., fo. 2r.
63. Ibid., fos. 2v, 3r.
64. Ibid., fo. 3v.
65. Ibid., fo. 4r.
66. Ibid., fo. 4r.
67. Ibid., fos. 4v–5r.
68. Ibid., fo. 5r.
69. Ibid., fo. 5v.
70. Ibid., fos. 5v–8r.
71. Ibid., fos. 9r–10r.
72. Ibid., fo. 10v.
73. Ibid., fos. 11v–13r.
74. Ibid., fos. 13r–13v.
75. Poonawala, *Biobibliography of Ismā'īlī Literature*, p. 229.
76. A. A. Engineer, *The Bohras* (Delhi: Vikas Publishing House, 1993), chap. 6.
77. Ibid., pp. 169–70.
78. Ibid., p. 137.

6. A Theology for the Mills and Dockyards

1. Chandavarkar, *The Origins of Industrial Capitalism in India*, chaps. 5 and 6.
2. Chakrabarty, *Rethinking Working-Class History*; Gooptu, *The Politics of the Urban Poor*.
3. R. D. Choksey, *Economic History of the Bombay Deccan and Karnatak (1818–1868)* (Poona: R. D. Choksey, 1945); V. V. Gupchup, *Bombay: Social Change, 1813–1857* (Bombay: Popular Book Depot, 1993).
4. J. Masselos, 'Migration and Urban Identity: Bombay's Famine Refugees in the Nineteenth Century', in S. Patel and A. Thorner (eds.), *Bombay: Mosaic of Modern Culture* (Delhi: Oxford University Press, 1995).

5. Chandavarkar, *The Origins of Industrial Capitalism in India*, pp. 140–4.
6. Rustom Pestanji Jehangir, *Short History of the Lives of Bombay Opium Smokers* (Bombay: J. B. Marzban & Co.'s Steam Printing Works, 1893), pp. 11, 19, 22, 24, 26, 28. The socio-economic milieu of a migrant Muslim butcher is reconstructed in A. Siddiqi, 'Ayesha's World: A Butcher's Family in Nineteenth-Century Bombay', *Comparative Studies in Society and History* 43, 1 (2001).
7. V. K. Bawa, *Hyderabad under Salar Jung I* (Delhi: S. Chand, 1996), pp. 50–1.
8. Mīr Lā'īq 'Alī Khān 'Imād al-Saltana [Sālār Jang II], *Safarnāma*, pp. 50, 54. He appears to have been an exception to the hotel's usual 'whites only' policy.
9. Green, 'Mystical Missionaries in Hyderabad State'.
10. On Konkanis in Bombay see Anonymous [Edwardes], *Gazetteer of Bombay City and Island*, vol. I, pp. 207–8, 254–62. More generally, see Khalidi, 'Konkani Muslims'. On later labour migration see M. S. Gore, *Immigrants and Neighbourhoods: Two Aspects of Life in a Metropolitan City* (Bombay: Tata Institute of Social Sciences, 1970); K. C. Zachariah, *A Historical Study of Internal Migration in the Indian Subcontinent, 1901–1931* (New York: Asia Publishing House, 1964).
11. W. W. Hunter, J. S. Cotton, R. Burn and W. S. Meyer (eds.), *Imperial Gazetteer of India* (Oxford: Clarendon Press, 1908–31), vol. XXI, p. 250.
12. Ibid.
13. M. Dossal Panjwani, 'Godis, Tolis and Mathadis: Dock Workers of Bombay', in S. Davies *et al.* (eds.), *Dock Workers: International Explorations in Comparative Labour History, 1790–1970* (Aldershot: Ashgate, 2000), p. 429.
14. Aubrey, *Letters from Bombay*, p. 270.
15. Mohiuddin, *Muslim Communities*, pp. 232–3, 265–8.
16. For this account of Mazagaon I have relied on Anonymous [Edwardes]. *Gazetteer of Bombay City and Island*, vol. I, p. 43, vol. II, pp. 161–90; and Edwardes, *The Rise of Bombay*.
17. *Bombay Gazette* newspaper, 14 July 1864, p. 2.
18. *Bombay Gazette* newspaper, 26 July 1864, p. 2 and 13 August 1864, p. 2.
19. On the development of Bombay's mills see Kooiman, *Bombay Textile Labour*; and M. D. Morris, *The Emergence of an Industrial Labor Force in India: A Study of the Bombay Cotton Mills, 1854–1947* (Berkeley: California University Press, 1965).
20. On the Konkanis in Bombay see Anonymous [Edwardes], *Gazetteer of Bombay City and Island*, vol. I, pp. 207–8, 254–62. On non-religious aspects of Bombay millworkers' identity see Upadhyay, *Existence, Identity, and Mobilization*.
21. Chakrabarty, *Rethinking Working-Class History*.
22. Cooper, *On the African Waterfront*.
23. Dossal Panjwani, 'Godis, Tolis and Mathadis', pp. 430–3.
24. On the life of Habīb 'Alī Shāh see Hājjī Muhammad Maqbūl, *Manāqib al-habībīn* (Delhi: Jahna Litho-Press, n.d. [c. 1910]); and Sayyid Muhammad

Muhyī al-dīn Habībī Hāfiz, *Zikr-e habīb* (n.p.: n.p., n.d.). I am grateful to Naeem Khan Sabiri of Durban for supplying me with copies of these Urdu texts; he has also translated *Zikr-e habīb* as *Life History of Khwaja Habib Ali Shah* (Durban: Soofie Saheb Badsha Peer Darbar, 1424/2004).

25. Habībī Hāfiz, *Zikr-e habīb*, pp. 8–9; Maqbūl, *Manāqib al-habībīn*, p. 152.
26. Maqbūl, *Manāqib al-habībīn*, pp. 153–6.
27. Interview, Muhammad Hanif Gaya, grandson-in-law of Habīb 'Alī Shāh and manager of the Dockyard Road *khanaqah*, 22 April 2009.
28. Ibid.
29. Wazīr Nawwāb Habībī, untitled MS, pp. 35–7, cited in Anonymous, *Tadhkirat'ul habīb* (Durban: n.p., n.d.), pp. 91–2.
30. I have been unable to gain direct access to this work. The following section relies on the extensive summary of the text provided in Anonymous, *Tadhkirat'ul habīb*, pp. 126–41.
31. *Bombay Gazette* newspaper, 13 October 1864, p. 3.
32. A. Bang, *Sufis and Scholars of the Sea: Family Networks in East Africa c. 1860–1925* (London: RoutledgeCurzon, 2003).
33. Cf. the classic statement in E. P. Thompson, 'Time, Work-Discipline and Industrial Capitalism', *Past and Present* 38 (1967).
34. Habībī Hāfiz, *Zikr-e habīb*, p. 12; Maqbūl, *Manāqib al-habībīn*, p. 172.
35. Mohiuddin, *Muslim Communities*, p. 117. On Sufi money-gathering techniques see also K. K. Aziz, *Religion, Land and Politics in Pakistan: A Study of Piri-Muridi* (Lahore: Vanguard, 2001), pp. 153–5.
36. Anonymous, *The Gadi of Mangrol*.
37. Ibid., p. 14.
38. Ibid.
39. Ibid.
40. Ibid., p. 15.
41. Ibid., pp. 15–16.
42. Ibid., p. 16.
43. Ibid., p. 16.
44. Paterson, *From Bombay through Babylonia*, p. 17.
45. See the listing in Naeem Khan Sabiri, *Life History*, p. 19.
46. Habīb 'Alī Shāh, *Habīb al-awrād*, Urdu trans. Ghulām Khwāja Mu'īn al-dīn Chishtī (Hyderabad: Khwāja Prēs, n.d.).
47. Anonymous, *Modern Hyderabad* (Hyderabad: n.d. [c. 1912]), p. 109.
48. Habīb 'Alī Shāh, *Habīb al-awrād*.
49. Ahmad 'Alī Shāh Chishtī, *Habīb al-in'ām* (n.p.: n.p., n.d. [c. 1910]), pp. 30–1.
50. Ibid., pp. 32–3.
51. Ibid., pp. 36–44.
52. Ibid., p. 46.
53. Ibid., p. 44.
54. Anonymous, *Awrād-e ihsānī* (Bombay: Matba'a-ye Haydarī, 1290/1873).
55. Ibid., p. 8.
56. Ibid., p. 35.
57. Thompson, 'Time, Work-Discipline and Industrial Capitalism'.

58. S. Sarkar, 'Renaissance and Kaliyuga: Time, Myth and History in Colonial Bengal', in Sarkar, *Writing Social History*.
59. Sūfī Sa'ādat 'Alī, *Asrār-e darwēsh mūsūma bih bahr al-ma'rifat* (Muradabad: n.p., 1898).
60. Ibid., pp. 18–27.
61. Ong, *Spirits of Resistance and Capitalist Discipline*.
62. *Bombay Gazette* newspaper, 20 October 1864, p. 2.
63. On the earlier genealogy of *tawassul* and its associated rituals among Naqshbandī Sufis see F. Meier, 'Die Herzensbindung an den Meister', in F. Meier, *Zwei Abhandlungen über die Naqshbandiyya* (Istanbul: Franz Steiner, 1994).
64. Sanyal, *Ahmad Riza Khan Barelwi*, pp. 91–3.
65. Green, *Indian Sufism since the Seventeenth Century*, pp. 92–102.
66. Hābīb 'Alī Shāh, *Habīb al-tālibīn*, Salar Jung Library, Hyderabad, Persian MS Tas. 50, fo. 1r.
67. Ibid., fo. 3r.
68. Ibid., fo. 3v.
69. For a contemporary Reformist discussion see Shaikh Muhammad Naasiruddin al-Albani, *Tawassul: Seeking a Means of Nearness to Allah* (Birmingham: al-Hidaayah, 1417/1996).
70. *The Quran*, Arabic text with English trans. by Muhammad Zafrulla Khan (London: Curzon Press, 1972), 5:36.
71. Hābīb 'Alī Shāh, *Habīb al-tālibīn*, fo. 5v.
72. Hābīb 'Alī Shāh, *Habīb al-barāzikh*, Salar Jung Library, Hyderabad, Persian MS Tas. 49.
73. This doctrine and terminology was also found in the teachings of Jamā'at 'Alī Shāh in Punjab. See A. F. Buehler, *Sufi Heirs of the Prophet: The Indian Naqshbandiyya and the Rise of the Mediating Sufi Shaykh* (Columbia: University of South Carolina Press, 1998), p. 200.
74. Hābīb 'Alī Shāh, *Habīb al-barāzikh*, p. 7.
75. On the spread of *tasawwur-e shaykh* see also Buehler, *Sufi Heirs of the Prophet*.
76. Hābīb 'Alī Shāh, *Habīb al-barāzikh*, p. 9.
77. J. Dewan, 'Sun Pictures from the City of Gold: Early Photography in Bombay', in Rohatgi *et al.* (eds.), *Bombay to Mumbai*, pp. 112–14.
78. A. F. Roberts, 'Mystical Reproductions: Photography and the Authentic Simulacrum', in A. F. Roberts and M. N. Roberts (eds.), *A Saint in the City: Sufi Arts of Urban Senegal* (Los Angeles: Fowler Museum of Cultural History, UCLA, 2003).
79. Reverend Canon H. U. Weitbrecht, 'Reform Movements in India', in Wherry *et al.* (eds.), *Islam and Missions*, p. 281, footnote.
80. P. Centlivres and M. Centlivres-Demont, 'Une étrange rencontre: la photographie orientaliste de Lehnert et Landrock et l'image iranienne du prophète Mahomet', *Études photographiques* 17 (2005).
81. B. D. Metcalf, 'Two Fatwas on Hajj in British India', in M. K. Masud, B. Messick and D. S. Powers (eds.), *Islamic Legal Interpretation: Muftis and their Fatwas* (Cambridge, MA: Harvard University Press, 1996), p. 189.

82. E.g. Maqbūl, *Manāqib al-habībīn*, pp. 154–9, 170–2. Habīb 'Alī's bio-graphical *Manāqib al-habībīn* is replete with uses of this term among his followers.
83. Ibid., pp. 170–2.
84. Ibid., p. 169.
85. Chakrabarty, *Rethinking Working-Class History*.
86. N. S. Green, 'Muslim Bodies and Urban Festivals: Sufis, Workers and Pleasures in Colonial Bombay', in T. Sevea and S. F. Alatas (eds.), *Sufism since the Eighteenth Century: Learning, Debate and Reform in Islam* (Singapore: National University of Singapore Press, forthcoming).
87. Quoted in D. Pinto, *Piri–Muridi Relationship: A Study of the Nizamuddin Dargah* (Delhi: Manohar, 1995), p. 150.
88. Chandavarkar, *The Origins of Industrial Capitalism in India*, pp. 100–9. On jobbers see also Kooiman, *Bombay Textile Labour*, pp. 11–30.
89. Interview, Muhammad Hanif Gaya, grandson-in-law of Habīb 'Alī Shāh and manager of the Dockyard Road *khanaqah*, 22 April 2009.
90. Nā'ib al-Sadr Shīrāzī, *Tarā'iq al-haqā'iq*, vol. III, p. 564.
91. G. Prakash, 'Reproducing Inequality: Spirit Cults and Labor Relations in Colonial East India', *Modern Asian Studies* 20, 2 (1986), p. 216.
92. For my understanding of patronage and the social structure of the mafia I have relied on J. Boissevain, 'Patronage in Sicily', *Man* 1, 1 (1966); and J. Dickie, *Cosa Nostra: A History of the Sicilian Mafia* (London: Hodder & Stoughton, 2004).
93. Lyon, *Anthropological Analysis*, pp. 209–24 and Pinto, *Piri–Muridi Relationship*.
94. Chakrabarty, *Rethinking Working-Class History*, pp. 110–14, 163.
95. Ibid., p. 112.
96. Ibid., p. 114.
97. Ibid., p. 112.

7. Bombay Islam in the Ocean's Southern City

1. On Frere see J. Martineau, *The Life and Correspondence of the Right Hon. Sir Bartle Frere, Bart.* (London: J. Murray, 1895); and Rekha Ranade, *Sir Bartle Frere and his Times: A Study of his Bombay Years, 1862–1867* (Delhi: Mittal Publishing, 1990). On Indian roles in colonial governance see R. G. Gregory, 'Co-operation and Collaboration in Colonial East Africa: The Asians' Political Role, 1890–1964', *African Affairs* 80, 319 (1981).
2. On Gandhi's sea journeys see Bose, *A Hundred Horizons*, pp. 152–70.
3. On the miraculous Gandhi see S. Amin, 'Gandhi as Mahatma: Gorakhpur District, Eastern UP, 1921–2', in R. Guha (ed.), *Writings on South Asian History and Society*, Subaltern Studies 3 (Delhi: Oxford University Press, 1984).
4. J. M. Arnold, *Kind Words and Loving Counsel to the Malays and Other Muslims* (Cape Town: Murray & St Ledger, 1879); J. B. Brain, *Christian Indians in Natal, 1860–1911: An Historical and Statistical Study* (Cape

Town: Oxford University Press, 1983), pp. 193–235; and C. Villa-Vicencio, 'Mission Christianity', in M. Prozesky and J. de Gruchy (eds.), *Living Faiths in South Africa* (New York: St. Martin's Press, 1995).

5. Brain, *Christian Indians in Natal*, p. 198 on Catholic mission schools, pp. 202–4 on Methodist mission schools, pp. 212–15 on Anglican mission schools and p. 223 on Baptist mission schools. Anglican missionaries were relative latecomers among Natal's indentured workforce, only establishing themselves there in 1883 (albeit with the well-funded and influential St Aidan's Mission), several decades after the Catholic and Methodist Churches. More generally, see A. R. Hampson, 'The Mission to Muslims in Cape Town', *The Moslem World* 24, 3 (1934); and W. J. Van der Merwe, 'Missions to Muslims in South Africa', *The Moslem World* 26, 3 (1936).

6. S. M. Zwemer, 'The Moslem Menace in South Africa', *Missionary Review of the World* 37 (1914).

7. The earliest source (in Urdu) on Ghulām Muhammad's life is Shaykh Dā'ūd bin Sulaymān, *Riyāz-e sūfi*. Several modern accounts of Ghulām Muhammad also exist. G. R. Smith, 'A Muslim Saint in South Africa', *African Studies* 28, 4 (1969) consists of a short study based largely on oral testimony collected in Durban during the 1960s. This oral tradition is expanded with documentation from Ghulām Muhammad's shrine by Shah Mohamed Saeid Soofie and Shah Abdul Aziz Soofie, *Hazrath Soofie Saheb & his Khanqahs* (Durban: Soofie Saheb Badsha Peer Darbar, n.d. [*c.* 2002]). I have previously discussed Ghulām Muhammad in N. S. Green, 'Saints, Rebels and Booksellers: Sufis in the Cosmopolitan Western Indian Ocean, *c.* 1850–1920', in K. Kresse and E. Simpson (eds.), *Struggling with History: Islam and Cosmopolitanism in the Western Indian Ocean* (London: Hurst & Co., 2007).

8. For a comparative overview of migration patterns see W. J. Argyle, 'The Migration of Indian Muslims to East and South Africa: Some Preliminary Comparisons', *Purusartha* 9 (1986).

9. A. Shodhan, 'Legal Formulation of the Question of Community: Defining the Khoja Collective', *Indian Social Science Review* 1, 1 (1999).

10. M. Hermansen, 'Common Themes, Uncommon Contexts: The Sufi Movement of Hazrat Inayat Khan (1882–1927) and Khwaja Hasan Nizami (1878–1955)', in P. Z. I. Khan (ed.), *A Pearl in Wine: Essays on the Life, Music and Sufism of Hazrat Inayat Khan* (New Lebanon: Omega Publications, 2001); de Jong-Keesing, *Inayat Khan*, p. 85.

11. D. A. S. Graham, 'Spreading the Wisdom of Sufism: The Career of Pir-o-Murshid Inayat Khan in the West', in Khan (ed.), *A Pearl in Wine*, p. 128.

12. F. R. Bradlow and M. Cairns, *The Early Cape Muslims: A Study of their Mosques, Genealogy and Origins* (Cape Town: A. A. Balkema, 1978); R. C-H. Shell, 'Islam in Southern Africa, 1652–1998', in N. Levtzion and R. L. Pouwels (eds.), *The History of Islam in Africa* (Oxford: James Currey, 2000).

13. A. Davids, *The Mosques of Bo-Kaap: A Social History of Islam at the Cape* (Cape Town: South African Institute of Arabic and Islamic Research, 1980);

and T. Gabriel, *The History of the Tana Baru* (Cape Town: Committee for the Preservation of the Tana Baru, 1985).

14. Davids, *The Mosques of Bo-Kaap.*
15. On Abū Bakr Effendī see Y. da Costa and A. Davids, *Pages from Cape Muslim History* (Pietermaritzburg: Shuter & Shooter, 1994), pp. 81–103; and Davids, *The Mosques of Bo-Kaap*, pp. 53–63.
16. For a reprint and translation respectively see Abū Bakr Effendī, *Abu Bakr se 'Uiteensetting van die Godsdiens': 'n Arabies–Afrikaanse Teks uit die Jaar 1869*, ed. A. Van Selms (Amsterdam: Noord-Hollandsche UM, 1979) trans. as *The Religious Duties of Islam as Taught and Explained by Abu Bakr Effendi: A Translation from the Original Arabic and Afrikaans*, ed. with introd. and notes by M. Brandel-Syrier (Leiden: E. J. Brill, 1960). On the earlier introduction of Roman-script printing to South Africa see A. C. G. Lloyd, 'The Birth of Printing in South Africa', *The Library* series 3, 5 (1914).
17. The literature on Indian migration to South Africa is now extensive. For the most effective overviews see S. Bhana and J. Brain, *Setting Down Roots: Indian Migrants in South Africa, 1860–1911* (Johannesburg: Witwatersrand University Press, 1990); H. Kuper, *Indian People in Natal* (Pietermaritzburg: University of Natal Press, 1960); and F. Meer, *Portrait of Indian South Africans* (Durban: Avon House, 1969). For a more politicized history of Indian labour in South Africa (which was banned under apartheid rule) see S. Marie, *Divide and Profit: Indian Workers in Natal* (Durban: University of Natal, 1986). On Indian Muslims in Natal see Argyle, 'The Migration of Indian Muslims'; S. A. Rochlin, 'Aspects of Islam in Nineteenth-Century South Africa', *Bulletin of the School of Oriental and African Studies* 10 (1940–2); and G. H. Vahed, 'Mosques, Mawlanas and Muharram: Indian Islam in Colonial Natal, 1860–1910', *Journal of Religion in Africa* 31, 3 (2001).
18. R. Ebr.-Vally, 'Migration of an Identity: South Africans of Indian Descent', in P. Gervais-Lambony, F. Landy and S. Oldfield (eds.), *Reconfiguring Identities and Building Territories in India and South Africa* (Delhi: Manohar, 2005), p. 224.
19. Shell, 'Islam in Southern Africa', p. 339.
20. A complete collection of Ships Lists data is preserved in the Documentation Centre, Westville Campus, University of KwaZulu-Natal, Durban. I am grateful to Mr K. Chetty for providing me with access to these and other documents.
21. For an archival survey of Indian mercantile expansion in Durban see K. Hiralal, 'The Natal Indian Trader: A Struggle for Survival, 1875–1910' (MA thesis, University of Durban-Westville, 1991).
22. As in many such individual migrations, it was Abū Bakr's family connections with Gandhi in their mutual home town of Porbandar that facilitated the latter's historic journey. The richest published source on Gandhi's activities in Natal is M. Gandhi, *The South African Gandhi: An Abstract of the Speeches and Writings of M. K. Gandhi, 1893–1914*, ed. F. Meer (Durban: Madiba, 1996). On Abū Bakr himself see G. Vahed, '"A Man of Keen Perceptive

Facilities": Aboobaker Amod Jhaveri, an "Arab" in Colonial Natal, circa 1872–1887', *Historia* 50, 1 (2005).

23. On these trade restrictions see Hiralal, 'The Natal Indian Trader', pp. 338–71.
24. Bhana and Brain, *Setting Down Roots*, p. 45.
25. On this class see V. Padayachee and R. Morrell, 'Indian Merchants and Dukawallahs in the Natal Economy, *c.* 1875–1914', *Journal of Southern African Studies* 17 (1991).
26. Anonymous, *Safarnāma-e Ūgandā wa Mumbāsā* (Lahore: Khādim al-Ta'līm Istīm Prēs, 1904).
27. Ibid., p. 6.
28. Ibid., pp. 6–9.
29. Ibid., pp. 11–12.
30. On the mosques see ibid., pp. 20–1.
31. Meer, *Portrait of Indian South Africans*, p. 189.
32. The complete song in Bhojpuri is cited in R. Mesthrie, 'New Lights from Old Languages: Indian Languages and the Experience of Indentureship in South Africa', in S. Bhana (ed.), *Essays on Indentured Indians in Natal* (Leeds: Peepal Tree, 1988), p. 205.
33. N. S. Green, 'The Dilemmas of the Pious Biographer: Missionary Islam and the Oceanic Hagiography', *Journal of Religious History* 34, 4 (2010).
34. Shaykh Dā'ūd bin Sulaymān, *Riyāz-e sūfi* (repr. 2001), pp. 4–5. Despite this, on the Certificate of Domicile issued to him in 1909 at Port Natal during one of his several sea journeys between India and South Africa, his age was recorded as being forty-six years, suggesting a year of birth around 1863: Colony of Natal, Immigration Restriction Department, Certificate of Domicile No. 4834, issued at Port Natal, 21 December 1909 (facsimile reprinted in Soofie and Soofie, *Hazrath Soofie Saheb*, p. 55).
35. On other Arab mercantile and Sufi interrelations in the west Indian Ocean during this period see Bang, *Sufis and Scholars of the Sea*.
36. G. H. Vahed, '"Unhappily Torn by Dissensions and Litigations": Durban's "Memon" Mosque, 1880–1930', *Journal of Religion in Africa* 36, 1 (2006), p. 35.
37. On the earlier maritime history of this community see R. Chakravarti, 'Merchants of Konkan', *Indian Economic and Social History Review* 23, 2 (1986); and R. Chakravarti, 'Coastal Trade and Voyages in Konkan: The Early Medieval Scenario', *Indian Economic and Social History Review* 35, 2 (1998).
38. Shaykh Dā'ūd bin Sulaymān, *Riyāz-e sūfi* (repr. 2001), p. 8.
39. Reproduced in Soofie and Soofie, *Hazrath Soofie Saheb*, p. 55.
40. 'Immigration Difficulties: Mahomedan Priest Sent Away', *Indian Opinion*, 2 December 1911, p. 453.
41. On the migration and transnationalization of a South Asian Sufi tradition between Pakistan and Britain see P. Werbner, *Pilgrims of Love: The Anthropology of a Global Sufi Cult* (London: Hurst, 2003).
42. On the foundation of this temple see Meer, *Portrait of Indian South Africans*, p. 175.

43. E. M. Mahida, 'History of Muslims in South Africa', typescript, Arabic Study Circle, Durban 1993, file 4741 (Grey Street), Local History Museums, Durban, p. 32.
44. Anonymous, 'Detailed Description of the Grey Street Mosque', typescript, file 5419 (Mosques), Local History Museums, Durban.
45. On the disputes see Vahed, '"Unhappily Torn by Dissensions and Litigations"'.
46. Ibid., pp. 32–5.
47. On Umgeni and other working-class Indian settlements see B. Freund, *Insiders and Outsiders: The Indian Working Class of Durban, 1910–1990* (Pietermaritzburg: University of Natal Press, 1995).
48. The biography of an Indian metalworker who established his own workshop in the region around 1914 can be found in the South African Indian magazine *Fiat Lux* 9, 8 (1974).
49. Shaykh Dā'ūd bin Sulaymān, *Riyāz-e sūfī* (repr. 2001), pp. 11–12.
50. Facsimile reproduced in Soofie and Soofie, *Hazrath Soofie Saheb*, p. 60. Gandhi's interest and expertise in 'Mahommedan Law' during this period are seen in a letter he wrote on the subject to the *Natal Witness* a few months before signing Ghulām Muhammad's documents. The letter is reprinted in Gandhi, *The South African Gandhi*, pp. 140–2. The signature at the bottom of the land-purchase deed for the property at which he built his mosque shows that the documentation had been prepared by none other than Mohandas Gandhi, who had arrived in Durban just two years before Ghulām Muhammad himself.
51. Facsimile reproduced in Soofie and Soofie, *Hazrath Soofie Saheb*, p. 60; the name of Narayam Samy as the former landowner was supplied to me in conversation with Ghulām Muhammad's descendants. Copies of legal documents relating to his other land purchases are preserved in an anonymous compilation entitled 'Soofie Sahib', file Islam/B 908/35, Documentation Centre, University of Durban-Westville, Durban.
52. Vahed, '"Unhappily Torn by Dissensions and Litigations"', pp. 29–30.
53. Shaykh Dā'ūd bin Sulaymān, *Riyāz-e sūfī* (repr. 2001), p. 11.
54. Quoted with minor amendments from Mesthrie, 'New Lights from Old Languages', pp. 205–6.
55. On early Indian mercantile settlement at Nottingham Road see Anonymous, *Nottingham Road: 100 Years, 1895–1995: Commemorative Brochure* (Nottingham Road: n.p., 1995); on the *madrasa* and mission see p. 10. Other Indian groups were also establishing their own distinctive schools at this time, such as the (predominantly Hindu) Tamil-medium school established in Durban in 1910 whose opening was reported in the *Indian Opinion* (14 May 1910, p. 163).
56. Sayyid Shujā' al-dīn Muhammad Rabbānī, *Selected Notices*.
57. R. S. O'Fahey, '"Small World": Neo-Sufi Interconnexions between the Maghrib, the Hijaz and Southeast Asia', in Reese (ed.), *The Transmission of Learning*.
58. S. S. Reese, 'Urban Woes and Pious Remedies: Sufism in Nineteenth-Century Benaadir (Somalia)', *Africa Today* 46, 3–4 (1999).

59. On the early settlement of Westville see B. O'Keefe, *Pioneers' Progress: Early Natal* (Durban: n.p., n.d.).
60. Soofie and Soofie, *Hazrath Soofie Saheb*, p. 130.
61. Shaykh Dā'ūd bin Sulaymān, *Riyāz-e sūfī* (repr. 2001), pp. 10–11, 13–14. The dates are given in Soofie and Soofie, *Hazrath Soofie Saheb*, p. 206.
62. B. Maharaj, 'From a Privileged to an Unwanted Minority: The Asian Diaspora in Africa', in Gervais-Lambony *et al.* (eds.), *Reconfiguring Identities*, p. 119.
63. In 1863 there were 78 Indians registered in Pietermaritzburg, a figure that had risen to 2,311 by 1891. See Bhana and Brain, *Setting Down Roots*, p. 59.
64. Ibid.; Soofie and Soofie, *Hazrath Soofie Saheb*, p. 139.
65. Anonymous, 'Origin and Development of Islam and Islamic Education in South Africa', typescript, file Religion: Islam (95/173), Durban Cultural and Documentation Centre, p. 11.
66. Y. da Costa, 'The Contribution of Maulana Abd al-Latif (RA) (1860–1916) of the "College" to the Religious Life of the Muslims at the Cape', in Y. da Costa (ed.), *Sufi Sahib: 100 Years of Service* (Durban: FA Print, 1416/1995), p. 18.
67. Q. Yen, 'Kinship and Organization: The History of the Gan (Yan or Yen) Clansmen in Singapore and Malaysia (1850–1993)', in Q. Yen, *The Chinese in Southeast Asia and Beyond* (Singapore: World Scientific Publishing, 2008).
68. Shaykh Dā'ūd bin Sulaymān, *Riyāz-e sūfī*.
69. Ibid. (repr. 2001), pp. 14–15.
70. Hunter *et al.* (eds.), *Imperial Gazetteer of India*, vol. XIV, pp. 322–3.
71. Mohiuddin, *Muslim Communities*, p. 266.
72. Cf. the Yemeni missions to Islamize uneducated Africans in the same period in U. Freitag, 'Hadhramaut: A Religious Center for the Indian Ocean in the Late 19th and Early 20th Centuries?', *Studia Islamica* 89 (1999), pp. 165–7.
73. Vahed, '"Unhappily Torn by Dissensions and Litigations"', p. 35.
74. Ibid., p. 38.
75. A. A. Soofie and O. M. Essop (eds.), *His Exalted Eminence Hazrath Sheikh Sayyid Ahmed Badsha Peer* (Durban: Impress Press, 2003), p. 11.
76. Ibid., pp. 12–13.
77. Metcalf, *An Imperial Vision*, chap. 4.
78. Shaykh Dā'ūd bin Sulaymān, *Riyāz-e sūfī* (repr. 2001), p. 8.
79. For a written version of this tradition see Soofie and Soofie, *Hazrath Soofie Saheb*, p. 42.
80. C.f. Green, 'Migrant Sufis and Sacred Space'.
81. Ship List *Truro*, in Ship Lists Files, Documentation Centre, University of Durban-Westville, Durban.
82. Ship List *Truro*, in Ship Lists Files, Documentation Centre, University of Durban-Westville, Durban, Coolie No. 283. No information is provided on either her home district in India or her employer in Natal.
83. Ship List *Lord George Bentinc* [sic], in Ship Lists Files, Documentation Centre, University of Durban-Westville, Durban, Coolie No. 962.
84. Hermansen, 'Common Themes, Uncommon Contexts'.

85. The text is reproduced in Soofie and Soofie, *Hazrath Soofie Saheb*, p. 76.
86. The photograph of the 1912 *ratiep* performers is preserved (uncatalogued) in the Soofie Saheb Archive at Riverside, Durban. For a colourful colonial account of the South African *ratiep* performances see A. W. Cole, *The Cape and the Kafirs, or Notes of Five Years Residence in South Africa* (London: Richard Bentley, 1852), pp. 44–6.
87. Shaykh Dā'ūd bin Sulaymān, *Riyāz-e sūfī* (repr. 2001), pp. 17–30.
88. Ibid., pp. 30–1.
89. For an account of the carnivalesque Muharram customs of nineteenth century India see Jaffur Shurreef, *Qanoon-e Islam, or the Customs of the Mussulmans of India*, trans. G. A. Herklots (Delhi: Asian Educational Services, 1991 [1863]), pp. 98–148.
90. On *kavadi* see Kuper, *Indian People in Natal*, pp. 217–35.
91. Gupchup, 'The Social Life of Bombay', pp. 634–5.
92. Kidambi, *The Making of an Indian Metropolis*, chap. 5. Also Masselos, 'Change and Custom', p. 59.
93. Shaykh Dā'ūd bin Sulaymān, *Riyāz-e sūfī* (repr. 2001), p. 8.
94. Ibid., p. 11. The story is repeated in Smith, 'A Muslim Saint in South Africa', p. 274 and Soofie and Soofie, *Hazrath Soofie Saheb*, p. 76. For Hyderabadi variants of the technique of breathing (usually Quranic words) on water, see J. Burkhalter Flueckiger, *In Amma's Healing Room: Gender and Vernacular Islam in South India* (Bloomington: Indiana University Press, 2006), pp. 64–105.
95. This story was recounted to the author by Faisal Yar Khan Habibi at the shrine of Habīb 'Alī Shāh in Hyderabad on 26 July 2005.
96. Shaykh Dā'ūd bin Sulaymān, *Riyāz-e sūfī* (repr. 2001), pp. 11–12.
97. A brief modern English version of the story printed in Durban nonetheless opts for the more rationalist reading of 'python'. See Soofie and Soofie, *Hazrath Soofie Saheb*, p. 77. In another early twentieth-century Indian Sufi biographical text, Haydar 'Alī Shāh of Jalalpur is also seen miraculously destroying an *izhdihā*. See Malik Muhammad Dīn, *Zikr-e habīb* (Lahore: al-Qamar Book Corporation, 1404/1983), p. 394.
98. Anonymous, *Safarnāma-e Ūgandā wa Mumbāsā*, pp. 51–4.
99. Green, 'Oral Competition Narratives'.

Conclusions

1. J. Douglas, 'Anglo-Indian Ghosts', in J. Douglas, *Bombay and Western India; A Series of Stray Papers*, 2 vols. (London: S. Low, Marston & Company, 1893), vol. II, pp. 363–6.
2. Ibid., p. 364.
3. M. Twain, *Tales of Wonder*, ed. D. Ketterer (Lincoln: University of Nebraska Press, 2003), p. xxvii.
4. Ibid., pp. 96–116.
5. On such 'domestication' in relation to Bombay exports to Zanzibar see J. Prestholdt, *Domesticating the World: African Consumerism and the*

Genealogies of Globalization (Berkeley: University of California Press, 2008), chap. 4.
6. S. Tejani, 'Re-Considering Chronologies of Nationalism and Communalism: The Khilafat Movement in Sind and its Aftermath, 1919–1927', *South Asia Research* 27, 3 (2007).
7. Cf. Roy, *Globalized Islam*.
8. Cf. Chakrabarty, *Rethinking Working-Class History*; Chandavarkar, *The Origins of Industrial Capitalism in India*; and Gooptu, *The Politics of the Urban Poor*.
9. Cooke and Lawrence (eds.), *Muslim Networks*.
10. Bang, *Sufis and Scholars of the Sea*; M. F. Laffan, *Islamic Nationhood and Colonial Indonesia: The Umma below the Winds* (London: RoutledgeCurzon, 2003); S. S. Reese, *Renewers of the Age: Holy Men and Social Discourse in Colonial Benaadir* (Leiden: Brill, 2008).
11. J. Butler, *Awash in a Sea of Faith: Christianizing the American People* (Cambridge MA: Harvard University Press, 1992); Hempton, *Methodism*.
12. Cf. J. Comaroff and J. Comaroff (eds.), *Modernity and its Malcontents: Ritual and Power in Postcolonial Africa* (Chicago: University of Chicago Press, 1993); and White, *Speaking with Vampires*.
13. T. E. Huff and W. Schluchter (eds.), *Max Weber and Islam* (New Brunswick: Transaction Publishers, 1999); Robinson, 'Islamic Reform and Modernities'; and B. S. Turner, *Weber and Islam: A Critical Study* (London: Routledge & Kegan Paul, 1974).
14. Van Bruinessen and Howell (eds.), *Sufism and the Modern in Islam*; Tschacher, 'From Local Practice to Transnational Network'.
15. Bayly, *The Birth of the Modern World*, chap. 9; Meuleman (ed.), *Islam in the Era of Globalization*; Robinson, 'Islamic Reform and Modernities'; Roy, *Globalized Islam*; Schaebler and Stenberg (eds.), *Globalization and the Muslim World*.

Bibliography

Primary Sources in Manuscript (Urdu, Persian, Arabic)

Anonymous. *Risāla-ye sūfiyya*, Bombay University Library, Arabic/Persian MS vol. 56, no. 99.

Untitled 'Hindustani' hagiographical *masnawī*, Asiatic Society, Bombay, MS Urdu 3.

Ḥabīb 'Alī Shāh. *Habīb al-barāzikh*, Salar Jung Library, Hyderabad, Persian MS Tas. 49.

Habīb al-tālibīn, Salar Jung Library, Hyderabad, Persian MS Tas. 50.

Ḥājjī Salāh al-dīn Ārā'ī. *Risālat al-tarjamat al-zāhira li firqati bohrat al-bāhira*, Asiatic Society, Bombay, MS Arabic 4.

Rashīd al-dīn ibn Ahmad Chishtī. *Mukhbir al-awliyā*, Asiatic Society, Bombay, MS Persian 14.

Sayyid Ibrāhīm al-Hussayni al-Madanī. *Zamīr al-insān*, Bombay University Library, Arabic MS vol. 56, no. 99.

Sayyid Yahyā ibn Sayyid Husayn. *Nasabnāma-ye Shāh Wajīh al-dīn*, Asiatic Society, Bombay, MS Persian 15.

Primary Sources in Print (Urdu, Persian, Arabic, English)

'Abd al-'Azīz Dihlawī. *Tafsīr-e fath al-'azīz sīpāra-e 'ām kī tarjama*. Bombay: Muhammadī Press, 1261/1845.

'Abd al-Karīm Munshī. *A Sketch of the Life of His Holiness Saint Syed Pedro Shah, and His Miraculous Deeds – Pēdrō Shāh Sāhib kī karāmāt*. Bombay: Gulzār Press, 1321/1903.

'Abd al-Majīd Qāzī. *Awliyā Allāh kē zinda karishmāt*. Bombay: Karīmī Press, n.d.

Abū Bakr Effendī. *Abu Bakr se 'Uiteensetting van die Godsdiens': 'n Arabies–Afrikaanse Teks uit die Jaar 1869*, ed. A. Van Selms. Amsterdam: Noord-Hollandsche UM, 1979; trans. as *The Religious Duties of Islam as Taught and Explained by Abu Bakr Effendi: A Translation from the Original Arabic and Afrikaans*, ed. with introd. and notes M. Brandel-Syrier. Leiden: E. J. Brill, 1960.

Ahmad 'Alī Shāh Chishtī. *Habīb al-in'ām*. n.p.: n.p., n.d. [*c.* 1910].

Ahmad Ghaffarī. *Tārīkh-e Nigāristān*. Bombay: n.p., 1245/1829.

Ahmad ibn Muhammad 'Alī ibn Muhammad Bāqir al-Bihbahānī. *Mir'āt al-ahwāl-e Jahān-numā*. Patna: n.p., 1225/1810.

Ahmad ibn Tuwayr al-Jannah. *The Pilgrimage of Ahmad, Son of the Little Bird of Paradise: An Account of a 19th Century Pilgrimage from Mauritania to Mecca*, trans. H. T. Norris. Warminster: Aris & Phillips, 1977.

Anonymous. *'Ajā'ib al-hikāyat*. Bombay: n.p., 1300/1883.

Ārā'ish-e mahfil ya'nī qissa-e Hātim Tā'ī bā taswīr. Bombay: Matba'a-e Karīmī, 1326/1908.

Awrād-e ihsānī. Bombay: Matba'a-e Haydarī, 1290/1873.

Brief Biography of Hazrat Khwaja Faqir Mohamed Ali Shah and Hazrat Khwaja Faqir Ahmed Ali Shah. Lenasia: Salim Miya Ahmed Bulbulia, n.d.

Jān-e Bombā'ī. Calcutta: n.p., *c.* 1820.

Majmū'a: Hālāt-e hazrat Shāh Wajīh al-dīn 'Alawī Gujarātī. Bombay: Matba'a-e Shihābī, n.d.

Modern Hyderabad. Hyderabad: n.p., n.d. [*c.* 1912].

Safarnāma-e Ūgandā wa Mumbāsā. Lahore: Khādim al-Ta'līm Istīm Prēs, 1904.

Sawānih al-Ayyām fī Mushāhadāt al-A'wām mawsūm bih Silsilat al-'Ārifīn. Bombay: n.p., 1307/1890; repr. in Aubin (ed.), *Matériaux*.

Tabarrukāt-e nūrānī al-ma'rūf bih gulzār-e Gīlānī. Bombay: Muzafarī Steam Press, 1330/1912.

The Gadi of Mangrol and Maulana Pir Mota Miya Saheb III alias Khwaja Syed Matauddin, being a Brief Description of the Biggest Chishtiya Gadi in the Bombay Presidency and a Small Account of the Life of the Present Sajjada Nashin. Bombay: n.p., 1922.

The Mahomedan and Hindu Riots in Bombay, Aug. 1893, from the Bombay Gazette. Bombay: Bombay Gazette, 1893.

'Aqil Hāshimī. *Sayyid Iftikhār 'Alī Shāh Watan: Hayāt aur kārnāmē*. Hyderabad: Shālīmār, 1968.

Arnold, J. M. *Kind Words and Loving Counsel to the Malays and Other Muslims*. Cape Town: Murray & St Ledger, 1879.

Aubin, J. (ed.). *Matériaux pour la biographie de Shâh Ni'matullah Walî Kermânî*. Tehran: Département d'Iranologie de l'Institut Francoiranien, 1956.

'De Kubahan à Bidar: la famille Ni'matullahī', *Studia Iranica* 20, 2 (1991).

Bābū Muhammad Husayn. *Risāla-e gōsht-khōrī*. Delhi: Muhammad Qasīm 'Alī, 1910.

Dargah Quli Khan. *The Muraqqa'-e Dehli*, trans. C. Shekhar and S. M. Chenoy. Delhi: Deputy, 1989.

Faqīr Muhammad. *'Alī Shāh Khumkhāna-e mahbūb*. Ahmadnagar: Shoa-e Tasawaf Publications, 1994.

Mureed-nama-e Saeed [*sic*]. Ahmadnagar: Shoa-e Tasawaf Publications, 1994.

Faquir M. Hunzai. *Shimmering Light: An Anthology of Isma'ili Poems*. London: Institute of Ismaili Studies/I. B.Tauris, 1997.

Fidā'ī, *see* Muhammad ibn Zayn al-'Ābidīn Khurāsānī Fidā'ī

Firishta, *see* Muhammad Qāsim Firishta

Ghulām 'Alī Shāh Chishtī Nizāmī. *Habīb al-wisāl* (Hyderabad: Chatta Bazār, n.d. [c.1910]).

Ghulām Husayn Khān. *Tārīkh-e Āsaf Jāhiyān (Gulzār-e Āsafiyya)*, ed. M. Mahdī Tawwasolī. Islamabad: Markaz-e Tahqīqāt-e Fārsī-ye Īrān wa Pākistān, 1377/1999.

Ghulām Husayn Mīrzā Sālih (ed.). *Tārīkh-e sifārat-e Hājjī Khalīl Khān wa Muhammad Nabī Khān bih Hindūstān*. Tehran: Kavir, 1379/2000 [1886].

Ghulām Muhammad Munshi. *Autobiography of Haji Ghulam Muhammad Munshi*. Bombay: Surat Mission Press, 1893.

Ghulām Samdānī Khān Gowhar. *Hayāt-e Māh Liqā*. Hyderabad: Nizām al-Matāba', 1324/1906.

Habīb 'Alī Shāh. *Habīb al-awrād*, Urdu trans. Ghulām Khwāja Mu'īn al-dīn Chishtī. Hyderabad: Khwāja Prēs, n.d.

Dīwān-e Habīb. Hyderabad: Khwāja Prēs, 1423/2002.

Hāfiz 'Abd al-Rahmān Sāhib. *Safarnāma-e bilād-e islāmiyya*. Lahore: Shaykh Imām Bakhsh, repr. 1338/1919 [1322/1904].

Haji Riazuddin Ahmed. *The Moslem Guide*. Bombay: Education Society's Press, 1891.

Hājjī Muhammad. 'Alī Pīrzāda *Safarnāma-ye Hājjī Pirzāda*, ed. Hāfiz Farmānfarmā'iyān, 2 vols. Tehran: Dānishgāh-e Tihrān, 1342–3/1963–5.

Hājjī Muhammad Maqbūl. *Manāqib al-habībīn*. Delhi: Jahna Litho-Press, n.d. [c. 1910].

al-Hajj Khwaja Kamal-ud-Din. *Islam and Other Religions*. Woking: Woking Muslim Mission and Literary Trust, n.d. [c. 1920].

Husein of Hamadān. *The Tarikh-i-jadid: or New History of Mirza Ali Muhammad the Bab*, trans. E. G. Browne. Cambridge: The University Press, 1893.

Iftikhār 'Alī Shāh 'urf Gharib al-Watan. *Irshādāt-e Watan*. Hyderabad: 'Imād Press, 1384/1964 [1363/1943].

'Imad al-Din. *A Mohammedan Brought to Christ: Being the Autobiography of a Native Clergyman in India, Translated from the Hindustanee*, trans. Robert Clark. London: CMS House, 1874.

Jaffur Shureef. *Qanoon-e Islam, or the Customs of the Mussulmans of India*, trans. G. A. Herklots. Delhi: Asian Educational Services, 1991 [1863].

Jawād ibn Sayyid Mujtaba Husaynī Mūsawī. *Kitāb matlūb al-zā'irīn*. Bombay: n.p., 1261/1845.

Khwāja Hasan Nizāmī. *Māzāmīn-e Khwāja Hasan Nizāmī*. Delhi: Ghulām Nizām al-dīn, 1912.

Malik Muhammad. Dīn *Zikr-e habīb*. Lahore: al-Qamar Book Corporation, 1404/1983 [1344/1925].

Maulana Shah Syed Waris Hassan. *A Guide for Spiritual Aspirants [Shamāmat al-ambar]*. Kuala Lumpur: A. S. Noordeen, 2001.

Mawlānā Jalāl al-dīn Balkhī. *Masnawī-ye ma'nawī*, ed. R. A. Nicholson. Tehran: Intishārāt-e Paymān, 1378/1999.

Mawlwī 'Abd al-Hayy. *Ādāt al-tanabbuh fī bayān ma'nī al-tashabbuh*. Delhi: Tuhfa-e Hind, 1326/1909.

Mīr Lā' īq 'Alī Khān 'Imād al-Saltana. *Safarnāma-ye 'Imād al-Saltana bih Urūpā*. Tehran: Nashr-e Pāband, 1383/2005.

Mirza Husayn Farahani. *A Shi'ite Pilgrimage to Mecca (1885–1886): The Safarnāmeh of Mirzā Mohammad Hosayn Farāhāni*, ed. and trans. M. Gulzar and E. L. Daniel. Austin: University of Texas Press, 1990.

Mohammad Abdullah Mama Paro Qaisary. *The Life History of Hazrat Shaikh Makhdum Ali Paro*. Mumbai: Ghazali Typesetters, 1999.

Moulavi Cheragh Ali. *The Proposed Political, Legal, and Social Reforms in the Ottoman Empire and Other Mohammadan States*. Bombay: Education Society's Press, 1883.

Muhammad Hasan al-Husaynī [Āghā Khān I]. *'Ibrat-afzā*. Bombay: n.p., 1278/1862.

Muhammad ibn Zayn al-'Ābidīn Khurāsānī Fidā'ī. *Kitāb-e tārīkh-e Ismā'īliyya, yā Hidāyat al-mu'minīn al-tālibīn*, ed. Aliksāndir Sīmiūnūf. Tehran: Intishārāt-e Asātīr, 1362/1983.

Muhammad Ismā'īl Khān. *A'zam al-karāmāt*. Aurangabad: Mu'īn Prēs, n.d. [c. 1921].

Muhammad Mahdī Wāsif. *Anīs al-zākirīn*. Bombay: Matba'a Haydarī, 1288/1871.

Muhammad Muhyī al-dīn. *Sawānih-e hayāt-e Khwāja Shams al-Dīn al-ma'rūf Khwāja Shamnā Mīrān*. n.p.: Khwāja Buk Dipō, n.d.

Muhammad Qāsim Firishta. *Tārīkh-e Firishta*, ed. Major-General John Briggs 'with the assistance of' Munshi Mir Kheirat Ali Khan Mushtak, 2 vols. Bombay: Government College Press, 1831.

Mullā Firōz bin Mullā Kāvus. *Risāla-ye istishhādāt*. Bombay: Matba'a-e Bombā'ī Samāchār, 1197/1828.

Munshī 'Abbās 'Alī. *Qissah-ye ghamgīn*, ed. S. C. Misra. Baroda: Maharaja Sayajirao University of Baroda, 1975.

Munshī Sīvanāth. *Sayr-e Ajmēr*. Ajmer: Matba'a Printing Company, 1892.

Murād 'Alī Tulū'. *Tazkira-e awliyā-e Haydarābād*. Hyderabad: Mīnār Buk Dipō, 1392/1972.

Nā'ib al-Sadr Shīrāzī. *Tarā'iq al-haqā'iq*, 3 vols. Tehran: Kitābkhāna-ye Baranī, 1339–45/1960–6.

  Tuhfat al-Harāmayn: Safarnāma-ye Nā'ib al-Sadr Shīrāzī dar ziyārat-e Makka wa siyāhat-e Īrān. Tehran: Bābak, 1361/1983 [1306/1899].

Nāsir al-dīn Shāh. *The Diary of HM the Shah of Persia During his Tour Through Europe in AD1873*, trans. J. W. Redhouse. Costa Mesa: Mazda, 1995.

Nawab Mohsin ul-Mulk. *Causes of the Decline of the Mahomedan Nation*. Bombay: Bombay Gazette Steam Printing Works, 1891.

Qāzī Muhammad Yūsuf. *Zayn al-majālis*. Bombay: n.p., 1868; repr. 1879.

Ra'ūf Ahmad ibn Shu'ūr Ahmad-e. *Tafsīr-e mujaddidī ma'rūf bih tafsīr-e Ra'ūfī*. Bombay: Matba'a-e Haydarī, 1876.

Safī 'Alī Shāh. *Dīwān-e Safī 'Alī Shāh hamrāh bā masnawī-ye Bahr al-haqā'iq*. Tehran: Intishārāt-e Safī 'Alī Shāh, n.d.

Zubdat al-asrār. Tehran: Intishārāt-e Safī 'Alī Shāh, 1379s/2000.

Sayyid Abul A'la Maududi. *Worship and Festivals in Islam*, trans. M. Durrani. Delhi: MMI Publishers, 1999.

Sayyid Ahmad Khan. *Selected Essays by Sir Sayyid Ahmad Khan*, trans. J. W. Wilder. Lahore: Sang-e Meel Publications, 2006.

Sayyid Muhammad Husaynī Gīsū Darāz. *Khātima-ye ādāb al-muridīn al-ma'rūf bih khātima*, Urdu trans. Mu'īn al-dīn Darda'ī. Karachi: Nafīs Akīdīmī, n.d.

Sayyid Muhammad Muhyī al-dīn Habībī Hāfiz. *Zikr-e habīb* n.p.: n.p., n.d.; trans. Naeem Khan Sabiri as *Life History of Khwaja Habib Ali Shah*. Durban: Soofie Saheb Badsha Peer Darbar, 1424/2004.

Sayyid Shāh Ghulām 'Alī Qādirī. *Mishkāt al-nabuwwa*, Urdu trans. Abū'l Fazl Mahmūd Qādirī, 8 vols. Hyderabad: I'jāz Printing Press, repr. 1982.

Sayyid Shujā'al-dīn Muhammad Rabbānī. *Sawānih-e Sayyid Mīrān 'Alī Dātār aur karāmāt wa munāqib*. Unava: Khayrō Kitābghar, n.d.

Selected Notices from the Newspaper Press of the Efforts made by Ghulam Muhammad Munshi to Spread Education among Mahomedans. Bombay: Fort Mercantile Press, 1880.

Shāh Kalīm Allāh Jahānābādī. *Maktūbāt-e kalīmī*. Delhi: Matba'a-e Yūsufī, 1301/1884.

Shāh Mahmūd Awrangābādī. *Malfūzāt-e naqshbandiyya: Hālāt-e hazrat Bābā Shāh Musāfir Sāhib*. Hyderabad: Nizāmat-e 'Umūr-e Mazhabī-e Sarkār-e 'Ālī, 1358/1939.

Shaikh Faizullah-Bhái. *A Moslem Present: An Anthology of Arabic Poems about the Prophet and the Faith of Islam*. Bombay: Moochâlâ & Co., 1893.

Shaykh Dā'ūd bin Sulaymān. *Riyāz-e sūfī*. Bombay: Mustafā'ī Steam Press, 1331/1913; facsimile repr. Durban, 2001.

Shaykh Yūsuf ibn Ismā'īl al-Nabahanī al-Naqshbandī. *Jamī' karāmāt al-awliyā*, 2 vols. Beirut: al-Maktaba al-Thaqafiyya, repr. 1411/1991.

Shihabu'd-Din Shah al-Husayni. *The True Meaning of Religion or Risala dar Haqiqati[sic] Din*, Persian text with English trans. by W. Ivanow. Bombay: Islamic Research Association, 1933.

Shihāb al-dīn Suhrawardī. *'Awārif-ul-ma'ārif*, trans. H. Wilberforce Clarke. Lahore: S. Muhammad Ashraf, 1991.

Sidi Ali Reïs. *The Travels and Adventures of the Turkish Admiral Sidi Ali Reïs*, trans. A. Vambéry. London: Luzac, 1899.

Sikandar ibn Muhammad. *Mir'āt-e Sikandarī*. Bombay: n.p., 1246/1831.

Sirajud Din, R. and Walter, H. A. 'An Indian Sufi Hymn', *The Moslem World* 9, 2 (1919).

Sorabjee Jamsetjee Jeejeebhoy. *Tohfa-e Jamsheed, being a Translation in Goozratee of a Persian Treatise entitled Kileed-e Danesh, Containing a Short Catechism on the Principles of Natural Theology & Morality for the Use of Parsee Youth*. Bombay: Sir Jamsetjee Jeejeebhoy, 1848.

Sūfī Sa'ādat 'Alī. *Asrār-e darwēsh mūsūma bih bahr al-ma'rifat*. Muradabad: n.p., 1898.

Sultān Muhammad Sayf al-Dawla. *Safarnāma-ye Makka*, ed. A. A. Khudāparast. Tehran: Nashr-e Nayy, 1363/1985.

'Uthmān ibn 'Umar al-Kahf. *Hikāyat al-sālihīn*. Bombay: Matba'a-e Haydarī, 1293/1876.

Wilson, John. *Rad-e dīn-e Musulmānī; or Refutation of Mohammadanism in Persian in Reply to Mohammad Hashim*. Bombay: Tract and Book Society, 1836.

Musulmānī dīn kā rad'iyya; or Refutation of Mohammadanism in Hindustani in Reply to Mohammad Hashim, 2nd edn. Bombay: Tract and Book Society, 1840 [1833].

Archival Documents, Newspapers and Official Publications

Ahmad Jalālī Farāhānī (ed.). *Asnādī az rawābit-i Īrān wa Hind dar dawrah-ye Muzaffar al-Dīn Shāh Qājār*. Tehran: Daftar-e Mutāla'āt-e Siyāsī wa Bayn al-Milalī, 1418/1997.

Anonymous. 'Detailed Description of the Grey Street Mosque', typescript, file 5419 (Mosques), Local History Museums, Durban.

'Hajee Sayed Mohideen Abdul Rahman' [obituary, 15 May 2003], file: Literature, Durban Cultural and Documentation Centre, Durban.

'Origin and Development of Islam and Islamic Education in South Africa since the Seventeenth Century', typescript, file: Religion: Islam (95/173), Durban Cultural and Documentation Centre, Durban.

Selected Notices from the Newspaper Press of the Efforts made by Ghulam Muhammad Munshi to Spread Education among Mahomedans. Bombay: Fort Mercantile Press, 1880.

The Mahomedan and Hindu Riots in Bombay, Aug. 1893, from the Bombay Gazette. Bombay: Bombay Gazette, 1893.

[S. M. Edwardes] *Gazetteer of Bombay City and Island*, 3 vols. Bombay: Times Press, 1909.

Bombay Almanac and Directory (Bombay: Bombay Gazette Press).

Bombay Gazette newspaper (Bombay).

Church Missionary Society. *Church Missionary Intelligencer*. London: Church Missionary House.

Committee of the District Benevolent Society [Bombay]. 'The Native Poor of Bombay: Reports of the Committee of the District Benevolent Society, for the years 1854 and 1855; Bombay 1855 and 1856', *The Bombay Quarterly Review* 4, 8 (1856).

Dawra-ye rūznāmahā'ī-ye Sharaf wa sharāfat. Tehran: Intishārāt-e Yasāwōlī Farhangsarā, n.d.

Edwardes, S. M. *Census of India*, vol. X, pt 4: *Bombay: History*. Bombay: Times of India Press, 1901.

Enthoven, R. E. *The Tribes and Castes of Bombay*. Bombay: Asian Educational Services, 1990.

Gazetteer of the Bombay Presidency: Musalmans and Parsis. Bombay: Government Central Press, 1899.

Hunter, W. W., Cotton, J. S., Burn, R. and Meyer, W. S. (eds.). *Imperial Gazetteer of India*. Oxford: Clarendon Press, 1908–31.

Indian Law Reports (Bombay Series). Bombay: Government Central Press.

Indian Opinion newspaper (Durban).

Lane-Smith, Rev. H. 'Papers of Henry Lane-Smith', Unofficial Papers, Acc. 33, Archives of the Church Missionary Society, Birmingham University Library.

Mahida, E. M. 'History of Muslims in South Africa', typescript, Arabic Study Circle, Durban, file 4741 (Grey Street), Local History Museums, Durban.

Reports on Native Newspapers Published in the Bombay Presidency, Maharashtra State Archives, Bombay.

Ship Lists Files [indentured labourer records], Documentation Centre, University of Kwa-Zulu Natal, Durban.

Memoirs, Speeches, Missionary Accounts, etc.

Anonymous. *Nottingham Road: 100 Years, 1895–1995: Commemorative Brochure*. Nottingham Road: n.p., 1995.

Modern Hyderabad. Hyderabad: n.p., n.d. [c. 1912].

Aubrey, D. *Letters from Bombay*. London: Remington & Co., 1884.

Barr, R. *In a Steamer Chair and Other Shipboard Stories*. New York: F. A. Stokes Co., 1892.

Browne, E. G. *A Year amongst the Persians*. London: Century Publishing, 1984.

Cole, A. W. *The Cape and the Kafirs, or Notes of Five Years Residence in South Africa*. London: Richard Bentley, 1852.

Colton, A. M. *Gordon Hall: A Memorial*. Northampton, MA: Bridgman & Childs, 1882.

Conan Doyle, A. *The History of Spiritualism*, 2 vols. London: Cassell, 1926.

Cox, M. and Gilbert, R. A. (eds.). *Victorian Ghost Stories: An Oxford Anthology*. Oxford: Oxford University Press, 1992.

Cust, R. N. *Missionary Address Delivered in Henry Martyn Hall, to Undergraduates of the University of Cambridge: The Hero-Missionary and Heroic Missionary Society: Allen Gardiner, Coleridge Patteson, John Williams, and the Moravian Missionary Society*. Hertford: Stephen Austin, n.d. [1888].

da Costa, Y. (ed.). *Sufi Sahib: 100 Years of Service*. Durban: FA Print, 1416/1995.

Damishky, P. J. E. 'The Moslem Population of Bombay', *The Moslem World* 1, 2 (1911).

Douglas, J. *Bombay and Western India; A Series of Stray Papers*, 2 vols. London: S. Low, Marston & Company, 1893.

Edwardes, S. M. *The Rise of Bombay: A Retrospect*. Bombay: Times of India Press, 1902.

By-Ways of Bombay. Bombay: D. B. Taraporevala Sons & Co., 1912.

French, A. J. P. 'The Problem of Islam in India (A Discussion of "Methods")', *The Moslem World* 6, 1 (1916).

Gandhi, M. *Satyagraha in South Africa*, trans. Valji Govindji Desaia. Ahmedabad: Navajivan Publishing House, n.d [1950].

The South African Gandhi: An Abstract of the Speeches and Writings of M. K. Gandhi, 1893–1914, ed. F. Meer. Durban: Madiba, 1996.

Hall, G. and Newell, S. *The Conversion of the World, or, The Claims of Six Hundred Millions and the Ability and Duty of the Churches Respecting Them*. Andover, MA: American Board of Commissioners for Foreign Missions, 1818.

Hampson, A. R. 'The Mission to Muslims in Cape Town', *The Moslem World* 24, 3 (1934).

Hart, F. *Rahator of Bombay, the Apostle to the Marathas.* London: The Epworth Press, 1936.

Headley, Lord 'Islamic Mission to South Africa: Khwaja Kamal ud-Din and Lord Headley at Cape Town', *The Islamic Review* 14 (1926).

Heber, R. *Narrative of a Journey through the Upper Provinces of India, from Calcutta to Bombay, 1824–1825*, 2 vols. London: John Murray, 1873.

Jehangir, R. P. *Short History of the Lives of Bombay Opium Smokers.* Bombay: J. B. Marzban & Co.'s Steam Printing Works, 1893.

Karkaria, R. P. *The Charm of Bombay: An Anthology of Writings in Praise of the First City in India.* Bombay: D. B. Taraporevala, 1915.

Keane, J. F. *Six Months in the Hejaz; Being Keane's Journeys to Meccah and Medinah.* London: Ward & Downey, 1887.

Kipling, R. *Plain Tales from the Hills.* Calcutta: Thacker Spink, 1888.

Lane-Smith, H. J. 'Illiteracy among Indian Moslems', *The Moslem World* 9, 2 (1919).

Martineau, J. *The Life and Correspondence of the Right Hon. Sir Bartle Frere, Bart.* London: J. Murray, 1895.

Narayan, G. *Govind Narayan's Mumbai: An Urban Biography from 1863*, ed. and trans. M. Ranganathan. London: Anthem Press, 2008.

Newell, H. *Memoir of Mrs Harriet Newell, Wife of the Rev. Samuel Newell, Missionary to India.* New York: American Tract Society, 1828.

Page, J. *Captain Allen Gardiner, Sailor and Saint.* London: S. W. Partridge & Co., n.d. [1897].

Paterson, J. G. *From Bombay through Babylonia.* Glasgow: David Bryce & Son, n.d.

Pinder, D. A. *The Visitor's Illustrated Guide to Bombay.* Bombay: G. Claridge & Co., 1904.

Rogers, C. *Christian Heroes in the Army and Navy.* London: S. Low, Son & Marston, 1867.

Shamrao Moroji Nayak, *A History of the Pattana Prabhus, Containing an Account of the Origin of this Caste, the Loss of their Principalities, and the Migration from Other Parts of India to Paitan, and thence Finally to Konkan.* Bombay: Family Printing Press, 1877.

Shepherd, W. A. *From Bombay to Bushire and Bussora.* London: Richard Bentley, 1857.

'Sleepy Sketches', in *Sleepy Sketches; or, How we Live and How we do not Live. From Bombay.* London: Sampson, Low, Marston, Searle, & Rivington, 1877.

Smith, G. *The Life of John Wilson, DD, FRS, for Fifty Years Philanthropist and Scholar in the East.* London: John Murray, 1878.

Smith, H. J. 'Moslem Missions in the Diocese of Bombay', *The Moslem World* 6, 1 (1916).

Soofie, A. A. and Essop, O. M. (eds.). *His Exalted Eminence Hazrath Sheikh Sayyid Ahmed Badsha Peer.* Durban: Impress Press, 2003.

Soofie, Shah Mohamed Saeid and Soofie, Shah Abdul Aziz. *Hazrath Soofie Saheb & his Khanqahs*. Durban: Soofie Saheb Badsha Peer Darbar, n.d. [c. 2002].

Stanhope, L. *Sketch of the History and Influence of the Press in British India*. London: C. Chapple, 1823.

Stock, E. *The History of the Church Missionary Society: Its Environment, its Men and its Work*, 3 vols. London: Church Missionary Society, 1899.

'The CMS Missions to Mohammedans', *The Moslem World* 2, 2 (1912).

Stocqueler, J. H. *A Review of the Life and Labours of Dr G. W. Leitner*. Brighton: Tower Press, 1875.

Sykes, P. M. *Ten Thousand Miles in Persia, or Eight Years in Iran*. London: John Murray, 1902.

Tacherkar, H. A. 'and others'. *A Brief Sketch of the Work of the Kāmgār Hitwardhak Sabhha, Bombay*. Bombay: Indu-Prakash Press, 1919.

Twain, M. *Tales of Wonder*, ed. D. Ketterer. Lincoln: University of Nebraska Press, 2003.

Van der Merwe, W. J. 'Missions to Muslims in South Africa', *The Moslem World* 26, 3 (1936).

Wacha, Sir D. E. *Shells from the Sands of Bombay, Being my Recollections and Reminiscences, 1860–1875*. Bombay: Indian Newspaper Co., 1920.

Wherry, E. M., Zwemer, S. M. and Mylrea, C. G. (eds.). *Islam and Missions: Being Papers Read at the Second Missionary Conference on Behalf of the Mohammedan World at Lucknow, January 23–28, 1911*. London: Fleming H. Revell Company, 1911.

Wilson, J. *The Pārsí Religion: As contained in the Zand-Avastá, and propounded and defended by the Zoroastrians of India and Persia, unfolded, refuted, and contrasted with Christianity*. Bombay: American Mission Press, 1843.

Zwemer, S. M. 'The Moslem Menace in South Africa', *Missionary Review of the World* 37 (1914).

Catalogues and Reference Works

Anonymous. *Catalogue of Native Publications in the Bombay Presidency up to 31st December 1864*. Bombay: Education Society's Press, 1867.

Arberry, A. J. *Catalogue of the Library of the India Office*, vol. II, pt 6: *Persian Books*. London: India Office, 1937.

Blumhardt, J. F. *Catalogue of the Library of the India Office*. London: Eyre & Spottiswoode, 1908.

Carter, L. *Chronicles of British Business in Asia, 1850–1960*. Delhi: Manohar, 2002.

Desai, S. P. *Handbook of the Bombay Archives*. Bombay: Government of Maharashtra, 1978.

Fyzee, A. A. A. 'A Descriptive List of the Arabic, Persian and Urdu Manuscripts in the Bombay Branch, Royal Asiatic Society', *Journal of the Bombay Branch, Royal Asiatic Society* 3 (1927).

Krek, M. A. *Gazetteer of Arabic Printing*. Weston, MA: privately printed, 1977.

Mushar, K. *Fihrist-e Kitābhā-ye Chāpī-ye Fārsī az Āghāz ta Ākhar-e Sāl-e 1345*. Tehran: Bungā-ye Tarjuma wa Nashr-e Kitāb, 1352/1974.

Poonawala, I. K. *Biobibliography of Ismāʿīlī Literature*. Malibu: Undena Publications, 1977.

Sambolle, L. *All India Press Directory*. Calcutta: Calcutta Exchange Gazette Press, 1935.

Sarafaraz, Shaikh Abdul Qadir. *A Descriptive Catalog of the Arabic, Persian and Urdu Manuscripts in the Library of the University of Bombay*. Bombay: Dar al-Qayyimah Press, 1935.

Articles and Books

Abu Manneh, B. 'A Note on "Rashahāt-i ʿAin al-Hayat" in the Nineteenth Century', in E. Özdalga (ed.), *Naqshbandis in Western and Central Asia*. Istanbul: Swedish Research Institute in Istanbul, 1999.

Ahmad, A. 'Afghānī's Indian Contacts', *Journal of the American Oriental Society* 89, 3 (1969).

al-Albani, Shaikh Muhammad Naasiruddin. *Tawassul: Seeking a Means of Nearness to Allah*. Birmingham: al-Hidaayah, 1417/1996.

Alam, M. and Subrahmanyam, S. *Indo-Persian Travels in the Age of Discoveries, 1400–1800*. Cambridge: Cambridge University Press, 2007.

Albin, M. W. (rev. N. S. Green). 'Book Publishing', in J. L. Esposito (ed.), *Oxford Encyclopaedia of the Islamic World*. Oxford: Oxford University Press, 2008.

Albuquerque, T. *Urbs Prima in Indis: An Epoch in the History of Bombay, 1840–1865*. Delhi: Promilla, 1985.

Algar, H. 'The Revolt of the Āghā Khān Mahallātī and the Transference of the Ismāʿīlī Imamate to India', *Studia Islamica* 29 (1969).

Alpers, E. A. 'Muqdisho in the Nineteenth Century: A Regional Perspective', *Journal of African History* 24, 4 (1983).

Amanat, A. *Resurrection and Renewal: The Making of the Babi Movement in Iran, 1844–1850*. Ithaca: Cornell University Press, 1989.

Amanat, A. (ed.). *Cities and Trade: Consul Abbot on the Economy and Society of Iran, 1847–1866*. London: Ithaca Press, 1983.

Amiji, H. M. 'Some Notes on Religious Dissent in Nineteenth-Century East Africa', *African Historical Studies* 4, 3 (1971).

Amin, S. 'Gandhi as Mahatma: Gorakhpur District, Eastern UP, 1921–2', in R. Guha (ed.), *Writings on South Asian History and Society*, Subaltern Studies 3. Delhi: Oxford University Press, 1984.

Anderson, C. '"The Ferringees are Flying – The Ship is Ours!": The Convict Middle Passage in Colonial South and Southeast Asia, 1790–1860', *Indian Economic and Social History Review* 41, 3 (2005).

'Sepoys, Servants and Settlers: Convict Transportation in the Indian Ocean, 1787–1945', in F. Dikotter and I. Brown (eds.), *Cultures of Confinement: A History of the Prison in Africa, Asia and Latin America*. London: Hurst, 2007.

'"Process Geographies" of Mobility and Movement in the Indian Ocean: A Review Essay', *Journal of Colonialism and Colonial History* 8, 3 (2008).

Anonymous. *Tadhkirat'ul habīb*. Durban: n.p., n.d.

Argyle, W. J. 'The Migration of Indian Muslims to East and South Africa: Some Preliminary Comparisons', *Purusartha* 9 (1986).

Asad, T. *Genealogies of Religion: Discipline and Reasons of Power in Christianity and Islam*. Baltimore: Johns Hopkins University Press, 1993.

Aubin, J. 'De Kubahan à Bidar: la famille Ni'matullahī', *Studia Iranica* 20, 2 (1991).

Avery, P., Hambly, G. and Melville, C. (eds.). *The Cambridge History of Iran*, vol. VII: *From Nadir Shah to the Islamic Republic*. Cambridge: Cambridge University Press, 1991.

Aziz, K. K. *Religion, Land and Politics in Pakistan: A Study of Piri-Muridi*. Lahore: Vanguard, 2001.

Azra, A. *The Origins of Islamic Reformism in Southeast Asia: Networks of Malay-Indonesian and Middle Eastern 'Ulama' in the Seventeenth and Eighteenth Centuries*. Honolulu: University of Hawaii Press, 2004.

Bang, A. *Sufis and Scholars of the Sea: Family Networks in East Africa c. 1860–1925*. London: RoutledgeCurzon, 2003.

Bankston, C. L. 'Rationality, Choice, and the Religious Economy: Individual and Collective Rationality in Supply and Demand', *Review of Religious Research* 45, 2 (2003).

Barq, 'A. K. *Justujū dar Ahwāl wa āsār-e Safī 'Alī Shāh*. Tehran: Intishārāt-e Ibn Sīnā, 1352/1973.

Barrow, L. *Independent Spirits: Spiritualism and English Plebeians, 1850–1910*. London: Routledge & Kegan Paul, 1986.

Basu, H. *Habshi-Sklaven, Sidi-Fakire: Muslimische Heiligenverehrung im westlichen Indien*. Berlin: Das Arabische Buch, 1995.

'Slave, Soldier, Trader, Faqir: Fragments of African Histories in Western India', in S. de S. Jayasuriya and R. Pankhurst (eds.), *The African Diaspora in the Indian Ocean*. Trenton, NJ: Africa World Press, 2003.

'Music and the Formation of Sidi Identity in Western India', *History Workshop Journal* 65, 1 (2008).

Bawa, V. K. *Hyderabad under Salar Jung I*. Delhi: S. Chand, 1996.

Bayly, C. A. *The Birth of the Modern World, 1780–1914: Global Connections and Comparisons*. Oxford: Blackwell, 2004.

Bazin, M. (ed.). *Métropoles et Métropolisation*, special edition of *Cahiers d'études sur la Méditerranée orientale et le monde turco-iranien* 24 (1997).

Bēgam, T. *Mīr 'Usmān 'Alī Khān aur unkā 'ahd*. Hyderabad: Commercial Book Depot, 2000.

Bhana, S. and Brain, J. *Setting Down Roots: Indian Migrants in South Africa, 1860–1911*. Johannesburg: Witwatersrand University Press, 1990.

Blyth, R. J. 'Aden, British India and the Development of Steam Power in the Red Sea, 1825–1839', in Killingray *et al.* (eds.), *Maritime Empires*.

Boissevain, J. 'Patronage in Sicily', *Man* 1, 1 (1966).

Boivin, M. 'The Reform of Islam in Ismaili Shī'ism from 1885 to 1957', in F. Delvoye (ed.), *Confluence of Cultures: French Contributions to Indo-Persian Studies*. Delhi: Manohar, 1994.

Les Ismaéliens: des communautés d'Asie du sud entre islamisation et indianisation. Turnhout: Brepols, 1998.

La rénovation du Shîisme ismaélien en Inde et au Pakistan: d'après les écrits et les discours de Sultan Muhammad Shah Aga Khan (1902–1954). London: RoutledgeCurzon, 2003.

Bose, S. *A Hundred Horizons: The Indian Ocean in the Age of Global Empire.* Cambridge, MA: Harvard University Press, 2006.

Boyce, M. 'Manekji Limji Hataria in Iran', in N. D. Manochehr-Homji and M. F. Kanga (eds.), *K. R. Cama Oriental Institute Golden Jubilee Volume.* Bombay: K. R. Cama Oriental Institute, 1969.

Bradlow, F. R. and Cairns, M. *The Early Cape Muslims: A Study of their Mosques, Genealogy and Origins.* Cape Town: A. A. Balkema, 1978.

Braginsky, V. 'Sufi Boat Symbolism: Problems of Origin and Evolution', *Indonesia and the Malay World* 26, 74 (1998).

And Sails the Boat Downstream: Malay Sufi Poems of the Boat. Leiden: Publicaties van Semaian, 2007.

Braginsky, V. and Suvorova, A. 'A New Wave of Indian Inspiration: Translations from Urdu in Malay Traditional Literature and Theatre', *Indonesia and the Malay World* 36, 104 (2008).

Brain, J. B. *Christian Indians in Natal, 1860–1911: An Historical and Statistical Study.* Cape Town: Oxford University Press, 1983.

Breckenridge, C. A. (ed.). *Consuming Modernity: Public Culture in a South Asian World.* Minneapolis: University of Minnesota Press, 1995.

Brenner, N. and Keil, R. (eds.). *The Global Cities Reader.* London: Routledge, 2005.

Broeze, F. (ed.). *Gateways of Asia: Port Cities of Asia in the 13th–20th Centuries.* London: Kegan Paul International, 1997.

Browne, E. G. *The Press and Poetry of Modern Persia.* Cambridge: Cambridge University Press, 1914.

Buck, C. 'The Kitab-i iqan: An Introduction to Baha'u'llah's Book of Certitude with Two Digital Reprints of Early Lithographs', *Occasional Papers in Shaykhi, Babi and Baha'i Studies* 2, 5 (1998).

Buehler, A. F. *Sufi Heirs of the Prophet: The Indian Naqshbandiyya and the Rise of the Mediating Sufi Shaykh.* Columbia: University of South Carolina Press, 1998.

Burkhalter Flueckiger, J. *In Amma's Healing Room: Gender and Vernacular Islam in South India.* Bloomington: Indiana University Press, 2006.

Butler, J. *Awash in a Sea of Faith: Christianizing the American People.* Cambridge, MA: Harvard University Press, 1992.

Cannadine, D. *Ornamentalism: How the British Saw their Empire.* London: Allen Lane, 2001.

Catlin-Jairazbhoy, H. and Alpers, E. A. (eds.). *Sidis and Scholars: Essays on African Indians.* Noida: Rainbow Publishers, 2004.

Centlivres, P. and Centlivres-Demont, M. 'Une étrange rencontre: la photographie orientaliste de Lehnert et Landrock et l'image iranienne du prophète Mahomet', *Études photographiques* 17 (2005).

Cesari, J. 'The Hybrid and Globalized Islam of Western Europe', in Y. Samad and K. Sen (eds.), *Islam in the European Union: Transnationalism, Youth and the War on Terror*. Oxford: Oxford University Press, 2007.

Chahārdihī, N. *Sayrī dar tasawwuf*. Tehran: Intishārāt-e 'Ishrāqī, 1361/1982.

Chakrabarty, D. *Rethinking Working-Class History: Bengal, 1890–1940*. Princeton: Princeton University Press, 1989.

Chakravarti, R. 'Merchants of Konkan', *Indian Economic and Social History Review* 23, 2 (1986).

'Coastal Trade and Voyages in Konkan: The Early Medieval Scenario', *Indian Economic and Social History Review* 35, 2 (1998).

Chandavarkar, R. *The Origins of Industrial Capitalism in India: Business Strategies and the Working Classes in Bombay, 1900–1940*. Cambridge: Cambridge University Press, 1994.

Chesnut, R. A. *Competitive Spirits: Latin America's New Religious Economy*. Oxford: Oxford University Press, 2003.

Chodkiewicz, M. *Seal of the Saints of South Asia: Prophethood and Sainthood in the Doctrine of Ibn 'Arabī*. Cambridge: Islamic Texts Society, 1993.

Choksey, R. D. *Economic History of the Bombay Deccan and Karnatak (1818–1868)*. Poona: R. D. Choksey, 1945.

Clarence-Smith, W. 'The Rise and Fall of Hadhrami Shipping in the Indian Ocean, c. 1750–c. 1940', in D. Parkin and R. Barnes (eds.), *Ships and the Development of Maritime Technology across the Indian Ocean*. London: RoutledgeCurzon, 2002.

'Middle-Eastern Entrepreneurs in Southeast Asia, c. 1750–c. 1940', in I. Baghdiantz, G. Harlaftis and I. P. Minoglou (eds.), *Diaspora Entrepreneurial Networks: Four Centuries of History*. London: Berg, 2004.

Cole, J. R. I. 'Mirror of the World: Iranian "Orientalism" and Early 19th-Century India', *Critique: Journal of Critical Studies of Iran and the Middle East* (1996).

"Abdu'l-Baha's "Treatise on Leadership": Text, Translation, Commentary', *Translations in Shaykhi, Babi and Baha'i Texts* 2, 2 (1998).

Modernity and the Millennium: The Genesis of the Baha'i Faith in the Nineteenth Century. New York: Columbia University Press, 1998.

'New Perspectives on Sayyid Jamal al-Din al-Afghani in Egypt', in Matthee and Baron (eds.), *Iran and Beyond*.

'The Provincial Politics of Heresy and Reform in Qajar Iran: Shaykh al-Rais in Shiraz, 1895–1902', *Comparative Studies of South Asia, Africa and the Middle East* 22, 1–2 (2002).

Comaroff, J. and Comaroff, J. (eds.). *Modernity and its Malcontents: Ritual and Power in Postcolonial Africa*. Chicago: University of Chicago Press, 1993.

Conlon, F. 'Industrialization and the Housing Problem in Bombay, 1850–1940', in K. Ballhatchet and D. Taylor (eds.), *Changing South Asia: Economy and Society*. London: School of Oriental and African Studies, 1984.

Cooke, M. and Lawrence, B. B. (eds.). *Muslim Networks: From Hajj to Hip-hop*. Chapel Hill: University of North Carolina Press, 2005.

Cooper, F. *On the African Waterfront: Urban Disorder and the Transformation of Work in Colonial Mombasa*. New Haven: Yale University Press, 1987.

da Costa, Y. and Davids, A. *Pages from Cape Muslim History.* Pietermaritzburg: Shuter & Shooter, 1994.

Daftary, F. *The Isma'ilis: Their History and Doctrines.* Cambridge: Cambridge University Press, 1992.

A Short History of the Ismailis: Traditions of a Muslim Community. Edinburgh: Edinburgh University Press, 1998.

Dale, S. F. 'The Hadhrami Diaspora in South-Western India: The Role of the Sayyids of the Malabar Coast', in U. Freitag and W. G. Clarence-Smith (eds.), *Hadhrami Traders, Scholars, and Statesmen in the Indian Ocean, 1750s–1960s.* Leiden: Brill, 1997.

Dangor, S. E. *Shaykh Yusuf of Makasar.* Durban: Iqra Publishers, 1994.

Dasnawī, Sayyid Shihāb al-dīn. *Anjuman-e Islām kē sau sāl: tārīkh ū jā'iza.* Bombay: Anjuman-e Islām, 1986.

David, M. D. *Bombay: The City of Dreams.* Bombay: Himalaya Publishing House, 1995.

Davids, A. *The Mosques of Bo-Kaap: A Social History of Islam at the Cape.* Cape Town: South African Institute of Arabic and Islamic Research, 1980.

Davis, P. *The Penguin Guide to the Monuments of India,* vol. II: *Islamic, Rajput and European.* London: Penguin Books, 1989.

de Groot, J. 'Kerman in the Late Nineteenth Century: A Regional Study of Society and Social Change', D.Phil. thesis, University of Oxford, 1978.

de Haan, A. *Unsettled Settlers: Migrant Workers and Industrial Capitalism in Calcutta.* Hilversum: Verloren, 1994.

de Jong, F. and Radtke, B. (eds.). *Islamic Mysticism Contested: 13 Centuries of Controversies and Polemics.* Leiden: E. J. Brill, 1999.

de Jong-Keesing, E. *Inayat Khan: A Biography.* London and The Hague: East–West Publications, 1974.

Dickie, J. *Cosa Nostra: A History of the Sicilian Mafia.* London: Hodder & Stoughton, 2004.

Diesel, A. and Maxwell, P. *Hinduism in Natal: A Brief Guide.* Pietermaritzburg: University of Natal Press, 1993.

Dirks, N. 'Annals of the Archive: Ethnographic Notes on the Sources of History', in B. Axel (ed.), *From the Margins: Historical Anthropology and its Futures.* Durham, NC: Duke University Press, 2002.

Dobbin, C. *Urban leadership in Western India: Politics and Communities in Bombay City 1840–1885.* Oxford: Oxford University Press, 1972.

Dossal, M. *Imperial Designs and Indian Realities: The Planning of Bombay City, 1845–1875.* Delhi: Oxford University Press, 1991.

Dossal Panjwani, M. 'Godis, Tolis and Mathadis: Dock Workers of Bombay', in S. Davies *et al.* (eds.), *Dock Workers: International Explorations in Comparative Labour History, 1790–1970.* Aldershot: Ashgate, 2000.

Dudoignon, S. A., Hisao, K. and Yashushi, K. (eds.). *Intellectuals in the Modern Islamic World: Transmission, Transformation, Communication.* London: Routledge, 2006.

Dumasia, N. J. *The Aga Khan and his Ancestors.* Bombay: Times of India Press, 1939.

Ebr.-Vally, R. *Kala-Pani: Caste and Colour in South Africa*. Cape Town: Kwela Books, 2001.

'Migration of an Identity: South Africans of Indian Descent', in P. Gervais-Lambony, F. Landy and S. Oldfield (eds.), *Reconfiguring Identities and Building Territories in India and South Africa*. Delhi: Manohar, 2005.

Eisenstein, E. L. *The Printing Press as an Agent of Change: Communications and Cultural Transformations in Early Modern Europe*, 2 vols. Cambridge: Cambridge University Press, 1979.

Engineer, A. A. *The Bohras*. Delhi: Vikas Publishing House, 1993.

Ernst, C. W. 'Ideological and Technological Transformations of Contemporary Sufism', in Cooke and Lawrence (eds.), *Muslim Networks*.

Etherington, N. (ed.). *Missions and Empire*. Oxford: Oxford University Press, 2005.

Ewing, K. P. 'The Politics of Sufism: Redefining the Saints of Pakistan', *Journal of Asian Studies* 42 (1983).

Farag, I. 'Private Lives, Public Affairs: The Uses of Adab', in Salvatore (ed.), *Muslim Traditions and Modern Techniques of Power*.

Farīd, Shaykh. 'Anjuman-e Islām Bombā'i aur Alīgarh', *Nawā-e Adab* 36 (April 1986).

Farooqui, A. *Opium City: The Making of Early Victorian Bombay*. Delhi: Three Essays Collective, 2006.

Feierman, S. 'Colonizers, Scholars, and the Creation of Invisible Histories', in V. E. Bonnell and L. Hunt (eds.), *Beyond the Cultural Turn: New Directions in the Study of Society and Culture*. Berkeley: University of California Press, 1999.

Fischel, W. J. 'Bombay in Jewish History in the Light of New Documents from the Indian Archives', *Proceedings of the American Academy for Jewish Research* 38 (1970–1).

Fischer-Tiné, H. and Mann, M. (eds.). *Colonialism as Civilizing Mission: Cultural Ideology in British India*. London: Anthem, 2004.

Floor, W. 'The Merchants (tujjār) in Qajar Iran', *Zeitschrift der Deutsche Morgenlandische Gesellschaft* 126 (1976).

Fortna, B. C. *Imperial Classroom: Islam, the State, and Education in the Late Ottoman Empire*. Oxford: Oxford University Press, 2002.

Franke, P. *Begegnung mit Khidr: Quellenstudien zum Imaginären in traditionellen Islam*. Stuttgart: Franz Steiner, 2000.

Freitag, U. 'Hadhramaut: A Religious Center for the Indian Ocean in the Late 19th and Early 20th Centuries?', *Studia Islamica* 89 (1999).

Frembgen, J. W. *Dervische und Zuckerbäcker: Bilder aus einem Orientalischen Basar*. Munich: Staatliches Museum für Völkerkunde, 1996.

Freund, B. *Insiders and Outsiders: The Indian Working Class of Durban, 1910–1990*. Pietermaritzburg: University of Natal Press, 1995.

Friedmann, Y. 'Medieval Muslim Views on Indian Religions', *Journal of the American Oriental Society* 95 (1975).

Fuccaro, N. 'Mapping the Transnational Community: Persians and the Space of the City in Bahrain, c. 1869–1937', in M. Al-Rasheed (ed.), *Transnational Connections and the Arab Gulf*. London: Routledge, 2005.

Fusfeld, W. 'The Boundaries of Islam and Infidelity', in K. P. Ewing (ed.), *Sharī'at and Ambiguity in South Asian Islam*. Berkeley: University of California Press, 1988.

Gaborieau, M. 'Criticizing the Sufis: The Debate in Early Nineteenth Century India', in F. de Jong and B. Radtke (eds.), *Islamic Mysticism Contested: 13 Centuries of Controversies and Polemics*. Leiden: E. J. Brill, 1999.

Gabriel, T. *The History of the Tana Baru*. Cape Town: Committee for the Preservation of the Tana Baru, 1985.

'Islamic Mystics of the Lakshadweep Islands', in C. Partridge and T. Gabriel (eds.), *Mysticisms East and West*. Carlisle: Paternoster Press, 2003.

Gandhi, L. *Affective Communities: Anticolonial Thought, Fin-de-Siecle Radicalism, and the Politics of Friendship*. Durham, NC: Duke University Press, 2006.

Gell, A. 'The Technology of Enchantment and the Enchantment of Technology', in J. Coote and A. Shelton (eds.), *Anthropology, Art and Aesthetics*. Oxford: Clarendon Press, 1992.

Ghosh, A. 'Cheap Books, "Bad" Books: Contesting Print Cultures in Colonial Bengal', in A. Gupta and S. Chakravorty (eds.), *Print Areas: Book History in India*. Delhi: Permanent Black, 2004.

Power in Print: Popular Publishing and the Politics of Language and Culture in a Colonial Society. Delhi: Oxford University Press, 2006.

Gilbar, G. G. 'The Opening up of Qājār Iran: Some Economic and Social Aspects', *Bulletin of the School of Oriental and African Studies* 49, 1 (1986).

Gilmartin, D. *Empire and Islam: Punjab and the Making of Pakistan*. Delhi: Oxford University Press, 1989.

Gooptu, N. *The Politics of the Urban Poor in Early Twentieth-Century India*. Cambridge: Cambridge University Press, 2001.

Gore, M. S. *Immigrants and Neighbourhoods: Two Aspects of Life in a Metropolitan City*. Bombay: Tata Institute of Social Sciences, 1970.

Gramlich, R. *Die Schiitischen Derwischorden Persiens*, 2 vols. Wiesbaden: Franz Steiner, 1965.

Greaves, R. 'Iranian Relations with Great Britain and British India, 1798–1921', in Avery *et al.* (eds.), *From Nadir Shah to the Islamic Republic*.

Green, E. *Prophet John Wroe: Virgins, Scandals and Visions*. Stroud: Sutton, 2005.

Green, N. S. 'The Survival of Zoroastrianism in Yazd', *Iran: Journal of Persian Studies* 38 (2000).

'Migrant Sufis and Sacred Space in South Asian Islam', *Contemporary South Asia* 12, 4 (2003).

'The Religious and Cultural Roles of Dreams and Visions in Islam', *Journal of the Royal Asiatic Society* 13, 3 (2003).

'Emerging Approaches to the Sufi Traditions of South Asia: Between Texts, Territories and the Transcendent', *South Asia Research* 24, 2 (2004).

'Geography, Empire and Sainthood in the Eighteenth Century Muslim Deccan', *Bulletin of the School of Oriental and African Studies* 67, 2 (2004).

'Oral Competition Narratives of Muslim and Hindu Saints in the Deccan', *Asian Folklore Studies* 63, 2 (2004).

'Stories of Saints and Sultans: Re-membering History at the Sufi Shrines of Aurangabad', *Modern Asian Studies* 38, 2 (2004).

'Who's the King of the Castle? Brahmins, Sufis and the Narrative Landscape of Daulatabad', *Contemporary South Asia* 13, 3 (2004).

'Making a "Muslim" Saint: Writing Customary Religion in an Indian Princely State', *Comparative Studies of South Asia, Africa and the Middle East* 25, 3 (2005).

'Mirza Hasan Safi 'Ali Shah: A Persian Sufi in the Age of Printing', in L. Ridgeon (ed.), *Religion and Politics in Modern Iran*. London: I. B. Tauris, 2005.

'Mystical Missionaries in Hyderabad State: Mu'īn Allāh Shāh and his Sufi Reform Movement', *Indian Economic and Social History Review* 41, 2 (2005).

Indian Sufism since the Seventeenth Century: Saints, Books and Empires in the Muslim Deccan. London: Routledge, 2006.

'Saints, Rebels and Booksellers: Sufis in the Cosmopolitan Western Indian Ocean, c. 1850–1920', in Kresse and Simpson (eds.), *Struggling with History*.

'Shi'ism, Sufism and Sacred Space in the Deccan: Counter-Narratives of Saintly Identity in the Cult of Shah Nur', in A. Monsutti, S. Naef and F. Sabahi (eds.), *The Other Shi'ites: From the Mediterranean to Central Asia*. Berne: Peter Lang, 2007.

'The Faqīr and the Subalterns: Mapping the Holy Man in Colonial South Asia', *Journal of Asian History* 41, 1 (2007).

'Breathing in India, c. 1890', *Modern Asian Studies* 42, 2–3 (2008).

'Making Sense of "Sufism" in the Indian Subcontinent: A Survey of Trends', *Religion Compass* (Blackwell Online, 2008).

Islam and the Army in Colonial India: Sepoy Religion in the Service of Empire. Cambridge: Cambridge University Press, 2009.

'Journeymen, Middlemen: Travel, Trans-Culture and Technology in the Origins of Muslim Printing', *International Journal of Middle East Studies* 41, 2 (2009).

'Transgressions of a Holy Fool: A Majzub in Colonial India', in B. D. Metcalf (ed.), *Islam in South Asia in Practice*. Princeton: Princeton University Press, 2009.

'Stones from Bavaria: Iranian Lithography in its Global Contexts', *Iranian Studies* 43, 3 (2010).

'The Dilemmas of the Pious Biographer: Missionary Islam and the Oceanic Hagiography', *Journal of Religious History* 34, 4 (2010).

'The Trans-Colonial Opportunities of Bible Translation: Iranian Linguists between the Russian and British Empires', in Michael Dodson and Brian Hatcher (eds.), *Trans-Colonial Modernities in South Asia, 1800–1940*. London: Routledge, forthcoming (2011).

'Muslim Bodies and Urban Festivals: Sufis, Workers and Pleasures in Colonial Bombay', in S. F. Alatas and T. Sevea (eds.), *Sufism since the Eighteenth Century: Learning, Debate and Reform in Islam*. Singapore: National University of Singapore Press, forthcoming.

Green, N. S. and Searle-Chatterjee, M. (eds.). *Religion, Language, and Power*. New York: Routledge, 2008.

Gregg, R. 'Uneasy Streets: Police, Corruption and Imperial Progressives in Bombay, London and New York City', in W. C. Jordan and E. Krieke (eds.), *Corrupt Histories*. Rochester: Rochester University Press, 2004.

Gregory, R. G. 'Co-operation and Collaboration in Colonial East Africa: The Asians' Political Role, 1890–1964', *African Affairs* 80, 319 (1981).

Greyling, C. 'Schech Yusuf: The Founder of Islam in South Africa', *Religion in Southern Africa* 1, 1 (1980).

Gupchup, V. V. 'The Social Life of Bombay in the First Half of the Nineteenth Century, 1813–1857', Ph.D. thesis, Bombay University, 1990.

    Bombay: Social Change, 1813–1857. Bombay: Popular Book Depot, 1993.

Haag-Higuchi, R. 'Religion in Public and Private Life: The Case of Yaghma-yi Jandaqi (1781–1859)', in R. Gleaves (ed.), *Religion and Society in Qajar Iran*. New York: RoutledgeCurzon, 2005.

Habermas, J. *The Structural Transformation of the Public Sphere: An Inquiry into a Category of Bourgeois Society*. Cambridge, MA: MIT Press, 1989.

Hakim Sharafuddin, S. A. *A Brief Survey of Urdu Translations of the Quran*. Bombay: Sharafuddin, 1984.

Hamès, C. (ed.). *Coran et talismans: Textes et practiques magiques en milieu musulman*. Paris: Karthala, 2007.

Hardiman, D. 'Purifying the Nation: The Arya Samaj in Gujarat, 1895–1930', *Indian Economic and Social History Review* 44, 1 (2007).

Harrison, M. 'Quarantine, Pilgrimage and Colonial Trade, 1866–1900', *Indian Economic and Social History Review* 29, 2 (1992).

Hasan, F. 'Madāris and the Challenges of Modernity in Colonial India', in J.-P. Hartung and H. Reifeld (eds.), *Islamic Education, Diversity and National Identity: Dini Madaris in India Post 9/11*. Delhi: Sage Publications, 2006.

Hasan, M. *A Moral Reckoning: Muslim Intellectuals in Nineteenth-Century Delhi*. Delhi: Oxford University Press, 2005.

Hempton, D. *Methodism: Empire of the Spirit*. New Haven: Yale University Press, 2005.

Hermansen, M. K. 'Common Themes, Uncommon Contexts: The Sufi Movement of Hazrat Inayat Khan (1882–1927) and Khwaja Hasan Nizami (1878–1955)', in Khan (ed.), *A Pearl in Wine*.

Hermansen, M. K. and Lawrence, B. B. 'Indo-Persian Tazkiras as Memorative Communications', in D. Gilmartin and B. B. Lawrence (eds.), *Beyond Turk and Hindu: Rethinking Religious Identities in Islamicate South Asia*. Gainesville: University of Florida Press, 2000.

Heyworth-Dunne, J. *An Introduction to the History of Education in Modern Egypt*. London: Luzac & Co., 1939.

Hinnells, J. R. 'The Flowering of Zoroastrian Benevolence: Parsi Charities in the 19th and 20th Centuries', *Acta Iranica*, series 2, 10 (1985).

    'Parsi Responses to Religious Pluralism', in H. G. Coward (ed.), *Modern Indian Responses to Religious Pluralism*. Albany: State University of New York Press, 1987.

    Zoroastrian and Parsi Studies. Aldershot: Ashgate, 2000.

Hinnells, J. R. and Williams, A. V. (eds.). *Parsis in India and the Diaspora*. London: Routledge, 2007.

Hiralal, K. 'The Natal Indian Trader: A Struggle for Survival, 1875–1910', MA thesis, University of Durban-Westville, 1991.

Ho, E. *The Graves of Tarim: Genealogy and Mobility across the Indian Ocean.* Berkeley: University of California Press, 2006.

Homāyūnī, M. *Tārīkh-e silsilahā-ye tarīqa-ye ni'matullāhiyya dar Īrān.* London: Bonyād-e 'Irfān-e Mawlānā, 1371/1992.

Home, R. K. *Of Planting and Planning: The Making of British Colonial Cities.* London: Taylor & Francis, 1997.

Hourani, A. H. *Arabic Thought in the Liberal Age, 1798–1939.* London: Oxford University Press, 1962.

'Shaikh Khalid and the Naqshbandi Order', in S. M. Stern, A. Hourani and V. Brown (eds.), *Islamic Philosophy and the Classical Tradition: Essays Presented by his Friends and Pupils to Richard Walzer on his Seventieth Birthday.* Columbia: University of South Carolina Press, 1972.

Huff, T. E. and Schluchter, W. (eds.). *Max Weber and Islam.* New Brunswick: Transaction Publishers, 1999.

Hunwick, J. 'The Arabic Literary Tradition of Nigeria', *Research in African Literatures* 28, 3 (1997).

Hurgronje, C. S. *The Achehnese*, trans A. W. S. O'Sullivan, 2 vols. Leiden: E. J. Brill, 1906.

Husain, S. A. 'Unani Physicians in Hyderabad State during Nizam IV, V and VI', *Bulletin of the Indian Institute of History of Medicine* 13, 1–4 (1983).

Hyslop, J. 'Steamship Empire: Asian, African and British Sailors in the Merchant Marine c. 1880–1945', *Journal of Asian and African Studies* 44, 1 (2009).

Irshād, F. *Muhājarat-e tārīkhī-ye Īrānīyān bih Hind: qarn-e hashtum tā hijdahum-e Mīlādī.* Tehran: Mu'assasah-ye Mutāla'āt wa Tahqīqāt-e Farhangī, 1365/1986.

Islam, R. *A Calendar of Documents on Indo-Persian Relations*, 2 vols. Karachi: Institute of Central and West Asian Studies, 1979–82.

Sufism in South Asia: Impact on Fourteenth Century Muslim Society. Delhi: Oxford University Press, 2002.

Ivanow, W. 'The Tombs of Some Persian Ismaili Imams', *Journal of the Bombay Branch of the Asiatic Society*, NS, 14 (1938).

Jackson, S. *The Sassoons.* London: Heinemann, 1968.

Jalal, A. 'Negotiating Colonial Modernity and Cultural Difference: Indian Muslim Conceptions of Community and Nation, c. 1870–1914', in Tarazi Fawaz and Bayly (eds.), *Modernity and Culture.*

Jayasuriya, S. de S. *African Identity in Asia: Cultural Effects of Forced Migration.* Princeton: Markus Wiener Publishing, 2008.

Johansen, J. *Sufism and Islamic Reform in Egypt: The Battle for Islamic Tradition.* Oxford: Oxford University Press, 1996.

Johnson, G. *Provincial Politics and Indian Nationalism: Bombay and the Indian National Congress, 1880 to 1915.* Cambridge: Cambridge University Press, 1973.

Jones, K. W. *Socio-Religious Reform Movements in British India.* Cambridge: Cambridge University Press, 1989.

Joshi, S. *Fractured Modernity: Making of a Middle Class in Colonial North India.* Delhi: Oxford University Press, 2001.

Kapur, S. *Witchcraft in Western India.* Hyderabad: Orient Longman, 1983.

Karandikar, M. A. *Islam in India's Transition to Modernity.* Westport, CT: Greenwood, 1969.

Keddie, N. R. *Sayyid Jamāl ad-Dīn 'al-Afghānī': A Political Biography.* Berkeley: University of California Press, 1972.

Khalidi, O. 'The Arabs of Hadramawt in Hyderabad: Mystics, Mercenaries and Moneylenders', in A. R. Kulakarni, M. A. Nayeem and T. R. De Souza (eds.), *Mediaeval Deccan History: Commemoration Volume in Honour of Purshottam Mahadeo Joshi.* Bombay: Popular Prakashan, 1996.

'Konkani Muslims: An Introduction', *Islamic Culture* 74, 1 (2000).

Khan, P. Z. I. (ed.). *A Pearl in Wine: Essays on the Life, Music and Sufism of Hazrat Inayat Khan.* New Lebanon: Omega Publications, 2001.

Kidambi, P. *The Making of an Indian Metropolis: Colonial Governance and Public Culture in Bombay, 1890–1920.* Aldershot: Ashgate, 2007.

Killingray, D., Lincoln, M. and Rigby, N. (eds.) *Maritime Empires: British Imperial Maritime Trade in the Nineteenth Century.* Rochester, NY: Boydell Press, 2004.

Kiong, T. C. *Rationalizing Religion: Religious Conversion, Revivalism and Competition in Singapore Society.* Leiden: Brill, 2007.

Knight, F. W. and Liss, P. K. (eds.). *Atlantic Port Cities: Economy, Culture, and Society in the Atlantic World 1650–1850.* Knoxville: University of Tennessee Press, 1991.

Kooiman, D. *Bombay Textile Labour: Managers, Trade Unionists, and Officials, 1918–1939.* Delhi: Manohar Publications, 1989.

Kopf, D. *British Orientalism and the Bengal Renaissance: The Dynamics of Indian Modernization, 1773–1835.* Berkeley: University of California Press, 1969.

Korom, F. J. *Hosay Trinidad: Muḥarram Performances in an Indo-Caribbean Diaspora.* Philadelphia: University of Pennsylvania Press, 2003.

Kresse, K. and Simpson, E. (eds.). *Struggling with History: Islam and Cosmopolitanism in the Western Indian Ocean.* London: Hurst & Co., 2007.

Kuper, H. *Indian People in Natal.* Pietermaritzburg: University of Natal Press, 1960.

Laffan, M. F. *Islamic Nationhood and Colonial Indonesia: The Umma below the Winds.* London: RoutledgeCurzon, 2003.

Laine, J. W. *Shivaji: Hindu King in Islamic India.* Delhi: Oxford University Press, 2003.

Lambton, A. K. S. 'The Case of Hājī 'Abd al-Karīm: A Study of the Role of Merchants in Mid-Nineteenth Century Iran', in C. E. Bosworth (ed.), *Iran and Islam: In Memory of the Late Vladimir Minorsky.* Edinburgh: Edinburgh University Press, 1971.

Lang, G. and Ragvald, L. *The Rise of a Refugee God: Hong Kong's Wong Tai Sin.* Hong Kong: Oxford University Press, 1993.

Larguèche, A. 'The City and the Sea: Evolving Forms of Mediterranean Cosmopolitanism in Tunis, 1700–1881', in J. Clancy-Smith (ed.), *North Africa, Islam, and the Mediterranean World: From the Almoravids to the Algerian War.* London: Frank Cass, 2001.

Lewisohn, L. 'An Introduction to the History of Modern Persian Sufism, Part I: The Niʿmatullāhī Order: Persecution, Revival and Schism', *Bulletin of the School of Oriental and African Studies* 61, 3 (1998).

Liebeskind, C. *Piety on its Knees: Three Sufi Traditions in South Asia in Modern Times.* Delhi: Oxford University Press, 1998.

Lings, M. 'The Qoranic Symbolism of Water', *Studies in Comparative Religion* 2, 3 (1968).

Lloyd, A. C. G. 'The Birth of Printing in South Africa', *The Library* series 3, 5 (1914).

Loimeier, R. 'Is There Something like "Protestant" Islam?', *Die Welt des Islams*, 45, 2 (2005).

Low, M. C. 'Empire and the Hajj: Pilgrims, Plagues, and Pan-Islam under British Surveillance, 1865–1908', *International Journal of Middle East Studies* 40, 2 (2008).

Lyon, S. M. *An Anthropological Analysis of Local Politics and Patronage in a Pakistani Village.* Lampeter: Edwin Mellen Press, 2004.

MacEoin, D. 'From Babism to Baha'ism: Problems of Militancy, Quietism and Conflation in the Construction of a Religion', *Religion* 13 (1983).

Machalski, F. *La littérature de l'Iran contemporain*, 2 vols. Wrocław: Zakład Narodowy Imienia Ossolinskich, 1965.

Maharaj, B. 'From a Privileged to an Unwanted Minority: The Asian Diaspora in Africa', in Gervais-Lambony *et al.* (eds.), *Reconfiguring Identities.*

Mahdavi, S. *For God, Mammon and Country: A Nineteenth Century Persian Merchant.* Boulder: Westview Press, 1999.

Manasseh, S. 'Religious Music Traditions of the Jewish-Babylonian Diaspora in Bombay', *Ethnomusicology Forum* 13, 1 (2004).

Mann, E. A. 'Religion, Money and Status: Competition for Resources at the Shrine of Shah Jamal, Aligarh', in C. W. Troll (ed.), *Muslim Shrines in India: Their Character, History and Significance.* Delhi: Oxford University Press, 1989.

Manuchehri, S. 'Historical Accounts of Two Indian Babis: Saʾin Hindi and Sayyid Basir Hindi', *Research Notes in Shaykhi, Babi and Baha'i Studies* 5, 2 (2001).

Marie, S. *Divide and Profit: Indian Workers in Natal.* Durban: University of Natal, 1986.

Markovits, C. *The Global World of Indian Merchants, 1750–1947.* Cambridge: Cambridge University Press, 2000.

Markovits, C. and Subrahmanyam, S. (eds.). *Society and Circulation: Mobile People and Itinerant Cultures in South Asia, 1750–1950.* Delhi: Permanent Black, 2003.

Masselos, J. 'The Khojas of Bombay', in I. Ahmad (ed.). *Caste and Social Stratification among Muslims in India.* Delhi: Manohar, 1978.

'Change and Custom in the Format of the Bombay Mohurrum during the Nineteenth and Twentieth Centuries', *South Asia* 5, 2 (1982).

'Appropriating Urban Space: Social Constructs of Bombay in the Time of the Raj', *South Asia* 14, 1 (1991).

'Migration and Urban Identity: Bombay's Famine Refugees in the Nineteenth Century', in S. Patel and A. Thorner (eds.), *Bombay: Mosaic of Modern Culture.* Delhi: Oxford University Press, 1995.

The City in Action: Bombay Struggles for Power. Delhi: Oxford University Press, 2007.

Massignon, L. 'Les pélerinages populaires à Baghdad', *Revue du Monde Musulman* 6, 12 (1908).

Matar, N. *Turks, Moors, and Englishmen in the Age of Discovery.* New York: Columbia University Press, 1999.

Matthee, R. P. *The Pursuit of Pleasure: Drugs and Stimulants in Iranian History, 1500–1900.* Princeton: Princeton University Press, 2005.

Matthee, R. and Baron, B. (eds.). *Iran and Beyond: Essays in Middle Eastern History in Honor of Nikki R. Keddie.* Costa Mesa: Mazda, 2000.

Mazharī, A. 'Hājjī Pīrzāda: Darwīsh-e Safī-zamīr', *Sūfī: Faslnāma-ye Khānaqāh-e Ni'matullāhī* 36 (1376/1997).

McFarlane, C. 'Governing the Contaminated City: Infrastructure and Sanitation in Colonial and Post-Colonial Bombay', *International Journal of Urban and Regional Research* 32, 2 (2008).

McPherson, J. W. *The Moulids of Egypt: Egyptian Saints-Days.* Cairo: Ptd. N. M. Press, 1941.

Meeker, M. E. *A Nation of Empire: The Ottoman Legacy of Turkish Modernity.* Berkeley: University of California Press, 2002.

Meer, F. *Portrait of Indian South Africans.* Durban: Avon House, 1969.

Meier, F. *Zwei Abhandlungen über die Naqshbandiyya.* Stuttgart: Franz Steiner, 1994.

Mesthrie, R. 'New Lights from Old Languages: Indian Languages and the Experience of Indentureship in South Africa', in S. Bhana (ed.), *Essays on Indentured Indians in Natal.* Leeds: Peepal Tree, 1988.

Metcalf, B. D. 'Islam and Custom in Nineteenth-Century India: The Reformist Standard of Maulāná Thánawí's Bihishtí Zewar', *Contributions to Asian Studies* 17 (1982).

Islamic Revival in British India: Deoband, 1860–1900. Princeton: Princeton University Press, 1982.

'The Pilgrimage Remembered: South Asian Accounts of the Hajj', in D. F. Eickelman and J. Piscatori (eds.), *Muslim Travellers: Pilgrimage, Migration and the Religious Imagination.* London: Routledge, 1990.

'Two Fatwas on Hajj in British India', in M. K. Masud, B. Messick and D. S. Powers (eds.), *Islamic Legal Interpretation: Muftis and their Fatwas.* Cambridge, MA: Harvard University Press, 1996.

'Traditionalist' Islamic Activism: Deoband, Tablighis, and Talibs. Leiden: ISIM, 2002.

Metcalf, B. D. (ed.). *Making Muslim Space in North America and Europe.* Berkeley: University of California Press, 1996.

Metcalf, T. R. *An Imperial Vision: Indian Architecture and Britain's Raj.* Oxford: Oxford University Press, 2002.

Imperial Connections: India in the Indian Ocean Arena, 1860–1920. Berkeley: University of California Press, 2007.

Meuleman, J. (ed.). *Islam in the Era of Globalization: Muslim Attitudes towards Modernity and Identity.* London: RoutledgeCurzon, 2002.

Minault, G. *The Khilafat Movement: Religious Symbolism and Political Mobilization in India.* New York: Columbia University Press, 1982.

Secluded Scholars: Women's Education and Muslim Social Reform in Colonial India. Delhi: Oxford University Press, 1998.

Minorsky, V. *Iranica: Twenty Articles.* Tehran: University of Tehran, 1964.

Mitchell, T. *Colonising Egypt.* Cambridge: Cambridge University Press, 1988.

Moaddel, M. 'Conditions for Ideological Production: The Origins of Islamic Modernism in India, Egypt, and Iran', *Theory and Society* 30, 5 (2001).

Mohiuddin, M. *Muslim Communities in Medieval Konkan: 610–1900 AD.* Delhi: Sundeep Prakashan, 2002.

Mohiuddin, M. and Poonawala, I. K. 'Bombay: Persian Muslim Communities', in E. Yarshater (ed.), *Encyclopaedia Iranica.* New York: Biblioteca Persica Press, 2009.

Moinuddin, K. *A Monograph on Muharram in Hyderabad City.* Delhi: Controller of Publications, 1977.

Momen, M. 'Jamāl Effendī and the Early Spread of the Bahā'ī Faith in Asia', *Bahā'ī Studies Review* 9 (1999–2000); repr. in J. Danesh and S. Fazel (eds.), *Search for Values: Ethics in Bahá'í Thought.* Los Angeles: Kalimat Press, 2004.

'The Baha'is and the Constitutional Revolution: The Case of Sari, Mazandaran, 1906–1913', *Iranian Studies* 41, 3 (2008).

More, J. B. P. *Muslim Identity, Print Culture and the Dravidian Factor in Tamil Nadu.* Hyderabad: Orient Longman, 2004.

Religion and Society in South India: Hindus, Muslims and Christians. Nirmalagiri: IRISH, 2006.

Morris, M. D. *The Emergence of an Industrial Labor Force in India: A Study of the Bombay Cotton Mills, 1854–1947.* Berkeley: California University Press, 1965.

Naidoo, T. *The Arya Samaj Movement in South Africa.* Delhi: Motilal Banarsidass, 1992.

Nizami, F. 'Madrasahs, Scholars, and Saints: Muslim Response to the British Presence in Delhi and the Upper Doab 1803–1857', D.Phil. thesis, Oxford University, 1983.

Nizāmī, K. A. *Tārīkh-e mashā'ikh-e chisht.* Delhi: Idāra-e Adabiyyat-e Dillī, 1405/1985.

Noorally, Z. 'The First Agha Khan and the British', MA thesis, University of London, 1964.

Numark, M. W. 'Translating Religion: British Missionaries and the Politics of Religious Knowledge in Colonial India and Bombay', Ph.D. thesis, UCLA, 2006.

O'Brien, S. 'A Transatlantic Community of Saints: The Great Awakening and the First Evangelical Network, 1735–1755', *American Historical Review* 91, 4 (1986).

Oddie, G. A. 'Anti-Missionary Feeling and Hindu Revivalism in Madras: The Hindu Preaching and Tract Societies, c. 1886–1891', in F. W. Clothey (ed.), *Images of Man: Religion and Historical Process in South Asia.* Madras: New Era, 1982.

Oesterheld, C. 'Bombay: Literarische Bilder einer Großstadt', in R. Ahuja and C. Brosius (eds.), *Mumbai–Delhi–Kolkata: Annäherungen an die Megastädte Indiens*. Heidelberg: Draupadi Verlag, 2006.

O'Fahey, R. S. *Enigmatic Saint: Ahmad ibn Idris and the Idrisi Tradition*. Evanston: Northwestern University Press, 1990.

'"Small World": Neo-Sufi Interconnexions between the Maghrib, the Hijaz and Southeast Asia', in Reese (ed.), *The Transmission of Learning*.

O'Hanlon, R. 'Narratives of Penance and Purification in Western India, c. 1650–1850', *Journal of Hindu Studies* 2, 1 (2009).

O'Keefe, B. *Pioneers' Progress: Early Natal*. Durban: n.p., n.d.

Oldenburg, V. T. *The Making of Colonial Lucknow, 1856–1877*. Delhi: Oxford University Press, 1989.

Ong, A. *Spirits of Resistance and Capitalist Discipline: Factory Women in Malaysia*. Albany: State University of New York Press, 1987.

Ostle, R. 'Alexandria: A Mediterranean Cosmopolitan Center of Cultural Production', in Tarazi Fawaz and Bayly (eds.), *Modernity and Culture*.

Özcan, A. *Pan-Islamism: Indian Muslims, the Ottomans and Britain, 1877–1924*. Leiden: Brill, 1997.

Padayachee, V. and Morrell, R. 'Indian Merchants and Dukawallahs in the Natal Economy, c. 1875–1914', *Journal of Southern African Studies* 17 (1991).

Palsetia, J. S. *The Parsis of India: Preservation of Identity in Bombay City*. Leiden: Brill, 2001.

'Parsi and Hindu Traditional and Nontraditional Responses to Christian Conversion in Bombay, 1839–45', *Journal of the American Academy of Religion* 74, 3 (2006).

Pankhurst, R. 'The Ethiopian Diaspora in India: The Role of Habshis and Sidis from Medieval Times to the End of the Eighteenth Century', in S. de Silva Jayasuriya and R. Pankhurst (eds.), *The African Diaspora in the Indian Ocean*. Trenton, NJ: Africa World Press, 2001.

Parveez, N. M. 'Indo-British Trade with Persia', *Imperial and Asiatic Quarterly Review*, 3rd series, 23 (1907).

Patel, S. and Thorner, A. (eds.). *Bombay: Mosaic of Modern Culture*. Delhi: Oxford University Press, 1995.

Pearson, H. O. *Islamic Reform and Revival in Nineteenth Century India: The Tariqah-i Muhammadiyah*. Delhi: Yoda Press, 2008.

Pearson, M. *The Indian Ocean*. London: Routledge, 2003.

Pemble, J. *The Mediterranean Passion: Victorians and Edwardians in the South*. Oxford: Oxford University Press, 1988.

Peters, F. E. *The Hajj: The Muslim Pilgrimage to Mecca and the Holy Places*. Princeton: Princeton University Press, 1994.

Peters, R. 'Religious Attitudes towards Modernization in the Ottoman Empire: A Nineteenth Century Pious Text on Steamships, Factories and the Telegraph', *Die Welt des Islams* 26, 1–4 (1986).

Picklay, A. S. *The History of the Ismailis*. Bombay: Popular Printing Press, 1940.

Pinto, D. *Piri–Muridi Relationship: A Study of the Nizamuddin Dargah*. Delhi: Manohar, 1995.

Porter, A. *Religion versus Empire? British Protestant Missionaries and Overseas Expansion 1700–1914*. Manchester: Manchester University Press, 2004.

Pourjavady, N. and Lamborn-Wilson, P. 'The Descendants of Shāh Ni'matullāh Wali', *Islamic Culture* 48, 1 (1974).

—— *Kings of Love: The Poetry and History of the Ni'matullahi Sufi Order*. Tehran: The Imperial Iranian Academy of Philosophy, 1978.

Powell, A. A. *Muslims and Missionaries in Pre-Mutiny India*. Richmond: Curzon Press, 1993.

Prabha Ray, H. 'Crossing the Seas: Connecting Maritime Spaces in Colonial India', in H. Prabha Ray and E. A. Alpers (eds.), *Cross Currents and Community Networks: The History of the Indian Ocean World*. Delhi: Oxford University Press, 2007.

Pradhan, A. 'Perspectives on Performance Practice: Hindustani Music in Nineteenth and Twentieth Century Bombay (Mumbai)', *South Asia* 27, 3 (2004).

Prakash, G. 'Reproducing Inequality: Spirit Cults and Labor Relations in Colonial East India', *Modern Asian Studies* 20, 2 (1986).

—— *Bonded Histories: Genealogies of Labor Servitude in Colonial India*. Cambridge: Cambridge University Press, 1990.

Prestholdt, J. *Domesticating the World: African Consumerism and the Genealogies of Globalization*. Berkeley: University of California Press, 2008.

Proudfoot, I. 'Malay Books Printed in Bombay: A Report on Sources for Historical Bibliography', *Kekal Abadi* 13, 3 (1994).

Radtke, B. and O'Kane, J. *The Concept of Sainthood in Early Islamic Mysticism*. London: Curzon, 1996.

Rahman, F. *Islam and Modernity: Transformation of an Intellectual Tradition*. Chicago: University of Chicago Press, 1982.

Rahman, T. 'Urdu as an Islamic Language', *Annual of Urdu Studies* 21 (2006).

Ranade, R. *Sir Bartle Frere and his Times: A Study of his Bombay Years, 1862–1867*. Delhi: Mittal Publishing, 1990.

Raval, R. L. *Socio-Religious Reform Movements in Gujarat during the Nineteenth Century*. Delhi: Ess Ess Publications, 1987.

Reese, S. S. 'Urban Woes and Pious Remedies: Sufism in Nineteenth-Century Benaadir (Somalia)', *Africa Today* 46, 3–4 (1999).

—— *Renewers of the Age: Holy Men and Social Discourse in Colonial Benaadir*. Leiden: Brill, 2008.

Reese, S. S. (ed.). *The Transmission of Learning in Islamic Africa*. Leiden: Brill, 2004.

Reeves, E. B. *The Hidden Government: Ritual, Clientelism and Legitimation in Northern Egypt*. Salt Lake City: University of Utah Press, 1990.

Reid, A. 'Nineteenth Century Pan-Islam in Indonesia and Malaysia', *Journal of Asian Studies* 26, 2 (1967).

Ringer, M. 'The Discourse of Modernization and the Problem of Cultural Integrity in Nineteenth Century Iran', in Matthee and Baron (eds.), *Iran and Beyond*.

'Reform Transplanted: Parsi Agents of Change amongst Zoroastrians in Nineteenth-Century Iran', *Iranian Studies* 42, 4 (2009).

Rizvi, S. A. A. 'The Breakdown of Traditional Society', in B. Lewis *et al.* (eds.), *The Cambridge History of Islam*, vol. II. Cambridge: Cambridge University Press, 1977.

Roberts, A. F. and Roberts, M. N. 'Flickering Images, Floating Signifiers: Optical Innovation and Visual Piety in Senegal', *Material Religion: The Journal of Objects, Art and Belief* 4, 1 (2008).

Roberts, A. F. and Roberts, M. N. (eds.). *A Saint in the City: Sufi Arts of Urban Senegal*. Los Angeles: Fowler Museum of Cultural History, UCLA, 2003.

Robinson, F. *Separatism among Indian Muslims: The Politics of the United Provinces' Muslims, 1860–1923*. Cambridge: Cambridge University Press, 1974.

'Technology and Religious Change: Islam and the Impact of Print', *Modern Asian Studies* 27, 1 (1993).

'Religious Change and the Self in Muslim South Asia since 1800', *South Asia* 20, 1 (1997).

The 'Ulama of Farangi Mahall and Islamic Culture in South Asia. Delhi: Permanent Black, 2001.

'Other-worldly and This-worldly Islam and the Islamic Revival', *Journal of the Royal Asiatic Society* 14, 1 (2004).

'Islamic Reform and Modernities in South Asia', *Modern Asian Studies* 41, 5 (2007).

Rochlin, S. A. 'Aspects of Islam in Nineteenth-Century South Africa', *Bulletin of the School of Oriental and African Studies* 10 (1940–2).

Rodrigues, L. 'Parsi Elite Leadership in the Politics of Western India in the Mid-Nineteenth Century', *Journal of the K. R. Cama Oriental Institute* 68 (2008).

Rohatgi, P., Godrej, P. and Mehotra, R. (eds.). *Bombay to Mumbai: Changing Perspectives*. Mumbai: Marg Publications, 2006.

Ross, R. and Telkamp, G. J. (eds.). *Colonial Cities: Essays on Urbanism in a Colonial Context*. Leiden: Martinus Nijhoff, 1985.

Roy, A. *The Islamic Syncretist Movement in Bengal*. Princeton: Princeton University Press, 1983.

Roy, O. *Globalized Islam: The Search for a New Ummah*. London: Hurst, 2004.

Royce, W. R. 'Mir Ma'sum 'Ali Shah and the Ni'mat Allahi Revival, 1776–77 to 1796–97', Ph.D. thesis, Princeton University, 1979.

Saiedi, N. *Logos and Civilization: Spirit, History, and Order in the Writings of Bahá'u'lláh*. Bethesda: University Press of Maryland, 2000.

Salvatore, A. (ed.). *Muslim Traditions and Modern Techniques of Power*. Piscataway, NJ: Transaction Publishers, 2001.

Sanyal, U. *Devotional Islam and Politics in British India: Ahmad Riza Khan Barelwi and his Movement, 1870–1920*. Delhi: Oxford University Press, 1996.

Ahmad Riza Khan Barelwi: In the Path of the Prophet. Oxford: Oneworld, 2005.

Sarkar, S. *Writing Social History.* Delhi: Oxford University Press, 1997.

Scarce, J. 'Bandar-e Tahiri: A Late Outpost of the Shahnama', in R. Hillenbrand (ed.), *Shahnama: The Visual Language of the Persian Book of Kings.* Aldershot: Ashgate, 2004.

Schaebler, B. and Stenberg, L. (eds.). *Globalization and the Muslim World: Culture, Religion, and Modernity.* Syracuse: Syracuse University Press, 2004.

Scheglova, O. 'Lithograph Versions of Persian Manuscripts of Indian Manufacture in the Nineteenth Century', *Manuscripta Orientalia* 5, 1 (1999).

'Lithography ii: In India', in E. Yarshater (ed.), *Encyclopaedia Iranica.* New York: Biblioteca Persica Press, 2009.

Schubel, V. J. *Religious Performance in Contemporary Islam: Shi'i Devotional Rituals in South Asia.* Columbia: University of South Carolina Press, 1993.

Sconce, J. *Haunted Media: Electronic Presence from Telegraphy to Television.* Durham, NC: Duke University Press, 2000.

'Mediums and Media', in M. Sturken, D. Thomas and Sandra Ball-Rokeach (eds.), *Technological Visions: The Hopes and Fears that Shape New Technologies.* Philadelphia: Temple University Press, 2004.

Searight, S. *Steaming East: The Forging of Steamship and Rail Links between Europe and Asia.* London: The Bodley Head, 1991.

Shakir, M. *Muslims and Indian National Congress: Badruddin Tyabji and his Times.* Delhi: Ajanta Publications, 1987.

Sharafi, M. 'Judging Conversion to Zoroastrianism: Behind the Scenes of the Parsi Panchayat Case (1908)', in Hinnells and Williams (eds.), *Parsis in India and the Diaspora.*

Shaw, G. M. 'The Printer of the First Book Published in Bombay', *The Library*, series 6, 1 (1979).

'Calcutta: Birthplace of the Indian Lithographed Book', *Journal of the Printing Historical Society* 27 (1998).

Shell, R. C-H. 'Islam in Southern Africa, 1652–1998', in N. Levtzion and R. L. Pouwels (eds.), *The History of Islam in Africa.* Oxford: James Currey, 2000.

Shodhan, A. 'Legal Formulation of the Question of Community: Defining the Khoja Collective', *Indian Social Science Review* 1, 1 (1999).

A Question of Community: Religious Groups and Colonial Law. Calcutta: Samya, 2001.

Siddiqi, A. 'Ayesha's World: A Butcher's Family in Nineteenth-Century Bombay', *Comparative Studies in Society and History* 43, 1 (2001).

Sikand, Y. S. 'The Fitna of Irtidad: Muslim Missionary Response to the Shuddhi of Arya Samaj in Early Twentieth Century India', *Journal of Muslim Minority Affairs* 17, 1 (1997).

The Origins and Development of the Tablighi Jama'at (1920–2000): A Cross-country Comparative Study. Delhi: Orient Longman, 2002.

Simpson, E. *Muslim Society and the Western Indian Ocean: The Seafarers of Kachchh.* London: Routledge, 2006.

Sirriyeh, E. *Sufis and Anti-Sufis: The Defence, Rethinking and Rejection of Sufism in the Modern World.* London: Curzon, 1999.

Smith, G. R. 'A Muslim Saint in South Africa', *African Studies* 28, 4 (1969).

Smith Diehl, K. 'Lucknow Printers, 1820–1850', in N. N. Gidwani (ed.), *Comparative Librarianship: Essays in Honour of Professor D. N. Marshall.* Delhi: Vikas, 1973.

Sontheimer, G. and Kulke, H. (eds.). *Hinduism Reconsidered.* Delhi: Manohar, 1997.

Stark, R. 'From Church-Sect to Religious Economies', in P. E. Hammond (ed.), *The Sacred in a Post-Secular Age.* Berkeley: University of California Press, 1985.

Stark, U. *An Empire of Books: The Nawal Kishore Press and the Diffusion of the Printed Word in India.* Delhi: Permanent Black, 2007.

Stein, S. J. *The Shaker Experience in America: A History of the United Society of Believers.* New Haven: Yale University Press, 1992.

Communities of Dissent: A History of Alternative Religions in America. Oxford: Oxford University Press, 2003.

Suvorova, A. *Muslim Saints of South Asia: The Eleventh to Fifteenth Centuries.* London: RoutledgeCurzon, 2004.

Tambe, A. and Fischer-Tiné, H. (eds.). *The Limits of British Colonial Control in South Asia: Spaces of Disorder in the Indian Ocean Region.* London: Routledge, 2009.

Tarazi Fawaz, L. *Merchants and Migrants in Nineteenth-Century Beirut.* Cambridge, MA: Harvard University Press, 1983.

Tarazi Fawaz, L. and Bayly, C. A. (eds.). *Modernity and Culture: From the Mediterranean to the Indian Ocean.* New York: Columbia University Press, 2002.

Tavakoli-Targhi, M. 'The Homeless Texts of Persianate Modernity', in R. Jahanbegloo (ed.), *Iran: Between Tradition and Modernity.* Lanham, MD: Lexington Books, 2004.

Tayob, A. *Islam in South Africa: Mosques, Imams and Sermons.* Gainesville: University of Florida Press, 1999.

Tejani, S. 'Music, Mosques and Custom: Local Conflict and "Communalism" in a Maharashtrian Weaving Town, 1893–1894', *South Asia: Journal of South Asian Studies* 30, 2 (2007).

'Re-Considering Chronologies of Nationalism and Communalism: The Khilafat Movement in Sind and its Aftermath, 1919–1927', *South Asia Research* 27, 3 (2007).

Tétreault, M. A. and Denemark, R. A. (eds.). *Gods, Guns, and Globalization: Religious Radicalism and International Political Economy.* Boulder: Lynne Rienner Publishers, 2004.

Thompson, E. P. *The Making of the English Working Class.* New York: Vintage Books, 1966.

'Time, Work-Discipline and Industrial Capitalism', *Past and Present* 38 (1967).

Customs in Common: Studies in Traditional Popular Culture. London: Merlin Press, 1991.

Thorner, D. *Investment in Empire: British Railway and Steam Shipping Enterprise in India 1825–1849.* Philadelphia: University of Pennsylvania Press, 1950.

Thorold, A. P. H. 'The Yao Tariqa and the Sukuti Movement in Southern Malawi', in D. Bone (ed.), *Malawi's Muslims: Historical Perspectives.* Blantyre: CLAIM, 2001.

Tschacher, T. 'From Local Practice to Transnational Network: Saints, Shrines and Sufis among Tamil Muslims in Singapore', *Asian Journal of Social Science* 34, 2 (2006).

Turner, B. S. *Weber and Islam: A Critical Study.* London: Routledge & Kegan Paul, 1974.

Tyabji, H. B. *Badruddin Tyabji: A Biography.* Bombay: Thacker, 1952.

Tromp, M. *Altered States: Sex, Nation, Drugs, and Self-Transformation in Victorian Spiritualism.* Albany: State University of New York Press, 2006.

Upadhyay, S. B. *Existence, Identity, and Mobilization: The Cotton Millworkers of Bombay, 1890–1919.* Delhi: Manohar, 2004.

Urban, H. *The Economics of Ecstasy: Tantra, Secrecy and Power in Colonial Bengal.* New York: Oxford University Press, 2001.

'The Marketplace and the Temple: Economic Metaphors and Religious Meanings in the Folk Songs of Colonial Bengal', *Journal of Asian Studies* 60, 4 (2001).

Vahed, G. H. 'Changing Islamic Traditions and Emerging Identities in South Africa', *Journal of Muslim Minority Affairs* 20, 1 (2000).

'Mosques, Mawlanas and Muharram: Indian Islam in Colonial Natal, 1860–1910', *Journal of Religion in Africa* 31, 3 (2001).

'"A Man of Keen Perceptive Facilities": Aboobaker Amod Jhaveri, an "Arab" in Colonial Natal, circa 1872–1887', *Historia* 50, 1 (2005).

'"Unhappily Torn by Dissensions and Litigations": Durban's "Memon" Mosque, 1880–1930', *Journal of Religion in Africa* 36, 1 (2006).

van Bruinessen, M. 'Kitab Kuning: Books in Arabic Script used in the Pesantren Milieu', *Bijdragen tot de Taal-, Land- en Volkenkunde* 146 (1990).

van Bruinessen, M. and Howell, J. D. (eds.). *Sufism and the Modern in Islam.* London: I. B. Tauris, 2007.

van den Bos, M. *Mystic Regimes: Sufism and the State in Iran, from the Late Qajar Era to the Islamic Republic.* Leiden: Brill, 2002.

van der Veer, P. *Gods on Earth: The Management of Religious Experience and Identity in a North Indian Pilgrimage Centre.* London: Athlone Press, 1988.

Imperial Encounters: Religion and Modernity in India and Britain. Princeton: Princeton University Press, 2001.

Vanzan, A. 'Hājjī Pirzāda', in E. Yarshater (ed.), *Encyclopaedia Iranica.* New York: Biblioteca Persica Press, 2009.

Villa-Vicencio, C. 'Mission Christianity', in M. Prozesky and J. de Gruchy (eds.), *Living Faiths in South Africa.* New York: St Martin's Press, 1995.

Voll, J. O. 'Linking Groups in the Networks of Eighteenth-Century Revivalist Scholars', in N. Levtzion and J. O. Voll (eds.), *Eighteenth-Century Renewal and Reform in Islam.* Syracuse: Syracuse University Press, 1987.

Weismann, I. *Taste of Modernity: Sufism, Salafiyya, and Arabism in Late Ottoman Damascus.* Leiden: Brill, 2001.

Werbner, P. 'Economic Rationality and Hierarchical Gift Economies: Value and Ranking among British Pakistanis', *Man* N.S. 25 (1990).

'Langar: Pilgrimage, Sacred Exchange and Perpetual Sacrifice in a Sufi Saint's Lodge', in P. Werbner and H. Basu (eds.), *Embodying Charisma: Modernity, Locality and the Performance of Emotion in Sufi Cults*. London: Routledge, 1998.

Pilgrims of Love: The Anthropology of a Global Sufi Cult. London: Hurst, 2003.

Werbner, P. and Basu, H. (eds.). *Embodying Charisma: Modernity, Locality, and Performance of Emotion in Sufi Cults*. London: Routledge, 1998.

White, G. E. 'The Mohammedan Conception of Saintship', *Muslim World* 8 (1918).

White, L. *Speaking with Vampires: Rumor and History in Colonial Africa*. Berkeley: University of California Press, 2000.

Whitehead, C. *Colonial Educators: The British Indian and Colonial Education Service, 1858–1983*. London: I. B. Tauris, 2003.

Williams, G. A. *Artisans and Sans-Culottes: Popular Movements in France and Britain during the French Revolution*. London: Edward Arnold, 1968.

Wilson, E. *The Sphinx in the City: Urban Life, the Control of Disorder, and Women*. Berkeley: University of California Press, 1992.

Wittenberg, H. 'Occult, Empire and Landscape: The Colonial Uncanny in John Buchan's African Writing', *Journal of Colonialism and Colonial History* 7, 2 (2006).

Worth, A. 'All India Becoming Tranquil: Wiring the Raj', *Journal of Colonialism and Colonial History* 9, 1 (2008).

Wright, T. P. 'Muslim Kinship and Modernisation: The Tyabji Clan of Bombay', in I. Ahmad (ed.), *Family, Kinship and Marriage among the Muslims in India*. Delhi: Manohar, 1976.

Yazdani, G. *Bidar: Its History and Monuments*. Delhi: Motilal Banarsidass, 1996 [1947].

Yegar, M. *The Muslims of Burma: A Study of a Minority Group*. Wiesbaden: Otto Harrassowitz, 1972.

Yen, Q. *The Chinese in Southeast Asia and Beyond*. Singapore: World Scientific Publishing, 2008.

Yeoh, B. S. A. *Contesting Space: Power Relations and the Urban Built Environment in Colonial Singapore*. Kuala Lumpur: Oxford University Press, 1996.

Young, L. A. (ed.). *Rational Choice Theory and Religion: Summary and Assessment*. New York: Routledge, 1997.

Zachariah, K. C. *A Historical Study of Internal Migration in the Indian Subcontinent, 1901–1931*. New York: Asia Publishing House, 1964.

Zaman, M. Q. 'Islamic Institutions of Learning: Religious Education and the Rhetoric of Reform: The Madrasa in British India and Pakistan', *Comparative Studies in Society and History* 41, 2 (1999).

Index

CPSIA information can be obtained at www.ICGtesting.com
Printed in the USA
LVOW06s0743250114

370902LV00001B/4/P

9 781107 627796